ISLAMIC LAW AND EMPIRE IN OTTOMAN CAIRO

For Helena

ISLAMIC LAW AND EMPIRE IN OTTOMAN CAIRO

◆ ◆ ◆

JAMES E. BALDWIN

EDINBURGH
University Press

Edinburgh University Press is one of the leading university presses in the UK. We publish academic books and journals in our selected subject areas across the humanities and social sciences, combining cutting-edge scholarship with high editorial and production values to produce academic works of lasting importance. For more information visit our website: edinburghuniversitypress.com

Edinburgh University Press Ltd
The Tun—Holyrood Road
12 (2f) Jackson's Entry
Edinburgh
EH8 8PJ

First published in hardback by Edinburgh University Press 2017

Typeset in 10/12.5pt Times by
Servis Filmsetting Ltd, Stockport, Cheshire,
and printed and bound in Great Britain by
CPI Group (UK) Ltd, Croydon CR0 4YY

A CIP record for this book is available from the British Library

ISBN 978 1 4744 0309 2 (hardback)
ISBN 978 1 4744 3213 9 (paperback)
ISBN 978 1 4744 0310 8 (webready PDF)
ISBN 978 1 4744 1907 9 (epub)

CONTENTS

ACKNOWLEDGMENTS

This book began life as a PhD dissertation at New York University. My first debt is to my advisers, Khaled Fahmy and Leslie Peirce, for their encouragement and support over many years. Khaled introduced me to the archives in Cairo, he taught me how to read court records at several levels, and he helped me to see the contemporary intellectual and political relevance of scholarship on Ottoman law. Leslie helped me to step back from Egypt and think about the wider Ottoman connections of my research, and she also taught me how to write, pushing me to tease out the overarching point from a tangle of observations and giving me the confidence to foreground and strengthen my own claims.

I would also like to thank all of the members of NYU's departments of Middle Eastern & Islamic Studies and History for the wonderful enriching graduate education they gave me. In particular, I am grateful to Zachary Lockman for the support and advice he has given me during and after my time at NYU, Michael Gilsenan for his encouragement and regular hospitality, Sibel Erol for teaching me Turkish in the best language classes I have attended anywhere, Everett Rowson and Bernard Haykel for helping me read fiqh, Hasan Karataş for teaching me to decipher Ottoman documents, and Lauren Benton for reading my dissertation and giving me feedback from a world historian's perspective. NYU also had a very supportive graduate community, and I thank all of my friends and colleagues who provided encouragement, conversation and criticism: On Barak, Robin Shulman, Kathi Ivanyi, Lale Can, Noah Haiduc-Dale, Sarah Tunney, Peter Valenti, Irfana Hashmi, Jeannie Miller, Omar Cheta, Guy Burak, Başak Tuğ, Ayelet Zoran-Rosen and Aaron Jakes.

I was fortunate to receive financial support from several organizations while working on my dissertation and revising it as a book. The bulk of the research was funded by a Leverhulme Trust Study Abroad Studentship that allowed me to spend two years in Cairo and Istanbul between 2007 and 2009. The Leverhulme Trust also supported me when I returned to the UK as a postdoctoral researcher with an Early

Career Fellowship. I'm very thankful to the Trust for its generosity and the freedom to follow my interests that its grants have allowed. I'm also grateful to New York University, which paid for my graduate education, and to NYU's Department of Middle Eastern & Islamic Studies, which gave me several grants to spend summers in Syria, Turkey and Egypt. I'm also grateful to Harvard Law School's Islamic Legal Studies Program and to Koç University's Research Center for Anatolian Civilizations for visiting fellowships during which I did much of my thinking about how to turn the dissertation into a book.

In the UK, I would particularly like to thank Yossi Rapoport, who has been a mentor and friend since I moved back to London, supporting me to find a post-doctoral and then a permanent position, and generally helping me to find my way in British academia. Yossi helped me to think about how to reframe my narrowly-focused dissertation on early modern Egypt to address historians of Islamic law more broadly, and he read drafts of every chapter in this book. I would also like to thank Miri Rubin for welcoming me to the wonderful history department at Queen Mary, University of London, and Colin Jones for his advice and support while I was based there. I'm grateful for the academic home Kate Fleet gave me at the Skilliter Centre for Ottoman Studies in Cambridge during my final year of dissertation-writing. The final stages of this book were completed in the supportive and dynamic environment of the University of Warwick's history department. I'd like to thank Maxine Berg and Giorgio Riello for their encouragement of my work and for pushing me to think in more global terms, and I'm especially grateful to Charles Walton for his advice, friendship and hospitality.

Various other friends and colleagues have helped to see this book to completion, by listening to my ideas, commenting on drafts, giving advice, or offering friendship and support during my extended trips away from home: Jessie Barnes, Alan Mikhail, Zaki Haidar, Denwood Holmes, Vanessa Larson, Brett Wilson and Cristina Corduneanu-Huci, Terry Walz, Fiona Cameron, Andrew Robarts, Nur Sobers-Khan, Abdurrahman Atçıl, Omri Paz, Dana Sajdi and Ariel Salzmann. Boğaç Ergene read most of the book's chapters in draft and then called me on Skype to discuss them. I'd also like to thank Tony Greenwood and Gülden Güneri at the American Research Institute in Turkey for hosting me during my first stint in Istanbul.

This book is informed in many ways by feedback and conversations at the workshops and conferences where I presented different parts of it. The list is extensive and I'm grateful to the organizers and participants at all of them. In particular, I would like to thank Khaled Fahmy and Amr Shalakany for organizing the conference on Egyptian legal history in Cairo in 2009; Mathieu Tillier for organizing a fascinating conference on judicial pluralism in Beirut in 2011; all those who participated in the panels I organized at the Middle East Studies Association meetings in 2011 and 2012, and Lale Can for co-organizing the 2012 one on petitions; Kent Schull and Safa Saraçoğlu for organizing the all-day panel-athon on Law and Legitimacy in the Ottoman Empire at the 2013 MESA, Nandini Chatterjee for including me in her wonderful 2015 workshop in Exeter on legal documents in the Persianate world, despite my inability to read Persian, and Michael Gilsenan for inviting me to his productive and sociable law workshops at New York University over several years.

I'm very grateful to Nicola Ramsey at Edinburgh University Press for taking on my book, and for her support and patience during its completion and the review process. I'm also thankful to the peer reviewers for their extensive comments which have refined many of the arguments in the book and greatly improved its presentation, and to Amir Dastmalchian whose meticulous copy-editing ironed out many mistakes.

Lastly, I want to thank my family. My parents, Pam and Mick Baldwin, were enormously supportive of my extended education and my long absences from the UK. I'm grateful to them for their love and encouragement over several decades, and for visiting me wherever I went. Most of all, I want to thank my partner Helena Wright, without whom I would not have finished graduate school, let alone this book. I don't find it easy to write and there have been several occasions when I have almost given up on finishing this project; Helena always offered emotional support and imaginative practical solutions. The ideas in this book were all tried on her first, and she is a ruthlessly effective editor. Now, she is also a wonderful mother to our children Zachary and Rufus. I'm very lucky and very grateful for her love and support.

ABBREVIATIONS

Archives

ENA	Egyptian National Archive, Cairo (Dār al-wathāʾiq al-qawmiyya)
PMA	Prime Ministry Archive, Ottoman Section, Istanbul (Başbakanlık Osmanlı Arşivi)

Archival units, Egyptian National Archive

BA	Sijillāt maḥkamat al-Bāb al-ᶜĀlī
BS	Sijillāt maḥkamat Bāb al-Shaᶜriyya
DA	Sijillāt al-Dīwān al-ᶜĀlī
MQ	Sijillāt maḥkamat Miṣr al-Qadīma

Archival units, Prime Ministry Archive

AŞD	Atik Şikayet Defterleri
DK	Divan Kalemi
MK	Mısır Kalemi
ŞD	Şikayet Defterleri
ŞK	Şikayet Kalemi

Published sources

Awḍaḥ	Aḥmad Shalabī ibn ᶜAbd al-Ghanī, *Awḍaḥ al-ishārāt fī man tawallā Miṣr min al-wuzarāʾ wa ʾl-bāshāt*, ed. ᶜAbd al-Raḥīm ᶜAbd al-Raḥmān ᶜAbd al-Raḥīm (Cairo: Maktabat al-Khānjī, 1978).

Damurdāshī A	Aḥmad al-Damurdāshī, *al-Durra al-muṣāna fī akhbār al-Kināna: fī akhbār mā waqaᶜa bi Miṣr fī dawlat al-mamālīk*, ed. ᶜAbd al-Raḥīm ᶜAbd al-Raḥmān ᶜAbd al-Raḥīm (Cairo: Institut français d'archéologie orientale, 1989).
Damurdāshī C	Aḥmad al-Damurdāshī, *Al-Damurdashi's Chronicle of Egypt: al-Durra al-musana fi akhbar al-Kinana*, ed. and trans. Daniel Crecelius and ᶜAbd al-Wahhab Bakr (Leiden: Brill, 1991).
Jabartī B	ᶜAbd al-Raḥmān al-Jabartī, *al-Tārīkh al-musammā ᶜAjāʾib al-āthār fī tarājim wa ʾl-akhbār* (Būlāq: n.p., 1297 AH).
Jabartī P	ᶜAbd al-Raḥmān al-Jabartī, *ᶜAbd al-Raḥman al-Jabartī's History of Egypt: ᶜAjāʾib al-athār fī ʾl-tarājim wa ʾl-akhbār*, ed. and trans. Thomas Philipp and Moshe Perlmann (Stuttgart: Franz Steiner Verlag, 1994).
Registerbuch	Hans Georg Majer (ed.), *Das osmanische Registerbuch der Beschwerden (Şikayet Defteri) vom Jahre 1675: Österreichische Nationalbibliothek Cod. mixt. 683* (Vienna: Verlag der Österreichischen Akademie der Wissenschaften, 1984).

Note on citation of archival documents

In the bound registers I used (i.e. BA, BS, DA, MQ and AŞD), for the most part the entries are individually numbered. I cite first the register number and then the number of the entry. I have not cited page or folio numbers as these are superfluous and not always given. In the case of the PMA, page numbers are unhelpful, as the registers are accessed digitally and the images are not arranged by page number. However, sometimes an entry is not numbered. In those cases I have described the position of the entry using page numbers and/or the numbers of the adjacent entries.

When citing loose documents in the DK and MK series, I first give the number of the box and then the number of the folder within the box. Documents in the Cevdet, İbnülemin and Ali Emiri collections are subdivided by subject matter or reigning Sultan, and then have a single number identifying the individual document.

NOTE ON TRANSLITERATION AND DATES

Ottoman Cairo was a multi-lingual society, in which both Arabic and Turkish were prominent. In my opinion, it is unnecessary, and even anachronistic, to insist rigidly on using either the Arabic or the Ottoman Turkish system for transliteration. I have used both. In general, the names of people from and places in Egypt or the Arab provinces are transliterated according to the Arabic system, whereas those from Istanbul, Anatolia, and Rumelia are transliterated under the Ottoman system. In the interests of readability, within the text I use the Ottoman system for some Turkish titles that appear within Egyptian/Arabic names. An example is the Egyptian chronicler Aḥmad Çelebi ibn ᶜAbd al-Ghanī. However, for accuracy's sake, in citations I transliterate consistently according to the language of the text cited (so the above chronicler becomes Aḥmad Shalabī ibn ᶜAbd al-Ghanī). When a name, title, or other word is well-known in an English rendering, I usually use the English form; hence Pasha, Sultan, ulema, Koran, and so on.

Although it may be hard on the non-specialist reader, I have often opted to retain many Arabic and Turkish technical terms rather than translate them into English. Because much of the argument of this book is concerned with the details of offices and institutions, English words could fudge the issue. Technical terms are transliterated according to my judgment as to whether, in Ottoman Cairo, they were understood as coming from the Arabicate or Ottoman tradition. So, for example: *ḳānūn* and *ḳānūnnāme* rather than *qānūn* and *qānūnnāma*, but *qāḍī* rather than *ḳaḍı*. In some cases, when a word is part of a proper noun, I transliterate it differently depending on context: the main example of this is that the governor's tribunal in Cairo is called al-Dīwān al-ᶜĀlī, but the imperial council in Istanbul is called the Dīvān-i Hümāyūn. Arabic and Turkish terms are explained in the glossary.

For Arabic, I transliterate according to the system of the *International Journal of Middle East Studies*, with some alterations. I transliterate *jīm* as g, following Cairene pronunciation, when it forms part of an Egyptian person or place-name. For example: the name Girgis. I do not assimilate the *lām* of the definite article to the sun letters (i.e. *al-shams* rather than *ash-shams*). I always use full diacritics, including in names and book titles. For Ottoman Turkish, I prefer full transliteration rather than modern Turkish spelling, and I follow the *IJMES* system.

Although it looks inelegant to readers of Arabic, I pluralize Arabic words in the English way to avoid confusion for non-specialist readers. The only two exceptions are *waqf*, which I pluralize in the Arabic way as *awqāf* (this word appears often in the plural, and the Anglicized waqfs is difficult to pronounce) and *shuhūd* (this is more familiar than the singular in the fixed phrases *shuhūd al-ḥāl* and *shuhūd ʿudūl*).

In general I use the CE calendar, but when discussing particular cases drawn from the archival records I prioritize the Muslim *hijrī* calendar (AH) that the documents use, with equivalent CE dates in parentheses. Documents issued by the imperial bureaucracy in Istanbul are often dated only to the early (*evāyil*), mid (*evāsiṭ*) or late (*evāhır*) part of the month, that is, the 1st–10th, the 11th–20th or the 21st–29th/30th.

INTRODUCTION

What was distinctive about Islamic law in the early modern period, the Muslim world's age of empire? How did Islamic law connect with the imperial power wielded by the great Turco-Persian dynasts, cultural descendants of Tamerlane and Genghis Khan, who ruled the vast swathe of Eurasia and north Africa from Algiers to Calcutta? This book explores this question through a study of legal practices in Cairo during the late seventeenth and early eighteenth centuries. Cairo was a long way from the Ottoman Empire's heartlands, but was one of its most important cities: the second largest in the empire after Istanbul, and the key to Egypt, the empire's most lucrative province. Moreover, the very contrast between the centrality of Cairo within Islamic history and its provinciality during the Ottoman period symbolizes one of the key dynamics animating Ottoman legal history. How did a dynasty from the far frontier of the Muslim world manage to harness the *sharīʿa* to imperial ends, in the very cities where that prestigious legal tradition was born and cultivated?

The book is centered around two interconnected lines of inquiry, which engage with important themes in Islamic legal studies and Ottoman historiography. The first is the relationship between Islamic law and political authority: what was the place of the Sultan and his government in what is often seen as a quintessential jurists' law? I argue that central and local political authorities were intimately involved in the formulation of legal doctrine and the day-to-day provision of justice. In contrast to prevailing models of Islamic legal history, I show that institutions resembling the ruler's *maẓālim* tribunal survived beyond the Middle Ages and throughout the Ottoman period, and that government intervention in Egypt's legal system began long before Meḥmed ʿAlī's reforms of the nineteenth century.

The second line of inquiry is the imperial relationship between Egypt and the Ottoman center: what sustained Ottoman rule over this distant province during a period in which most historians describe a shift in power from the government in Istanbul to provincial political forces? I demonstrate that law and legal practice were central to this relationship, as government edicts shaped Egypt's laws and the Grand Vizier, the Ottoman governor and military officers handled lawsuits and disputes originating in Egypt. I argue that, to a greater extent than is recognized by scholarship, this relationship was driven from below: it was Egyptian subjects who demanded that the Sultan and his agents engage in their disputes.

Islamic law and political authority

As with most stereotypes, there is some truth in the assertion that Islamic law is a jurists' law. The great scholarly edifice of *fiqh* was the bedrock of Islamic law until the late nineteenth century, and even in the age of codification and the secular nation-state, the primary sources, hermeneutics, and doctrines of the fiqh tradition remain significant points of reference.[1] The medieval model of Muslim scholarship and education was idiosyncratic and marked by its distance from political authority. In this model institutions and patrons, let alone states and kings, were marginal. The context for the generation and transmission of knowledge was the study-circle that formed around an individual professor. A jurist's authority was drawn not from official appointment or certification, but from his scholarly lineage: the record of personal pedagogical relationships with esteemed teachers.[2]

The problem with the notion of Islamic law as a jurists' law lies not in its empirical accuracy, but in its operation as a central organizing concept in Islamic legal history. As the notion transformed from a description of a particular dimension of pre-modern Muslim intellectual culture into a normative statement about Islamic law, it hardened into a litmus test of authenticity. An assumption became embedded in modern scholarship that "genuine" Islamic law was produced by jurists. By contrast, any observable input by any other authority was considered not a part of Islamic law, but an external intrusion. Intervention into the law by rulers and political authorities was seen either as corruption or as a "secular" alternative to "Islamic" law.

This model was most glaring in the work of earlier generations of scholars in the Orientalist and Islamic Studies traditions, who wrote legal history solely on the basis of fiqh texts. This textual orientation reduced Islamic law to fiqh, treating it in isolation from other contemporaneous intellectual traditions as well as from the institutional structures and practical applications of law in historical Muslim societies. This paradigm resulted in broad characterizations of Islamic law that became infamous: that it was impractical, that it was immutable, and that there was a wide chasm between Islamic law and Muslim legal practice.[3]

Over the last four decades, scholarship on Islamic law, including that conducted using the textual, fiqh-centered approach, has become much more sophisticated. Post-classical fiqh is now treated much more seriously. Meanwhile, the burgeoning output of scholarship based on the Ottoman sharīʿa court records, which are often known as *sijill*s after the name for the registers in which they were kept, has transformed our understanding of Muslim legal practice. Together, these developments have upended the image of Islamic law as moribund, impractical, and divorced from real social conditions.

Sijill-based Ottoman legal historiography has modified the straightforward equation of Islamic law with fiqh, showing that Ottoman ḳānūn and local custom formed part of the law administered by the sharīᶜa courts. Nevertheless, the binary outlined above, between law as the domain of scholars and political power as the domain of rulers, remains visible, especially at the level of judicial institutions. Most Ottomanists have focused squarely on the sharīᶜa court as the central institution of Ottoman justice and on the *qāḍī* (judge), who was drawn from the same scholarly milieu as the jurist, as its key actor.[4] Some historians have gone so far as to claim that rival jurisdictions familiar in the medieval Middle East, such as the maẓālim tribunal and the *muḥtasib*, disappeared under the Ottomans, their functions subsumed by the qāḍī and his court. Others have simply not addressed the question of jurisdictions other than the sharīᶜa court, or have portrayed them as marginal.

Recently, Wael Hallaq published the most significant synthesis of Islamic legal history for a generation, with his 2009 book *Sharīᶜa: Theory, Practice, Transformations. Sharīᶜa* sums up the recent advances in scholarship, while presenting them through Hallaq's unique perspective on the subject. Hallaq's model is premised on the understanding that Islamic law was primarily fiqh, produced by jurists who were largely independent of rulers, and applied by qāḍīs who, although appointed by the ruler, operated autonomously. Hallaq's model is much more sophisticated than earlier accounts. Not only does he identify evolution and dynamism in fiqh over the long term, but his description of the relationship between Islamic law and legal practice is more complex and draws on the insights of legal anthropology as well as the sijill-based Ottoman historiography. Hallaq argues that features such as the recognition of local custom, the orientation towards mediation that allowed local communal values to find expression in legal practice, and the firm grounding in morality, were vital structural features that made Islamic law a very effective system of ordering, commanding respect and obedience while using minimal coercion. Hallaq's Islamic law is not simply a jurists' law, therefore, even if the jurist is the most prominent figure in his narrative. Rather, Hallaq characterizes Islamic law as a "non-state, community-based, bottom-up, jural order."[5] Hallaq's jurists were independent of political authority, but they were not isolated in ivory towers. They were deeply rooted in their societies, and the law they crafted was inextricably interwoven with the communal moral order.

While Hallaq celebrates local, communal influences on Islamic law, the binary of jurist/ruler remains central to his narrative. Hallaq regards significant influence by the ruler on the law as illegitimate, and he minimizes it in his narrative of Islamic legal history before the nineteenth century. Hallaq admits the importance of *siyāsa sharᶜiyya*—the exercise of political power in accordance with the sharīᶜa—but he insists that this was a limited concept, which allowed the ruler to control his governors and officials while also granting him authority over "tax collection, public order, land use, and at times criminal law and some aspects of public morality that could affect social harmony."[6] The qāḍī and the sharīʿa, which Hallaq distinguishes from siyāsa, governed everything else. In other words, Hallaq convincingly reverses the Orientalist stereotype by presenting Islamic law as a dynamic legal tradition that was absolutely central to social life and governance in the Muslim world, but he retains the definition of Islamic law as fiqh. The supremacy of sharīʿa was qualified only slightly by the strictly circumscribed jurisdiction of the ruler under siyāsa.

The Ottoman Empire plays a significant role in Hallaq's grand narrative of Islamic legal history. Hallaq argues that, with few exceptions, the near-monopoly of the qāḍī and the sharīʿa over legal life was the norm in the pre-modern Muslim world, true of the Mamluk Sultanate, Safavid and Qajar Persia, and Mughal India. But for Hallaq, the authority of the sharīʿa reached its zenith in the Ottoman Empire, when the jurisdiction of the qāḍī was extended to include state officials as well as subjects. In Hallaq's words,

> The Ottomans' perfection of this system was largely due to one of their reforms, namely, the abolishment of the *maẓālim* court, the extra-judicial tribunal of grievances. Instead of placing a political/military body in a position to judge the misconduct of government officials, the Ottomans located this function firmly within the jurisdiction of the Sharīʿa judge. The *qāḍī* became the only government official empowered to hear cases and to adjudicate them, and, more importantly, to decide on the legality of conduct of the highest provincial officials, including the governor.[7]

If the early modern Ottoman Empire represents the pinnacle of sharīʿa for Hallaq, then the Tanzimat was its undoing. The nineteenth-century legal reforms in the Ottoman Empire and Egypt, undertaken by Ottoman Muslim statesmen, represent the intrusion of alien, European concepts and ideals into the Islamic legal sphere just as much as the reforms of colonial governments in Algeria, India, and Indonesia. The subjection of the law to state authority, codification, the founding of modern law schools, the introduction of new tribunals staffed by bureaucrats in the Ottoman Empire and by British judges in India: these changes constitute a single phenomenon across the Muslim world and are the fundamental rupture in Hallaq's narrative. The intrusion of the modern state is so alien to Hallaq's concept of Islamic law that he regards the reformed legal systems of the modern Muslim world as inauthentic by definition, regardless of the claims they make about compliance with Islamic law.[8]

Ottoman legal historiography

Hallaq's assessment of the Ottoman legal system is a synthesis of the sijill-based Ottoman legal historiography of the past few decades, albeit skewed towards the earlier works of the 1970s–90s, which suit Hallaq's model better. In particular, Hallaq relies on the work of Ronald Jennings and Haim Gerber, pioneering scholars of the sharīʿa court records who both emphasized the autonomy of the qāḍī and his sharīʿa court. In a series of articles in the late 1970s, Jennings used the sijills of

Kayseri in central Anatolia to explore the structure and operation of Ottoman justice at a local level and the use of the courts by women and non-Muslims.[9] In two articles focusing on the role of the qāḍī, Jennings argued that although he was appointed by the Sultan and could be dismissed, in practice the qāḍī did not suffer interference in his judicial business. Jennings found imperial orders sent to the qāḍī concerning specific cases, but they only instructed the qāḍī to try the case, never to reach a particular decision.[10]

Haim Gerber gave a similar picture of judicial autonomy in two books and several articles published between 1980 and the early 2000s.[11] Gerber's research focused on the sijills of Bursa; unlike most sijill-scholars, he also connected this with research on Ottoman-era fiqh.[12] Gerber argued that Ottoman qāḍīs applied the law impartially, consistently and without interference from the Sultan or other political authorities. Gerber also, in common with many other scholars of the sijills, stressed the primacy of the qāḍī's jurisdiction. While Gerber discussed the Dīvān-i Hümāyūn as a tribunal, he portrayed its function as primarily to receive complaints from subjects against Ottoman officials. Otherwise, the sharīᶜa court was the only legal institution available to Ottoman subjects, and the qāḍī the only official able to resolve disputes and convict offenders. According to Gerber, other jurisdictions that had existed in the medieval Middle East—including the maẓālim tribunal presided over by medieval rulers, and the muḥtasib who oversaw both market trading and public morality—disappeared under Ottoman rule, their functions subsumed into the sharīᶜa court.[13] The qāḍī's near-monopoly on dispute resolution was connected with his alleged autonomy: the lack of rivals with parallel or superior jurisdictions meant that his judgments could not be overruled.

The emphasis placed on judicial autonomy by Jennings and Gerber should be seen in the context of the earlier scholarship on the Ottoman Empire and Islamic law that they were writing against. Gerber in particular engaged explicitly with the image of Ottoman rule as despotic and arbitrary, and with Weber's model of *kadijustiz*, which held that Muslim qāḍīs made judgments based on expediency rather than on a settled and coherent body of law.[14] First and foremost, their aim was to demonstrate that Ottoman sharīᶜa courts were not arbitrary but operated according to clear procedures and relied on a coherent body of law that was widely understood, at least in its broad outlines. They portrayed the sharīᶜa courts not only as effective mechanisms of governance but also as useful resources for Ottoman subjects who willingly brought their disputes and complaints to the qāḍī. If these claims seem unremarkable now it is only because other scholars have built on the foundations laid by Jennings and Gerber.

The autonomy of the qāḍī was a central part of this argument. For Jennings and Gerber, the qāḍī was the key guarantor of the rationality and impartiality of Ottoman justice. The qāḍī was a check on the power of the government, and his autonomy prevented arbitrary rule. A similar picture of the qāḍī was also given by historians who were not writing legal history specifically, but were offering a broader theory of an Ottoman system of governance.[15] In these accounts, the Ottoman qāḍī took the role of the independent judiciary that is deemed an essential component of constitutional government and the rule of law today. In other words, when trying to prove that Ottoman rule was not arbitrary, historians tended to project back a modern conception of the separation of powers on to the early modern Ottoman Empire. In this book, I question this image of an autonomous qāḍī as the pivot of the Ottoman justice system. I argue instead that qāḍīs in Ottoman Cairo played a limited, though certainly vital, role within a complex network of legal institutions with overlapping jurisdictions. Questioning the central position accorded to the qāḍī by previous historiography does not mean that I hope to restore the title of arbitrary despotism to the Ottoman Empire. It only means an attempt to define the roles of different actors within the legal system more precisely, in order to uncover an indigenous and contemporary Ottoman understanding of just governance.

The literature on Ottoman legal practice has tended, for the most part, to confirm the picture given by Gerber of the sharīᶜa court's monopoly on dispute resolution, at least by implication. Historians working on the sharīᶜa court records have naturally made that institution the focus of their study. And the sharīᶜa court was undoubtedly an important institution, acting as a property registry as well as being a popular venue for dispute resolution, at least for the urban populations of the Ottoman Empire. But, despite important methodological critiques of the sharīᶜa court records, it is often forgotten that the primary reason that scholars foreground the sharīᶜa courts is because the sharīᶜa court records give them the vast majority of their evidence.[16] Due to their disproportionate bulk, the sharīᶜa court records obscure the view of other institutions and practices in the Ottoman legal system. Recently, several scholars have recognized the existence of other forums alongside the sharīᶜa court. With a couple of exceptions, those working on the provinces have made only tentative suggestions about them: lacking sources produced by these institutions, they have been able only to cull limited information about them from narrative sources or from the sharīᶜa court records themselves.[17] Historians working on Istanbul have had access to a wider range of sources and have begun to produce detailed studies of the relationships between different legal institutions.[18]

Cairo makes an ideal provincial site for an investigation of how sharīᶜa courts fitted in to a broader web of legal institutions and practices, because a particularly rich and varied range of sources relevant to this city has survived. In Cairo, in addition to the extensive collection of sharīᶜa court records, a much smaller but very interesting collection of records from the Ottoman governor of Egypt's tribunal, al-Dīwān al-ᶜĀlī, has survived. The role of the Dīvān-i Hümāyūn, the Imperial Council in Istanbul, in Egyptian legal affairs can be traced through its records in Istanbul's Ottoman archives. Furthermore, Cairo life is chronicled in several surviving narrative accounts. All of these sources are explained in more detail later in this chapter.

Based on these sources, I portray Ottoman Cairo's legal system as a complex network of judicial forums and practices with poorly-defined and therefore overlapping jurisdictions: the sharīᶜa court, the governor's tribunal, the imperial council which received petitions from Egypt and across the empire, several military officials who shared responsibility for policing and market regulation, and political notables who offered justice as part of their cultivation of client networks. Rather than viewing this system from an institutional perspective, in order to make sense of it I explore the roles of different individuals who worked within them. Particular individuals were not necessarily associated with single institutions: the qāḍī, for example, worked in or on behalf of several of these institutions. I argue that the qāḍī was primarily responsible for determining facts through the application of legal procedure. When adjudicating litigation, qāḍīs did not play a significant role in determining or interpreting the legal doctrine that would be applied to the case. This job was often played by the government, which instructed qāḍīs which doctrines from the accumulated body of fiqh should be applied in Ottoman courts. In cases where the government had not issued instructions, and the answer was not straightforward, the qāḍī would refer to a mufti for guidance. Lastly, enforcement of judgments and penalties was largely the responsibility of the governor and Cairo's military officials; this was true of judgments issued by the sharīᶜa courts as much as those issued by other authorities.

Law and empire

The second of the two themes running through this book is the role of law in the imperial relationship between Cairo and the Ottoman capital. Unusually for an imperial historiography, and thanks in large part to the sharīᶜa court records, the provinces feature as prominently as the center in Ottoman historiography. Center–province relations during the seventeenth and eighteenth centuries have been a particular focus of study. This period was the age of the supposed decline of the Ottoman Empire, a narrative that described a progressive loss of central control over the provinces. Revisionist scholarship challenging the decline thesis from a provincial perspective has reinterpreted this period as one of decentralization. Far from weakening the empire, historians have argued that this process of decentralization integrated provinces into the empire, by creating provincial elites who identified with the Ottoman dynasty and recognized it as the source of their power and prosperity.[19]

Egyptian historiography has seen a particular variant of the development outlined above. Due to the influence of Egyptian nationalism, the Ottoman period was long seen as a period of stagnation, an anomalous hiatus during which Egypt was a distant province rather than an imperial center.[20] Early works focusing on the Ottoman period adopted the decline paradigm, portraying a vigorous assertion of Ottoman imperial power during the sixteenth century, followed by a gradual relinquishing of control and drift towards eventual autonomy during the seventeenth and eighteenth centuries.[21] Beginning in the 1970s, studies based on Ottoman Egypt's sharīᶜa court records upended the image of stagnation, demonstrating that Ottoman rule saw Egypt's economy and trade thrive, while Cairo grew substantially in population and area.[22] In these sijill-based studies, however, aspects of the Ottoman decline paradigm were retained: in particular, the distance, or even irrelevance, of the Ottoman center from Egyptian life.

The first major revision to the image of Ottoman Egypt as a province set apart politically and culturally from the rest of the empire was Jane Hathaway's monograph *The Politics of Households in Ottoman Egypt*. Hathaway presented the elite households of seventeenth and eighteenth-century Egypt as a provincial variant on the contemporary households that dominated political life in the center of the Ottoman Empire, rather than as a throwback to the Mamluk Sultanate. Far from being antagonistic to Ottoman rule, they were another hyphenated Ottoman-provincial elite, jockeying for a greater share of power and resources within the Ottoman system, but not seeking to overthrow it.[23]

More recently, Alan Mikhail's *Nature and Empire in Ottoman Egypt* demonstrated the remarkably intimate connections between Egyptian villagers and the imperial government through which Egyptian agriculture was managed.[24] Beyond demonstrating the Ottomanization of the province within a context of decentralizing power, Mikhail questions the extent of decentralization. Officials in the capital were involved in decisions concerning local irrigation infrastructure in the rural areas of a distant province: infrastructure that was crucial to the food security of the entire empire. The metropolitan officials were not simply issuing orders: rather, this relationship was a collaboration that allowed the government to draw on peasant expertise in local water management.

This book builds on this trajectory to question further whether the decentralization paradigm can accurately describe the relationship between Egypt and the Ottoman Empire during the seventeenth and eighteenth centuries. I explore how both the imperial government, in the form of its council the Dīvān-i Hümāyūn and the governors it sent to run the provincial administration in Cairo, was intimately involved in the day-to-day legal affairs of this distant province. As with Mikhail's story of peasant agency, the involvement of these imperial authorities in often mundane disputes was not a top-down process imposed on Egyptian society. Rather, Egyptians sought to draw the imperial government into their disputes, recognizing the symbolic weight and the practical might of the empire and its Sultan as a useful resource in pursuing their disputes.[25] In this way, the imperial relationship was perpetuated and strengthened from below, by the provincial population, even as Istanbul's ability to impose its will on Egypt's political elite was flagging.

The decentralization paradigm fails to explain the behavior of the many Cairene litigants who saw it as advantageous to involve the Sultan or the governor in their disputes. Insofar as it suggests a linear, progressive transfer of power from center to province, it also fails to convey the oscillation in the government's ability to project its will in Egypt. In the context of Egypt, the decentralization narrative proposes that there was a period of intensive Ottomanization in the half-century immediately following the conquest, which saw powerful governors remake Egypt's administration and military, impose the Ottoman ḳānūnnāme, and imprint the urban landscape of Cairo with grand mosques in the neo-Byzantine style of the capital.[26] From the late sixteenth century on, the power of the governors weakened in favor of the corporate power of the Janissary and ᶜAzabān regiments and the patronage-dispensing political households. The governor was reduced to attempting to manipulate the internecine factional conflicts of the households and regiments; Muḥammad Nūr Faraḥāt claims that in the eighteenth century he was little more than an "ambassador from Istanbul."[27]

The legal system has played a significant role in this rise and decline narrative. Nelly Hanna and Michael Winter have both argued that in the decades immediately following the conquest the Ottoman government made a concerted attempt to Ottomanize legal practice in Cairo. This project of Ottomanization involved reorganizing the sharīᶜa courts, imposing Ottoman ḳānūn and privileging the Ḥanafī *madhhab* (school of law), enhancing the qāḍī's authority at the expense of other individuals such as the muḥtasib, imposing the Turkish language in some areas of legal practice, and appointing "Ottoman Turks," trained in the central lands of the empire, to key posts in Cairo's judicial hierarchy. From the late sixteenth century on, however, the legal system underwent a reverse process of Egyptianization as Ottoman influence dwindled. The Ottoman chief qāḍī become a less significant figure, the Arabic language became increasingly dominant, and Ḥanafī supremacy was undermined. According to Winter, "more significantly, the number of Turkish qāḍīs decreased; in 1798 only six qāḍīs were Ottoman Turks, the rest being Arabs."[28]

In this book I suggest a more complicated story of imperial influence over Cairo's legal system waxing and waning during the course of Ottoman rule. The central authorities and their agents in Cairo reasserted their control at several points, trying different strategies at different times. Reem Meshal has recently shown that attempts to mold Cairene legal practice into an Ottoman shape, in particular by promoting the Ḥanafī madhhab at the expense of the others, continued into the early seventeenth century.[29] I extend this story by describing a further wave of Ḥanafizing pressure in Egypt beginning in the 1690s and continuing into the eighteenth century. Meanwhile, the involvement of Ottoman imperial authorities in the day-to-day legal affairs of Cairo was not significantly affected by the weakening of central control over Egypt's discordant political elite. The earliest surviving register of the governor's Dīwān dates from the 1740s, a period when according to traditional narratives the governor was very weak in comparison with Cairo's leading political households. Indeed, chronicles tell of the most powerful figure in Cairo politics of this period, ᶜUthmān Bey Dhū ᵓl-Faqār, setting up his own tribunal in what was both a direct provocation to the governor and an ambitious act of self-aggrandizement.[30] Nevertheless, the first register of the governor's Dīwān reveals it to be a bustling center of legal activity used especially by the very elites that the governors struggled to control. Part of the explanation of this apparent dissonance is that, as mentioned above, Egyptian subjects actively sought the involvement of Ottoman authorities in their affairs: imperial influence was not simply a top-down projection.

Legal pluralism

If the jurisdictional boundaries between different legal forums in Cairo were ill-defined, then how should we understand the relationships between them? An explanatory framework drawn from outside the field of Islamic legal studies—legal pluralism—can help us to make sense of the legal system as a whole.[31] In this section I will briefly lay out how I think this concept can apply to the case of Ottoman Cairo.

The concept of legal pluralism emerged within the study of European colonial societies, primarily as a way of understanding the relationship between the law imposed by the colonial government and the customary laws used by indigenous subject populations. For this reason, the binaries of formal/informal and state/non-state have been central to the concept. John Griffiths, who wrote a detailed and influential definition of legal pluralism, insisted that the term could only be legitimately applied to societies where at least one of the bodies of law in operation lay entirely outside the control of the state. A situation in which multiple bodies of law coexist, but all are recognized by the state, constitutes legal diversity, but not legal pluralism, according to Griffiths.[32]

Highlighting state recognition as the crucial factor distinguishing between diverse and plural legal systems betrays a very modern conception of the state, its objectives, and its capabilities. It relies on there being a clear distinction between state law and non-state law, one fully controlled by the state, the other entirely independent. The Ottoman Empire, a pre-modern state administering a prestigious legal tradition that predated it and that the ruling dynasty identified with, does not fit into this binary. Did the Ottoman state control Islamic law? We cannot answer simply yes or no; indeed, the situation is wholly unlike the colonial and postcolonial situations imagined by most theorists of legal pluralism. Islamic law was not imposed from on high by the Ottomans; at least, not in the Islamic heartlands that they conquered in the sixteenth century. But neither was it an "indigenous" law that persisted underneath a top layer of imperial law: the Ottomans recognized Islamic law as supreme, and much of the development and application of the law was undertaken by Ottoman institutions.

In an article focusing on the Muslim world, Ido Shahar proposed a different definition that looked at the issue from the litigant's perspective. Shahar argued that the key question is whether the litigants can choose between two or more forums. If yes, then this is a case of "strong," that is, genuine, legal pluralism. If litigants are automatically allocated to one of several forums, according to religious identity or some other characteristic of the litigant or the dispute, then this is "weak" legal pluralism, which is not really pluralism at all.[33] This definition better suits the weak capacities of early modern states. It also points to one of the most interesting questions about legal pluralism: how do litigants navigate a system where they can choose different forums that will give different judgments? However, as I demonstrate in this book, the ability of Ottoman litigants to choose between forums, while real in some circumstances, was constrained. For one thing, in many circumstances cases were, in effect, automatically assigned to a particular forum. This was often true of the "choice" between judges of different madhhabs which, I argue in Chapter 4, fits the model of forum-shopping less well than is commonly assumed. Furthermore, to a large extent pluralism in Ottoman Cairo concerned different forums that applied the same body of law. This does not mean that litigant choice had no effect on outcome, but it means that the effect did not come via doctrinal differences. Instead, as I discuss in Chapter 6, it relied on a litigant's canny manipulation of a system with poorly-defined jurisdictional boundaries.

Recently, Paul Schiff Berman has formulated a concept of global legal pluralism as an attempt to explain the increasingly globalized law of today's world, where transnational, national, and sub-national jurisdictions frequently clash and lawyers must increasingly work within "hybrid legal spaces." Although conceived for the contemporary age of globalization, I think this model has much to offer the early modern Ottoman Empire. Berman sidesteps the distinction between state and non-state law, crucial to Griffiths' formulation, by writing instead of "norm-generating communities." These norm-generating communities include recognizable law-making bodies ranging from international institutions such as the United Nations through nation-states to municipalities. They also include many other entities that create norms, which can be formal or informal and national, transnational, or subnational: religious institutions, industry standard-setting bodies, accreditation agencies, professional organizations, and so on. While there may appear to be a clear line between state and non-state, in practice there is not: for example, conventions and standards agreed privately between companies in a particular economic sector often create obligations that can be enforced by national courts.[34] Berman's model of legal pluralism is cosmopolitan, in that he recognizes that all people are simultaneously members of multiple norm-generating communities, and that he refuses to privilege, a priori, any particular community over another. Instead, he argues that legal activity consists of constant interaction, exchange, and conflict between different sets of norms, which takes place in the "hybrid spaces" where they overlap.

I find Berman's model attractive because the blurring of the lines between state and non-state, formal and informal, helps make sense of the indeterminate boundaries between different jurisdictions and different bodies of law in the Ottoman Empire. For a start, consider the difficulty of categorizing Islamic law as transnational, national, or subnational; or rather, to avoid the anachronistic term "national," as trans-state, state, or sub-state. In one sense, Islamic law was clearly trans-state, both in theory—as a divine law of universal applicability—and in practice, as jurists in different empires were in dialogue and rules created in one state could be applied in another. In another sense, Ottoman Islamic law was a state law: it was applied by judges appointed and paid by the state, and the state shaped the doctrines of Islamic law that were applied within Ottoman territory. And yet, in another sense, Islamic law was a sub-state law: multiple Islamic legal traditions existed within the empire, by which I do not mean madhhabs (which of course were themselves trans-state), but different scholarly cultures in different regions. Recently, Guy Burak explored the interactions between an Ottoman and a Syrian tradition of Ḥanafism, while both Ahmed Ibrahim and Reem Meshal have pointed to a distinctive early modern Egyptian understanding of Islamic law: Chapter 4 of this book contributes to this discussion.[35] Consider also the interactions between Islamic law and other normative traditions that had currency among Muslim ruling elites: in the Ottoman case, the Persian and Turco-Mongol in particular, associated with the concepts of siyāsa and ḳānūn. Here too, much of the development of law as well as litigation and other legal activities took place precisely in the "hybrid spaces" between different normative traditions.

There are several possible contexts where legal pluralism can be located in Ottoman Cairo. The most obvious is the Ottomans' well-known willingness to allow Christians and Jews to arrange their affairs according to their own religious laws. This is the terrain on which many previous scholars have discussed legal pluralism in the Ottoman Empire.[36] Many scholars have demonstrated that Ottoman Christians and Jews made extensive use of the empire's sharīᶜa courts, choosing between them and communal courts when resolving intra-communal disputes.[37] While Muslims had no corresponding right, Christians and Jews in large Ottoman cities were able to forum-shop between different bodies of religious law. Of all the types of legal pluralism that existed in the Ottoman Empire, this most closely resembled the colonial situations where the concept of legal pluralism was first discussed, with Islamic law serving as the imperial law, and church and rabbinical laws serving as the indigenous law. Ottoman Cairo was home to substantial Christian and Jewish communities, so this form of legal pluralism was certainly a reality there. However, it does not strike me as the most fruitful ground on which to discuss Ottoman legal pluralism, because we currently know very little about Christian or Jewish courts in Cairo or, with a handful of small exceptions, anywhere else in the Ottoman Empire.[38]

The second manifestation of legal pluralism in Ottoman Cairo was the pluralism of madhhabs. The four Sunnī madhhabs—Ḥanafī, Shāfiᶜī, Mālikī and Ḥanbalī—were all practiced in the city's sharīᶜa courts despite the Ottoman dynasty's endorsement of Ḥanafism. This is the other aspect of legal pluralism that has been widely commented on by historians of the Ottoman Empire, and litigants were sometimes able to exercise choice, therefore complying with Shahar's definition.[39] In Chapter 4, I qualify the image of unrestricted choice between madhhabs by showing that in certain important contexts the Ottoman authorities controlled access to non-Ḥanafī doctrines. Moreover, Ottoman control over non-Ḥanafī doctrines was tightened during the period I study: the element of choice was gradually restricted in the interests of Ḥanafī uniformity.

The third type of legal pluralism in Ottoman Cairo differs from the first two, as it did not concern different bodies of law. Rather, it involved different institutions that applied the same body of law, but which had overlapping jurisdictions. Ottoman subjects in Cairo could choose to submit complaints to several different institutions, as they could in most other major cities in the empire. These all applied the same body of law: Islamic law combined with Ottoman ḳānūn (dynastic law). Yet the choice was still significant, and litigants could hope to achieve different outcomes depending on which forum they chose. In order to understand this we have to think not about differing legal doctrines, but about different enforcement capabilities and about the relationship between judgment and compromise; or, in other words, the distinction between the court ruling and the ultimate resolution of the dispute within the community.

I explore this "institutional pluralism" in Chapters 3 and 6. This subject has not been discussed extensively by Ottomanists, with a few recent exceptions.[40] It has received greater attention from scholars of medieval Muslim societies, whose attention has often focused on the relationships between sharīᶜa courts and maẓālim tribunals, although these scholars have mostly not used the terminology of legal pluralism.[41] Although much of the detailed empirical work has suggested otherwise, this relationship in the medieval period is still generally understood through a model of distinct jurisdictions—the sharīᶜa court adjudicating disputes among the general population while the maẓālim tribunal heard complaints against officials—and it is assumed to involve different procedural law, with the maẓālim procedure making the conviction of criminals easier. This definition of maẓālim follows the theory of the eleventh-century jurist and administrator Māwardī.[42] Rather than assuming clear jurisdictional boundaries, I think that legal pluralism is a better model for this relationship before and during the Ottoman Empire. Recently, Mathieu Tillier has developed this as an approach to pre-modern Muslim legal systems in general.[43] Berman's model of cosmopolitan legal pluralism is particularly appropriate. Ottoman subjects were members of multiple "norm-generating communities." For a start, all were both subjects of God's universal law and subjects of a patrimonial Sultan personally responsible for ensuring justice; the recognition of "ancient traditions" specific to locality, trade, profession and other identifiers added further complexity. They made claims according to the norms, rights, and rhetoric of more than one of these communities, exploring and exploiting the "hybrid spaces" in between them.

Sources

As a central goal of this study is to explore the plurality of legal institutions in Ottoman Cairo, I have used a broader range of sources than the sharīᶜa court records which have been the focus of Ottoman legal historiography. As mentioned above, an exceptionally diverse set of legal records relevant to Cairo has survived.

Although I have tried to cast my net wider, the sharīᶜa court records necessarily remain central to my research. As one of the largest cities in the Ottoman Empire, Cairo had many sharīᶜa courts. These included the main court, known as al-Bāb al-ᶜĀlī and the seat of the chief qāḍī; two courts specializing in inheritance, al-Qisma al-ᶜAskariyya and al-Qisma al-ᶜArabiyya; eleven neighborhood courts within the city of Cairo; and one court in each of Cairo's two suburbs, Būlāq and Miṣr al-Qadīma.[44] I focused on the records of two of these, the neighborhood court of Bāb al-Shaᶜriyya and al-Bāb al-ᶜĀlī, while briefly surveying some of the others. Bāb al-Shaᶜriyya was a neighborhood in the northwest of the city, named after one of the gates in the medieval wall. In the seventeenth and eighteenth centuries, its population was dominated by small-scale artisans, especially those working in the textile industry. The registers of al-Bāb al-ᶜĀlī are somewhat idiosyncratic, due to its status as the main sharīᶜa court and seat of the chief qāḍī. As well as the disputes and contracts found in all court registers, they contain a large amount of administrative record-keeping, including appointments to positions in the provincial government and in the administration of endowments, and official correspondence with Istanbul.

The sharīᶜa court records have been a staple source of Ottoman social and economic history since they were first subjected to scholarly study in the 1970s. Existing in voluminous quantities, often in near-complete runs, for almost every major city in the empire and for many minor towns, they have provided an intimate view into the homes, streets, and markets of every corner of the empire. They have opened up fields of inquiry that have revolutionized our understanding of life in the Ottoman Empire; for example, the history of women and family life.

Given the great historiographical weight that sharīᶜa court records bear, it is worth reflecting on why they exist, why they survived, and the implications of this for their use as historical sources. The court registers contain copies of documents issued by the court, including both contracts notarized by the court or lawsuits heard by it. These registers were the working archives of the court, enabling litigants to prove their claims and qāḍīs to check the veracity of documents.

The circumstances of the production of these registers have important implications for how we use them as historical sources. Much of the early use of court records was uncritical; the records were simply mined for factual data. Several critiques, in particular those by Dror Ze'evi, Boğaç Ergene, and Iris Agmon, highlighted the flaws in this approach, and pointed the way to the critical study of these records that is sensitive to the social, institutional, and textual constraints within which they were produced.[45] To summarize these critiques very briefly, the sharīᶜa court records are not transparent descriptions of reality, but have been filtered through several layers of representation and translation. A single record of a dispute represents a real situation that two litigants have presented to the qāḍī, each in the way that best suits his or her objectives. This has then been summarized by the scribe, translated into legal terminology and structured according to legal procedure, recording only what was procedurally relevant. The greater scholarly attention paid to the operation of Ottoman sharīᶜa courts since the mid-1990s has helped historians to read these records with a more critical eye, but they remain problematic and sometimes infuriating sources.

Here I want to point out another important feature of the sharīᶜa court registers: their survival in such great numbers. The particular shape of Ottoman legal historiography, which places the sharīᶜa court and its qāḍī squarely at the center of the Ottoman legal system, has emerged because legal historians have worked primarily, often exclusively, on the sharīᶜa court records. In a basic sense, the survival of the records itself tells us that the sharīᶜa courts were important. But the relative rate of survival of sharīᶜa court records versus other categories of legal document should not be attributed to the relative importance of the institutions that produced them, but rather to the stability and longevity of the sharīᶜa courts, which was much greater than that of any other Ottoman legal institution. The courts remained in existence into the late nineteenth and in most cases well into the twentieth century, and so they preserved their registers—which were their working archives—until that time. In some cases, Ottoman court registers are still in the possession of functioning sharīᶜa courts that are the institutional descendants of their early modern equivalents.[46] But even in places where sharīᶜa courts were eventually abolished or transformed into something unrecognizably different, this happened at a time when modern national archives existed to take care of the documents.

This record of institutional continuity is remarkable, and compares very favorably with that of any other institution of Ottoman governance. Let us take the governor of Egypt's Dīwān al-ᶜĀlī as an example. This racked up quite an impressive continuous existence from its establishment in 1524 until the early nineteenth century. At this point, the reforming governor Meḥmed ᶜAlī Pasha replaced it with the Dīvān-i Hıdīvī, which itself was eclipsed by the emergence of a modern bureaucracy during the nineteenth century. Despite being one of the longer-lasting Ottoman institutions, the Dīwān al-ᶜĀlī fell well short of the longevity of Cairo's sharīᶜa courts, which were not abolished until 1956. Moreover, unlike the qāḍī, the governor of Egypt was frequently involved in violence, much of which took place in the vicinity of the citadel where his residence and the Dīwān were located. For example, the Janissary barracks, located at the foot of the citadel, were heavily bombarded by the rival ᶜAzab regiment during the war of 1711.[47] It is quite likely that documents may have been damaged or destroyed during such incidents. Indeed, the chronicler Aḥmad Çelebi tells us that a fire in the citadel in 1670 burned the Dīwān's files.[48] Of course, the violent destruction of sharīᶜa courts and their records was not unheard of: the case of the sharīᶜa court records of Smyrna, which burned in the great fire when the Turkish National Movement took the city from the Greek occupation force in 1922, is well known. But the Dīwān al-ᶜĀlī and similar institutions associated with provincial governorships elsewhere in the empire were much more frequently the targets of political violence. And just as we would be wrong to conclude from the absence of Smyrna's court records that the city's sharīᶜa courts were not important, we must also hesitate before dismissing the importance of provincial governors' tribunals on the grounds that there are few surviving records.[49]

Although the surviving quantity of records from the Dīwān al-ᶜĀlī looks meager compared to the sharīᶜa court records, we are fortunate to have any at all. The registers of the Dīwān al-ᶜĀlī are not quite unique, but they are a very rare example of extant documents from a provincial governor's tribunal prior to the nineteenth century.[50] The earliest surviving register dates from 1741–3, and is held at the Egyptian National Archive. I have used this register, and its dates give the chronological terminus of this study. After the first register, there is a gap of several decades, with the second register dating from the 1780s. The remaining ten registers in the series date from the early nineteenth century. In addition to the registers, there are a handful of surviving *ḥujja*s issued by the Dīwān, held at both the Egyptian

National Archive and the Prime Ministry Archive in Istanbul. I have found twelve ḥujjas dating from earlier than the Dīwān's first register, including three from the seventeenth century, the earliest of which dates from 1621.[51] The similarity between these ḥujjas and the register's entries establishes that the Dīwān performed the same judicial role much earlier than the first register; it probably performed this role since the early days of Ottoman rule.

The physical shape of the Dīwān's register is different from those of Cairo's sharīᶜa courts: it is an elongated, narrow register similar to the *defter*s used by the imperial bureaucracy in Istanbul, whereas the court registers are a thicker rectangular shape, 40cm x 50cm. However, the records contained within the register are very similar to those in the court registers. They are copies of ḥujjas detailing both contracts notarized by the Dīwān and disputes heard by the Dīwān. The register also contains a few records concerning administrative business specific to the Dīwān, such as the annual measurement of the Nile. There were some differences between the Dīwān and the sharīᶜa courts, in terms of their caseloads and personnel, which I discuss in Chapter 3.

Records related to petitioning are a significant body of sources useful for historians of all regions of the Ottoman Empire. They include the original petitions sent to the Sultan and registers containing copies of the imperial orders sent in response.[52] The registers have received some attention from historians, though nowhere near as much as the sharīᶜa court records.[53] The original petitions have hardly been studied at all.[54]

The petitioning records pose different challenges to the researcher. Petitions are also formulaic, but their formula is utterly different to that of the court records. They are highly stylized, adopting a supplicant tone suited to the patrimonial nature of the institution, emphasizing the humble gratitude of the petitioner and the magnanimity of the Sultan. Even by the standards of the sharīᶜa court records, they are very terse, often obscuring the precise details of the complaint behind passive-voiced clichés such as "the noble sharīᶜa has been violated." Petitions are usually undated,[55] and some petitioners signed their petitions using only their first name.[56] Moreover, petitions are one-sided, giving the complainant's story but not the opponent's response. The imperial orders issued in response to petitions are similarly formulaic and concise. As with sharīᶜa court records, careful attention to the circumstances of production and the purpose of these documents is necessary if we are to use them effectively as historical sources.[57] Nevertheless, these documents are vital to reveal the role of the imperial government in the resolution of disputes across the empire.

In order to deal with these challenges, the approach I have adopted is to select particular cases and read them closely. I have tried as far as possible to reconstruct the circumstances surrounding legal actions, relying on normative legal texts, chronicles, and the work of previous scholars for the contextual knowledge that this requires. The micro-historical approach to Ottoman legal records is exemplified by Leslie Peirce's *Morality Tales*, a study of the sharīᶜa court of ᶜAyntāb over a single year in the mid sixteenth century. While I have attempted to emulate Peirce's methods, this book is certainly not a micro-history either spatially or chronologically: its subject is a great metropolis over the course of some eighty years. I have tried to take the techniques of micro-history—the close reading and reconstruction of particular cases—and apply them to this larger subject. Much of micro-history's potential for rich description is lost in the process, but the longer time frame allows me to discuss long-term processes of change.

The micro-approach has been the more common method of dealing with Ottoman court records, at least since the focus of sijill-studies shifted from economic to legal history in the 1990s.[58] Recently, Boğaç Ergene has called for a return to quantitative methods in order to unlock the full potential of the sijills.[59] Ergene's method, as displayed in recent articles, is promising, but I am skeptical of its applicability to larger Ottoman cities at this stage.[60] Ergene works on the small northern Anatolian town of Kastamonu, and he has a complete set of the Kastamonu court records. Such a comprehensive view is not possible in Cairo or other large cities. This is partly for reasons of accessibility, but even if a full set of records were obtainable, the sheer quantity would make it impossible for one scholar to tackle. Smaller, manageable sets of records could be identified, but this would lead to several problems. First, the chronological scope would be considerably truncated.[61] Second, there are so many unknowns that it would be difficult to interpret the results. For example, we have only a very limited understanding of the extent to which there was a division of labor between the different courts, or whether particular sections of the population preferred particular courts.[62] Consequently, the representativeness of any sample would be very difficult to judge.[63] The application of Ergene's methods to the empire's major cities will have to wait for records to be made both more accessible and more manipulable, through digitization, cataloging, and indexing.[64]

Lastly, I found it helpful to use narrative sources in addition to archival materials. As a historian of Cairo I am fortunate in having access to a large number of contemporary chronicles in Arabic and Turkish written in and about this large and wealthy city, several of which have been published. This is primarily an archival study, and time precluded a full survey of these texts. I focused on two of the more widely-known contemporary chronicles: Aḥmad Katkhudā al-Damurdāshī's *al-Durra al-muṣāna fī akhbār al-Kināna* and Aḥmad Çelebi ibn ᶜAbd al-Ghanī's *Awḍaḥ al-ishārāt fī man tawallā Miṣr al-Qāhira min al-wuzarāʾ wa ʾl-bashāt.* I also used ᶜAbd al-Raḥman al-Jabartī's famous work of the early nineteenth century, *ᶜAjāʾib al-āthār fī tarājim wa ʾl-akhbār*; Jabartī himself drew on seventeenth and eighteenth-century chronicles for his coverage of that period.

I have used chronicles for two main purposes. One is for details of legal institutions and actors that did not leave any documentary records. One example is the various individuals involved in policing, including the Janissary Āghā, the muḥtasib, and the *multazim* of the Khurda tax-farm, all of whom are described in detail in Chapter 2. Another example is the unofficial dispute resolution activities carried out by prominent political figures, which I discuss in Chapter 5. Chronicles are our main insight into these individuals and their activities. The other purpose is as a source of contemporary attitudes and opinions of the legal system and its wider political context. The court records necessarily present what happened within court as orderly and procedurally correct. Corruption or intimidation that influenced the outcome of a case would not be recorded; indeed it *could not* be recorded given the textual constraints within which the scribe worked. Even if we disregard the potential for outright corruption, there is also the question of whether the courts, with their overwhelming reliance on eye-witness testimony and on personal integrity, were seen as fair by the population. The implicit assumption of much of the scholarship based on sharīᶜa court records has been that, because the courts were so widely and consistently used, and because there is little documentary evidence of corruption on the part of court officials, the courts must have been mostly trusted by Ottoman subjects. Chronicles give us a different perspective. The meaning of justice was controversial, and Ottoman-Egyptians were often critical of their courts and qāḍīs. The venal judge is, of course, a trope found in Muslim literature across the ages. But the stories in these chronicles go beyond the issue of straightforward corruption, describing justice as deeply entwined in the factional political struggles of Ottoman Cairo. The chronicles themselves were also entwined in these factional politics, and their stories must be read with an eye for their polemic, but they deserve to be taken seriously.

Outline of chapters

Chapter 1 provides a brief overview of the history of Ottoman Cairo, its key social, economic, and political structures and practices, and its place within the wider Ottoman Empire. This will help readers place the material presented in the rest of the book in its historical context.

Chapter 2 gives an overview of the various institutions, actors, and practices that made up Ottoman Cairo's legal system. As well as the sharīᶜa courts, this chapter introduces the reader to the Ottoman governor's tribunal (al-Dīwān al-ᶜĀlī), the Dīvān-i Hümāyūn (Imperial Council), the muḥtasib (market inspector), the role of the military regiments in policing, and *ṣulḥ* (mediation).

Chapter 3 examines in more detail the role of two institutions—the Ottoman governor's tribunal (al-Dīwān al-ᶜĀlī) and the Imperial Council (Dīvān-i Hümāyūn)—in Cairo's legal system. These two institutions both represented the direct involvement of the empire's executive authorities in the mundane administration of justice.[65] The chapter demonstrates considerable overlap between the workloads of these institutions and the sharīᶜa courts. I suggest that rather than asking what was each institution's specific role, a better way to understand their relationships to one another is to delineate the precise role of the different individuals who worked within them: the qāḍī, the governor, and the Grand Vizier.

Chapter 4 explores the ways in which the Ottoman executive authorities attempted to influence and control the legal doctrines, drawn from fiqh, that were applied in Cairo. The fact that the production of fiqh was the domain of scholars did not prevent executive authorities from influencing how fiqh as an intellectual discipline was translated into applied law. I investigate in particular the issue of madhhab pluralism: a feature of Cairo's legal system with a long, pre-Ottoman history, which the Ottomans at various points tried to control, contain, or eliminate in favor of Ḥanafī uniformity. I place this struggle in a wider context of attempts by executive authorities to produce legal change by instructing judges to follow particular opinions drawn from the fiqh tradition.

In Chapter 5, I investigate how prominent figures among the Egyptian political elite began to resolve disputes among Cairo's population in the late seventeenth and eighteenth centuries, encroaching on the jurisdictions of long-established Ottoman legal institutions. This development saw justice become enmeshed in the patron-client networks and factional antagonism of Cairo politics. Based on chronicles, this chapter also explores what contemporary Cairenes thought of their city's legal system.

Chapter 6 examines how Cairene litigants navigated the multiplicity of forums and practices with overlapping jurisdictions that constituted Cairo's legal system. Moving away from the state-centrism of Ottoman historiography, this chapter adopts the perspective of a legal consumer in order to discover how legal institutions were used, rather than the role the state intended them to play. I argue that there was little in the way of formal hierarchies or defined relationships between the different institutions, and that this jurisdictional imprecision offered litigants opportunities to manipulate the system's pluralism.

In the conclusion, I reflect on the implications of my findings for longer-term narratives of Islamic legal history and Ottoman history. Placing my research in the context of recent works on both the medieval period and the Ottoman nineteenth century, I suggest that a new grand narrative of Islamic legal history is being constructed. This grand narrative emphasizes legal practice as much as doctrine and places the relationship between law and political authority at the center of the story.

The appendix reproduces six key documents in transcription and translation. These documents illustrate the range of genres of legal document used in this study, introducing readers to some types of document that are not commonly used in Ottoman legal historiography.

CHAPTER

1

A BRIEF PORTRAIT OF CAIRO UNDER OTTOMAN RULE

Unsurprisingly, for a city that has been a political, economic, and cultural center for over a millennium, Cairo has a fortunate location. Sited where the Nile opens up into the branches that flow into the Mediterranean, one of the most naturally fertile regions in the world, for most of its history Cairo's significance was founded on the enormous agricultural output of the Nile valley and delta that was amassed, processed and distributed in the city. As well as being the key to the natural wealth of Egypt, Cairo was also an intermediary in long-distance trade networks. The Nile gave Cairo easy access to Africa and the Mediterranean; Cairo was also a short desert crossing from the Red Sea, and a terminus of the trans-Saharan caravan trade. Goods from Africa, Arabia, and India passed through Cairo on their way to the markets of the Mediterranean and northern Europe, until the Suez Canal allowed long-distance trade to circumvent the city. Cairo was, and still is, one of the great cultural centers of Islam and the Muslim world. The famous mosque-university of al-Azhar attracted scholars and students from all corners of the Muslim world. Before the carbon age, Cairo was the assembly point for one of the two major caravans to Mecca for the annual pilgrimage, which saw Muslims of all backgrounds passing through the city. Meanwhile, Cairo's graveyards are filled with the tombs of illustrious figures from Islam's past, many of which became pilgrimage sites in their own right.

Books on the history of Cairo tend to dismiss the Ottoman era prior to 1798, claiming that in addition to being marginalized politically, economic and cultural life in the city stagnated.[1] But the list of assets outlined above meant that although, after the Ottoman conquest of 1517, Cairo found itself in the unusual position of being provincial, it lost little of its global significance and quickly became one of the most important cities in the Ottoman Empire. While Vasco de Gama's discovery of the Cape route to the Indies created competition in trade routes to western Europe, the traditional sea and land routes through the Middle East remained vital and healthy under Ottoman rule. After all, the Ottoman Empire itself was one of the key markets for Asian commodities, and this trade did not involve western Europeans. In fact, far from suffering from western European competition during the early modern period, Cairo's transit trade boomed due to Ottoman and western European demand for coffee, a new commodity. Introduced into the major Ottoman cities in the 1550s, and spreading from there to western Europe over the following half-century, coffee was grown in Yemen and Egypt was its main route west. The fashion for coffee, as well as tea, also created demand for one of Egypt's indigenous commodities: sugar, the export of which was also conducted via Cairo. The real threat to the prosperity of Cairo's transit trade was not the circumnavigation of the Cape in 1498, but the introduction of coffee plantations in the French Caribbean in the mid eighteenth century.[2]

Rather than the stagnation assumed by historians working within the interpretive straitjacket of "Ottoman decline," prosperity and expansion is a more appropriate summation of Cairo's early modern history. Cairo's prosperity was reflected first and foremost in its geographic and demographic expansion between the early sixteenth and late eighteenth centuries. André Raymond estimated a population increase of roughly 50% between the end of Mamluk rule and the French invasion in 1798. This figure masks a lot of volatility in the city's population due to recurrent plagues, famines, and other disasters, including a series of crises in the 1780s and 1790s which probably means that the figure recorded by the French expedition is somewhat lower than the population was in the mid eighteenth century. The increased population required, of course, an increase in the quantity of both housing and commercial buildings. Because the historic center of Cairo had already reached very high densities in the Middle Ages, most of the building was accommodated through outward expansion. The east and northeast were ruled out by hills and distance from the Nile, the city's only water source, so Cairo expanded south and west. The southern area between Bāb Zuwayla and the citadel had long been settled but changed from being a sparsely-populated elite suburb of mansions to a much more densely-populated urban district. As a consequence, some of those elites began building mansions around the shores of the Azbakiyya lake to the west, and their move attracted further development west of the Khalīj canal.

Ottoman Cairo's wealth was also reflected in the diversity of its population: the city's prosperity attracted immigrants from across the Ottoman Empire and beyond. Large communities of Turkish, Maghribī, and Syrian residents were engaged in commerce. The Turkish community consisted mostly of people who had migrated after the Ottoman conquest and their descendants. Due to historic links and proximity, the Maghribī and Syrian communities were much longer standing. Syrian Muslims and Christians lived in Cairo; the population of Syrian Christians increased markedly during the eighteenth century due to the 1724 schism in the Orthodox Church, which led to many Melkites emigrating from Aleppo and Damascus.[3] Smaller communities of Greeks and Armenians were engaged in a variety of specialized artisan trades: tailors, jewelers, clockmakers; the city was also home to a Sephardi Jewish community and a base, albeit a minor one, for the Sephardi merchant diaspora.[4] Before Meḥmed ᶜAlī's determined attempt to draw European capital and expertise to Egypt, the population of western European migrants in Cairo was very small, but nevertheless there was a more or less permanent community of French merchants in the city, along with a handful of other western European nationals.

Cairo's Islamic religious and intellectual life was another draw for migrants. In particular, the Azhar mosque-university attracted students and scholars from across the Muslim world, housing and feeding many of them at the various *riwāq*s associated with the mosque. Many of these riwāqs were founded to support a specific group of immigrants, from Maghribīs to sub-Saharan Africans to Central Asians.[5] Cairo was also a vibrant center of Sufi mystic activity, and its *zāwiyya*s provided accommodation and fraternity to visiting Sufis, some of whom settled in Cairo permanently. The city's Sufi networks cultivated particularly close ties with Sufis in the central lands of the Ottoman Empire (Rūmīs), but Sufis also visited from Syria, Arabia, India, and other parts of the Muslim world.[6]

Political and military society was also highly diverse. Unsurprisingly, Turks were again a significant presence, and included soldiers in the various regiments and scribes in the provincial government and the households of the elite. Some of these Turks came and went with the ever-changing governors and chief qāḍīs. But many, even if they originally arrived in the entourage of an Ottoman official posted to Cairo, settled permanently. The other Muslim ethnicities of the Ottoman Empire, including Bosnians and Albanians, were represented in Cairo. Meanwhile, the city's great political households continued to recruit *mamlūk*s from the Caucasus, and so many of the most powerful members of the political elite were Georgian, Circassian, or Abkhazian. Lastly, an immigrant group whose influence far outshone its small numbers was the community of African eunuchs; after a lifetime's service in the imperial harem, eunuchs spent their later years in Egypt where, despite their formal retirement, they continued to wield influence due to their great wealth and extensive contacts.[7]

Lastly, of course, we must not forget internal migration within the province of Egypt, much of which saw Egyptians from the rural villages and the smaller towns up and down the Nile move to Cairo. Egyptians moved to Cairo for all manner of reasons; scholarship and commerce were the most prominent. Cairenes from elsewhere in Egypt continued to identify with their roots, most obviously through *nisba*s formed from their place of origin—Damanhūrī, Ṭanṭāwī, Saᶜīdī, and so on—which could become surnames used by Cairo-based families over several generations.

Economic life

What were the sources of Cairo's wealth, and the activities that created it? Of course, the agriculture of the Nile valley and delta remained the cornerstone of Egypt's economic life. Egypt was an important producer and exporter of staple foods including grain, rice, and lentils. It was also an important source of the luxury sugar, and of agricultural commodities used in manufacturing such as cotton, hemp, and flax.[8] Although it obviously took place in rural areas, Egyptian agriculture enriched Cairo's economy. A significant proportion of Egypt's agricultural output was traded in Cairo, for distribution within the province or for export. Moreover, many of the elites who controlled the collection of revenue from agriculture, including the multazims (tax-farmers) and the administrators of the great blocs of *awqāf* (endowments), resided in Cairo.[9] Therefore, the proportion of revenue that remained in Egypt—the tax-farmer's profit and the *waqf*-administrator's salary—accumulated in Cairo where it funded construction, philanthropy, the patronage of scholars and poets, and the cultivation of client networks, as well as being spent on consumption. Furthermore, the revenues of some rural awqāf were designated to support religious and educational institutions in Cairo, which far outshone any other urban center in Egypt in size and prestige. Via the rentier classes and the endowments, Egyptian agriculture funded Cairo's political, religious, and cultural life.

The most profitable economic activity that took place within Cairo was undoubtedly trade. Probate inventories show that the wealth of the leading merchants far outstripped that of artisans.[10] Coffee surpassed spices as the most lucrative commodity during the seventeenth century, though the latter retained an important position in Cairo's commerce. Other significant commodities included sugar, tobacco, soap, and cloth.[11] The biggest coffee merchants attained fabulous wealth, investing the proceeds from the coffee trade in tax-farms and real estate. The Sharāybīs, a family of Maghribī origin who migrated to Cairo in 1630, became the most significant dealers in the coffee market during the first half of the eighteenth century. The Sharāybī household was extensive and several of their mamlūks became prominent political players; most as regimental officers, with one becoming a bey.[12] The Sharāybī mansion in Azbakiyya was a social center for Cairo's political elite; poets would attend the parties there and compete for the attention and patronage of the distinguished guests by reciting verses in praise of them. According to Jabartī, the mansion consisted of twelve apartments, each of which would have been a sizeable house in itself, and it contained a rich scholarly library, the books of which were lent to any student who asked. The Sharāybīs were apparently so gracious that if a student failed to return a borrowed book and instead sold it, they would simply buy it back from the book market and excuse the student on the grounds of his poverty.[13] The Sharāybīs were involved in developing the commercial infrastructure of Cairo. Muḥammad Dādā al-Sharāybī, who died in 1725, built a caravanserai in the Faḥḥāmīn district consisting of fourteen shops on the ground floor, with two storeys of apartments above; the family also owned the nearby Ḥamzāwī marketplace. And they were also engaged in philanthropy; Qāsim al-Sharāybī, the head of the family at its apogee in the 1720s and 30s, built a mosque and a *sabīl-kuttāb* (public fountain and elementary school) in Azbakiyya, funded by an adjacent bathhouse, apartment building, and shops.[14] In addition to enriching the merchants who dealt in it, coffee also generated wealth through the customs dues paid on imports at Suez, transit through the Nile ports, and exports at the Mediterranean ports. These customs-posts were farmed out, as were most revenue-sources, and the value of the coffee passing through made them very lucrative posts. The customs-farms of the Red Sea and Nile ports were dominated by Janissary officers during the late seventeenth and early eighteenth centuries, forming one of the bases of the regiment's power and influence.[15]

The wealth generated by commerce was reflected spatially in the concentration of expensive housing in the center of historic Cairo, close to the main marketplaces. While the very largest mansions were built on the southern and western fringes of the city, the bulk of elite housing was concentrated in the commercial center.[16] Merchants of middling wealth who wanted to live near to the markets were accommodated in the distinctive form of housing known as the *rabᶜ* (pl. *urbūᶜ*), multi-storey apartment buildings containing modestly-sized, vertically-arranged apartments with their own private roof terraces, a compromise between bourgeois expectations of comfort and the very high land values in the city center.[17]

Manufacturing was generally less rewarding than commerce. It was possible for an artisan to build a great fortune: the powerful Jalfī household of the early eighteenth century was founded an oil-presser.[18] But most artisans lived comfortable but not extravagant lifestyles. They tended to reside in a middle belt, outside the expensive historic center but not as far out as either the exclusive suburbs or the shantytowns populated by poor rural migrants. Artisanal activity was concentrated in the same areas; the exceptions were fine woodwork and coppersmithing, which shared the central commercial district, and trades deemed noxious to public health or the atmosphere, such as tanneries, potteries, slaughterhouses, and butchers, which were located on the outskirts of the city.[19]

Artisans organized themselves in *ṭāʾifa*s (guilds). The guild played a number of roles, including collecting the taxes due from its members, enforcing quality standards, and using collective resources to support members who were unable to work through age or ill health. Each guild was led by a shaykh who would represent the trade's interests before the authorities. In certain businesses, much of the production took place within families. Textiles are an example: a lot of women worked as weavers within their homes for businesses run by family members.

The scourge of artisan communities was the *ḥimāyāt*, technically illegal additional levies imposed on guilds by the officials, usually regimental officers, in charge of collecting their taxes. A barely-legitimized shake-down, the literal translation of the word ḥimāyāt is indeed "protection." The prevalence of ḥimāyāt had several consequences. It provided a strong incentive for artisans to join a regiment, and so become a protector rather than protected, and was therefore one of the key factors driving the interpenetration of artisan and military societies. And the demand for higher authorities to abolish the exploitative practice became one of the key political dynamics of the period. Individual officials could make considerable political capital out of abolishing the ḥimāyāt, if they were powerful enough to do so. On the other hand, the ḥimāyāt becoming too oppressive was one of the conditions that could spark an urban riot.

Scholarship, culture, and religious life

The concentration of wealth in Cairo enabled a vibrant intellectual life, as prosperous political figures and merchants made endowments to support education and scholarship.[20] The central institution in Cairo's intellectual life was undoubtedly al-Azhar. The great mosque-university complex was founded by the Fāṭimid dynasty in 972 CE. But by the time of the Ottoman conquest it had grown substantially from the original foundation as subsequent rulers and notables had made further endowments to support new madrasas, hostels, and other facilities attached to al-Azhar. Indeed it is incorrect to understand al-Azhar as a single institution; rather, it was a complex of institutions clustered around the Azhar mosque. Nevertheless, the complex was understood to have a degree of unity, and the scholars and students connected with it identified as Azharites (often using the nisba "Azharī"). In common with most pre-modern Muslim educational institutions, al-Azhar's madrasas were largely sources of financial support and accommodation for otherwise independent scholars and students. There was no organized curriculum that students were obliged to follow. There was no overall degree certificate indicating completion of a student's studies. Rather, each professor gave classes on whatever texts he wanted, students chose to study what they wanted, and they received an *ijāza* (certificate) for each text they mastered.[21]

The various madrasas that made up al-Azhar were supported by a huge number of awqāf. These awqāf varied in size from the huge benefactions of the ruling classes and the rich, to small donations by people of modest wealth. The awqāf paid for the upkeep of the buildings and provided stipends for the scholars and students. Many of the books in the madrasas' libraries had been donated as waqf. Al-Azhar's members were well integrated into broader Cairene society: many were active in production and commerce. The most obvious examples of this were the trades directly connected with education and scholarship: many Azharī scholars worked as booksellers, copyists, or bookbinders, and the book market was located immediately behind the mosque.

Much of the energy of al-Azhar's scholars was devoted to Muslim religious subjects: Arabic grammar and lexicography, Koranic exegesis, theology, and fiqh. But while these subjects, in particular fiqh, were the most prestigious and considered the most important, many of the scholars also enjoyed broader interests. Subjects studied in Ottoman Cairo included mathematics, the natural sciences such as astronomy and medicine, and occult sciences.[22] Other scholars wrote literature, a field they shared with the educated classes more broadly. History was one popular branch of literature, written by professional scholars such as Muḥammad ibn Abī ᵓl-Surūr al-Bakrī al-Siddīqī, by highly literate laymen such as Aḥmad Çelebi ibn ᶜAbd al-Ghanī and ᶜAlī al-Shādhilī, and, in colloquial Arabic, by soldiers of rudimentary education.[23] Poetry was the most widespread form of literary production, and the ability to compose poetry was the essential mark of an educated person.

If scriptural Islam in Cairo revolved around al-Azhar, the other major dimension of Muslim religious activity, Sufi mysticism, had no comparable central organization. There were multiple *ṭarīqas* (Sufi orders) in the city engaged in forms of worship ranging from the sedate, intellectual spirituality of the Shādhiliyya, who were quite comfortable with material wealth, to the antinomian Rifāᶜiyya, who practiced self-mortification. Integration into the Ottoman cultural world led to the introduction of two new ṭarīqas in Cairo, the Baktāshiyya and the Mawlawiyya, and the rapid growth of a third, the Khalwatiyya, which had first spread to Cairo during the last decades of Mamluk rule. A distinctive feature of Sufism in Cairo was the existence of two Sufi clans: the Bakriyya and the Sādāt al-Wafāʾiyya. These were illustrious extended families, which traced their genealogies back to the first caliph Abū Bakr and the fourth caliph ʿAlī respectively. Sufi ṭarīqas were not exclusive and it was common for someone to be a member of several. Plenty of ulema were involved with Sufi orders: there was no strict separation between scriptural and mystical Islam.[24]

There does not seem to have been widespread antipathy towards Sufism, as emerged in Istanbul and the central provinces during the seventeenth century. In 1711, in what may have been a late echo of Istanbul's seventeenth-century militant anti-Sufi Kadızadeli movement, a group of students under the influence of a Rūmī preacher attacked a number of Sufi gatherings.[25] But this was an unusual event and the momentum of the Rūmī preacher's campaign appears to have dissipated quickly. Indeed, Sufi mysticism was the normal, mainstream form of religiosity among Cairo's Muslims: even people who were not members of ṭarīqas engaged in Sufi practices, in particular shrine visitation, and participated in the *mawlid* festivals (saints' days). The more important mawlids, in particular the *mawlid al-nabī* (Prophet's birthday) were major events in Cairo's social calendar that saw the streets brightly decorated and free food dispensed to the public.

The madrasa-educated ulema dominated all genres of literature, as they did in most pre-modern Muslim societies. But although, famously, the Muslim world did not adopt print technology until the nineteenth century, early modern Cairo still saw some degree of democratization of writing and reading comparable to, if not as extensive as, contemporary developments in Europe. Probate inventories reveal a sharp decline in the average value of books between the sixteenth and the eighteenth century. The increased demand for paper to feed Europe's printing presses led to the introduction of lower quality, lower priced paper; this enabled the production of cheaper books for a wider market in Cairo, notwithstanding the persistence of the manuscript culture.[26] The middling classes not only consumed more literature, they also wrote more. The chronicle of Damurdāshī, which I used for this book, is a good example: written in an inelegant, colloquial Arabic, and without much attention to structure or causation, Damurdāshī's chronicle combines a skeleton narrative of political events with what appears to be a collection of anecdotes and legends circulated orally among the ʿAzabān regiment, of which Damurdāshī was a member. There are comparable examples from the civilian world: Nelly Hanna has described a humorous compendium written by a literate but not scholarly artisan called Muḥammad ibn Ḥasan Abū Dhākir.[27] André Raymond, meanwhile, suggests that author of a short chronicle detailing a major armed conflict between Cairo's elite in 1711, ʿAlī al-Shādhilī, was a merchant or artisan who was well educated, but not a scholar.[28]

Cairo's place in the Ottoman Empire

The fertility of the delta made Egypt the empire's breadbasket: Egyptian grain fed Ottoman soldiers on campaign in Hungary and Persia, while Egyptian rice maintained the poor of Mecca and Medina, and Egyptian sugar sweetened the drinks of the princes and princesses in Topkapı Palace.[29] Cairo was the hub in which the products of Egyptian agriculture were collected and transferred to the imperial palace, to the holy cities, and to the private merchants who would ship them for sale in all corners of the empire. The city was also home to many of the tax-farmers and waqf-administrators who controlled and profited from this process.[30]

Cairo was also a key transit point in the long-distance trade networks that brought high-value goods from Africa, Arabia, and India into the Ottoman Empire. Chief among these commodities in the seventeenth and eighteenth centuries was coffee from Yemen; spices from India were also significant. The centrality of Egypt to the Ottoman trade in exotic foodstuffs is reflected in the name of the Istanbul bazaar where they were sold, which survives today: the Mısır Çarşısı or Egyptian bazaar.[31] From sub-Saharan Africa, the key commodities were gold and slaves. Many African slaves ended up as domestic servants in households throughout the empire and beyond: a few were, after castration in Upper Egypt on the way to Cairo, destined to become eunuchs in the harems of the Ottoman political elite, including the harem of the Sultan himself. Cairenes grew wealthy from both passive investment and active participation in all of these trades, while the customs posts at the ports of Suez, Rosetta, Damietta, and Alexandria provided lucrative opportunities for tax-farmers.[32]

Cairo also played a vital role in the Ottomans' administration of their broader empire. The Ottoman administration of the Muslim holy cities in the Hejaz, which was crucial to Ottoman legitimacy, was conducted via Cairo. The holy cities were under the authority of the *sharīf*s of Mecca, who were subject to Ottoman suzerainty. Hejazi affairs were supervised by the governor of Egypt, who appointed a governor of Jidda from among the Egyptian beys to act as the local representative of Ottoman power. Furthermore, a large military force was barracked in Cairo, and the Egyptian army took part in many major Ottoman campaigns. In the sixteenth century Egypt was the staging post for the conquest and occupation of Yemen. While the withdrawal from Yemen meant fewer demands on the Egyptian army in the late seventeenth and eighteenth centuries, Egyptian soldiers were frequently called for service in the Mediterranean and eastern Europe.[33]

As well as facilitating the control of the holy cities, Cairo played a further role in securing the Ottoman dynasty's religious legitimacy, as it was the assembly point for one of the two great caravans that made the annual pilgrimage to Mecca (the other caravan departed from Damascus). The political significance of administering the pilgrimage was reflected in the fact that the position of *amīr al-ḥājj* (commander of the pilgrimage) was one of the most senior and prestigious positions in the Egyptian administration. It was also one of the most coveted, as it allowed the holder to cultivate personal ties in the Hejaz that could prove crucial to getting ahead in the coffee trade.

The departure of the pilgrimage caravan was a major event in Cairo's calendar. For one thing, it brought a huge number of temporary visitors from across north and west Africa, who stayed in the city while they waited for the caravan to depart. This would have provided a significant boost to Cairo's markets, as the pilgrims both fed themselves while in the city and purchased supplies for the journey. The departure was accompanied by a lavish ceremony in Rumayla Square in the southeastern corner of Cairo, at the foot of the Muqaṭṭam hill where the citadel stood. The caravan commander (*serdar al-ḥājj*) and the soldiers who would accompany the pilgrims paraded with their cannon before the governor, who watched from his tent which was pitched on the Square. The governor draped the *maḥmal* (ceremonial palanquin) over a camel and led it walking around the Square. The caravan commander repeated this action, and then the caravan departed.[34]

The political structure of Ottoman Cairo

As the provincial capital, Cairo was the seat of the Ottoman governor of Egypt. Governors were appointed from among the imperial elite and usually served terms of one to three years before being rotated to another appointment. The governor was an outsider: unlike in some other Ottoman provinces, local or localized elites did not manage to take control of this post during the seventeenth and eighteenth centuries.[35] The Egyptian governorship was an important position in the imperial hierarchy and was filled by some of the empire's leading statesmen; several governors also served as Grand Viziers.[36] The governor was based in the citadel, a complex originally built during the Ayyūbid period, on the Muqaṭṭam hill to the southeast of the city of Cairo.

The governorship was one of only two senior posts in the Egyptian administration to which outsiders were routinely appointed; the second being the chief judgeship, the *qāḍī ʾl-quḍā*, which is discussed in the following chapter. The other positions, including *defterdār* (treasurer), amīr al-ḥājj (commander of the pilgrimage), and the governorships of Egypt's regions, were appointed from among the provincial political elite. This political elite was organized in households, which were patronage networks formed through slavery, kinship, and other types of patron–client relations. Many of the most powerful men within this system, who were often but not always freed mamlūks, attained the rank of *ṣancaḳbeyi*, which was usually shortened to bey. Unlike elsewhere in the Ottoman Empire, in Egypt the rank of bey did not correspond with control of a particular territory, but the number of beys was limited to twenty-four at any one time.[37]

Overlapping with the households as loci power within elite political society were the military regiments. There were seven regiments, the largest of which were the Janissaries and the ʿAzabān.[38] The regiments were institutions that had been implanted by the Ottomans after their conquest of Egypt. But by the seventeenth century they had developed strong corporate identities and would mobilize to defend their corporate interests. The days when the Janissaries were filled exclusively with Christian-born slaves recruited from the Balkans via the *devşirme* child-levy were long past, and the Cairo Janissaries and other regiments contained a mix of slaves and free-born Muslims from various parts of the empire including Egypt itself. As was the case across the empire, there was a great deal of overlap between the regiments and the urban commercial class in Egypt. Soldiers and officers increasingly entered trade from the late sixteenth century on to supplement their debased salaries, while merchants and artisans increasingly sought regimental membership for the financial and social benefits it offered.[39] Regiments and households were not distinct sections of Ottoman-Egyptian society. Rather, they were two different organizational forms through which the elite created and exerted power. They overlapped with one another considerably: many regimental soldiers were affiliated with a household, some regimental officers led their own households, and beys sought to place their protégés in key positions in the regiments.

Politics in Ottoman Cairo consisted mainly of a struggle to control revenue sources. As detailed above, the Ottoman government had several key interests in Egypt connected with their religious legitimacy and regional domination, but the maximization of revenue from Egypt's rich agriculture and trade was one of the governor's key objectives. The provincial elites, by contrast, wanted to retain as big a proportion of revenue as possible within the province, in order to line their own pockets and to dispense the patronage necessary to build their client networks.

Competition for control of resources, between the provincial elite and the Ottoman government, and among different groups and factions within the provincial elite, was the key dynamic that animated the political history of Egypt between 1517 and 1805.[40] This is not the place for a narrative history of Ottoman Egypt, but I will highlight what I think are the main contours of this history, and point out how this differs from traditional accounts of Egyptian history.[41] Many traditional accounts describe Ottoman Egypt's history with a model of rise and decline. In effect, they borrow the now-discredited rise and decline model of Ottoman history: Ottoman Egypt's history latches on to the last half-century of the empire's rise, and then participates more than fully in its decline.[42]

As discussed above, the economic component of this supposed long decline in Cairo is untenable: Ottoman Cairo enjoyed a prosperous economy that supported the expansion of the city and its population. In political terms, the rise and decline model focuses on the degree of control exercised over Egypt by the imperial government in Istanbul and its governor in Cairo. The traditional narrative holds that this central control was strongest in the sixteenth century. After the two rebellions in 1523 that threatened to undo the Ottoman conquest, the Grand Vizier Ibrāhīm Pasha arrived in 1524 to consolidate the Ottoman conquest with a series of administrative reforms and the introduction of a provincial law-code: the Ottoman ḳānūnnāme for Egypt.[43] This was followed by fifty or so years of vigorous and assertive Ottoman rule in Egypt, during which time the province acted as the base for further expansion into Yemen and the eastern coast of Africa. From the late sixteenth century onwards, however, Ottoman rule became increasingly ineffective, and the governor an increasingly weak figure. The space was filled by the reassertion of the power of

Egypt's provincial elite, in particular the beys and their households.[44] By the time of the regime of ᶜAlī Bey al-Kabīr in the late eighteenth century, the imperial ties linking Egypt to the Ottoman Empire were threadbare, leaving the province open to French conquest in 1798.

While it suited the prejudices of Egyptian nationalism, which assumed Ottoman rule to be decadent, the rise and decline model is far too simplistic to convey the texture of Ottoman Egypt's political history over almost three centuries. It is true that no later Ottoman governor enjoyed the degree of control exercised by Sulaymān Pasha and Daᵓūd Pasha, the two governors who completed the consolidation of Ottoman power in Egypt, serving exceptionally long terms from 1525–38 and 1538–49 respectively.[45] But this does not mean that there was a simple, linear decline of Ottoman power during the seventeenth and eighteenth centuries. Rather, Istanbul's authority over the province waxed and waned: there were periods during which Ottoman control slackened, and periods when it was vigorously reasserted. I explore this model with respect to the legal system in Chapter 4.

The political narrative is punctuated by several military rebellions, especially during the last decades of the sixteenth century and the first half of the seventeenth, which represent the low points of Ottoman control of the province. After the mid seventeenth century armed insurrection was less frequent, but a pattern developed of the relatively peaceable deposition of governors who seriously offended the provincial elite. The soldiery would mass in Rumayla Square, blocking the entrance to the citadel, the governor would be arrested, the beys would select an acting governor (*qāᵓimmaqām*) from among themselves, and the beys and regimental officers would send a petition to the Sultan detailing their complaints against the deposed governor, emphasizing their continued loyalty to the Ottoman dynasty, and requesting the appointment of a new governor.[46] The substance of the ongoing tensions between provincial elite and governor was almost always resources: the levies the regiments could charge Egypt's population, the proportion of tax-revenues that remained in the tax-farmers' hands, the skimming of revenue from the major awqāf.

While the provincial political elite were assertive, the pressure was not all one-way. There were also several moments when the imperial government made a determined attempt to reassert its influence in Cairo. The most significant was the period of the Köprülü Grand Viziers in the late seventeenth century, which saw several reformist governors of Egypt, including Ḳara Ibrāhīm Pasha, the lieutenant (*katkhudā*) of the Grand Vizier Köprülü Fāẓıl Aḥmed Pasha himself, attempt to implement the Köprülü reform program that the government was pushing across the empire. The reformers managed to punish some of the worst examples of revenue-skimming, take control of Egypt's financial administration, and place allies in charge of the biggest awqāf. More usually, however, the governors pursued Istanbul's interests more subtly, by attempting to manipulate the factional conflicts within provincial political society rather than impose their will by brute force.

It was these internecine rivalries and conflicts within the political elite that formed the substance of politics in the city. As described above, the two main units of political organization were the household and the regiment. But these were not stable units. Households evolved and frequently split, consolidated or disintegrated. Although the regiments enjoyed continuity as institutions, they saw infighting and factionalism within them: a split within the Janissary regiment sparked one of the most serious conflagrations in the history of Ottoman Cairo, the war of 1711.[47] The trajectory of provincial politics during the period covered in this book sees the beys dominant in the mid-seventeenth century. This was followed by the rise to prominence of regimental officers, in particular Janissaries, towards the end of the century. The power of the Janissary regiment then enabled the emergence during the eighteenth century of the household founded by the Janissary katkhudā Muṣṭafā al-Qāzdughlī.[48] The Qāzdughlī household grew to a position of overwhelming dominance by the 1750s, and it eventually shifted its power base away from the Janissary regiment by promoting one of its own as a bey, ᶜAlī Bey al-Kabīr, who asserted his autonomy from Istanbul in 1768, causing the biggest crisis in Ottoman control of Egypt since the conquest.[49] This broad schema masks, however, a much more complicated story which saw a great deal of turnover of factions, alliances, and feuds.

The implications of political struggle for wider Cairene society were many. The client networks of political leaders, and consequently the political elite's factionalism, stretched deep into Cairene society, a dynamic assisted both by the interpenetration of the commercial and military classes and by the reliance of intellectuals on the patronage of the wealthy. The fact that local power-brokers were almost always highly partisan helps explain why, to many Cairenes, imperial authority in the form of the Sultan and the governor, was very attractive as a comparatively neutral resource. As I will demonstrate in subsequent chapters, in many ways it was the demands of civilian Cairene subjects, who approached the imperial authorities with their problems, that drove the imperial relationship between Cairo and Istanbul during this period. When politics turned violent, which it did frequently, the consequences for the city could be grave. Most political violence was contained within the political classes, but the larger disturbances led to widespread property damage, caused shortages, and could sometimes confine people to their homes as movement around the city became too dangerous.[50]

Cairo, the Empire, and the Law

Law was essential to enable the crucial political and economic roles played by Cairo in the Ottoman Empire, as well as being central to the daily lives of Cairenes. Law was the basis for the extraction of the agricultural revenues that made Cairo rich: it governed the contracts of the tax-farmers and the structure of the awqāf that owned much of the Egyptian countryside. Law structured the urban economic activities of manufacturing and trade. The courts provided the basis for the authority of the guilds and were the place where Cairo's merchants signed and enforced their contracts; Ottoman legal institutions even mediated disputes between Egyptian merchants and distant foreign governments.[51]

Law also regulated the relations between the imperial government and its servants. The most widespread structure within which Egyptians held local political office was the tax-farm: purchased by the holder for an upfront payment, the rights and duties of a tax-farmer were laid out in a contract that was drawn up and enforced by a qāḍī.[52] Beyond tax-collection and local administration, other services performed for the imperial government by the Egyptian elite, such as the provision of military forces, were also often arranged as contracts overseen by qāḍīs.[53] Moreover, legal institutions provided a means for the imperial government to monitor and control the actions of its provincial officials. The classic principal-agent problem, whereby local administrative officers abuse their authority in order to further their own rather than the central government's interests, was aggravated in a situation where those local administrative officers had invested significant financial capital in the acquisition of their offices: investments which they then sought to recoup. The empire's legal system enabled ordinary taxpayers to challenge unwarranted exactions.[54]

Lastly, the Ottomans' successful exploitation of Egypt's potential rested on the stability of their rule, which relied on the acquiescence of Egypt's large population. The key component of Ottoman legitimation, alongside the claim to defend and expand Islam, was the provision of justice. This involved providing security for people and property by suppressing crime, and providing facilities that enabled subjects to resolve their disputes.[55]

CHAPTER

2

CAIRO'S LEGAL SYSTEM: INSTITUTIONS AND ACTORS

Ottoman Cairo's legal system was a complex web of overlapping jurisdictions. This feature of Ottoman legal practice has been overlooked by many historians, who have focused overwhelmingly on the sharīʿa court as the central institution of Ottoman justice. The sharīʿa courts were undoubtedly important, but their high profile in Ottoman legal historiography is a result of the survival of many thousands of sharīʿa court registers, which have become the main source for Ottoman social and economic history. Other legal institutions and actors left few records, and so have been marginalized in the historiography. In the case of Egypt, the contrast with the legal historiography of the preceding Mamluk Sultanate is striking. With a few exceptions, sharīʿa court records from the Mamluk period have not survived.[1] Mamluk legal historians have therefore relied largely on normative legal texts, chronicles, and biographical dictionaries. The resulting historiography has placed far more emphasis on jurisdictions other than the sharīʿa court, including the maẓālim tribunals, the courts of the Mamluk *amīrs* and the muḥtasib.[2]

It is worth imagining what the legal historiography of Ottoman Egypt would look like if the Ottoman sharīʿa court records had not survived. The image of legal practice painted by the available chronicles would look more similar to that given by Mamlukists: Janissary officers, the police chief, and the muḥtasib play a key role in suppressing crime and regulating the markets; the beys hold courts in their private residences. Small archival collections in Cairo, such as the few registers of the governor's Dīwān, would assume far greater importance: most likely one or more monographs on the Dīwān would have been written, instead of a handful of footnotes. Lacking significant archival material in Egypt, far more historians would use the Prime Ministry Archive in Istanbul, and so the role of the imperial government in Egyptian legal affairs would loom much larger. This exercise is not intended to denigrate scholarship based on sharīʿa court records, nor to claim that they are exhausted as sources: given their great number and the intimate detail of legal, social, and economic life that they contain, Ottoman sharīᶜa court records are inexhaustible. I simply wish to point out that the dominant role accorded by historians to the sharīᶜa courts in the Ottoman legal system is the result of the volume of their records and the ease of access to them.[3] Given the relative lack of sources for most other legal institutions, this imbalance is impossible for historiography to overcome entirely. But in what follows I attempt to give a more comprehensive portrayal of the variety of legal institutions and actors in Ottoman Egypt.

The courts and tribunals of Cairo and Istanbul

The sharīᶜa courts

As noted above, the best-known Ottoman legal institution is the sharīᶜa court (*maḥkama* or *majlis al-sharᶜ*), and Cairo was well-supplied with these. There were fifteen sharīᶜa courts in the city of Cairo and its suburbs. The main sharīᶜa court, al-Bāb al-ᶜĀlī, was presided over by the chief qāḍī of Cairo (qāḍī ᵓl-quḍā), and was held at his official residence, the late fifteenth-century palace of the Mamluk Amīr Māmāy al-Sayfī, located just north of the Khān al-Khalīlī market in the center of Cairo. While the chief qāḍī personally heard many of the lawsuits presented to al-Bāb al-ᶜĀlī, the court also employed deputy qāḍīs (*nāᵓib*, pl. *nuwwāb*) of the Ḥanafī, Mālikī, Shāfiᶜī, and Ḥanbalī madhhabs, whom the chief qāḍī appointed. In addition to al-Bāb al-ᶜĀlī, there was a network of neighborhood courts around Cairo, as well as courts in the suburbs of Būlāq and Miṣr al-Qadīma.[4] Most of these courts were held in mosques. For example, the court of Jāmiᶜ al-Ḥākim was held at the tenth-century Ḥākim mosque just south of Bāb al-Futūḥ, the court of Qūṣūn was held at the fourteenth-century Amīr Qūṣūn mosque south of Bāb Zuwayla, and the Miṣr al-Qadīma court was held at the fourteenth-century al-Nāṣirī al-Jadīd mosque, which stood on the bank of the Nile.[5] There were also two specialized courts which dealt only with inheritance matters: al-Qisma al-ᶜAskariyya handled the inheritances of members of the ruling class (the *ᶜaskerī*), while al-Qisma al-ᶜArabiyya handled the inheritances of civilian subjects. These were held at two madrasas: respectively, the Ẓāhiriyya madrasa and the Kāmiliyya madrasa. Both stood on the central street of commercial Cairo, al-Muᶜizz li ᵓl-Dīn Allāh, close to al-Bāb al-ᶜĀlī: the former was virtually next door.[6] Thus, there were no dedicated courthouses in Ottoman Cairo: courts were held in other public buildings or, in the case of al-Bāb al-ᶜĀlī, in the reception area of an official residence.

Cairo's sharīᶜa courts were sites where the imperial met the local: they were one of the most important venues in which Egyptian subjects could interact with the Ottoman authorities.[7] They were a conduit through which the imperial government imposed its authority on the province, but they also offered subjects the means to engage with and make demands on the government. The combination of imperial and local attitudes and interests can be found in the law applied by the courts. The law applied was, of course, Islamic law, but this was inflected by Ottoman *ḳānūn*, imperial priorities, and local Egyptian traditions. Moreover, the normative order enforced by the courts was drawn not only from legal texts, but also from custom, which was recognized as authoritative within the Islamic legal tradition, and which obviously varied across time and space. Lastly, as I discuss in more detail below, a large number of disputes heard in the sharīᶜa courts were settled not by adjudication, but rather by *ṣulḥ* (mediation), performed by influential local people who were guided by local values.

The combination of imperial and local can also be seen in the personnel of the sharīᶜa courts. The position of chief qāḍī of Cairo was one of the highest-ranking judgeships in the empire: at the beginning of our period it was, along with Mecca, Edirne, and Bursa, one of the *Bilād-i Erbāᶜa* judgeships, which ranked below only Istanbul and the chief qāḍīs (*ḳāżᶜasker*) of Rumelia and Anatolia.[8] The chief qāḍī of Cairo was always a senior Ottoman qāḍī from the imperial ilmiye hierarchy, who served a short term, usually one to two years, after which he would be reassigned.[9]

While the chief qāḍī heard some cases himself at the court of al-Bāb al-ᶜĀlī, he appointed deputies from among the local population who were responsible for the bulk of the caseload in Cairo's courts. These deputy qāḍīs, or nāᵓibs, staffed the main sharīᶜa court al-Bāb al-ᶜĀlī and all the neighborhood courts, as well as the Dīwān al-ᶜĀlī.[10] They were, for the most part, local men educated within Egypt, and they were drawn from the Shāfiᶜī, Mālikī, and Ḥanbalī madhhabs as well as the official Ḥanafī madhhab.[11]

This contrast between the Ottoman chief qāḍī and the local nāᵓibs does not, however, imply a strict divide between Ottomans and Egyptians, or between Turks and Arabs. The chief qāḍī was an Ottoman by virtue of his education and cultural identity, not due to his regional, ethnic, or linguistic background. The members of the imperial ilmiye hierarchy were trained at imperial medreses, where they assimilated to the culture of the ruling elite if they did not already belong to it.[12] But this career route was open to talented Muslim students from across the empire. It was possible for Egyptians to train at these institutions and so become "Ottoman" qāḍīs. Egyptians served as chief qāḍī in Damascus, Jerusalem, Aleppo, Skopje, Salonica, Bursa, Edirne, and Istanbul, and even as ḳāżᶜasker of Anatolia, one of the two senior judges in the empire.[13] One such Egyptian-born qāḍī was appointed as chief qāḍī of Cairo in the mid-seventeenth century. Although he was active a few decades before the period under focus in this book, it is worth examining his biography in more detail as it illustrates the fluidity of the boundaries between imperial and local in the legal profession.

Shihāb al-Dīn Aḥmad ibn Muḥammad al-Khafājī was born in or near Cairo around 1571, to a father who hailed from Siryāqūs, a village near the city. He was educated initially by his father, Muḥammad ibn ᶜUmar al-Khafājī,[14] and his maternal uncle, Abū Bakr ibn Ismāᶜīl al-Shanawānī, from whom he learned grammar and philology. He went on to study Shāfiᶜī and Ḥanafī law with noted scholars including the Shāfiᶜī Shams al-Dīn al-Ramlī and the Ḥanafī Ghānim al-Maqdisī al-Khazrajī. He continued his studies in Mecca and Medina after traveling there on pilgrimage, and later he moved to Istanbul where he studied not only law and religious sciences with Saᶜd al-Dīn ibn Ḥasan, but also Euclidean geometry with a rabbi called Dāwūd.

He then embarked on a career as a qāḍī, serving in Rumelia, Skopje, and Salonica, before being appointed chief qāḍī in Cairo, a position he held for a year. He then spent a year in Damascus before returning to Istanbul via Aleppo. He felt that the intellectual climate had deteriorated since his student days, and he made no friends by writing *al-Maqāma al-Rūmiyya*, which satirized the capital's scholars. He fell out with the Şeyhulislām Yaḥyā ibn Zakariyyāᵓ, failed to get the Grand Vizier to intervene on his behalf, and was banished back to Cairo. There, he found work as a nāᵓib and teacher, with the great biographer Muḥibbī's father numbering among his students. He died in Cairo on 3 June 1659.[15]

Al-Khafājī's career illustrates the mobility possible within the Ottoman scholarly world. The son of a minor Shāfiᶜī scholar in Egypt, he was not born into elite Ottoman circles. Nevertheless, he was able, after training in Cairo and in the imperial medreses of Istanbul, and after switching to the Ḥanafī school of law, to enter the imperial ilmiye hierarchy. Initially he was successful, obtaining the prestigious position of chief qāḍī of his native city Cairo. But mobility worked both ways, and a lack of political nous led to his fall into professional obscurity despite the fact that his scholarship was respected: from chief qāḍī of Cairo to a simple court nāᵓib. That both the imperial and the local aspects of the personnel of Cairo's courts were represented in one man's career illustrates how these boundaries were permeable. Acceptance into the ilmiye hierarchy did not depend solely on background, but was open to anyone with suitable talent and education, and a little good luck. Succeeding within the ilmiye hierarchy depended not only on legal expertise but also on the cultivation of patrons and on savvy political maneuvering.

The courts also relied on local educated men to fill the important positions of scribe and court witness. The scribe's primary duty was to record proceedings both in the court register and in the form of *ḥujja*s that were issued to the litigants. Much of the courts' workload consisted of the notarization of contracts rather than adjudication, and the scribe may often have performed this role alone, without any input from the qāḍī or nāᵓib.[16] The court witnesses, known as *shuhūd al-ḥāl* or *shuhūd ᶜudūl*, were official appointees whose role was to witness the conduct and conclusion of every litigation and contract that came before the court. Their role was different from that of circumstantial witnesses, who provided testimony in support of litigants' claims. The court witnesses performed an important role, which certified the validity of the proceedings while preventing judicial corruption and the fabrication of judgments.[17] The names of the court witnesses present were inscribed at the bottom of every record in the court register, and also at the bottom of all ḥujjas issued by courts to litigants.[18]

Who were the people who filled these positions? We have more information on the court witnesses than on the scribes, for the former were named at the end of each entry in the registers. The scribes who wrote the entries, on the other hand, were not named within the records, although sometimes their appointments were noted in the sijill. The names given for court witnesses were not as detailed as those given for the litigants and circumstantial witnesses who appeared in court proceedings: they consisted only of title, name, and surname, lacking patronyms, places of origin, professions, and places of residence. This is because the court witnesses were appointees of the court and therefore such identifying details were unnecessary. The court witnesses almost always bore the title of *shaykh* or *faqīr*, indicating membership of the learned class. Titles indicating military rank, or distinction in the merchant elite, are not found. On the basis of the registers of the courts of Bāb al-Shaᶜriyya and al-Bāb al-ᶜĀlī, it seems that the office may have been associated with particular families.[19] At least one of the court witnesses at Bāb al-Shaᶜriyya was succeeded by his son. Fāyid al-Buḥayrī served in the 1660s, while Muḥammad al-Buḥayrī served in the 1690s and 1700s: in one entry there is a rare example of the inclusion of a patronym in a court witness's name, and Muḥammad is identified as ibn Fāyid.[20] There were also other court witnesses with the family name al-Buḥayrī: ᶜAbd al-Bāqī al-Buḥayrī served at Bāb al-Shaᶜriyya in the 1660s and 1670s, while another Muḥammad al-Buḥayrī served at Bāb al-Shaᶜriyya and al-Bāb al-ᶜĀlī in the 1670s.[21]

In seventeenth and eighteenth-century Cairo, both scribes and court witnesses were legal professionals appointed by the court.[22] In some cases, they were the same people. In 1699, a man called ᶜUmar al-Qāḍiri was appointed to serve as both court witness and as chief scribe (*raᵓīs al-kuttāb*) at the court of Bāb al-Shaᶜriyya.[23] There was a good deal of overlap between the roles. Court witnesses frequently wrote the contracts that were notarized by the courts: orders from the chief qāḍī instructing court personnel on what kinds of contract to draw up were addressed to the court witnesses as well as to the scribes and nāᵓibs.[24] There is some evidence that, as the least qualified and poorest paid court personnel, the court witnesses were the weak link in the integrity of the court system. The chronicler Damurdāshī reports a story of a court witness who was pressured into conducting an illegal marriage.[25] The authorities were aware of corruption among court witnesses and took some steps to combat it: the chronicler Aḥmad Çelebi describes an incident in 1696 in which a court witness, guilty of producing fraudulent documents, had his beard shaved before being paraded through Cairo's markets on a camel, accompanied by a crier announcing his offenses to the crowds.[26]

As well as the evidence of their involvement in drafting legal documents, there is also further evidence that court witnesses had received formal legal training. One court witness, ᶜAlī al-Rifāᶜī, was sufficiently qualified to also practice as a Mālikī nāᵓib at Bāb al-Shaᶜriyya.[27] Others were described in the court records as imāms, which indicates at least a basic grounding in the religious sciences, including law.[28]

The Dīwān al-ᶜĀlī

As well as the sharīᶜa courts, Cairene litigants also had access to the Ottoman governor's council, known as the Dīwān al-ᶜĀlī. The obligation to hold the Dīwān at least four days a week was imposed on the governor by the ḳānūnnāme of Egypt.[29]

The governor's Dīwān is mentioned in several chronicles of the seventeenth and eighteenth centuries, where it is usually described as a consultative council, at which the governor met with various officials and dignitaries to discuss matters of state such as the transfer of revenues to Istanbul, the administration of the pilgrimage, and the receipt of orders from the imperial government. The mid-eighteenth-century chronicler Damurdāshī describes a meeting of the Dīwān in 1169/1755 to inaugurate the regime of the newly-arrived governor Ḥekīmoğlu ᶜAlī Pasha and to arrange the collection of taxes for Istanbul and grains for the holy cities. Damurdāshī lists the composition of the Dīwān on this occasion as follows: the shaykhs of the Sādāt and the Bakriyya, the shaykhs of the Sufi orders, the heads of the guilds, the senior muftis of each madhhab, the ulema, the beys, the commanders and senior officers of the seven regiments, and the lieutenants of the Janissary and ᶜAzabān regiments.[30] The Dīwān also had a staff of functionaries, including the *firmāniyya*, who wrote up the edicts issued by the Dīwān, and the *mahrdār*, who was responsible for the seals.[31] Modern historians, relying on the chronicles, have followed them in describing the Dīwān as a consultative forum.[32]

The Dīwān al-ᶜĀlī also functioned as a tribunal. Tribunals presided over by the executive authorities were found in many pre-modern Muslim societies, often called maẓālim or siyāsa tribunals. In the Ottoman Empire this tradition was continued by the councils of provincial governors and by the Imperial Council (*Dīvān-i Hümāyūn*) in the capital. In contrast with that of other pre-modern Islamic societies, Ottoman historiography has paid very little attention to executive tribunals, instead focusing on the sharīᶜa court as the paradigmatic Ottoman legal institution. Indeed, some historians have suggested that the maẓālim jurisdiction was abolished by the Ottomans.[33] One reason that provincial governors' councils have received little attention from historians is that few of their records have survived. In this respect, Cairo's Dīwān is unusual. Two of the Dīwān's eighteenth-century registers have survived: one from the 1740s and one from the 1780s. Compared to the hundreds of registers left by Ottoman Egypt's sharīᶜa courts, this is a meager quantity. It is, however, far more documentation than has survived from any other provincial governor's council in the Ottoman Empire, which makes it significant.[34] A scattering of individual ḥujjas issued by the Dīwān in the late seventeenth and early eighteenth centuries have survived and can be used to complement the registers.[35]

When functioning as a tribunal, the Dīwān al-ᶜĀlī was presided over by the governor himself, by his lieutenant (katkhudā), or when there was no governor present in Cairo, by the acting governor (qāʾimmaqām). When simply registering transactions, the governor was not always present, although in many cases the record states that the transaction was concluded with his knowledge (*bi maᶜrifat al-wazīr*). But when the Dīwān heard a lawsuit, the governor or his representative almost always attended. The governor or his representative was always accompanied by a qāḍī. The qāḍī was usually either the Dīwān's own qāḍī or the chief qāḍī of Egypt. Reflecting the pluralism found in Cairo's sharīᶜa courts, some cases were heard by nāʾibs from the Mālikī, Shāfiᶜī, and Ḥanbalī madhhabs. Often, a group of other notables was present at hearings. These notables attended simply as observers and witnesses: similar groups of notables sometimes attended hearings at Cairo's sharīᶜa courts. Lastly, when sitting as a tribunal the Dīwān employed scribes to write up the records of litigations and contracts, and court witnesses to sign off on them, as did the sharīᶜa courts.

The Dīwān was held at the citadel, which was the governor's official residence, and contained the barracks of the Janissary and ᶜAzabān regiments. The citadel is located on the Muqaṭṭam hill which, during the seventeenth and eighteenth centuries, was just outside the southeastern boundary of the city. Constructed by Saladin in the 1180s, the citadel remained the seat of government in Cairo until 1874, when the Khedive Ismāᶜīl moved it to the ᶜAbdīn Palace.[36] The Dīwān differed from the sharīᶜa courts in being located at some distance from the homes and businesses of the civilian population. The main sharīᶜa court, al-Bāb al-ᶜĀlī, was located in the city's central commercial district, one block away from the main thoroughfare, al-Muᶜizz li ᵓl-Dīn Allāh Street. It was convenient for those working or trading in the nearby markets as well as those who lived in the city center's densely-packed houses and apartment buildings. The other sharīᶜa courts were located in residential neighborhoods, and were held in the mosques that were central to community life. Distant from Cairo's centers of commerce and social life, the Dīwān was a less convenient venue for ordinary Cairenes. However, the citadel was a hub of elite political activity: as mentioned above, the Dīwān was not only a tribunal but also a council of state. Cairo's elites were often in attendance at the Dīwān on official business; they were also familiar with its personnel. Unsurprisingly, the litigants who used the Dīwān were disproportionately drawn from the city's elites.

The Dīvān-i Hümāyūn

As an expression of the jurisdiction of the sovereign, the Dīwān al-ᶜĀlī in Cairo was the provincial counterpart of the Dīvān-i Hümāyūn (Imperial Council) in Istanbul. Despite the great distance between Cairo and the capital, Egyptian litigants could also present their disputes to the Dīvān-i Hümāyūn itself, which accepted petitions from subjects from across the empire. The availability of the Sultan to his subjects, and his duty to respond to grievances and injustices from across his realm, was an ancient ideal of kingship shared across many pre-modern societies. In the late seventeenth and eighteenth-century Ottoman Empire, a complex bureaucracy had developed to handle this function, which for the most part was only notionally connected with the Sultan himself. Petitions were addressed to the Sultan, but the Dīvān-i Hümāyūn was in fact presided over by the Grand Vizier. Meetings of the Dīvān-i Hümāyūn were held at the Topkapı Palace, in a chamber adjoining the harem, which was the Sultan's private quarters. A window covered with a grille allowed the Sultan to view the Dīvān's proceedings without being noticed himself, so that the members of the Dīvān would never know whether or not they were being observed. We don't know how frequently the Sultans really did surreptitiously supervise the Dīvān's meetings, and we might guess that the answer is not very often, particularly when the agenda consisted of the mundane problems of ordinary subjects. But the viewing grille preserved the ideal of the Sultan's control over the process, and his ultimate responsibility for justice.

Some Egyptians went to the trouble of personally traveling to Istanbul to submit their petitions; usually when the stakes were particularly high. For example, during the regime of Silāḥdār Ḥasan Pasha (1707–9 / 1119–21 AH), the six Cairo regiments other than the Janissaries composed a petition complaining that the Janissaries were monopolizing urban tax-farms and protecting certain merchants against the city's authorities. A group of six soldiers, one representing each regiment, traveled to Istanbul to submit the petition. The Janissary officers found out and came up with a counter-petition, demanding that if they lost any privileges, their rivals should lose something too. A Janissary of Istanbul origin was selected to take this petition to the palace; he bumped into the six rival petitioners in Alexandria and they traveled together on the same boat.[37] In another example from the regime of Murādī Ḥusayn Pasha (1698–9 / 1109–11 AH), the people of Banī Suwayf and Bahnasā petitioned the Sultan to complain that they suffered frequent bedouin raids and that the local authorities were failing to prevent them due to bribes from the bedouin. They elected a local shaykh called Muḥammad to convey their petition, and he traveled to Alexandria and thence to Istanbul by sea.[38] The petitioning records kept by the Dīvān-i Hümāyūn sometimes indicate that Egyptian petitioners had attended in person to deliver their petitions.[39] While in the idealized image of the petitioning process the Sultan would receive petitions personally while riding to mosque, in the sprawling Ottoman Empire of the seventeenth and eighteenth centuries this function was delegated and bureaucratized. During the seventeenth century the chief white eunuch was charged with receiving petitions at the outer door to the palace grounds.[40] Given the great distance, however, most Egyptian petitioners did not travel to the palace in person, but sent their petitions via couriers.

Previous scholars have portrayed petitioning as a process that allowed Ottoman subjects to bring the misdeeds and abuses of provincial officials to the government's attention.[41] However, many petitions concerned private disputes among subjects. Egyptians of various social strata sent petitions on matters including real estate, waqf administration, debts, and petty neighborhood quarrels. The procedures followed by the Dīvān-i Hümāyūn in responding to petitions are discussed at length in the following chapter. Suffice it to say here that, when handling disputes involving Egypt, the Dīvān-i Hümāyūn's procedures were very different from those of the courts and tribunals based in Cairo. Given the great distance, the process was conducted entirely through paperwork, and decisions were often, though not always, delegated to officials on the ground in Cairo.

Military officers and the prosecution of crime

The sharīᶜa courts, the Dīwān al-ᶜĀlī and the Dīvān-i Hümāyūn had a limited role to play in the prosecution of crime and the punishment of criminals.[42] The Dīvān-i

Hümāyūn did not handle criminal matters in Cairo on a regular basis, although Egyptians occasionally sent petitions complaining about gangs of bandits who continually terrorized their communities when they felt that the provincial authorities were not doing enough to suppress them.[43] The sharīᶜa courts and the Dīwān al-ᶜĀlī handled cases of petty theft, verbal abuse, assault, and occasionally homicide.[44] However, crime was not a large part of their caseloads, which were dominated by property and family disputes. More importantly, both the sharīᶜa courts and the Dīwān al-ᶜĀlī were reactive. They did not investigate or prosecute, they merely responded to claims brought by private litigants. Policing—the active investigation and prosecution of crime, undertaken with the intention of deterring criminals and ensuring security for the residents of Cairo—was the responsibility of military officers. The irrelevance of qāḍīs to the suppression of criminality and the securing of public order is illustrated by an anecdote told by Damurdāshī about the visit of Yirmi Sekiz Çelebi, agent of the imperial government and former Ottoman ambassador to France, to Cairo in 1744. Yirmi Sekiz Çelebi was outraged by the behavior of Egyptians, both soldiers and civilians, who would openly smoke in front of senior officers and notables, so the governor issued a *fermān* prohibiting smoking in the streets and in public buildings. To enforce the order, the Janissary Āghā toured the streets three times a day. In order to catch offenders unawares, the Āghā made his rounds in disguise: as a Qarandalī dervish, as a Sufi, as a cavalryman, and as a qāḍī.[45] Clearly, it did not occur to the Āghā that the presence of a qāḍī would deter people from petty law-breaking.

Police officials and their jurisdictions

Policing duties were assigned to military officers in the ḳānūnnāme promulgated for Egypt shortly after the Ottoman conquest. The Egyptian ḳānūnnāme ordered the commander and lieutenant of each regiment to take turns in organizing a night-watch, patrolling the city in order to prevent disorder in the streets, house-breaking, and theft.[46] While the specific provisions of the sixteenth-century ḳānūnnāme were not directly relevant to seventeenth and eighteenth-century Cairo, the principle of military responsibility for public order and policing remained.

The jurisdiction of the police officials covered public order, public morality, and marketplace regulation; the police were also employed to apprehend rebels and fugitives and deliver them to the governor. The combination of public morality and marketplace regulation corresponded to the medieval Islamic jurisdiction of *ḥisba*, overseen in most medieval polities by the *muḥtasib*. Haim Gerber, whose research has focused primarily on Bursa, has claimed that under Ottoman rule the muḥtasib's jurisdiction was subsumed under that of the qāḍī.[47] In Ottoman Cairo, however, the ḥisba jurisdiction was alive and well in the eighteenth century: the term ḥisba was used, and there was an official with the title muḥtasib, who was also known by its synonym *amīn al-iḥtisāb*, and who was active in the regulation of markets. The Ottoman conquest of Cairo was marked by continuity in this institution: the last muḥtasib of Mamluk Cairo, the famous Zaynī Barakāt, was immediately reappointed by the city's new rulers.[48] The continuing relevance of ḥisba in Ottoman Cairo is also illustrated by the fact that Mamluk-era manuals for the use of muḥtasib were copied and read during the late sixteenth, seventeenth, and eighteenth centuries.[49] Over the course of the Ottoman period, the importance of the muḥtasib himself declined. But his jurisdiction neither disappeared nor was subsumed within the qāḍī's. Rather, it was gradually taken over by other military officials. During the period studied here, the task of ḥisba was shared between three officials: the Janissary Āghā, the police chief (known as the *wālī*, the *zaᶜīm*, or the *ṣubaşı*), and the muḥtasib.[50] They were assisted by various subordinate officials, including the *odabāshī al-bawwāba*, who manned the city gates under the command of the police chief, the *nawbatjī*, who carried out the night watch, and Janissary soldiers who assisted their Āghā in making arrests and implementing corporal punishments.

The precise boundaries between the jurisdictions of the Janissary Āghā, the police chief and the muḥtasib were blurred and subject to change. The general trend during the late seventeenth and early eighteenth centuries saw the Janissary Āghā achieving predominance over the police chief and the muḥtasib, unifying the responsibility for market regulation that had been the jurisdiction of the muḥtasib with the responsibility for public order that had traditionally fallen to the Janissaries.[51] The governor also frequently tasked the Janissary Āghā with arresting and punishing disobedient and corrupt officials.

By contrast, the muḥtasib's responsibilities had by 1742 diminished to regulating and collecting taxes from most perishable food markets, along with woodworkers and candle-makers.[52] He did not even have authority over the entire marketplace. An assortment of markets, including those for timber, salt, camels, saddle-makers, and confectionery, along with the entertainment business, which encompassed dancers, snake-charmers, monkey-trainers, drummers, jugglers, acrobats, strongmen, and hashish merchants, were regulated by the multazim of the Khurda tax-farm.[53] The police chief regulated and taxed other professions viewed as lowly or morally dubious, including merchants of black slaves, street-lighters, street-sweepers, donkey-shearers, beggars, and prostitutes.[54]

The police chief's primary responsibility, however, was for maintaining public order and security. As well as running night patrols, he also managed a fire brigade, and was called to quiet disturbances. When, in 1743, the house of ᶜUthmān Bey Dhū ᵓl-Faqār was on fire after a battle between him and Ibrāhīm Çavuş Āghā, the police chief was called to extinguish the fire and to remove the bodies of ᶜUthmān Bey's slain mamlūks, the stench from which was offending his neighbors.[55] In March 1709, a dispute between two groups of al-Azhar students supporting rival candidates for the professorship of the Aqbughāwiyya madrasa descended into a gunfight within the Azhar mosque: the police chief arrived to disperse the students and remove the dead bodies.[56] Like the Janissary Āghā, the police chief was also employed by the governor to apprehend and summarily execute rebels and disobedient notables and officials. Among other examples, when Ibrāhīm Bey Abū Shanab refused to pay outstanding taxes or appear before the governor ᶜAlī Pasha in 1698, ᶜAlī Pasha ordered the police chief to guard the Qanāṭir al-Sibāᶜ bridge to prevent his escape from Cairo.[57] In 1726, the governor Nişāncı Meḥmed Pasha sent the police chief to behead the mint supervisor Muᶜallim Dāwud for minting the gold *janzīrlī* coin after it had been withdrawn.[58] Lastly, the police chief had various ceremonial duties. Most importantly, he escorted messengers from Istanbul and visiting dignitaries from the port at Būlāq to Cairo,[59] and he also served at public occasions, such as during the celebration of the circumcision of the sons of governor Ismāᶜīl Pasha in 1109 (1697–8), when the police chief, the muḥtasib, and various other officials, dressed in yellow sashes embroidered with gold and silver thread and carrying bamboo canes, welcomed guests entering the citadel compound.[60]

However, to a certain extent the jurisdiction of a particular office depended on the charisma and ambitions of its holder: aggressive and successful individuals could temporarily expand their roles and secure more power. Thus Yūsuf Āghā, appointed muḥtasib in 1740, took back many of the functions that had been appropriated by the Janissary Āghās during the first half of the eighteenth century.[61] Indeed, according to Damurdāshī, assertive officials sometimes insisted on expanded jurisdictions as a condition of their accepting office or particular duties. When ᶜAlī Āghā, a Janissary Āghā discussed in more detail below, was asked to take charge of a currency crisis in 1703, he demanded the right to take action against the *ḥimāyāt* (illegal protection taxes), alcohol consumption, and prostitution. Meanwhile, Damurdāshī claims an unnamed amīr nominated as police chief during the rule of ᶜAbdullāh Pasha Köprülü (1142–4 / 1729–31) insisted that Miṣr al-Qadīma and Būlāq be added to his jurisdiction, and that he be allowed to undertake a campaign against bars and brothels.[62]

The imprecision and flexibility of these jurisdictional boundaries also meant that officials other than the Janissary Āghā, police chief, and muḥtasib sometimes played a significant role in policing. The famous and unorthodox *başodabaşı* (senior officer) of the Janissaries, Küçük Muḥammad, took action on his own initiative to bring wheat and corn prices under control after the failure of the Nile flood in 1694. When the Būlāq grain market responded to his price ceiling of sixty niṣf fiḍḍa per *ardabb* by ceasing trade, Küçük Muḥammad executed three boat captains and two customs officers to set an example.[63] Küçük Muḥammad's attempt to intervene in market regulation failed due to his assassination, procured by the Hawwāra bedouin and the multazims who controlled the grain trade.[64]

The predominance of the Janissary Āghā was formalized a decade after Küçük Muḥammad's death, in 1703, when ᶜAlī Āghā was granted authority over weights, prices, and public morality, in the midst of an inflation crisis caused by coin-clipping.[65] At the request of the market traders, a delegation of ulema from al-Azhar approached the governor and demanded action. A meeting of the governor's katkhudā, the beys, the āghās and other leading officials was convened; they decided to issue a new silver coin to replace the discredited *maqāṣīṣ* (clipped) currency.[66] ᶜAlī Āghā was charged with enforcing use of the new currency and adherence to the official exchange rates and prices. According to Damurdāshī, the decision to give control of weights and prices to the Janissary Āghā was inspired by the example of Istanbul.[67] ᶜAlī Āghā insisted on also being permitted to undertake a general campaign against corruption and vice, abolishing the *ḥimāyāt* (the "protection" taxes levied on merchants by the regiments), and closing the bars, būẓa-cafes, and brothels.[68] The assembly accepted his conditions, and the qāḍī drew up a ḥujja confirming this.

ᶜAlī Āghā inaugurated his new role with a procession through the streets of Cairo, Būlāq, and Miṣr al-Qadīma, which served both to announce the new official prices for the major commodities and to impose ᶜAlī Āghā's new order through the summary punishment of offenders. ᶜAlī Āghā was accompanied by the police chief and his men, the muḥtasib, a *çavuş* from each of the seven regiments,[69] the çavuş of the *naqīb al-ashrāf*,[70] a nāᵓib, the executioner (*mashāᶜilī*), two money-changers and a group of mamluks.[71] Both Damurdāshī and Aḥmad Çelebi agree that the procession was marked by extreme violence. Aḥmad Çelebi claims that anyone found trading contrary to the regulations was laid face down on the ground and beaten with a stick: most culprits died of their injuries immediately or within a few days. Damurdāshī specifies that on the first day ᶜAlī Āghā had two public weighers and three oil merchants beaten to death for using fraudulent weights; Jabartī adds also a butcher to the list of victims. According to Damurdāshī, on the following days ᶜAlī Āghā turned his attention to moral infractions, closing down or demolishing bars, būẓa-cafes, and brothels throughout the city and driving out the prostitutes who worked there. He also raided the house of al-ᶜAnza, the head of the guild of women singers (*shaykhat al-maghānī*), but was unable to arrest her as she took refuge in the house of ᶜAlī Ḥasan Katkhudā.[72]

The procession undertaken by ᶜAlī Āghā illustrates the hierarchy of police officials that held during most of the eighteenth century: the police chief and the muḥtasib participated in the procession, but under ᶜAlī Āghā's command. In normal circumstances, the police chief and the muḥtasib undertook their daily activities in providing security and regulating the market individually, but they worked under the Janissary Āghā's overall supervision. When the three acted as a group in response to major events, the Janissary Āghā was in charge.

Punishments

The key tool used by the Janissary Āghā, police chief, muḥtasib, and all other police officials to keep order in Ottoman Cairo was violence, which was sometimes ferocious. This comes across strongly in the story of ᶜAlī Āghā's procession, in which miscreants were beaten to death on the spot. Despite his violence, and the apparent relish with which he used it, ᶜAlī Āghā was praised by the chroniclers for his honesty and for his success in controlling prices and preventing fraud. Aḥmad Çelebi states that he was tyrannical (*jabbār*) and that people obeyed him through fear. But he claims that he imposed order on Cairo, that there were no shortages of vital commodities under his rule, and that the prices he set were never exceeded. In fact, Aḥmad Çelebi notes approvingly, when he declared that coffee should be sold at 1,200 niṣf fiḍḍa, the price dropped from 1,500 to 1,100. For Aḥmad Çelebi, ᶜAlī Āghā was the yardstick by which one measured the success of other police officials. Some years later, Aḥmad Çelebi witnessed the arrival of Yaḥyā Sharīf in Mecca, having traveled with him on the same boat from Egypt, and he praises Yaḥyā in his chronicle by claiming that he accomplished in Mecca what ᶜAlī Āghā had achieved in Cairo.[73] Similarly, Damurdāshī compares the muḥtasib Yūsuf Āghā (who played a more active and prominent role in policing than most other muḥtasibs of the period) with ᶜAlī Āghā in order to emphasize his effectiveness.[74] Jabartī, meanwhile, claims that ᶜAlī Āghā never accepted a bribe, and he quotes a eulogy composed by Shaykh Ḥasan al-Ḥijāzī after ᶜAlī Āghā's death on 12 Shawwāl 1123 (23 November 1711), which justified ᶜAlī Āghā's violence as inflicted only on evil-doers for the greater benefit of the community:

> Because of him, you enjoyed abundance, bounty, and security, under a regime unopposed by any other regime.
> He caused affliction, disaster, calamity, and suppression to alight on oppressors,
> On the evil and unclean rabble who were out to cheat and cause loss.
> He established fair weights and full measures; he quenched fires and established peace.
> None hated him but those who deviated from the truth or whose beliefs were unsound.[75]

But while ᶜAlī Āghā's ferocity was lauded, the chroniclers did not praise violence indiscriminately. Violence had to be targeted and successful if it was to receive approval. A later Janissary Āghā called Ismāᶜīl, a protégé of Ismāᶜīl Bey ibn ᶜIwaḍ, was described by Aḥmad Çelebi as a depraved and unjust tyrant.[76] Cairene merchants were so scared of his violence, which included punishing offenders by impaling and flaying, that they simply shut up shop and stayed at home. As an example of Ismāᶜīl Āghā's brutality, Aḥmad Çelebi recounts a story about him that circulated in Cairo. When traveling from Cairo to Miṣr al-Qadīma on one of his processions, he passed the garbage dump that lay just outside the city boundary, and noticed a man coming down tying his trousers. He sent his men to investigate, and they discovered that the man had just visited a prostitute; Ismāᶜīl Āghā beat the prostitute one hundred times with a wooden club (*nabbūt*), and nailed the man's penis to a tree. When Ismāᶜīl Āghā was deposed and replaced by Muḥammad Āghā ibn al-Jīᶜān, Cairenes rejoiced and economic life returned to the city.[77]

As well as beating, often to the soles of the feet, punishments employed by police officials included nailing an offender's ear to his shop door in such a way that he could only just touch the ground with his toes, piercing the nose of a baker with a spike from which was hung a loaf of bread; cutting a chunk of flesh from the body of a butcher equal in weight to the amount by which he had short-sold a customer; bleeding an oil-merchant of a volume of blood equivalent to the amount of oil missing from his measures; and cutting off the noses, ears, and hands of repeat offenders.[78] It is clear that, regardless of the stipulation in the Egyptian ḳānūnnāme of 1524 that police officials should not take action without a judgment from a qāḍī, in the seventeenth and eighteenth centuries the police punished offenders on the spot, without a trial.[79]

This does not indicate that the police were acting outside the law, as it was conceived in eighteenth-century Cairo. Again, the story of ᶜAlī Āghā's procession is illustrative: the chief qāḍī sanctioned his jurisdiction and his grand procession in advance with a ḥujja, and according to Aḥmad Çelebi, a nāʾib accompanied him on his procession.[80] The right of the police to summarily punish offenders whom they caught red-handed was widely accepted.[81] The impression of ruthless violence given by the chroniclers should not be taken to indicate that Cairenes lived in permanent terror of the police, however. The chroniclers' accounts of violent punishment focus on particular individuals famed for their effectiveness or brutality. Meanwhile, the chronicles are full of complaints about out-of-control prices and widespread immorality. Aggressive policing was the exception rather than the norm. Indeed, the police were often in league with unscrupulous traders and petty criminals, operating protection rackets in which the unofficial taxes known as the ḥimāyat (protection dues) were extracted in return for lax enforcement of regulations.[82] Such a conflict of interest was inevitable given the venality of public office during this period: having spent financial as well as political capital on obtaining their positions, most police officials were keen to maximize their returns. While we must accept that many of the chronicles' descriptions of punishments were accurate, we should hesitate to assume that such punishments were common.

Appointments, patronage, and factional politics

As military men, those who held office as Janissary Āghā, police chief, and muḥtasib were all to some degree integrated into the factional politics of Cairo. The Janissary Āghā was appointed by the central government in Istanbul: a haṭṭ-i şerīf (imperial order written in the Sultan's own hand) would be sent to the governor in Cairo notifying him of new appointments.[83] In order that he be independent of the regiment he controlled, the Janissary Āghā was usually either sent from Istanbul or appointed from among the Müteferriḳa or Çavuşān regiments.[84]

The police chief was formally appointed by the governor, but on many occasions the governor's choice appears to have been dictated by one of the leading beys. In fact, Damurdāshī describes Çerkes Muḥammad Bey al-Kabīr as making Muḥammad Āghā Lahlūba police chief in 1136/1723–4; this probably means that Çerkes Muḥammad prevailed upon the governor to appoint Muḥammad Āghā, rather than that he appointed him himself.[85] A bey could wield influence over this decision even when there was tension between him and the governor. For example, Muḥammad Bey Qaṭāmish's nomination of a candidate for police chief was accepted by the governor ᶜAbdullāh Pasha Köprülü in 1731. This was despite the fact that the reason for the vacancy was the absconding of the previous police chief after the governor attempted to arrest him for murdering the governor's protégé, ᶜAbd al-Ghaffār Āghā, on the orders of Qaṭāmish. According to Damurdāshī, Qaṭāmish nominated the new police chief in the very same conversation in which the governor reprimanded him for ordering the killing.[86]

After having been held by qāḍīs during the first few decades of Ottoman rule in Egypt, the position of muḥtasib was made an iltizām (tax-farm) in 1581. This iltizām was reserved for members of the Çavuşān regiment.[87] Damurdāshī describes the selection process for the appointment of Yūsuf Āghā in 1740. The governor Ḥekīmoğlu ᶜAlī Pasha asked the lieutenant of the Çavuşān regiment to find an honest man to serve as muḥtasib. The lieutenant summoned the chief officers of the seven watch-stations run by the Çavuşān: they agreed that Yūsuf Āghā was the most suitable candidate. The lieutenant of the Çavuşān then brought Yūsuf Āghā to the Dīwān where, before the senior officers of the Çavuşān and Müteferriḳa regiments, the governor presented him with the robes of office.[88]

Unlike the governor and the chief qāḍī, who stood outside Cairene society as representatives of the government in Istanbul (though they intervened in the city's fractious politics on many occasions), the military officers who carried out policing functions were fully integrated into Cairo's violent factionalism. It is perhaps not surprising that their police powers were sometimes used to further political disputes. In particular the police chief, whose claim on the office was often the result of his clientage to a bey, seems often to have been willing to use the coercive force he controlled to serve his patron's interests. The example given above, of an unnamed police chief assassinating ᶜAbd al-Ghaffār Āghā on the order of Muḥammad Bey Qaṭāmish, is only one of several similar stories. During a feud between Dhū ʾl-Faqār Bey and Çerkes Muḥammad Bey al-Kabīr in the 1720s, Ibrāhīm Āghā, the lieutenant of Yūsuf Bey al-Jazzār and ally of Çerkes Muḥammad Bey, escaped to his villages in Sharqiyya province after the latter's defeat. Dhū ʾl-Faqār Bey invited Ibrāhīm Āghā to his house for talks, promising that nothing untoward would happen to him. But he arranged for the police chief to ambush Ibrāhīm Āghā as he was leaving and cut off his head. Dhū ʾl-Faqār Bey then appropriated Ibrāhīm Āghā's villages after paying the ḥulvān tax; the police chief profited in a more modest way, by taking Ibrāhīm Āghā's cloak, turban, and horse.[89]

As well as sometimes directing their efforts towards the private interests of their patrons, police officials' entanglement in the political struggles of Cairo could also constrain their effectiveness. The efforts of the police could be obstructed by powerful beys or other notables. In such circumstances the ability of the police to enforce the law or the orders of the governor depended on whether they could mobilize sufficient support: in many cases they could not. ᶜAlī Āghā's story is informative again: he was prevented from arresting al-ᶜAnza, the shaykhat al-maghānī, during his campaign against prostitution because she took refuge in the house of ᶜAlī Ḥasan Katkhudā.[90] Another example of a grandee offering protection from police action is the case of the attempted pilgrimage of the Coptic Patriarch to Jerusalem in 1748. The Patriarch set off from Hārat al-Rūm with many Copts in a great procession, riding in specially-constructed wooden carriages mounted atop camels, accompanied by a band, dancers, and young boys carrying torches. The ulema complained that the procession was an illegitimate innovation and an unacceptable imitation of the Muslim pilgrimage caravan, and so the acting governor issued a fermān ordering the Janissary Āghā to prevent the Christians from traveling and to confiscate everything they were carrying. The Janissary Āghā and the police chief headed to al-ᶜĀdiliyya outside Cairo to intercept the pilgrimage. The Christians, however, appealed to ᶜUthmān Bey Abū Sayf, who was guarding the Sabīl ᶜAllām fortress on the road out of Cairo. While they were unable to proceed with their pilgrimage, ᶜUthmān Bey protected them and their possessions.[91]

Beyond the intercession of powerful figures in particular cases, the character of particularly powerful beys could affect the nature of policing more broadly. According to Jabartī, Riḍwān Katkhudā al-Jalfī, one half of the duumvirate that dominated Cairo in the late 1740s and 1750s, was a hedonist who openly drank wine and "associated with beautiful girls and debauched boys," and he forbade the police from taking action against alcohol and sexual transgression. Jabartī claims that under his sway Cairo became "a pasture for gazelles and a home for nymphs and effete boys," and that it was as if Cairenes "had been released from the Day of Judgment."[92] While we should allow for the rhetorical memorialization of a legendary figure in Jabartī's biography, which was written more than half a century after Riḍwān Katkhudā al-Jalfī's ascendancy, the weight of evidence concurs that prominent notables like Jalfī had great influence over how Cairo was policed.

Christian and Jewish Courts

There were communal courts serving Cairo's Jewish and Christian communities: these have not been studied extensively and consequently little is known about them. Although they suffered some procedural handicaps such as the invalidity of their testimony in many cases, Christians and Jews were entitled to use Ottoman Cairo's official legal institutions. They were obliged to appear before a qāḍī if they sued or were sued by a Muslim, but many chose to use the sharīᶜa courts even in disputes with co-religionists. There are several reasons why Ottoman Christians and Jews generally preferred Muslim legal institutions over their own communal courts.[93] The Ottoman sharīᶜa courts, as the official courts of the empire, were more prestigious and had a greater air of institutional permanence, which was important to people arranging their legal affairs. The Ottoman authorities recognized and were willing to enforce judgments from sharīᶜa courts but not from non-Muslim communal courts. While the Ottomans allowed Christians and Jews to arrange their affairs according to their own religious laws if they wished, they did not grant any legal validity to the decisions of their communal courts: this meant that the authority of such courts depended on the consent of the parties to a dispute, either of whom could decide to resort to the sharīᶜa court whose qāḍī would ignore the outcome of earlier communal court litigation.[94] Moreover, some significant areas of legal life were necessarily conducted according to Islamic law, such as real estate; for example, Church properties in Muslim territory were held as waqf, as this was the only form of charitable endowment that was recognized by Muslim rulers and which would therefore secure Church property from seizure.[95] And in some domains, non-Muslims found Islamic legal doctrines favorable to their interests. A major example is divorce: Islamic law granted women greater rights to divorce than either Jewish or Christian law.[96]

However, Church and rabbinical courts existed in parallel, and could be used to resolve disputes between Christians or Jews if both parties agreed. Recent scholarship, focusing on the extent to which non-Muslims used the sharīᶜa courts, has downplayed the significance of Christian and Jewish courts.[97] This neglect is partly due to a lack of sources: very few records from Christian or Jewish courts survive. However, there are sufficient records to establish that such institutions existed. For Cairo, a handful of legal records produced by Jewish institutions in the seventeenth century have survived as part of the Geniza, but have not been studied by modern historians.[98] As they are in Hebrew and Aramaic, I was not able to use them for this study.[99] To my knowledge, the documentary evidence for Christian courts in Ottoman Cairo is slimmer still, although there is evidence in narrative sources that the Coptic Patriarch possessed some degree of legal jurisdiction over Christians.[100] Beyond the fact of their existence, however, we know little about the role of Jewish and Christian courts and legal practices in Ottoman Cairo, or about their interaction with the sharīᶜa courts and other Ottoman-Islamic institutions; it is a worthy subject for future research.[101]

Mediation

In common with other Ottoman cities, many disputes in Cairo were resolved not by adjudication but by mediation: a process known as ṣulḥ. Mediation was not an extra-judicial method of dispute resolution: the sharīᶜa courts and the Dīwān al-ᶜĀlī were involved in the process, registering agreements that litigants reached through ṣulḥ. Islamic law sanctioned mediation, and indeed promoted it as preferable to adjudication, following the Prophetic tradition *al-ṣulḥ khayr* (ṣulḥ is best). Jurists instructed qāḍīs to encourage litigants to try to resolve their disputes through ṣulḥ before adjudicating.[102] The records of Cairo's sharīᶜa courts and the Dīwān al-ᶜĀlī abound with disputes that were resolved through ṣulḥ, as do sharīᶜa court records from many other Ottoman cities.[103]

It is an open question whether ṣulḥ was a process directed by the qāḍī, or whether it was a communal process undertaken by community elders, with the result simply brought to the qāḍī for registration. Recently, Boğaç Ergene has recently suggested that Ottoman qāḍīs led ṣulḥ negotiations themselves; the tendency among most scholars has been to assume that mediators were prominent people from the community.[104] The evidence does not allow me to offer a conclusive answer for Cairo. The formulaic court records usually do not identify the mediators, referring to them generically as the *muṣalliḥūn* or the *mutakallimūn fī ṣulḥ*.[105] In the one case where the mediators were identified, the qāḍī was not among them. The record does not give a lot of information about them, but they appear simply to be local people of at least moderate status.[106] Of course, even if the qāḍī was not considered as a mediator, he may have facilitated the mediation process.

While Cairo's records cannot give a definitive answer to this question, they offer clues that suggest that the initiative to enter ṣulḥ, and the mechanism by which the ṣulḥ was conducted, varied from case to case. The clues are in differences in the structure of different records involving ṣulḥ. They suggest that often ṣulḥ took place without any input from the qāḍī at all, apart from his formalization of the final agreement. But in other cases, the qāḍī may well have encouraged the litigants to undergo ṣulḥ and directed them towards mediators; just as, according to fiqh, he was supposed to.

The ṣulḥ process resulted in an agreement that was then formalized before the court. The agreement usually consisted of two parts: the negotiated resolution of the dispute, and the mutual renunciation of future claims connected with the dispute. In many entries in the court registers, the ṣulḥ agreement is the first thing mentioned in the record, before even the content of the underlying dispute is explained. An example is a dispute between the shopkeeper Jamāl al-Dīn ibn Sulaymān and his wife Dallāl ibnat ᶜAbd al-Karīm that was brought to the Mālikī nāʾib at the court of Bāb al-Shaᶜriyya on 29 Ṣafar 1085 (4 June 1675).[107] No precise details of the dispute are given, but the agreement reached between the couple shows that it concerned the ownership of jewelry and the husband's payment of maintenance. At the conclusion of the ṣulḥ process they agreed that Jamāl al-Dīn's total debt to Dallāl, covering both the jewelry she had sold him and his maintenance obligations, was 360 silver niṣf, which he would pay in monthly installments of 15 niṣf. The couple then renounced all other claims against each other, with the exception of Dallāl's claims for future payments for clothing of 5 niṣf per month and for her delayed dower of 8 *ghurūsh*.[108] The formulaic beginning of the record simply states that a dispute emerged between the couple and that the dispute continued, so a mediator intervened and persuaded them to undergo ṣulḥ.[109] The fact that the ṣulḥ agreement is the only thing mentioned in such records, without any description of the dispute, the parties' opposing claims, or evidence, suggests that the disputants made their ṣulḥ agreement outside the court, and then brought it before the qāḍī for notarization.

Other entries begin as a litigation, with the claim of the plaintiff, the response of the defendant and, if necessary, the presentation of evidence. At some point during the course of the litigation, either before or after the qāḍī's judgment, the record states that mediators intervened and the dispute was resolved through ṣulḥ: the ṣulḥ agreement is then confirmed before the qāḍī. For example, on 10 Ramaḍān 1078 (23 February 1668), Muḥammad ibn Sulaymān al-Ḥāyik complained to the Ḥanafī nāʾib at Bāb al-Shaᶜriyya that his neighbor Khadīja bint Aḥmad had assaulted him, called him a pimp, and called his wife and niece harlots. Khadīja denied the charge, but Muḥammad provided two witnesses who corroborated his claim. The qāḍī sentenced Khadīja to *taᶜzīr*, but at this point the record states that mediators intervened. The ṣulḥ agreement resulted in Muḥammad lifting his demand that Khadīja be punished.[110] In such cases, the fact that litigation commenced and that recourse to ṣulḥ was made at a later stage suggests that the qāḍī may well have played a role in the ṣulḥ process, either by encouraging the litigants to try to resolve their differences through ṣulḥ or by actually leading the mediation process.

Ṣulḥ was used to resolve a wide range of disputes, including debts, property claims, marital disputes, assaults, and even homicides. Recourse to ṣulḥ made sense when neither party to a dispute was obviously in the right. In such cases, the parties had a strong incentive to undergo ṣulḥ, since neither could be confident of winning.[111] Ṣulḥ also offered a broader social benefit. In such difficult cases adjudication was a rather blunt instrument: as a zero-sum process, it would lead to a judgment in favor of one party, but this might not be accepted either by the loser or the wider community, and so could lead to resentment and tension. A widely-derided judgment could also prove difficult to enforce. A good example of these considerations is a lawsuit brought by Ḥasan ibn ᶜAlī al-Ḥāyik against his neighbors, the Christians Yaᶜqūb ibn Shaḥāda and Ghāzir ibn ᶜArḍ, at the court of Bāb al-Shaᶜriyya on 24 Ramaḍān 1077 (20 March 1667). Ḥasan claimed that Yaᶜqūb and Ghāzir had built an extension which included a window that overlooked the house belonging to Ḥasan and his wife Sulṭāna. Privacy was highly valued in Ottoman societies: the seclusion of private space was a right that could be defended in court.[112] Yaᶜqūb and Ghāzir conceded that they had built an extension, but they denied that the window overlooked Ḥasan and Sulṭāna's property. We cannot know the precise location of the window with respect to Ḥasan's house, but it seems likely that he and Yaᶜqūb and Ghāzir genuinely disagreed. Cairo was a tightly-packed city and windows and rooftops unavoidably provided views of neighboring houses: the point was that the views should not intrude unreasonably into the private spaces inside homes. But what constituted intrusive overlooking? In some cases this would be obvious, but in many it would come down to subjective opinion. In this case, while Ḥasan felt that his privacy had been violated, Yaᶜqūb and Ghāzir thought his expectations were unreasonable. The resolution reached through ṣulḥ was a compromise. Yaᶜqūb and Ghāzir got to keep their extension, but they agreed to build a new wall to the side of Ḥasan's house at their own expense. The wall blocked the view of Ḥasan's house from Yaᶜqūb and Ghāzir's window. Ḥasan declared that the window no longer offended him, and renounced any future claims against Yaᶜqūb and Ghāzir concerning the window. The compromise reached through ṣulḥ allowed all parties to feel satisfied with the outcome, with both sides having made and received a concession.

While the benefits to both the litigants and to wider social harmony are obvious in ambiguous cases such as the dispute between Ḥasan and Yaᶜqūb and Ghāzir, ṣulḥ was also used to resolve cases where there would be a clear winner under adjudication. As mentioned above, ṣulḥ was sometimes even used *after* the qāḍī had issued his judgment, so that there was no doubt as to who would win the case. The resort to ṣulḥ in such cases is more intriguing: why would a litigant voluntarily give up a right that he or she could be confident of winning, or even that he or she had already won? In the case cited above between Muḥammad ibn Sulaymān al-Ḥāyik and Khadīja bint Aḥmad, the right that Muḥammad had won in court was to have Khadīja corporally punished. In this case, we can assume that Muḥammad's waiving that right was a simple act of mercy. He had already established publicly that Khadīja was in the wrong, and had caused her some embarrassment; he had also defended his and his family's honor. He had no direct interest in having Khadīja flogged. But in other cases, litigants voluntarily gave up real property or money to which they had an unquestionable legal right: on the face of it, they acted against their own interests. Why?

One example is a dispute between Muḥammad ibn al-Ḥājj Aḥmad, who went by the name Ibn Khalīl, and a local sieve-maker called Muḥammad ibn ᶜAlī and the wife of his paternal uncle Sālima bint Sālim. The dispute was heard at the court of Miṣr al-Qadīma on 14 Dhū ᵓl-Qaᶜda 1091 (6 December 1680). Ibn Khalīl appeared on behalf of himself and also as the agent of his wife Riḍā bint al-Shaykh Muḥammad. Ibn Khalīl accused Muḥammad and Sālima of insulting Riḍā, falsely accusing her of *zināᵓ* (illegal sexual intercourse), and physically assaulting her while she was pregnant. Ibn Khalīl claimed that these attacks led to Riḍā miscarrying a formed (*mukhallaq*) male fetus.[113]

The second part of Ibn Khalīl's claim suggests that he and Riḍā were far from naïve in legal matters. When they specified that the fetus was "formed" (mukhallaq), they used a technical legal term describing the stage in the development of the fetus at which it became "ensouled." An ensouled fetus was considered a person; its miscarriage therefore incurred *diya* (blood-money) if it had been caused by a third party.[114] By asserting that the fetus was formed, Ibn Khalīl was attempting to make Muḥammad and Sālima responsible not just for the verbal and physical assaults on Riḍā, but also for the death of a child. If proved, this would make them liable to pay diya, in addition to punishment for insult, slander, and physical assault.[115]

However, Muḥammad and Sālima denied the charges, and Ibn Khalīl was unable to prove them. We can assume that Ibn Khalīl knew in advance that he would not be able to establish his claim. He knew enough about the legal niceties of fetus development to construct a claim that created the maximum liability for his adversaries: he must surely have known the basic requirements for evidence. Without evidence, all Ibn Khalīl could do was hope that Muḥammad and Sālima confessed, and if they did not, demand that they take an oath of innocence. If they took the oath, they would be cleared of the charges.

Before judgment was passed, however, mediators intervened and the dispute was resolved through ṣulḥ. The resulting agreement, according to the court record, was simply the mutual renunciation of all claims between the two parties, including the charges that Ibn Khalīl had made. What did each side gain from this agreement? Ibn Khalīl apparently gained nothing. Having failed to prove his charges, the ignominy he had caused Muḥammad and Sālima by publicizing their behavior was all he had to show for his lawsuit. By retracting the charges, he gave up even that. It is possible, however, that he received a payment from Muḥammad and Sālima in return for dropping the charges. The fact that payment is not mentioned in the court record does not mean that no payment was made. The purpose of formalizing the ṣulḥ agreement before the qāḍī was to make it binding, and to produce evidence of what had been agreed, in the form of the court record. Therefore, only those aspects of the agreement which the parties wished to make binding needed to be included. For this purpose, the important aspect of this agreement was the mutual renunciation of claims, which ensured that Ibn Khalīl could not reissue the lawsuit. If payment was made in cash on the spot, there was no need for it to be recorded as it would not need to be enforced at a later date.[116] In fact, Muḥammad and Sālima may well have preferred not to publicize the payment, in case it was seen as a tacit admission of guilt.

Muḥammad and Sālima's gains from the agreement are more obvious: they cleared their names. However, if they had taken an oath of innocence, they could have cleared their names with a judgment from the qāḍī in their favor. Legally, the effect of either a qāḍī's judgment or Ibn Khalīl's retraction of the claim through the ṣulḥ agreement would have been identical: both would have prevented Ibn Khalīl pursuing them. But it is likely that ṣulḥ agreement was more desirable for two reasons. First, the oath was not taken lightly by many Cairenes of this period. For believers, swearing a false oath to God had far weightier consequences than telling a simple lie to a fellow human being. Let us assume that Ibn Khalīl's claims were true, or partially true. Muḥammad and Sālima may have felt comfortable denying the claims before the qāḍī, but remained loath to take an oath of innocence. Indeed, there are examples in the court records of defendants who lost cases that they could have won because they refused to take an oath.[117] Second, the ṣulḥ agreement may have been more valuable socially than a judgment from the qāḍī. The publicity surrounding the court case would have been embarrassing for Muḥammad and Sālima: their reputations had been tarnished. Through the ṣulḥ agreement, they publicly made amends with Ibn Khalīl, and he assured the community that their relations were repaired. This may have done more to restore their reputations than winning an adjudication would have done, as everyone would have known that their victory was only due to Ibn Khalīl's lack of evidence and their oaths. In fact, if the community was sympathetic to Ibn Khalīl, then winning a court judgment on the basis of an oath could have been even more damaging to Muḥammad and Sālima's reputations, since they would have been suspected not only of obnoxious and violent behavior, but also of swearing false oaths, with all that implied about their impiety and dishonesty.

As noted above, both the sharīᶜa court system, and Ottoman-Islamic legal culture more generally, favored ṣulḥ over adjudication as a means of dispute resolution. Ibn Khalīl, Muḥammad, and Sālima were probably encouraged to undergo ṣulḥ by members of the community and by the qāḍī. Their decision to undergo ṣulḥ was a result of both social pressure and a recognition that it would serve their own interests. It seems that for Ibn Khalīl it was the prospect of a resolution through ṣulḥ that motivated him to initiate the lawsuit, despite knowing that he could not prove his claim.[118] Of course, it was not necessary to go to court in order to conduct ṣulḥ negotiations. But court action was useful to cajole reluctant adversaries into ṣulḥ negotiations, through the embarrassment of publicity, and through the social pressure applied by the qāḍī and other local figures of influence.[119]

Conclusion

Cairenes involved in disputes had a great number of options during the late seventeenth and early eighteenth centuries. They could approach one of the many sharīᶜa courts to have their dispute adjudicated according to one of the four orthodox Sunni madhhabs. They could, if they desired the involvement of the higher executive authorities, appeal to the Ottoman governor's Dīwān al-ᶜĀlī. If they could bear the delay, they could petition the Sultan in Istanbul. For matters involving market trading and petty crime, they could demand the help of the Janissary Āghā, the police chief, the muḥtasib, or one of the many other military officials working under them. Christians and Jews could approach their own religious authorities if both parties agreed. Disputants who preferred a negotiated solution to adjudication could undergo mediation and have the result ratified and rendered enforceable by a qāḍī.

The theme that emerges most strongly from this overview of Cairene legal life is plurality. There was institutional plurality, with several tribunals and authorities available to litigants. To a great extent, these different tribunals and authorities had overlapping jurisdictions: litigants had a genuine choice of forum. There was also doctrinal plurality. The majority of the population who were Muslim had access to Ḥanafī, Shāfiᶜī, Mālikī, and Ḥanbalī law, although they did not have a free choice in all circumstances, as I explain in Chapter 4. The Christian and Jewish minorities had the same choices, albeit tempered by their institutionalized disabilities within an Islamic legal context, while also having the further option of their own religious-legal traditions. Lastly, there was a plurality of dispute resolution methods: in addition to adjudication there was court-sanctioned ṣulḥ. The contention of this book is that this range of institutions and practices constituted a single sphere of legal activity. Disputants moved back and forth between the different forums and approaches according to their calculation of their best interests. Pluralism was a key feature of this legal system, and it relied not only on the multiplicity of legal forums, but also on the lack of clear jurisdictional boundaries between them: this is what enabled litigants to exercise choices as they pursued their disputes.

The best way to seek to understand this complex is perhaps not to call it a "legal system," which calls to mind rules, formal procedures, and clearly demarcated jurisdictions, but rather a "culture of disputing," a phrase which leaves this field open to input from a range of actors and sources: rulers and subjects as well as judges and jurists, cultural norms and expectations as well as legal texts and government edicts. In Chapter 6, I explore in more detail the strategies devised by litigants to navigate this plural system. First, however, the next three chapters will zoom in more closely on some of the legal institutions and authorities I have described.

CHAPTER

3

ROYAL JUSTICE: THE DĪVĀN-İ HÜMĀYŪN AND THE DĪWĀN AL-ᶜĀLĪ

In the last chapter I described the range of forums and practices, formal and informal, that Cairenes could use to resolve disputes. Previously, only one of these forums—the sharīᶜa court—has received sustained attention from scholars of Egypt or any other region of the Ottoman Empire. In this chapter I examine two of the other forums—the Dīvān-i Hümāyūn in Istanbul, headed by the Grand Vizier, and the Dīwān al-ᶜĀlī in Cairo, presided over by the Ottoman governor—in more detail. These two institutions have significant implications for our understanding of Ottoman legal history, yet their judicial functions have never been studied in detail. Ottoman legal historiography has privileged the sharīᶜa court as the central institution of Ottoman justice. The impression given by the historiography is of a separation of judicial from executive authority, with sharīᶜa courts and their qāḍīs gaining a near-monopoly on dispute resolution. This impression is, in part, due to the lack of coverage of other forums and jurisdictions. Some historians have suggested that the Ottomans abolished the maẓālim and ḥisba, jurisdictions prominent in earlier Muslim polities, and assigned their functions to the sharīᶜa court.[1]

In the introduction, I discussed Hallaq's model of the Islamic legal system, exemplified by the Ottoman Empire but more broadly applicable throughout the pre-modern Muslim world. Hallaq's model rests on a binary opposition between sharīᶜa (law, the domain of jurists and qāḍīs), and siyāsa (political power, the domain of rulers). For Hallaq, the supremacy of sharīᶜa over siyāsa is what constituted the rule of law in pre-modern Muslim societies: this judicial supremacy was partially realized in pre-Ottoman polities, perfected by the Ottomans, and catastrophically undermined by the legal reforms of the nineteenth century.

Hallaq's model, in particular his description of the pre-Ottoman maẓālim tribunal as "extra-judicial," rests on a number of assumptions that are not borne out by recent scholarship. First, Hallaq equates the function of the qāḍī with the jurisdiction of the sharīᶜa court, implying that qāḍīs were not involved in the maẓālim tribunals.

But scholarship based on documentary and biographical sources has shown that qāḍīs were involved in the maẓālim tribunals of several medieval societies, including ᶜAbbāsid Iraq, Umayyad Spain, and Mamluk Egypt.[2] Second, Hallaq assumes that the primary role of pre-Ottoman maẓālim tribunals was to hear cases against government officials. This was no doubt an important function of maẓālim tribunals, but the notion that there was a formal division of jurisdiction between maẓālim tribunals and sharīᶜa courts is also not supported by recent research. Maẓālim tribunals heard a range of cases involving both officials and civilians.[3] Hallaq's definition of maẓālim—which reflects the portrayal of medieval maẓālim tribunals in much of the secondary literature—relies on the theory of maẓālim offered by the eleventh-century jurist and diplomat Māwardī in his famous treatise *al-Aḥkām al-sulṭāniyya*. This was a normative work intended to justify maẓālim and to reconcile the wielding of siyāsa power by the ruler with the demands of the sharīᶜa: it was not a description of how maẓālim tribunals actually functioned in the late ᶜAbbāsid caliphate.[4] A better definition of pre-Ottoman maẓālim tribunals, which allows for considerable variation over time and space, is that they were tribunals over which the ruler or a military official presided, rather than a qāḍī. They represented the jurisdiction of the sovereign and his ultimate responsibility for justice.

Once we dispense with ideal types and understand the role of legal institutions based on the empirical evidence of actual practice, we can see continuities between pre-Ottoman and Ottoman legal systems. Legal forums presided over by executive officials were a feature of the Ottoman Empire just as they were of most pre-modern Muslim societies. Contemporaries did not see these institutions as "extra-judicial" or as following a law substantially different from or inferior to the sharīᶜa. Rather, they were an integral part of the practice and development of the sharīᶜa, as rulers sought to integrate the sharīᶜa within their state-building projects.[5] It is within this framework, and with the intention of normalizing the role of executive authorities within Islamic law, that I investigate the role of the Dīwān al-ᶜĀlī and the Dīvān-i Hümāyūn in Ottoman Egypt. My assertion that these institutions represent continuity does not imply that nothing changed: the Ottomans did not simply replicate pre-Ottoman institutions.[6] I simply claim that a narrative framed around a radical break—the abolition of maẓālim or the supremacy of the qāḍī—is not a helpful way to understand the Ottoman contribution to Islamic legal history.

The questions I ask in this chapter are somewhat different to those taken up by previous scholarship. I am not asking what law each institution applied: in all cases sharīᶜa provided the procedural and doctrinal framework. I am primarily interested in how the institutional plurality of Cairo's legal system functioned. Were there clear jurisdictional boundaries between different institutions? How did different institutions interact with each other: were they arranged in a hierarchy, and did they respect each other's judgments? What were the roles of the different actors involved in these institutions: qāḍīs, governors, Grand Viziers, and court functionaries? In this chapter I discuss these questions by focusing on personnel and formal institutional relationships. I explore the same questions in Chapter 6 from the perspective of litigants, asking how they sought to maneuver within and manipulate the plurality of legal life in Cairo.

Rather than think in terms of the functions of different institutions, I think it is easier to understand Cairo's legal system by focusing on the functions of individuals who worked within those institutions. In Ottoman Cairo, the qāḍī had a specific and limited role connected with the assessment of evidence: the qāḍī's expertise was in procedure. Indeed, the concept of *qaḍā*ʾ (judging), as defined by the jurists, was focused on the assessment of evidence in order to ascertain facts. Although qāḍīs were most closely associated with the sharīᶜa courts, they also played this role at the Dīwān al-ᶜĀlī and on behalf of the Dīvān-i Hümāyūn. This role was crucial to the operation of the legal system, but it does not justify the qāḍī's status in Ottoman and Islamic legal historiography as the pivot of the legal system and guarantor of the rule of law. The qāḍī had little input into the legal doctrine that was applied in any of Cairo's dispute resolution forums, including the sharīᶜa court over which he presided. While the textual foundation of the law was created by jurists, the translation of this tradition into applied law was undertaken by muftis, the Şeyhulislām and the Sultan.[7] The doctrines they produced were equally applicable in a sharīᶜa court, the governor's Dīwān, or the Dīvān-i Hümāyūn. Moreover, the qāḍī had only a limited part to play in the enforcement of judgments and rulings. This was generally the responsibility of the local executive and military authorities who carried out this role on behalf of the sharīᶜa courts and other tribunals. The roles played by these actors within the legal system were all crucial: the legal system could not have functioned effectively without the contribution of any one of them.

The Dīvān-i Hümāyūn

The Dīvān-i Hümāyūn, or Imperial Council, was the central formal organ of Ottoman government: an assembly of high officials presided over by the Grand Vizier which issued orders in the name of the Sultan. It was held in the council chamber (Dīvān Odası) of Topkapı Palace or, when on campaign, in the Grand Vizier's tent.[8] Alongside the Grand Vizier, the members of the Dīvān were the chief judges (ḳażᶜasker) of Rumelia and Anatolia, the treasurers (*defterdār*) and chancellors (*nişāncı*).[9] While the Sultan was not directly involved in the Dīvān's deliberations, the council chamber was located next to his private quarters and, famously, had a *mashrabiya*-covered window through which he could observe proceedings without being seen himself, so that the members of the Dīvān would always have to assume that they were being supervised.

The Dīvān-i Hümāyūn dealt with many different aspects of imperial business, but one of its chief functions was to respond to petitions sent to the Sultan by subjects from across the empire. Many of these petitions survive at the Prime Ministry Archive in Istanbul; also extant are copies of the orders sent in response to petitions, which were carefully filed by the Dīvān's staff in bound registers.[10] Petitioning was an expansive concept: the petition was the paradigmatic form of communication between subjects or officials and the Sultan. Ottomans sent petitions on many different kinds of issues, including to request employment or pensions, to object to tax demands, or to demand a new governor.[11] Converts to Islam sent petitions to request the gift of clothing that the government routinely provided.[12] Many petitions concerned disputes, and when the Dīvān-i Hümāyūn responded to these it functioned as a tribunal. It is this function of the Dīvān that I examine here.

What kinds of disputes did petitioners bring to the Dīvān-i Hümāyūn? The limited previous scholarship on petitioning has focused on complaints against officials, arguing that the main role of the petitioning system was to allow subjects to bring official abuses to the central government's attention, and so to assist the central government in supervising the behavior of its provincial officials; in this way, it reflects the conventional understanding of the medieval maẓālim jurisdiction.[13] The evidence regarding Egypt confirms that complaints against officials formed part of the Dīvān-i Hümāyūn's remit. An example is the petition of the two sisters Fāṭima and Zeyneb, who complained that political notable Muṣṭafā Bey had confiscated the possessions of their father Ömer Efendī when he died in Cairo en route to Mecca for the pilgrimage.[14] Another example is ᶜAlī, the warden of the citadel at Medina, who claimed that Qāsim Bey, the governor of the sub-province of Girga in Upper Egypt, refused to repay a debt of 100 Spanish reals.[15] And a third is the unnamed supervisor of the Doğancılar endowment, who sought to reclaim a debt of 3,500 ghurūsh owed to the endowment by the qāḍī of Bilbays in Lower Egypt.[16] But the Dīvān-i Hümāyūn's jurisdiction was not restricted to complaints against officials, and in fact this does not appear to have been the primary role of the petitioning system. Plenty of petitions concerned private disputes between subjects.[17] These disputes revolved around a range of issues: property, endowments, inheritances, debts, and even petty neighborhood quarrels.[18] The Dīvān-i Hümāyūn's jurisdiction was unlimited—open to petitions from anyone on any issue—reflecting the unbounded sovereignty of the Sultan.[19]

The ability of subjects to bring their grievances directly to the monarch via a petition was a key component of legitimacy in many pre-modern political cultures.[20] The petition formed part of a patrimonial ideal: the monarch as patriarch was personally responsible for the execution of justice within his realm. During the fourteenth and fifteenth centuries, Ottoman Sultans received petitions in person while riding to the mosque, on campaign, or while hunting. By the seventeenth century, this ancient royal ideal had been bureaucratized. The practices surrounding petitioning retained aspects of political theatre: some petitioners undertook a dramatic ritual in which they ran through the palace grounds holding a burning mat, the smoke from which would alert the Sultan to the injustice they suffered.[21] But for the most part, petitioning was an impersonal and bureaucratic encounter. Petitioners could submit their petitions in person, and many did: some even traveled from as far afield as Egypt.[22] But most such petitioners engaged in no elaborate ceremony, and none met the Sultan in person. The important and influential may have been admitted to submit their petitions to the Dīvān in the ᶜArż Odası, the reception hall dedicated to that function.[23] The majority presented their petitions to the chief white eunuch, who collected them at the outer door to the palace grounds.[24] More commonly, given the great distance involved, Egyptians mailed their petitions, using either the official postal system or private couriers connected with merchant networks.[25] However it was effected, the physical journey of the petition to the palace in Istanbul added considerably to the time it took for the underlying dispute to be resolved. The sea voyage from Alexandria to the capital took twelve days; from Cairo there was the additional journey along the Nile to Rosetta and then along the coast to Alexandria.[26] Evidence from chronicles suggests that urgent news from Istanbul could arrive in Cairo in not much more than twelve days.[27] Cairo's court records, however, suggest that more mundane official correspondence could take two months or more.[28]

Petitions were formulaic documents that confirmed the submission of the petitioner to the power of the Sultan. While the performance of a ritual such as the burning mat was not necessary in order to have one's grievance heard, the language of petitions was performative. Written in formal Ottoman Turkish, petitions included more or less elaborate variations on a set of conventions. First, a prayer was given for the long life and reign of the Sultan: at its simplest this was *devletlü, merḥametlü, Sulṭānım ḥażretleri sağ olsun* (long live His Excellency, my Sultan, the illustrious and merciful), but it could often take up five or more lines.[29] Second, the petitioner described him or herself as a humble slave. Third, the petitioner requested intervention in his or her problem as an act of benevolence on the Sultan's part. Sandwiched between these formulae was an account of the petitioner's grievance or dispute. Intriguingly, when petitions concerned private disputes between subjects, rather than complaints against officials, petitioners often failed to name their antagonists, instead describing them using stock phrases such as "people who bear grudges and ill-will" (*baᶜżı garaż ve buğż ṣāḥibleri*).[30] Petitions were usually undated and some petitioners identified themselves using only their first names.[31] Furthermore, while the substance of the dispute behind a petition could be described in some detail, the rhetorical conventions of petition-writing did not allow for precise legal argument. The complainant always stated simply that his or her antagonist had violated the law or broken with tradition. This marks a striking contrast with most other genres of Ottoman legal documents, in which legal concepts and doctrines form the structure and vocabulary of the text. The distinctive language of petitions reflects the patrimonial ideology that the petitioning system propagated: the petitioner did not confidently assert his or her rights based on clear legal principles, but rather made a plaintive appeal for an abstract justice.

These conventions had consequences for the accessibility of the petitioning system, particularly among non-Turkish-speaking communities. Even literate petitioners would usually have had to hire a scribe competent in the correct register of Turkish and the appropriate formulae: either one of the professional petition-writers known as *ᶜarżuḥālci*s, of whom there were forty-five in Cairo when Evliyā Çelebi visited the city in the 1670s, or a qāḍī or nāᵓib, whose role included the production of official documents for a fee.[32]

However, the patrimonial idiom in which petitions were written obscures the bureaucratic procedures through which petitions were processed. The Dīvān-i Hümāyūn did not respond to petitions on a patrimonial basis, by selectively bestowing its favor in order to build and secure a client base. Rather, it evaluated a petitioner's claim and supported it if it deemed it justified. When it could not adequately assess the claim, which was a frequent occurrence with petitions sent from the provinces, it delegated the process of adjudication to the appropriate qāḍī.

How could a tribunal in Istanbul plausibly evaluate the claim of an Egyptian petitioner? Not only was the distant great, but petitions were one-sided documents. They presented only the claim of the petitioner, giving his or her antagonist no space to offer a response. It was possible for both sides to a dispute to send separate petitions. Chronicles suggest that this occasionally happened when the stakes in a dispute were particularly high. For example, Damurdāshī reported that during the governorship of Ḥasan Pasha al-Silāḥdār (1707–9), the six Cairo regiments other than the Janissaries sent a petition complaining about the Janissaries' monopolization of lucrative urban tax-farms. The Janissaries learned of this and sent a counter-petition; a resolution to the dispute was then brokered after reviewing both petitions.[33] However, judging from the archival evidence, this was rare. I have not found any examples in the archives where two antagonists sent petitions about the same dispute. Moreover, the Dīvān-i Hümāyūn responded to each petition individually, and never solicited input from the opposing side.

The Dīvān-i Hümāyūn could, however, evaluate a petitioner's claim when it rested on a title to property or office that had been granted by an imperial fermān. The palace scrupulously kept copies of all fermāns and other outgoing correspondence that it issued. When a petitioner claimed entitlement to hold a particular property or position based on a previously-issued fermān, the Dīvān's staff could check by looking up the fermān cited by the petitioner in the palace archives. A good example of this is a petition sent by Muṣṭafā ibn al-Shaykh Aḥmad Muḥammad during the first half of 1676. Muṣṭafā's petition, which survives in the Prime Ministry Archive in Istanbul, contains a particularly rich set of annotations made by Dīvān bureaucrats which illustrate the process the petition went through when it reached the palace.[34]

In his petition, Muṣṭafā claimed to have been granted the supervisorship (neẓāret) of the endowment of Muḥammad Abū ʾl-Saʿūd al-Jāriḥi in Cairo by the Sultan. He explained that this position, which the Sultan had made permanent and hereditary, was granted to him in recognition of his having repaired the endowment's buildings and mosque, and restored its finances, after a period of mismanagement had impoverished it. Muṣṭafā claimed to possess ample documentation of his right to this position: four appointment deeds (*berāts*) and an imperial fermān, as well as an order issued by the governor of Egypt; his position was also recorded in the official register in Cairo. However, people who bore him "grudges and ill-will" were attempting to seize his position from him. Muṣṭafā requested a further decree guaranteeing his position and that of his descendants.

Muṣṭafā identified the previous fermān granting him the position by its date: mid Rabīᶜ al-Awwal 1077 (11–20 September 1666). The fact that his claim rested on a title granted by the Sultan meant that it could be verified by checking the palace archives. The Dīvān official who initially reviewed his petition looked up the copy of this fermān that was filed there: he copied out this fermān on to the side of Muṣṭafā's petition for the benefit of the senior official who adjudicated the case. This earlier fermān confirmed Muṣṭafā's claim. The Dīvān-i Hümāyūn therefore decided in Muṣṭafā's favor, issuing a further order that reconfirmed his hereditary right to the supervisorship. This decision was annotated at the top of the petition, which was then passed to the scribe who would write the imperial order.

Another example is the case of Aḥmad Nūr al-Dīn, who sent a petition in late 1674 or early 1675. Aḥmad claimed that he had endowed a mosque and two colleges in Cairo, and had stipulated in the endowment deed that the supervisor of the endowment should be from his male line. When his father, ᶜAlīm, the previous supervisor, died, someone unrelated to Aḥmad had been appointed to replace him, contrary to the stipulation. Aḥmad had previously been issued with an imperial order supporting his family's right to the supervisorship: the Dīvān staff were able to look up a copy of the order in the palace archives to verify his claim. Having done so, the Dīvān-i Hümāyūn issued a new imperial order directing the qāḍī and the governor in Cairo to prevent any interference from outsiders in Aḥmad's endowment.[35]

In addition to cases where the petitioner's claim rested on a title granted by the Sultan, the Dīvān-i Hümāyūn could also investigate a petitioner's claim if that claim was based on another kind of document, and the petitioner produced the relevant document as evidence. For example, a woman called ᶜĀyisha sent a petition during late 1697, claiming that she held the usufruct (*taṣarruf*) of a merchant hostel, several shops and some other properties around the Khān al-Khalīlī market in Cairo, and that she possessed a ḥujja (a certificate issued by a qāḍī) confirming this. She demanded that her agent in Cairo be given possession of these properties. While the document ᶜĀyisha possessed was not issued by the Dīvān-i Hümāyūn, and so would not have been available in its archives, the imperial order reveals that ᶜĀyisha delivered her petition in person, and so she was presumably able to show her ḥujja to the appropriate official. The document allowed the Dīvān-i Hümāyūn to evaluate her claim, and accordingly it ordered the qāḍī and governor in Cairo to grant possession of the properties to ᶜĀyisha's agent.[36]

In order to establish a claim with documents other than those issued by the Dīvān-i Hümāyūn itself, a petitioner had to be physically present at the Dīvān. Petitioning was therefore particularly convenient for residents of Istanbul, and it offered them a means to carry out their business in distant parts of the empire, including Cairo. One such petitioner, who lived exceptionally close to the Dīvān-i Hümāyūn, was the imperial harem eunuch Beşīr Ağa, the chief eunuch of the Ottoman princess Gevher Cān Sulṭān. In 1675, Beşīr petitioned the Dīvān after he purchased a long-term lease on a house called Ḥayātiyye near Bāb Zuwayla in Cairo. Beşīr's investment in distant Cairo was no doubt made in anticipation of his retirement there: the city was the usual destination of ex-harem eunuchs, whom the Sultans preferred to keep away from the political intrigues of the capital.[37] The house belonged to the endowment of the late İdrīs Ağa; Beşīr had given the endowment's supervisor an upfront payment of 3,000 ghurūsh to secure the lease.[38] Beşīr possessed a ḥujja and a title-deed (*temessük*) confirming his right to the house, However, some unnamed "people with vested interests" (*eṣḥāb-i ağrāż kimesneler*) were preventing Beşīr's agent in Cairo from taking possession of the house. As the Dīvān-i Hümāyūn was able to verify Beşīr's claim by checking his documents, it was able to decide in his favor and order the qāḍī and governor in Cairo to ensure that no one interfered with his possession of the house.[39]

In many cases, however, it was not possible for the Dīvān-i Hümāyūn to adjudicate a dispute itself, because it did not have sufficient information. When a case did not rest on a title granted by an official document, or when the relevant document was not accessible to the Dīvān's staff, the Dīvān-i Hümāyūn would delegate adjudication to a qāḍī in Cairo, by issuing an imperial order to the qāḍī to "hear the matter according to the sharīᶜa" (the typical phrase was *şer'le görülmek*). The circumstances in which the Dīvān-i Hümāyūn could get to the bottom of a dispute in a distant province were limited, and so delegation was the most common response to petitions from Egypt.

One example is the case of Ḥācī Muṣṭafā, a veteran of the Bostāncı regiment, who claimed in a petition sent during mid-1675 that two Cairo money-changers called Ḥaydar and Dāwīd were refusing to repay a debt of 247,000 Egyptian *para*, the outstanding amount of a loan of 322,000 para. Ḥācī Muṣṭafā possessed a deed (temessük) confirming the loan, but proof that a debt had once existed could not prove that it still existed. Ḥaydar and Dāwīd might claim that they had repaid the sum, or at least had repaid more than the 75,000 para that Ḥācī Muṣṭafā conceded. Unable to evaluate Ḥācī Muṣṭafā's claim itself, the Dīvān-i Hümāyūn sent an imperial order to the governor and chief qāḍī in Cairo, instructing them to hear the matter according to the sharīᶜa.[40]

Another example is a contested inheritance case from 1697. A man called Muṣṭafā sent a petition reporting that the Rosetta resident Sīdī ᶜUthmān had died childless. Sīdī ᶜUthmān was the manumitted slave of Muṣṭafā's late uncle, and in the absence of prior heirs his estate should have passed to the uncle, who inherited as ᶜUthmān's *mawlā* (patron), and thence to Muṣṭafā. Moreover, ᶜUthmān's wife had also died without children, and her estate should have passed to ᶜUthmān, thence to the uncle, and thence to Muṣṭafā. However, another man called Muṣṭafā Çorbacı had seized both estates on behalf of his wife, on the grounds that she was also a manumitted slave of the same owner. Muṣṭafā claimed that he had won a court case against Muṣṭafā Çorbacı in Rosetta, and possessed a ḥujja confirming this, but that Muṣṭafā Çorbacı had refused to relinquish the estates. Despite the fact that the petitioner in this case claimed to possess a legal document establishing his right to the estates, the Dīvān-i Hümāyūn did not have access to this document because Muṣṭafā was not present in Istanbul and had sent his petition by mail from Egypt. As the Dīvān-i

Hümāyūn did not have sufficient evidence to evaluate Muṣṭafā's claim, it delegated the case, ordering the governor and chief qāḍī in Cairo to hear the matter according to the sharīᶜa.[41]

Another example is the complaint of al-Ḥājj Muṣṭafā, a resident of the Lower Egyptian town of Ziftā, sent in 1742. Muṣṭafā claimed that his Christian neighbor Banūb had built a house, located in the Muslim quarter, that was taller than the houses of his Muslim neighbors, violating established custom.[42] This was not a dispute that the Dīvān-i Hümāyūn could adjudicate itself, as proof of the relative heights of Banūb's and his Muslim neighbors' houses required eye-witnesses, and possibly also the expert testimony of an architect or builder.[43] Unless all relevant witnesses traveled to Istanbul, which was not plausible for such a trivial problem, the Dīvān-i Hümāyūn could not evaluate Muṣṭafā's claim. It therefore delegated the case, ordering that the matter be heard according to the sharīᶜa in Egypt.[44]

An order delegating the matter back to the provincial qāḍī, whom the petitioner could have approached directly, might seem a disappointing outcome given the effort and expense involved in petitioning. Egyptians, and other Ottoman subjects, would have known that this was what would happen if their case did not rest on a document accessible to the Dīvān-i Hümāyūn. Why, then, did petitioners go to the trouble of petitioning? The principal motivation for petitioners seems to have been to obtain an additional tier of oversight of the resulting court case: the imperial orders sent to Egypt were always doubly addressed to the governor and the qāḍī. The governor was charged with ensuring that the case was handled fairly and, more importantly, that the qāḍī's decision was enforced.[45]

The Dīwān al-ᶜĀlī

The Ottoman governor's council, al-Dīwān al-ᶜĀlī, was the central institution in the administration of Ottoman Egypt. Established by the Ottoman ḳānūnnāme for Egypt of 1524,[46] the Dīwān al-ᶜĀlī remained the institution through which the Ottoman governor's power was formally projected through to the early nineteenth century. Modern historians have followed contemporary chronicles in describing the Dīwān al-ᶜĀlī as a consultative body where the Ottoman governor met with various notables of Egypt—the beys, the shaykhs of the Sufi orders, senior ulema, and the commanders of the seven regiments—to discuss affairs of state.[47] This consultative or advisory role was an important part of the institution's function. However, the Dīwān al-ᶜĀlī also functioned as a tribunal, and this aspect of its activity has not received much attention from scholars.[48]

We can study its operation as a tribunal through the documentation it created: registers which detail its judicial activities. The extant documentation from the Dīwān al-ᶜĀlī is, unfortunately, less voluminous than that produced by Cairo's sharīᶜa courts. Only two registers from the eighteenth century survive at the Egyptian National Archive; the earliest dates from 1741–3, covering parts of the governorships of Yaḥyā Pasha and Ḥekīmoğlu ᶜAlī Pasha.[49] A scattering of individual ḥujjas issued by the Dīwān al-ᶜĀlī survive at the Egyptian National Archive and the Turkish Prime Ministry Archive.[50] These show that the Dīwān al-ᶜĀlī was operating as a tribunal much earlier than the 1740s: the earliest ḥujja I have seen is dated 1621, and there is no reason to think that the Dīwān al-ᶜĀlī was not performing a judicial function much earlier still. While this quantity of surviving documentation is meager by the standards of the sharīᶜa court records, it is nevertheless significant when compared to governors' councils in other Ottoman provinces. While scholars have demonstrated that governors' councils in cities including Sofia, Salonica, and Aleppo functioned as tribunals, they have not found any documentation created by these councils, and instead have relied upon narrative sources and upon references to these institutions found within sharīᶜa court records.[51] I know of only one source comparable to the registers of Egypt's Dīwān al-ᶜĀlī from elsewhere in the Ottoman provinces before the nineteenth century: a single register containing responses to petitions sent to the Kaymakam of Rumelia between 1781 and 1783, published by Michael Ursinus.[52]

The Dīwān al-ᶜĀlī was held in the citadel, on the Muqaṭṭam hill at the south-eastern outskirt of the city. When functioning as a tribunal, the Dīwān was formally presided over by the governor, who was accompanied by a qāḍī. Unsurprisingly, the governor was not always in attendance. There were other demands on his time, and there were also frequent periods when no governor was present in Cairo, as the sitting governor stepped down immediately when a new governor was appointed, even though the new governor would not arrive in Egypt for another month or more.[53] When the governor was not attending, he was sometimes represented by his lieutenant (*katkhudā*). When neither the governor nor his lieutenant were present, the record usually states that the details of the case were communicated to the governor: the case was heard *bi maᶜrifat al-wazīr*. During the periods between the deposition of the sitting governor and the arrival of his replacement, the incoming governor appointed one of Egypt's beys to serve as acting governor (qāʾimmaqām): the acting governor or his lieutenant would then preside at the Dīwān al-ᶜĀlī. As for the qāḍī who accompanied the governor at the Dīwān, this could be the holder of one of several different offices. Sometimes it was the Dīwān's own qāḍī, and sometimes it was the chief qāḍī of Cairo; both of these offices were necessarily held by Ḥanafīs. On other occasions, it was a nāʾib of the Shāfiᶜī, Mālikī or Ḥanbalī school. As with the sharīᶜa courts, the Dīwān al-ᶜĀlī's judicial function involved both the adjudication of lawsuits and the notarization of contracts.

Some of the cases brought to the Dīwān al-ᶜĀlī involved alleged misconduct by government officials, in line with Māwardī's theory of maẓālim. For example, a merchant from Upper Egypt called ᶜAbdullāh ibn Makkī sued Muḥammad Āghā, the commander of the Muwayliḥ fortress, at the Dīwān in September 1672. ᶜAbdullāh claimed that a boat carrying a load of cloth, coffee, and cash belonging to him had been attacked and plundered by bedouin in the vicinity of the Muwayliḥ fortress. Far from protecting river traffic as he was supposed to, Muḥammad Āghā was accused of protecting the bedouin and supplying them with the necessary equipment and provisions, in return for a cut of their booty.[54] In another example, a large group of officers from Cairo's regiments, accompanied by several beys, came to the Dīwān to complain about the behavior of the recently deposed governor Defterdār Aḥmed Pasha. The officers and beys alleged that the former governor, and several minor officials, had conducted meetings in secret in violation of the "ancient customs" of Egyptian political conduct (*al-ᶜāda wa ᵓl-qānūn al-qadīm*).[55]

However, the majority of cases brought to the Dīwān al-ᶜĀlī involved private disputes between subjects. These cases covered a variety of issues. To start with the less common, there are two cases of homicide in the Dīwān's earliest register. In one case, two Christians were accused of accidentally shooting dead a passer-by when one of them fired a gun during a drunken argument in the street. They denied the charge, but the victim's siblings produced witnesses to the incident. The Christians were ordered to pay blood-money (diya); a resolution which was adjusted after mediation (ṣulḥ) with the victim's heirs.[56] In the other case, Yūsuf ibn ᶜAbdullāh of the ᶜAzabān regiment was accused by ᶜAlī ibn Ḥasan of killing his father with three blows to the head. The charge was confirmed by witnesses, and so Yūsuf was sentenced to retaliation (*qiṣāṣ*), that is, death. The record does not detail how the sentence was carried out.[57] Two unusual cases in the same sijill involved slaves who managed to secure their freedom by proving that they had been enslaved illegally. In August 1741, Aḥmad ibn Jarkas, a slave belonging to the former Cairo police chief (*zaᶜīm*) ᶜAbdullāh Āghā, produced witnesses who testified that he was of free origin and had converted to Islam prior to his enslavement, making it illegal.[58] The Dīwān al-ᶜĀlī ordered that Aḥmad be freed, and told ᶜAbdullāh Āghā to pursue the slave-dealer from whom he had bought him for compensation.[59] In the other case, a woman called Fāṭima, who was in the possession of the notable Azhar professor Aḥmad ibn ᶜAbd al-Munᶜim al-Damanhūrī, claimed to be a free-born Muslim from Anatolia.[60] Again, she was able to provide witnesses to testify to this, and so Damanhūrī was ordered to free her and to seek redress from the slave-dealer who had sold her.[61]

Most common, however, were cases involving property or the control of endowments. In a typical case, a woman called Sāfiya Khātūn bint Sulaymān claimed, via her agent (*wakīl*),[62] that a man called Shaykh Yūsuf ibn Ḥijāzī had taken several things from her late brother's estate that should have formed part of her inheritance, including a house and a slave, whom Yūsuf had married to his son. By providing documents and witnesses, Yūsuf proved that before his death Sāfiya's brother had endowed the house and manumitted the slave; the Dīwān al-ᶜĀlī therefore rejected Sāfiya's lawsuit.[63] In another example, a woman called Janas bint ᶜAbdullāh, the manumitted slave of the late Amīr Ḥassan Āghā, sued the Qāḍī Muḥammad Efendī for the return of shares in a series of properties in the area around Rumayla Square and in the Muskī market. Muḥammad Efendī denied that the shares belonged to the plaintiff, claiming that before his death her husband, who was also a slave of Ḥassan Āghā, had sold them to the late ᶜAlī Çorbacı, who in turn had donated them to an endowment of which Muḥammad was the beneficiary. Muḥammad Efendī produced both the document detailing the sale of the shares to ᶜAlī Çorbacı, and the deed with which ᶜAlī endowed them. Janas, however, refused to accept the documents as evidence. Muḥammad Efendī then produced three witnesses: one man and two women, all of whom were manumitted slaves of Janas's former owner. They confirmed Muḥammad's story, and so the Dīwān al-ᶜĀlī ruled against Janas.[64]

As the above examples suggest, the procedure followed by the Dīwān al-ᶜĀlī was the same as that followed by the sharīᶜa courts. In contrast to the Dīvān-i Hümāyūn, at the Dīwān al-ᶜĀlī there was always a public hearing attended by both the plaintiff and the defendant or their agents. When contracts were notarized, this was done publicly with both parties to the contract either present or represented by agents. In a dispute, in the absence of the defendant's acknowledgment of the plaintiff's claim, the plaintiff was obliged to produce evidence. And as with the sharīᶜa court, but unlike the Dīvān-i Hümāyūn, oral testimony took precedence over paper. Documents were frequently introduced by litigants at the Dīwān al-ᶜĀlī, but in line with the procedures of qaḍāᵓ, only oral testimony was considered conclusive proof. If the plaintiff could not produce acceptable evidence, the defendant could absolve him or herself of the charge by taking an oath.[65] Although the Dīwān al-ᶜĀlī was the Ottoman governor's tribunal, it was the qāḍī who accompanied him who oversaw the implementation of judicial procedure, demanding and assessing the evidence, asking for an oath when necessary, and then adjudicating in favor of one party or the other.[66]

Jurisdictional boundaries

It is tempting for a legal historian, when confronted with a complex set of judicial institutions, to try to reconstruct the precise jurisdiction of each. In modern legal systems, institutions have clearly defined jurisdictional boundaries. Jurisdictions can be defined around subject matter—commercial courts, criminal courts, and so forth—or in terms of hierarchy—courts of first instance, appellate courts, supreme courts. Both systems of arrangement have seemed alluring for historians seeking to make sense of the legal systems of the Ottoman Empire and other pre-modern Muslim societies. As discussed above, one common assumption about medieval legal systems has been that while sharīᶜa courts handled cases between private subjects, maẓālim tribunals dealt with complaints against abusive officials. This dichotomy had an echo in Ottoman historiography in early studies of the petitioning system, which focused on how petitioning allowed Ottoman subjects to bring official misdeeds to the central government's attention.[67] Ottoman historians have also portrayed the system as hierarchical, describing the Dīvān-i Hümāyūn as a forum in which litigants could appeal a verdict from a sharīᶜa court.[68]

Neither of these frameworks suits the legal system of Ottoman Cairo. The caseloads of the Dīvān-i Hümāyūn and the Dīwān al-ᶜĀlī overlapped considerably with that of Cairo's sharīᶜa courts. Both dealt with private disputes between subjects as well as complaints against officials. Cases involving property and endowments formed the majority of the workload of all these institutions. Nor is there any evidence of an appellate hierarchy among these institutions. Of course, judicial appointments within the Ottoman Empire were ranked in a hierarchy that was expressed in title, status, and salary. Within this hierarchy the chief qāḍīship of Cairo was one of the highest ranks, and the two qāḍīships associated with the Dīvān-i Hümāyūn, the *ḳaẓᶜaskerliks* of Rumelia and Anatolia, ranked higher still: all three were far more prestigious than any other judicial position in Cairo.[69] It was also possible, as detailed above, for the Dīvān-i Hümāyūn, in response to a petition, to direct the qāḍī in Cairo to issue a particular judgment. But this did not amount to an institutional appellate hierarchy, which would have meant both a certain sequence—a case must be heard by a court of first instance before it can proceed to an appeal court—and the ability of the superior institution to overrule the judgments of the lower. Neither of these conditions applied to the relationships between the Dīvān-i Hümāyūn, the Dīwān al-ᶜĀlī and the sharīᶜa courts of Cairo. A litigant could approach any of these institutions at any point in a dispute. And the overruling of the judgments of inferior courts was not a routine part of the function of either the Dīvān-i Hümāyūn or the Dīwān al-ᶜĀlī. While there are examples of cases brought to the Dīvān-i Hümāyūn after having been heard previously at a sharīᶜa court in Egypt, these involved the winner of the court case attempting to have the judgment enforced, not the loser trying to have it overturned.[70]

Some differences are observable in the caseloads of these different institutions. But these were the result of the choices, strategies, and needs of litigants, rather than of formal definitions of jurisdiction. For example, when compared with the neighborhood sharīᶜa courts, the caseload of the Dīwān al-ᶜĀlī included a relatively high proportion of cases of high value, and its clientele was disproportionately drawn from the city's social and political elites.[71] Al-Bāb al-ᶜĀlī, the main sharīᶜa court, also attracted a greater proportion of elite clients than the neighborhood courts, but the difference was not as pronounced. This difference did not, however, represent a formal division of labor between the two institutions. Rather, it reflected the fact that the Dīwān al-ᶜĀlī was a hub of elite political activity in Cairo. The Dīwān al-ᶜĀlī was located in the citadel outside of the city, in contrast to the sharīᶜa courts which were housed within mosques and other public buildings in Cairo's commercial center and residential neighborhoods. The Dīwān was therefore less convenient for most litigants, who would have had to walk or ride some distance, and then climb the Muqaṭṭam hill, to reach it. Given the Dīwān al-ᶜĀlī's additional function as a consultative council, however, members of the political and scholarly elites were in frequent attendance. Those who were there on other business, and were familiar with the institution's personnel and procedures, may have chosen to use the Dīwān for their private lawsuits and contracts. Meanwhile, other people might have chosen to bring their cases to the Dīwān if they wanted the dispute aired before the audience of notables that was typically gathered there; they would more likely have seen the extra effort of going to the Dīwān as worthwhile when the stakes were high.

The lack of clear jurisdictional boundaries reflected the intertwining of a patrimonial ideology with the Islamic legal tradition in the Ottoman conception of justice. The Ottoman government appointed qāḍīs to sharīᶜa courts across the empire in order to hear disputes among the populace, as any Muslim ruler was expected to do. But at the same time, the Sultan bore the ultimate responsibility for upholding justice within his realm. The Perso-Islamic notion of the "circle of justice," according to which the prosperity and vitality of the state depended on benign conditions for the subjects who filled the treasury with the taxes that paid the soldiers, placed justice at the very core of the monarch's purpose.[72] Therefore, it was inconceivable to place limits on the jurisdiction of the Sultan: he had to be available to all litigants for all cases, or risk undermining a central plank of Ottoman legitimacy. The Dīvān-i Hümāyūn and the Dīwān al-ᶜĀlī were the bodies that acted on behalf of the Sultan in Istanbul and Cairo respectively: they represented his universal jurisdiction and so had to receive subjects with cases on all matters, at any stage of a dispute.

The role of the qāḍī

Rather than looking at the particular characteristics of these three institutions, a better way to understand their relationships with one another is to examine the roles of the different individuals who worked within them and for them. As described above, the institutions themselves had only vaguely defined characteristics. But the roles of the individuals who made up Cairo's legal system were more clearly delineated. The qāḍī played a particular and distinct role within all three institutions.

By focusing on the role of the qāḍī, we achieve a clearer view of the relationship between judicial and political power, avoiding the misperceptions that have characterized previous literature. The most important misperception is that which associates the qāḍī exclusively with the sharīᶜa court and assumes that the tribunals associated with political authorities—maẓālim tribunals, siyāsa courts, or dīvāns, depending on polity and period—represented an alternative form of justice. This assumption is seen in Wael Hallaq's description of the medieval maẓālim tribunals as "extra-judicial." This term suggests that these tribunals operated without a proper judge, and implies that their standards of justice were inferior, or at least different. In fact, as detailed above, qāḍīs were involved in the operation of maẓālim tribunals in most of the medieval Islamic legal systems that have been studied; although we do not have much archival evidence that could show us exactly what qāḍīs did within these institutions.[73] Ottoman Egypt, however, is amply supplied with archives, so we can investigate exactly what qāḍīs did within and on behalf of the sharīᶜa courts, the Dīwān al-ᶜĀlī, and the Dīvān-i Hümāyūn.

Another misperception, at least where the Ottoman period is concerned, is that the qāḍīs represented legal knowledge, or more specifically, that expertise in fiqh was crucial to their role. This idea is linked with the previous one: qāḍīs knew fiqh and so applied that in the sharīᶜa courts, while other tribunals, lacking qāḍīs, applied something else. In fact, interpreting fiqh was not a significant part of the qāḍī's function. Qāḍīs had a legal education, of course. Qāḍīs in the higher-ranking posts were products of elite schools, and some produced important legal scholarship.[74] Some individuals moved from qāḍīships to other posts, such as chief mufti (Şeyhülislam), in which they were called upon to produce applied law from fiqh.[75] But whatever a particular individual may have achieved in other spheres of his life, *in his capacity as a qāḍī* the interpretation of fiqh was not particularly significant.

The key function and expertise of the qāḍī lay in procedure. The qāḍī's job was to establish truth by mechanically applying the rules of evidence drawn from fiqh. The qāḍī had a further role that was subsidiary to this: he could authenticate statements of truth by issuing ḥujjas. Litigants could subsequently use these ḥujjas as proof. Faced with two litigants with conflicting stories, the qāḍī could use his procedures to evaluate their claims and decide who was right. Crucially, he then had the authority to transform the winning litigant's claim into an incontrovertible legal fact.

Once this was done, the qāḍī's judgment (*ḥukm*) would award rights or impose penalties based on this legal fact, and these rights and penalties were drawn, for the most part, from fiqh. In the vast majority of cases a broad but basic understanding of fiqh was sufficient to do this correctly. The great bulk of the courts' caseload was mundane, and the resolution of most cases was legally straightforward: misappropriated goods should be returned, debts should be repaid.[76] The complication in solving these cases was to do with the facts, not the law: to whom did the goods belong? Had the debt been repaid? For many cases where the legal principle was not immediately obvious, because there were multiple credible opinions in the relevant fiqh or divergent authoritative customs, qāḍīs were instructed to follow a particular doctrine by the higher judicial and executive authorities; this is discussed in the next chapter. In the minority of cases where a controversial or unclear legal doctrine was crucial to the correct solution of a case and there was no publically-available guidance, the qāḍī would refer the legal question to a mufti.[77] It was not the qāḍī's job to interpret fiqh or to choose from among contrary opinions within his madhhab.[78] The interpretation of fiqh was the mufti's domain; the responsibility of the qāḍī was only to apply procedure to the contested facts of the dispute.[79]

In Ottoman Cairo, qāḍīs performed this limited but vital role of establishing truth through the implementation of legal procedure wherever it was required within the city's complex network of legal forums. They performed this role within the sharīᶜa courts as the presiding official. They performed this role within the Dīwān al-ᶜĀlī: although this institution was identified with the governor, it was the qāḍī who evaluated the evidence presented by litigants. And qāḍīs performed this role on behalf of the Dīvān-i Hümāyūn, when it referred cases to the qāḍī in Cairo for adjudication. The only exceptions to this, in which the Dīvān-i Hümāyūn would decide a case itself rather than delegating adjudication to a local qāḍī, were cases which rested on a title granted by the imperial government, which could be verified by consulting the palace archives, and cases when the petitioner could prove to the Dīvān with documents that the dispute had already been adjudicated by a qāḍī. In the former situation, the presentation of evidence to a qāḍī was unnecessary: the relevant witness was the imperial government, and the Dīvān-i Hümāyūn trusted its own archives as accurate guides to what the government had previously done. In the latter situation, the Dīvān-i Hümāyūn was not technically adjudicating: rather, it was ordering the enforcement of a right that had already been established.

Once we recognize the consistent role of qāḍīs within all the institutions that made up the legal system, the distinctions between the institutions suggested by the sharīᶜa/siyāsa binary that has been central to Islamic legal historiography start to dissolve. All institutions drew on the same legal tradition. The doctrines they applied were drawn largely from the vast body of fiqh scholarship. The process of interpretation that produced positive rules that could be applied to particular cases was undertaken by muftis, who would resolve problems posed to them by courts or litigants on a case-by-case basis, and by the imperial government, which directed legal institutions across the empire to follow particular opinions that it favored. Furthermore, all these institutions had similar expectations regarding procedure and evidence. The process of qaḍāᵓ, through which evidence was received and weighed according to clearly defined rules, was common to all institutions as the standard means of establishing the truth from conflicting accounts. In all institutions, a fact established through qaḍāᵓ was considered to be true, and all relied on qāḍīs to conduct qaḍāᵓ.

Meanwhile, it is important to consider what the qāḍī did *not* do. I have already mentioned the limited role of the qāḍī with regard to the substantive law that was applied in Cairo's legal institutions: the qāḍī simply needed a broad understanding of the basic features of substantive law, and a willingness to defer to a mufti or to the imperial government on complex or contentious issues. The qāḍī also had a limited role in the enforcement of judgments. In this sphere, the executive authorities, including the provincial governor and the officials under his command, took the lead. Again, this was true across all legal institutions: not only in the Dīvān-i Hümāyūn and the Dīwān al-ᶜĀlī, but also in the sharīᶜa court that was the qāḍī's domain. The sharīᶜa court records demonstrate that there were only two types of judgment that were routinely enforced by the qāḍī himself. The first was orders to repay a debt. When the debtor refused, the qāḍī would order his or her imprisonment at the request of the creditor.[80] This would take place in a jail operated by one of the military regiments; the task of physically restraining the prisoner fell to a member of the sharīᶜa court's staff called the *muḥḍir*, who was also responsible for compelling the attendance of defendants at court.[81] The second was the corporal punishment of minor offenses such as insults, public indecency, and physical assaults that did not cause serious injury. Such punishment was governed by the concept known as taᶜzīr or discretionary punishment. Taᶜzīr typically meant corporal punishment, and it was administered immediately.[82] Here, the qāḍī may have had some discretion. Fiqh texts gave expansive definitions of what taᶜzīr could encompass, with the understanding that punishment would vary with status: the lower the social standing of the offender, the harsher the punishment required to deter.[83] Unfortunately, the sharīᶜa court records do not detail how Cairene qāḍīs responded to this wide latitude, noting simply that offenders were punished with taᶜzīr "*al-lāyiq bi ḥālihi/ha*": taᶜzīr appropriate to his or her station.

Apart from these two instances, however, enforcement was not part of the qāḍī's remit. The qāḍī did not enforce his judgments in disputes over property and control of endowments. Nor did he compel compliance with negotiated settlements (ṣulḥ) that were formalized before him. In such cases, litigants depended primarily on the voluntary compliance of the opposing party: usually this was forthcoming, but sometimes it was not, as the examples of winning parties taking the same case to another authority demonstrate. Also, the qāḍī did not generally administer the punishments for serious crimes or for persistent troublemakers. When such cases were heard within the sharīᶜa court, the qāḍī's role was limited to establishing the facts. Once he had done this, the case would be passed on to another authority to implement the punishment. The language used by the sharīᶜa court scribes did not identify who this authority was: the phrase was *man lahu walī al-amr* (the person with the authority to take action). Most likely, a senior officer in one of the regiments would carry out arrests and punishments, under the command of the governor. Similarly in the Dīwān al-ᶜĀlī, the qāḍī established the facts, with the military authorities responsible for implementing the judgment. And the imperial orders issued by the Dīvān-i Hümāyūn show that it too expected this division of responsibility: they were always jointly addressed to the governor and the qāḍī, as the input of both was necessary to resolve a dispute successfully.

The qāḍī's role in this legal system was vital: the establishment of truth via the correct implementation of legal procedure was crucial in preventing false claims and fraud, and in providing Ottoman subjects with a commonly accepted and understood framework within which they could plan and manage their affairs. But to elevate the qāḍī to guardian of the rule of law overstates his importance, while to draw a stark contrast between judicial and "extra-judicial" authority, or between sharīᶜa and siyāsa, mischaracterizes the relationship between the judicial and executive authorities. Juristic, judicial, and executive power were intertwined in ways that do not match modern ideals of the separation of powers or the rule of law. If we divide the administration of law into the three areas of doctrine, procedure, and enforcement, we find that authority over doctrine was shared between the jurists and the executive; that procedure was the responsibility of the judiciary; and that enforcement was shared between the judiciary and the executive. All three of these areas were crucial if the legal system was to function effectively.

My attempt here to qualify the importance of the qāḍī is not intended to undermine the notion of an Islamic rule of law in the Ottoman Empire. The intimate involvement of the executive authorities in the quotidian administration of the law did not make the legal system arbitrary or despotic: on the contrary, these authorities shared their understanding of evidence and proof with the qāḍīs, and constructed positive law in dialogue with the jurists. My intention is rather to understand this Ottoman-Islamic rule of law on its own terms, without the binaries imposed by the Orientalist tradition of Islamic legal studies on the one hand, and modern conceptions of what constitutes the judicial and the political on the other. It is also an attempt to integrate into the history of Islamic law actors such as Sultans, provincial governors, and military officers, who have been sidelined by the textual and idealist approaches.

CHAPTER

4

GOVERNMENT AUTHORITY, THE INTERPRETATION OF FIQH, AND THE PRODUCTION OF APPLIED LAW

The previous chapter demonstrated that the Ottoman Sultan and the governor of Egypt, whom I call the executive authorities, were intimately involved in the day-to-day administration of justice in Cairo, via the institutions of the Dīvān-i Hümāyūn in Istanbul and the Dīwān al-ᶜĀlī in Cairo. Cairenes chose to involve the executive authorities in their disputes by petitioning the Sultan or by issuing their lawsuit at the governor's Dīwān. I also argued that we might best understand how the different components of Egypt's legal system fit together if we thought not in terms of the different institutions, but in terms of the different personnel and the functions they carried out. The sharīᶜa court was not the only sphere of the qāḍī's activities. There were qāḍīs present at the governor's Dīwān al-ᶜĀlī, and the Dīvān-i Hümāyūn referred cases to the chief qāḍī of Egypt when the facts of the case could not be clearly established with documentation in Istanbul.

I divided the administration of justice into three essential functions: (1) doctrine, that is, the production of the substantive law that was applied; (2) procedure, which determined whether a claim was, legally, true; (3) enforcement of any penalties or actions that a judgment imposed. I am interested in how these different functions were shared between three spheres of power: the juristic, the judicial, and the executive. I argued that procedure lay firmly within the judicial sphere: the correct implementation of procedure was the qāḍī's key responsibility, which he performed within, or on behalf of, all of the formal institutions of justice. I argued that enforcement was shared between the judicial and executive spheres. While the qāḍī imposed penalties and commanded actions in his judgments, his ability to enforce these judgments was limited. The debtor's prison lay under his control, and the minor corporal punishments imposed as taᶜzīr were performed immediately at the court. But beyond this, the qāḍī had no power to enforce a judgment. A successful litigant was issued with a ḥujja confirming their right, but it was up to him or her to enforce it. When coercion was required, litigants relied on the executive authorities to provide it. This explains the desire of many litigants to involve the executive authorities in their disputes, even though they could not influence or alter the qāḍī's judgment.

I also suggested that the production of doctrine was shared between the juristic and the executive spheres. This chapter is an attempt to substantiate that claim. The bulk of the doctrine applied in Ottoman courts was produced by the jurists, a global scholarly community that transcended the Ottoman Empire. The Ottoman executive authorities intervened in the way that judges interpreted that body of doctrine. In other words, while Islamic law was to some extent a jurists' law, its transformation into applied law in the Ottoman Empire was shaped and manipulated by the state. These interventions could take various forms, but in late seventeenth and early eighteenth-century Cairo the primary site for intervention was the system of madhhab pluralism which the Ottomans had inherited from the defeated Mamluk Sultanate. Instructions on when and how doctrines particular to different madhhabs could be applied served to control the way that law as a system of ordering was derived from the law as an intellectual tradition. In this broad respect, the Ottoman period saw the continuation of processes that had begun under Mamluk rule. But the Ottomans used this tool for rather different purposes: while the Mamluks had favored doctrines from different madhhabs on a pragmatic basis in order to pursue particular policies, the Ottomans sought to privilege the Ḥanafī madhhab as far as they could within an Egyptian legal culture that resisted uniformity. This model of the manipulation of the existing body of doctrine by the state authorities is important in the context of the historiographical debates surrounding the problem of change in Islamic law. Whereas most recent contributions to that debate have focused on doctrinal development, the examples of intervention by the Ottoman and Mamluk authorities in Cairo's courts demonstrate that at the level of applied law, legal change could be achieved simply by manipulating the existing body of doctrine, rather than by creating new doctrine.[1]

Before proceeding, it is important to clarify what I mean by the executive, juristic, and judicial spheres. These are categories that I am imposing on our material in order to make sense of it, and the boundary between them is blurred. The categories should be understood in terms of function, not person. The juristic and judicial spheres consisted of legal scholarship and the day-to-day practice of judgeship, while the executive sphere consisted of imposing the will of the imperial government. Therefore, certain people had a foot in both camps: practicing law either as a jurist or judge placed them within the juristic or judicial sphere, while wielding power on behalf of the government pushed them into the executive sphere. Here, I am not referring simply to the fact that all qāḍīs were appointed by the state. This is true, but the simple fact of official appointment did not make an ordinary provincial qāḍī or nāʾib, who operated only within his court, a member of the executive sphere as I define it. His appointment licensed him to apply the law, but he did not wield the authority of the Sultan, and he was not a member of the imperial elite that staffed the government. The people who straddled the boundary between judicial and executive spheres were, primarily, the Şeyhulislām and the chief qāḍīs. While both were products of a legal education and continued to engage in juristic and judicial activities, in certain of their functions they acted on behalf of the state.[2] The Şeyhulislām's fatwās were considered binding on points of law within Ottoman courts, and many of these fatwās were issued in coordination with, or at the prompting of, the Sultan or other departments of the central government. In such cases, I think it is fair to characterize the Şeyhulislām as producing government policy.[3] As I will explain below, the Şeyhulislām's fatwā was one of the main ways in which the imperial government intervened in legal doctrine within the empire. The chief qāḍī, meanwhile, not only practiced as a qāḍī but also administered the court system in whatever town he served. In a large city such as Cairo, this was a considerable administrative role: managing a network of courts, recruiting and managing the nāʾibs and other court functionaries. Again, in doing so the chief qāḍī acted to implement the imperial government's policies. This administrative role, in particular the managing and disciplining of the nāʾibs, was another means by which the government intervened in legal doctrine.

At the most general level, the idea that responsibility for doctrine was shared between the juristic and executive spheres is not controversial. There is an extensive literature on the relationship between fiqh and ḳānūn: the two most substantial bodies of positive law that informed Ottoman court practice.[4] In this dyad, fiqh belongs in the juristic sphere and ḳānūn belongs in the executive sphere.[5] This debate is important, but it has some limitations. The first is that the discussion takes place at a textual level: how did the production and circulation of ḳānūn texts affect the production of fiqh texts and vice versa, and what did the attempts to "reconcile" the two bodies of literature entail? This discussion takes place at some remove from the level of court practice. The second limitation is that ḳānūn covered only a circumscribed set of domains: principally administration, land tenure, taxation, and crime. Vast, important areas of law have therefore not been included in this discussion: family law, urban property, endowments, and finance, for example. Did the executive authorities intervene in these areas of law? At the level of texts, it appears that their involvement was limited. But at the level of practice, we find more evidence of their interventions. These interventions were not directly textual; rather, they were interventions in how the texts were used in court practice.

There were two main ways in which the government could intervene in and shape court practice. One was to set limits on the circumstances in which the courts could act. The other was to give instructions on how qāḍīs should read the textual tradition for the purposes of applying it in court. There were also several tools that the government could use to intervene. The first was through a generally-applicable *emr-i şerīf* issued by the Sultan: this would be addressed either to all qāḍīs, or to the qāḍīs within a particular region, and it was intended to have a general effect and to remain in force until canceled or superseded by a further emr-i şerīf. Such an emr-i şerīf was therefore different to those, usually issued in response to petitions, which were addressed to a particular qāḍī and concerned a particular dispute, and which I discussed in the previous chapter. The second means was through a fatwā issued by the Şeyhulislām. This could address either all qāḍīs empire-wide or the qāḍīs within a specified region. All fatwās have a general applicability, because they clarify a point of law, rather than addressing a particular case. The special quality of the Şeyhulislām's fatwas was that Ottoman qāḍīs were obliged to follow them.[6] The third means by which the government could intervene in court practice was via instructions issued by the chief qāḍī of a city to the qāḍīs and deputy qāḍīş who worked under him. Such an instruction clearly only affected those qāḍīş working within a particular city or province. To some extent, chief qāḍīs appear to have had some latitude to set their own agendas. However, as we will see later in this chapter, in some cases similar instructions were issued by the chief qāḍīs of different cities during the same period, suggesting that they were following a broader government policy.

An example: the statute of limitations

Sometimes more than one of these means could be used to make the same intervention; for example, a fatwā might cite, and so reinforce, an emr-i şerīf; or a chief qāḍī might instruct his subordinates to follow one. A good illustration of how different elements within the government worked together to create new legal doctrine is the statute of limitations for claims that was established in 957 AH (20 January 1550–8 January 1551). Included in the fatwā collections of the great Şeyhulislām Ebūᵓs-suᶜūd is a petition he sent to Sultan Suleyman and the latter's response. The petition requested a clear time limit for claims to replace the ambiguous prevailing position that the time lapsed should not be excessive. Suleyman responded with an emr-i şerīf declaring that henceforth the limit would be fifteen years for most cases, but only ten years for cases involving land.[7] The Şeyhulislām and Sultan worked together to establish a new rule that governed how qāḍīs should apply the law in the courts.[8]

The statute of limitations was permanent and applicable throughout the empire. Historians have seen it cited in courts across Anatolia and Rumelia during the seventeenth and eighteenth centuries.[9] It was still being cited in Cairo almost two centuries later. On 18 Jumādā ᵓl-Thānī 1154 (31 August 1741), a Christian merchant called Sarāwī walad Bālī Māzaḥīoghlū sued ᶜAbd al-Raḥīm ibn Abū ᵓl-Khayr for the sum of eighty ghurūsh, the bill for a quantity of fabric he had sold to him twenty-one years previously, at the Dīwān al-ᶜĀlī. The qāḍī informed him that, on the authority of the emr-i şerīf, his claim could not be heard as it exceeded the fifteen-year time limit.[10] In another case, heard at the Dīwān al-ᶜĀlī on 17 Rajab 1154 (28 September 1741), Riḍwān ibn Ḥusayn, a retainer of the late Yāqūt Āghā, sued al-Ḥājj Ibrāhīm ibn Haykal al-Maydūmī for 100 *zinjīrlī dīnārs*, the value of 100 *ardabb* of wheat that he had purchased from Riḍwān's late father, Ḥusayn. Riḍwān produced a *tamassuk* (receipt) detailing the transaction of wheat, dated 20 Ramaḍān 1120 (3 December 1708): almost 34 lunar years prior to the date of the lawsuit. The Ḥanafī nāᵓib dismissed Riḍwān's claim, again citing the emr-i şerīf.[11]

Although the statute of limitations came from a Sultan's order rather than from fiqh, it was accepted by subsequent jurists. The seventeenth-century Palestinian mufti, Khayr al-Dīn al-Ramlī, and Ḥāmid al-ᶜImādī, a mufti operating in Damascus in the early eighteenth century, both cited the emr-i şerīf in fatwās concerning claims delayed longer than fifteen years.[12] The fifteen-year time limit became so entrenched within Ottoman legal practice that it was eventually incorporated into the *Mecelle-yi Aḥkām-i ᶜAdliyye*, the Ottoman civil code produced during the Tanzimat.[13] The Mecelle, which codified the Ḥanafī law of contract and procedure, is considered a major rupture in the history of Islamic law. Previous scholars have described how codification radically transformed the fundamental nature of law by subordinating juristic authority to the power of the centralized state.[14] However, the fact that the Mecelle incorporated the statute of limitations, which had no basis in Ḥanafī fiqh and was instead the product of a Sultanic order, illustrates that the codification project drew on a longer tradition of intervention by the executive authorities into legal doctrine.

Interventions in the reading of fiqh

The fifteen-year limit was drawn from outside the textual tradition of fiqh; probably from custom or from a previous ruler's practice. The Ottoman Sultan, via an emr-i şerīf, imposed this external rule on to the courts, which obviously affected how the qāḍīs could apply the textual tradition that was the basis for their rulings. In other circumstances, the Ottoman government intervened within the textual tradition itself: instructing qāḍīs and muftis on how they should read, interpret, and implement fiqh.

The most famous example of this is the problem of the cash waqf. Although the majority of Ḥanafī authorities prohibited endowing awqāf with cash, it had nonetheless become a widespread practice in the central regions of the empire by the early sixteenth century. Therefore, when in the late 1540s the ḳażᶜasker of Rumelia Çivizāde issued a fatwā declaring the cash waqf illegal, he caused a crisis. The crisis was swiftly resolved with another joint effort from Şeyhulislām Ebūᵓs-suᶜūd and Sultan Suleyman. Ebūᵓs-suᶜūd issued a fatwā declaring the practice legitimate on the basis of its current widespread acceptance and support from some early Ḥanafī jurists. Meanwhile, Suleyman issued a decree in May 1548 declaring the cash waqf licit. Henceforth, while the debate among scholars rumbled on into the seventeenth century, for the purposes of applied law within the empire, the cash waqf was unambiguously legal. With this coordinated maneuver, Ebūᵓs-suᶜūd and Suleyman did not fabricate a new legal doctrine: opinions favoring the cash waqf already existed within the Ḥanafī textual tradition. What they did was to intervene in the reading of that tradition, promoting what had previously been considered a weak opinion and ordering Ottoman judges to follow it.[15]

Islamic law, or more accurately fiqh, was a jurists' law in the sense that legal doctrine was created by jurists with little input from rulers. But the legal tradition the jurists created was vast and contained many different, often mutually contradictory, opinions on many subjects. This left room for the Ottoman and other governments to shape the way that the textual tradition was translated into applied law. Even within the central lands of the empire, where the courts were exclusively Ḥanafī, the Ḥanafī madhhab itself contained sufficient diversity of opinion for the government to have an impact on the law that qāḍīs applied, by choosing from among the existing opinions. In Egypt and the Arab provinces, there was an even greater diversity of legal doctrines and opinions available to be applied, due to the madhhab-pluralist court system that the Ottomans inherited from their Mamluk predecessors.

Madhhab pluralism and government intervention

Madhhab pluralism was the primary site in which the Ottoman authorities intervened in the sphere of legal doctrine in Cairo. They intervened by instructing qāḍīs to favor the opinion of one madhhab over another, and by circumscribing the circumstances in which particular doctrines from non-Ḥanafī madhhabs could be used. In manipulating madhhab pluralism, the Ottoman authorities were following the example of their predecessors in Cairo. The Mamluk Sultanate had also prioritized particular doctrines within their madhhab-pluralist legal system, commanding that relevant cases should be referred to a qāḍī of the appropriate madhhab.[16] Whereas the Mamluks did so on a pragmatic basis, selecting doctrines from any madhhab where they furthered the government's objectives, Ottoman interventions were largely ideological, seeking to promote the doctrines of the Ḥanafī madhhab in order to foster Ḥanafī uniformity across the empire. This concern for Ḥanafization and uniformity led the Ottomans to attempt to make rigid some areas of the law where the flexibility afforded by the plurality of madhhabs had long been exploited for the benefit of ordinary people and the wider society. One example is the sphere of marriage and divorce, where court practice in Egypt and the eastern Arab lands had long combined doctrines from different madhhabs in order to create more possibilities for women.[17] As Judith Tucker and others have demonstrated, these practices continued into the Ottoman period, and were endorsed by Ottoman-era Syrian jurists of the seventeenth century.[18] The Ottoman imperial authorities attempted on several occasions to close down this flexibility in favor of rigid adherence to Ḥanafism. Prior to the legal reforms of the Tanzimat era, they were never completely successful, but periodic attempts gradually shifted legal practice in the direction of Ḥanafī uniformity.

The Ottoman government's interventions in this period prefigured the much more aggressive, and ultimately successful, Ḥanafization of the nineteenth-century legal reforms. Sticking with the topic of family law, Kenneth Cuno has demonstrated that women's rights within marriage and after divorce shrank significantly in Egypt during the nineteenth century, due to the Ḥanafization and codification of law. This was because Ḥanafī doctrines in family law were usually more restrictive, and codification saw them imposed where previously litigants had been able to choose among more generous options from the other madhhabs.[19] The experience of Egypt and the other Arab provinces during the early modern period shows that the codifying and Ḥanafizing projects of the nineteenth century did not constitute the implantation of European concepts in an alien soil. Rather, these projects drew on longer-term trends within Islamic legal history: of government intervention into legal doctrine, of legal standardization as a facet of state-formation, and of the increasing preference for the Ḥanafī madhhab among imperial elites.[20]

Before I relate the story of Ḥanafization in early modern Egypt, it is worth reflecting on the nature of the madhhab and on what it meant for an Ottoman Muslim to identify with a madhhab. There were significant differences in attitudes to these questions between the juristic culture of the Ottoman center and that of Egypt. These differences lay behind the ongoing struggles over Ḥanafization.

Madhhab identity

What did it mean for a person living in the Ottoman Empire to be affiliated to a particular madhhab? There has been little research on what the madhhabs meant to Muslims living in any historical society, or on how understandings of madhhab-affiliation might have varied between different regions or periods, or between ulema, members of the government apparatus, and ordinary people. Did the identification of jurists with a particular madhhab entail an ideological commitment to it? What did the well-known but little-explored fact that Ḥanafism was the "official" madhhab of the Ottoman Empire actually mean?[21] Did ordinary Cairenes, who were part of neither the scholarly nor the political establishments, consciously identify with a madhhab? Asking these questions is vital if we are to understand how madhhab-pluralism worked within Cairo's legal system.

I will start with the last question: did ordinary people in Ottoman Cairo consciously identify with a madhhab? While this question has received little attention, many scholars have assumed that madhhab affiliations were present among the general populations of historical Muslim societies. Much scholarship on the Arab provinces of the Ottoman Empire has contained the implicit assumption that the pluralism of the legal system was a reflection of the multicultural population in large cities such as Cairo, Damascus, and Aleppo. Thus, Rudolph Peters writes that in the sixteenth century the Ḥanafī monopoly on Ottoman courts was not extended to the newly-conquered provinces "with Muslim populations following different madhhabs."[22] Abdul-Karim Rafeq writes that in Ottoman Damascus the majority of the population were Shāfiʿīs, while the city also contained a small number of Ḥanbalīs who had moved from Nablus and a number of Moroccan migrants who were Mālikīs.[23] Meanwhile, Sherman Jackson describes a treatise written by the sixteenth-century Mālikī jurist al-Qarāfī as "addressed exclusively to the Mālikī community in Cairo."[24]

It is not at all clear, however, whether members of the general Muslim population in the Ottoman Empire, or in other societies, consciously identified with a particular madhhab. Of course, each madhhab's doctrines encompassed religious practice and ritual as well as law in the modern sense of the word. Therefore, to the extent that a particular madhhab dominated the religious institutions of a community, the doctrines of that madhhab would be reflected in the community's religious practices. For this reason, particular madhhabs are often associated with geographic regions and/or ethnic-linguistic groups. But such a community bound by common religious practice need not be at such a large scale; it could also be a small group such as the community described by Daniella Talmon Heller which centered around a popular Ḥanbalī preacher in medieval Nablus and Damascus.[25] More importantly, it is not clear whether observance of certain religious practices necessarily entailed a conscious identification with the relevant madhhab. An ordinary native-born Cairene might have recognized the way his or her religious practices differed from those of a Maghribī immigrant without ascribing this to a difference in madhhab. Someone living in a more homogeneous small town might not have realized that diversity in practice existed. The Syrian community studied by Heller was united more by devotion to a charismatic shaykh than by an ideological commitment to Ḥanbalism, although Ḥanbalī doctrine would have informed the shaykh's teaching.

What is clear from Cairo's sharīᶜa court records is that even if ordinary Cairene Muslims identified with a certain madhhab with regard to their worship, they did not feel obliged to organize their worldly legal affairs according to the doctrines of any one madhhab. In the court records, the choice of madhhab correlates clearly with certain types of cases. Court users chose a particular madhhab according to the remedies it could offer, not according to their own affiliation.[26]

By contrast, it is clear that identification with a madhhab was the norm for jurists and for scholars in other disciplines. The madhhabs did not have any institutional form, but a scholar's affiliation meant having been trained in, and continuing to work within, the particular body of scholarship that grew out of the works of the madhhab's eponymous founder and his disciples.[27] The reference points of a scholar's writings were the previous works produced by his madhhab, while qāḍīs and muftis were expected to give judgments or fatwās according to the doctrines of their own madhhabs; they were often obliged to do so by the terms of their appointments.[28]

Nonetheless, the implications of jurists' affiliations to madhhabs have not been much explored by modern historians. Did affiliation entail an ideological commitment to the madhhab: would a jurist have believed that his madhhab's doctrines were superior or that following them was a more righteous path? Or was madhhab-affiliation akin to a professional qualification, such as a modern lawyer practicing Scottish law, who need not have any view on its relative merits vis-à-vis English law, and would certainly not feel any compunction about arranging her own affairs according to English law if it were more convenient? There is no clear answer to this question, and it seems that the meaning of madhhab-affiliation varied between different societies, and possibly from individual jurist to jurist. In the local juristic culture of Ottoman Cairo, madhhab-affiliation tended towards my latter definition: simply a professional qualification. But the same was not true of Ḥanafī jurists educated within the ilmiye system who were more attached to the Ottoman state and its institutions. At least some of these jurists were more ideologically and emotionally committed to the Ḥanafī madhhab, and they worked to establish its supremacy.

Plenty of evidence suggests that among Cairene scholars, madhhab-affiliation was primarily a professional qualification. First, it was fairly common for jurists to change madhhab. One reason a jurist might change madhhab was to secure a particular position. For example, ᶜAbd al-Barr ibn ᶜAbd al-Qādir al-Fayyūmī al-ᶜAwfī, a scholar born in Cairo during the first half of the seventeenth century, was trained as a Ḥanafī in Cairo, Mecca, Damascus, Aleppo, and Istanbul, but became a Shāfiᶜī later in his career in order to accept appointments as Shāfiᶜī qāḍī and as professor of Shāfiᶜī fiqh in Jerusalem.[29] In the eighteenth century, Muṣṭafā Raᵓīs al-Būlāqī switched the other way: he began his career as a Shāfiᶜī and then became a Ḥanafī. His biographer, Jabartī, does not claim explicitly that the switch was motivated by career opportunities, but he notes that he became a Ḥanafī deputy qāḍī at the sharīᶜā court of Būlāq.[30]

Another reason was falling out with one's colleagues within the madhhab. Muḥammad ibn Ibrāhīm al-ᶜAwfī, a scholar of the mid eighteenth century praised by Jabartī as a versatile jurist and a bawdy poet, began his career as a Shāfiᶜī. He was close to Shams al-Din al-Ḥifnī, the most prominent Shāfiᶜī in eighteenth-century Cairo who served a long tenure as Shaykh al-Azhar. But ᶜAwfī's standing within the madhhab collapsed when several colleagues accused him of fraud, producing as evidence legal documents in ᶜAwfī's hand, and earning him censure from Ḥifnī. ᶜAwfī responded by switching to the Mālikī madhhab, within which he had a long career. Late in his life he returned to the Shāfiᶜī madhhab after suffering a stroke.[31] ᶜAwfī's return to his original madhhab in the face of serious illness suggests that his earlier decision to move had been a fraught one. But it is not clear what was the source of ᶜAwfī's regret: it could well have been the social consequences of switching, or a disappointment that he had run away rather than facing and overcoming his challenges, rather than a belief that Shāfiᶜī doctrine was superior.

Another biography by Jabartī also suggests that switching madhhab could be anguished. Muḥammad ibn ᶜAbd Rabbih ibn ᶜAlī al-ᶜAzīzī, a jurist born in Cairo in the early eighteenth century, was a Mālikī scholar. Early in his career, he decided to switch to the Shāfiᶜī madhhab, but its founder the Imam al-Shāfiᶜī appeared to him in a dream and told him not to, so he changed his mind and remained a Mālikī.[32] Of course, most jurists affiliated with the same madhhab throughout their careers. But even so, Jabartī's biographies show that it was not unusual for jurists—particularly the more accomplished—to study more than one madhhab during their educations.[33]

The jurist Aḥmad ibn ᶜAbd al-Munᶜim al-Damanhūrī, who began his studies at al-Azhar as a young orphan in the early eighteenth century and died in 1778–9 (1192 AH), did not affiliate with any particular madhhab, but instead lectured and gave fatwās in all four. According to his biographers, he was a polymath, excelling not only in all four schools of law but also in alchemy, medicine, philosophy, and other sciences, in addition to serving as Shaykh al-Azhar. Damanhūrī was unusual—his biographer Murādī described him as unique in his age—but nevertheless, the fact that he was both able to practice all four madhhabs simultaneously and was celebrated for doing so demonstrates that the boundaries between the madhhabs were fluid in eighteenth-century Cairo.[34]

Jabartī also reveals tensions between the madhhabs in Cairo. When the great Damanhūrī fell ill, a dispute broke out over who should succeed him as Shaykh al-Azhar. ᶜAbd al-Raḥmān ibn ᶜUmar al-ᶜArīshī, a Ḥanafī, was frontrunner, having secured the backing of the shaykh of the Sādāt clan, the *shaykh al-balad* Ibrāhīm Bey, and many senior ulema and amīrs. But Shāfiᶜī scholars protested against his appointment on the grounds that the position had traditionally been held by a Shāfiᶜī, and that as a native of al-ᶜArīsh near Gaza, he was a foreigner; instead, they demanded that the local Shāfiᶜī Aḥmad al-ᶜArūsī be appointed. The Shāfiᶜīs won the backing of Murād Bey, Ibrāhīm Bey's partner in the Qāzdughlī duumvirate that dominated Cairo in the 1770s, and for seven months both ᶜArīshī and ᶜArūsī claimed the post. The standoff only came to end when ᶜArīshī fell out with the amīrs backing him; they withdrew their support, ᶜArūsī won the position, and ᶜArīshī retreated into obscurity.[35] For all the bitterness of this dispute, it is not clear that the tension reflected competing beliefs about the relative merits of Ḥanafī and Shāfiᶜī law. It seems more likely that the dispute was about two corporate bodies fighting over their respective privileges: the Shāfiᶜī protestors wanted to defend the opportunities for employment and prestige that were reserved for themselves and their colleagues.

While the biographies of Cairene jurists show that many studied different madhhabs during their educations, and that some switched madhhabs during their careers, evidence from Cairo's court records demonstrates that jurists did not feel obliged to observe the doctrines of their madhhabs in their private lives. When arranging their private legal affairs, jurists were happy to use whichever madhhab was most convenient.

For example, an entry dated 16 Dhū ᵓl-Ḥijja 1106 (28 July 1695) details the lease of a plot of land in the Bakrī neighborhood that belonged to the waqf of the late Imām Abū ᵓl-Surūr al-Ṣadīqī, to Zaynī Ṣāliḥ ibn ᶜAlī al-Shaᶜrānī al-Mawārdī of the Tüfekçiyān regiment. The lessor, ᶜAbd al-Munᶜim al-Bakrī al-Ṣadīqī, was a Shāfiᶜī mufti, yet he drew up the contract according to Ḥanbalī law, following common practice in Cairo at the time.[36] Another entry shows that the Mālikī scholar ᶜAbd al-Ḥalīm al-Shaᶜrānī issued a lawsuit through his agent before a Shāfiᶜī judge, to recover taxes due to a waqf he controlled.[37] In another entry, the Ḥanbalī deputy judge at al-Bāb al-ᶜĀlī, Muḥammad Abū Surūr, took his dispute with al-Ḥajj Muḥammad ibn Shams al-Dīn over an unpaid debt to the Ḥanafī judge at Bāb al-Shaᶜriyya.[38]

The practice of following a madhhab other than one's own in a specific case for reasons of utility—called *tatabbuᶜ al-rukhaṣ*—was also treated explicitly in the writings of several jurists in Egypt and the other Arab provinces of the Ottoman Empire. For the most part, jurists allowed the practice. Some held that it was only allowed if a person had a pressing need, while others were more permissive. The sixteenth-century Egyptian Ḥanafī, Ibn Nujaym, allowed a litigant to withdraw a claim he had made before one qāḍī and then present it to a qāḍī of a different madhhab with a more favorable doctrine, as long as he did so before the first qāḍī had issued a judgment. Another Egyptian Ḥanafī, Ḥasan ibn ᶜAmmār al-Shurunbulālī, who was active in the early seventeenth century, allowed people to choose to follow a doctrine from any of the four madhhabs based on their preference, regardless of whether they had an urgent need or not. These opinions drew on a longer tradition of acceptance of tatabbuᶜ al-rukhaṣ by many post-classical jurists in the late medieval Middle East.[39] The sixteenth-century Egyptian Shāfiᶜī mystic and jurist Shaᶜrānī elaborated a more expansive concept of tatabbuᶜ al-rukhaṣ, which Ahmed Ibrahim has described as a theory of legal pluralism. For Shaᶜrānī, the availability of "easier" and "harder" rulings among the doctrines of the four madhhabs was designed to accommodate the range of ability and moral strength within the Muslim community: God created a law that could be calibrated so that all people could abide by it. Those of weaker faith or limited ability could choose to follow the easier rulings, while the more pious and intelligent could choose the more demanding route.[40] A few jurists, such as the Egyptian Ḥanbalī, Marᶜī ibn Yūsuf al-Karmī (d. 1623), were even willing to endorse *talfīq*—the combination of doctrines from different madhhabs within one legal affair—which would become an important tool of modernist reformers in the late nineteenth century but remained highly controversial during this period.[41]

Madhhab identity in the ilmiye system

The above picture of fluid boundaries between the madhhabs relates specifically to the ulema of Cairo. Jurists in other regions of the empire may have felt more of an ideological commitment to their madhhabs. In Syria, the local scholarly culture was similarly pluralist.[42] But many, if not all, of the jurists who were trained and spent their careers within the Ottoman ilmiye system showed a more fervent commitment to the Ḥanafī madhhab.

The ilmiye system was an innovation in the Muslim Middle East. While previous rulers had patronized individual madrasas, the Ottoman Empire's ilmiye was much more ambitious: a hierarchical network of madrasas that constituted a cohesive system.[43] Ilmiye madrasas attained a much greater significance in the certification of students. The medieval Islamic model of education centered on personal relationships, in which the measure of a scholar's accomplishment was the particular professors he had studied with, remained relevant in the Ottoman Empire, and biographers continued to trace the movements of peripatetic students.[44] But increasingly, placement in prestigious judgeships and professorships depended on graduation from particular madrasas within the ilmiye system.

This meant that the Ottoman government was increasingly able to define the curriculum for the students who would fill the upper ranks of the judiciary, and so shape their intellectual outlook. A fermān issued in 1565, which prescribes the books to be studied at the highest level of madrasa in the ilmiye system, is the earliest evidence of the Ottoman government's attempt to define a canon of Islamic learning for the empire's judicial elite.[45] The syllabus shows that the legal education offered by imperial madrasas—both legal theory (*uṣūl al-fiqh*) and positive law (*furūᶜ al-fiqh*)—was exclusively Ḥanafī. This became the norm in ilimiye madrasas: a curriculum of 1741, prepared at the French ambassador's request to demonstrate what was studied in the madrasas of the Ottoman capital, was equally Ḥanafī-centric.[46]

An increasing number of Ottoman jurists and judges, particularly at the higher levels of the hierarchy, received their education primarily, or even exclusively, within the ilmiye madrasas. The intellectual culture fostered by these madrasas was much narrower than that in older madrasas that were not government-sponsored. The scholars produced by imperial madrasas were trained in an almost exclusively Ḥanafī environment, in which they did not develop social and intellectual relationships with representatives of other madhhabs, and may never have studied a non-Ḥanafī legal text. The intellectual experience and outlook of ilmiye graduates was very different from that of scholars, including Ḥanafīs, who trained in Cairo or Damascus: ilmiye graduates were much less familiar with non-Ḥanafī scholarship, particularly in the field of fiqh, and what knowledge they had of it would have come largely via rebuttals penned by Ḥanafīs. It is not surprising that some scholars in this milieu developed a pronounced favoritism towards Ḥanafism, believing in its intellectual superiority, and willing to promote its superiority in practice by marginalizing the other madhhabs within the Ottoman legal system.[47]

In addition to an exclusively Ḥanafī education, ilmiye graduates also shared an identification with the Ottoman imperial project, which deployed law as its key legitimation strategy and which saw legal uniformity as a desirable goal, even if it was quite willing to shelve it in the short term if political circumstances demanded that. This clash of intellectual cultures, between the positive pluralism of Cairo and the Ḥanafizing instinct of the ilmiye graduates who tolerated plurality as a regrettable necessity, was the context for struggles over the place of the Ḥanafī madhhab in the Egyptian legal system that erupted periodically throughout the sixteenth, seventeenth, and eighteenth centuries.

Ḥanafization in Ottoman Egypt

By the late sixteenth century, the Ḥanafī madhhab had a virtual monopoly on legal life in the central lands of the empire. As late as the early sixteenth century, Shāfiᶜī law was still being used in some circumstances in Anatolia, with the approval of Şeyhulislām Kemālpaşazāde (in office 1527–34). However, an imperial order banned this practice during the tenure of Şeyhulislām Ebūᵓs-suᶜūd.[48] In the Arab provinces conquered in 1517, the Ottomans were more hesitant. Egypt and Syria were old Muslim countries, whose heritages far outshone that of the Ottomans. The new rulers faced the task of incorporating the prestigious scholarly cities of Cairo and Damascus, both of which had rich, madhhab-pluralist intellectual cultures. They also had to win the allegiance of populations who were used to the flexibility of a madhhab-pluralist court system that had existed for two and a half centuries. But although they trod carefully in the Arab provinces, the Ottoman rulers nonetheless saw Ḥanafization as the goal.[49]

Previous scholars have placed Ḥanafization within the traditional narrative of the rise and decline of Ottoman power in Egypt. In this narrative, limited Ḥanafization of Egypt's legal system took place in the early years of Ottoman rule, as part of a package of legal reforms that included the reorganization of the courts, the extension of the qāḍī's competence at the expense of the muḥtasib, the introduction of court fees, the appointment of Turkish-speaking qāḍīs to key posts, and the promulgation of the ḳānūnnāme of Egypt. The Ḥanafizing element of these reforms consisted in ensuring the supremacy of the Ḥanafī madhhab without abolishing the others: Cairo would have only one chief qāḍī, a Ḥanafī, as opposed to the four chief qāḍīs of the Mamluk Sultanate, and all non-Ḥanafī judges would be subordinate to him. As Ottoman influence began to fade by the end of the sixteenth century, according to this narrative, so did attempts to promote Ḥanafism.[50]

In fact, rather than taking the simple form of rise and decline, the story includes several periods between the sixteenth and nineteenth centuries when the Ottoman government reasserted its Ḥanafizing drive, followed by periods when it backed off. On some occasions, the Ottoman government sought to appoint more Ḥanafīs to the courts while dismissing non-Ḥanafīs; on other occasions, it sought instead to restrict the use of non-Ḥanafī doctrines. Rather than a linear decline, the Ottoman government's pursuit of Ḥanafization fluctuated over time. These fluctuations reflected changing political dynamics in Istanbul and in Cairo, and also the personalities and views of particular senior officials.

The first action the Ottomans took against the non-Ḥanafī madhhabs in Egypt was on 14 Ṣafar 923 (5 March 1517), two months after the conquest, when an imperial order dismissed Cairo's four chief qāḍīs, the Shāfiʿī Kamāl al-Dīn al-Ṭawīl, the Ḥanafī Maḥmūd ibn al-Shiḥna, the Mālikī Muḥyī ʾl-Dīn ibn al-Damīrī, and the Ḥanbalī Shihāb al-Dīn al-Futūḥī.[51] They were replaced by a single Ḥanafī qāḍī, called initially the Qāḍī ʾl-ʿArab, who held court at the Ṣāliḥiyya madrasa.[52] This situation remained until 1522, when Sultan Suleymān appointed Sīdī Çelebi to the renamed post of Qāḍī ʾl-ʿAskar of Egypt.[53] At the same time, Suleymān dismissed all of the nāʾibs in Cairo except four, one from each madhhab, who would work under Sīdī Çelebi's supervision at the Ṣāliḥiyya court. Suleymān also dismissed most of the court witnesses (shuhūd), leaving in post only two for each nāʾib.[54]

Two years later, Pīr Aḥmed Çelebi was appointed chief qāḍī in the wake of the failed rebellion of Aḥmed Pasha al-Khāʾin, arriving in Egypt on 25 Dhū ʾl-Qaʿda 930 (24 September 1524). He dismissed all the Shāfiʿī, Mālikī and Ḥanbalī nāʾibs and court witnesses, with the exception of those who served under him at al-Bāb al-ʿĀlī, which had now been established as Cairo's main sharīʿa court.[55] This suggests that either Suleymān's order of 1522 had been ineffective, or that the dismissed nāʾibs and court witnesses had returned to work during the brief interregnum under Aḥmed Pasha's rule.

Pīr Aḥmed Çelebi's reform did not last either, and non-Ḥanafī deputy qāḍīs were soon working in Cairo's local neighborhood courts again. But the actions undertaken by the Ottomans in the first years of their rule in Egypt set a pattern of recurrent attempts to suppress the non-Ḥanafī madhhabs. None enjoyed more then temporary or partial success, and for much of the time the Ottoman chief qāḍīs and governors found it prudent to refrain from openly targeting the non-Ḥanafī madhhabs for fear of raising tension with their Egyptian subjects. However, the ideal of Ḥanafization remained, ready to be activated by ambitious or ideological administrators when they saw an opportunity.

Attitudes to non-Ḥanafī judges, and to the indigenous Egyptian judiciary in general, form a major theme in the biographical dictionary of sixteenth and early seventeenth-century chief qāḍīs composed by Ḥusayn ibn Muḥammad al-Damīrī. For example, Damīrī reports that in 1601, the first act of newly-appointed chief qāḍī ᶜAbd al-Wahhāb ibn Ibrāhīm al-Rūmī was to dismiss the Shāfiᶜīs, Mālikīs, and Ḥanbalīs working in the neighborhood courts, so that the non-Ḥanafī madhhabs were again represented only in the main court al-Bāb al-ᶜĀlī. Along with further reforms to cut both the total number of deputy qāḍīs and court witnesses working in Cairo's courts, and to enforce strict limits on the fees they could charge, this made Rūmī deeply unpopular, the subject of satirical poems and offensive graffiti.[56]

After 1601, there were no further attempts to dismiss the Shāfiᶜī, Mālikī, and Ḥanbalī nāʾibs. The Ottoman government instead turned its attention to particular doctrines that varied significantly from the Ḥanafī positions. Initially, the Ottomans did not attempt to prohibit these doctrines, but rather to monitor and control them by placing them under the supervision of the Ḥanafī chief qāḍī. In the last decade of the seventeenth century, they would tighten restrictions on these doctrines, with the aim of marginalizing them. This was not an easy task for the Ottoman authorities: it was resisted by Cairenes who valued these doctrines, particularly those connected with waqf. In the following section of this chapter, I will examine two doctrines as examples of Ottoman policy. These are judicial divorce (*faskh*) for abandoned wives, and the long-term rental contract (*al-ijāra al-ṭawīla*) on waqf-owned properties. These were not the only non-Ḥanafī doctrines that drew the imperial government's attention.[57] I focus on judicial divorce because it has been discussed at some length in the secondary literature; I offer some qualifications to its portrayal. I examine the long-term rental contract because it was so ubiquitous in Cairo's real estate market: given its popularity, it is a good example of the tensions created by the Ottoman commitment to Ḥanafization.

Judicial divorce for abandoned wives

While pre-modern Islamic law gave husbands the right to repudiate their wives unilaterally for any reason (known as *ṭalaq*), women's access to divorce was much more restricted. Two types of divorce gave wives in the Ottoman Empire certain limited opportunities to escape an unwanted marriage. The more common of the two was *khulᶜ*, a transaction in which the husband repudiated his wife at her request in exchange for compensation. The other type of divorce was faskh or judicial divorce: the dissolution of a marriage by a qāḍī at the request of the wife, on the grounds of a defect in the husband.[58] From a woman's perspective faskh was preferable to khulᶜ as it did not require the husband's agreement and the wife did not have to compensate him financially. The wife was, however, required to demonstrate a legitimate cause for a judicial divorce, and there were very few grounds on which it could be granted. They varied from madhhab to madhhab, and the Ḥanafīs were the most restrictive.[59]

Ḥanafī jurists accepted the husband's impotence as grounds for judicial divorce, as impotence undermined the central purpose of marriage, which was legitimate sexual relations and procreation. Ottoman-era Ḥanafī jurists also saw a husband's blasphemy as grounds for the dissolution of a Muslim woman's marriage: by blaspheming the husband became an apostate, which rendered the marriage invalid because the law forbade the marriage of a Muslim woman to a non-Muslim man. Ḥanafī jurists rejected other defects of the husband such as insanity and scrofula as they did not undermine sexual relations and reproduction. They also refused to consider the prolonged absence of the husband, even if his wife knew neither his whereabouts nor whether he was alive or dead, as grounds for dissolution. According to Ḥanafī doctrine, in cases of abandonment a judicial divorce could only be granted once the husband could be presumed dead. This, according to various opinions, was after a period of ninety-nine years, 120 years or once all members of his peer group had died. By contrast, jurists of other madhhabs drew an analogy between abandonment and impotence, as both prevented sexual relations.[60]

The Ḥanafīs' restrictive approach to judicial divorce was impractical: the presumption in Islamic law was that women relied on their husbands for financial support, and consequently many women did not have the opportunity to earn their own living.[61] In many cases it may not have been the abandoned woman herself who was harmed by the difficulty of judicial divorce, though no doubt many such women did wish to re-marry. A family whose daughter had been abandoned might find providing for her a financial burden, and so might want to find a new husband to take responsibility for her. Moreover, the family of a man who had disappeared might hope that his wife would receive a judicial divorce and re-marry, as this would preclude her from inheriting a share of the man's property and so allow it to remain intact and within the family. In short, there were numerous parties who might have an interest in an abandoned wife being able to obtain a judicial divorce. It is not surprising, therefore, that Ottoman societies found legal ways to evade the restrictive Ḥanafī doctrines.

In Cairo, along with the rest of Ottoman Egypt and Syria, the solution was to resort to a non-Ḥanafī judge. The Ḥanafī madhhab was alone in restricting judicial divorce so severely, and Mālikī, Shāfiᶜī, and Ḥanbalī nāʾibs were able to dissolve the marriages of abandoned wives after a relatively short period of time. Judith Tucker has documented how eighteenth-century Syrian women who had been abandoned would approach a Shāfiᶜī or Ḥanbalī judge.[62] In Cairo, women usually went to a Mālikī or Ḥanbalī nāʾib. This was not a new solution: abandoned women in Mamluk Egypt and Syria had done the same thing, and indeed the Mamluk authorities specifically charged Mālikī and Ḥanbalī qāḍīs with providing this service.[63]

This solution was also used outside the Ottoman Arab provinces: Ḥanafī muftis in nineteenth-century British India suggested that abandoned women seek judicial divorce under Mālikī doctrine.[64] It had once been the preferred solution in the central regions of the Ottoman Empire. In the early sixteenth century, it had been common practice for abandoned wives in Anatolia and Rumelia to go to a Shāfiᶜī qāḍī or mufti to obtain a dissolution, and the Şeyhulislām Ebūʾs-suʿūd endorsed the practice in a fatwā, with the condition that the wife had a genuine need for financial support.[65] However, during Ebūʾs-suʿūd's tenure (1545–1574), an imperial decree banned this practice within Anatolia and Rumelia.[66] People in Anatolia subsequently found a new solution to the problem that could be enacted within the confines of Ḥanafī doctrine. Başak Tuğ has shown that Ḥanafī qāḍīs in eighteenth-century Ankara were willing to declare that an abandoned wife was widowed or divorced if she could demonstrate that she had received information that her husband had either died or divorced her while away. Crucially, she did not have to provide eye-witnesses to the actual death or divorce, but could rely on hearsay transmitted from afar.[67] In other words, Anatolian legal practice dealt with this issue by allowing women to use a lower standard of proof than usually required by Ottoman sharīʿa courts; Selma Zečević described the same procedure being used in eighteenth-century Bosnia.[68] It was also possible for women in Anatolia and Rumelia, as elsewhere, to insert a stipulation into their marriage contracts that they would be divorced if the husband should ever disappear for a certain period of time. In these cases, the husband's absence would automatically trigger a pre-arranged repudiation, so there was no need to refer to the concept of faskh. But a woman's ability to obtain divorce in this way obviously depended on her having had the foresight and the legal knowledge to request the stipulation at the time of marriage, and having been able to convince her husband to accept it.[69]

In the empire's Arab provinces, recourse to non-Ḥanafī qāḍīs for a judicial divorce was not banned in the mid sixteenth century, and Cairenes continued to use Mālikī or Ḥanbalī qāḍīs for this purpose. Ḥanafī jurists from the Ottoman Arab provinces advocated this practice. The sixteenth-century Egyptian jurist Ibn Nujaym argued that a judicial divorce performed by a non-Ḥanafī qāḍī to end the marriage of an abandoned woman should be treated as valid by Ḥanafi qāḍīs. It was therefore legitimate for a Ḥanafī qāḍī to marry such a woman to someone else; a Ḥanafī qāḍī should also dismiss any claim by her first husband, should he subsequently return, to annul her second marriage and reclaim her as his wife.[70] Khayr al-Dīn al-Ramlī, a jurist active in seventeenth-century Palestine, issued a fatwā declaring that, if a woman's husband was failing to provide her with adequate maintenance due to his poverty, a Ḥanafī qāḍī should appoint a Shāfiʿī deputy to dissolve her marriage.[71] Like Ibn Nujaym, Ramlī also argued that a judicial divorce performed by a Shāfiʿī in case of abandonment was decisive and irreversible: if the husband subsequently returned from his absence he could not have the dissolution declared void.[72]

While the Ottoman authorities did not ban judicial divorce outright in the Arab provinces, the discomfort they felt with non-Ḥanafī doctrines was reflected in their attempts to control the practice. Abandoned wives in Cairo could not go directly to a Mālikī or Ḥanbalī qāḍī to request a dissolution. Rather, they were supposed to petition the Ḥanafī chief qāḍī, who would then refer the case to a Mālikī or Ḥanbalī deputy. Sharīʿa court registers from the early seventeenth century contain orders addressed to the deputy qāḍīs and scribes of Cairo's various courts, instructing them that they should not deal with a range of issues that included judicial divorce without the permission of the Ḥanafī chief qāḍī.[73]

By the late 1660s, the procedure that was followed when an abandoned wife wanted to obtain a judicial divorce was well established. It is illustrated by the following case, which was heard at Bāb al-Shaᶜriyya on 19 Ṣafar 1078 (10 August 1667). A woman called Hiba ibnat Muḥammad al-Ḥāyik submitted a petition (*ᶜarḍ al-ḥāl*) to the Ḥanafī chief qāḍī, seeking a judicial divorce on the grounds that her husband Muḥammad ibn Muḥammad al-Ṣawwāf had been absent from Cairo and the surrounding area for a period of one year and two months, leaving Hiba without any money or source of income for maintenance. Her petition stated that during this period she had stayed in the marital home, leaving it only for necessities and in order to request the divorce. This was an important point, because jurists conceived maintenance as compensation for a wife's confinement in the marital home.[74] If Hiba had left the house without her husband's permission, then as a disobedient wife (*nāshiza*) she would have forfeited her right to maintenance, although in the case of abandonment, the jurists made an exception for essential excursions.[75] Upon receiving the petition, the chief qāḍī referred the case to the Mālikī nāᵓib at Bāb al-Shaᶜriyya, Nūr al-Dīn ᶜAlī al-Rifāᶜī, who heard the case of 19 Ṣafar 1078 (10 August 1667). Hiba brought two witnesses, al-Ḥājj ᶜAlī ibn Sharaf al-Dīn al-Kaᶜkī and Sulaymān ibn Muḥammad al-Ṣawwāf.[76] They testified to the truth of Hiba's claim. Hiba asked the nāᵓib to permit her to dissolve her marriage. In the obligatory stage of the procedure that followed, the nāᵓib cautioned Hiba against divorce and urged patience, but in the face of Hiba's insistence he then acceded to her request. Hiba then pronounced a formula dissolving the marriage, recorded by the court scribe in the first person: *fasakhtū nikāḥī min ᶜismat zawjī Muḥammad al-madhkūr faskhan sharᶜiyyan malaktū bihi nafsī* (I dissolve my marital bond to my husband the aforementioned Muḥammad with a legal dissolution, and by this act I assume ownership of myself). The nāᵓib confirmed the dissolution, and the court record specifies that his judgment was according to the doctrines of the Mālikī madhhab.[77]

The same Mālikī nāᵓib handled a Damascene woman's request for judicial divorce on 13 Ramaḍān 1078 (26 February 1668). Ḥalīma bint ᶜAbd al-Karīm al-Ḥāyik followed the same procedure as Hiba in the previous example: she petitioned the Ḥanafī chief qāḍī, who then referred the case to the Mālikī nāᵓib. Ḥalīma was a resident of Damascus, where she had married her husband Ibrāhīm ibn ᶜAbdullāh al-Ḥāyik.[78] Ibrāhīm disappeared from Damascus, and after an absence of a year Ḥalīma traveled to Cairo to look for him. Ḥalīma stated that she had stayed in Cairo for three months looking for him without success. She had no means of support and requested a dissolution. Two witnesses, al-Sayyid Aḥmad ibn al-Shāmī al-Khabbāz and Muḥammad ibn ᶜAlī al-Ḥāyik, confirmed the truth of Ḥalīma's claim, and she also swore an oath. The nāᵓib cautioned Ḥalīma and urged patience, and then permitted her to dissolve her marriage. Ḥalīma then effected the dissolution by pronouncing the required formula.[79]

Long leases on waqf-owned property

Another controversial non-Ḥanafī doctrine which was permitted but supervised by the Ottoman authorities in Cairo was the long lease on property owned by a waqf. Long-term leases on waqf-owned property were controversial due to restrictions, common to the classical doctrine of all four madhhabs, that were created in order to protect the interests of awqāf. The standard position limited leases to three years, although some opinions distinguished between agricultural land and urban buildings, allowing only one-year leases on the latter. The primary reason for this limit was to protect the principle of the inalienability of waqf property: that properties were endowed to a waqf in perpetuity, and the waqf was not allowed to sell them.[80] A long lease could tend towards the effective ownership of a property by the lessee, and so long leases were prohibited. For this purpose, three years might seem an excessively cautious limit, but another reason for mandating very short leases was to protect the waqf's commercial interests by ensuring frequent re-negotiation of terms.

There were many reasons why waqf supervisors and beneficiaries might want more flexibility in managing their property than the classical doctrine allowed. Some of these reasons were more legitimate, from the perspective of a waqf's purpose, than others. The restriction to three years limited the attractiveness of a lease and the waqf supervisor's freedom to bargain, and so limited the amount of money that could be raised in the short term. Current beneficiaries might well prefer to boost current income at the expense of future income that would go to their descendants. Even a conscientious supervisor, determined to safeguard the long-term value of the waqf, might want to raise a large amount of money in the short term in order to finance renovations or to invest in further properties.

There was also a public interest in easing the rule of three-year leases. A recurrent problem with urban awqāf was the ruin or decay of waqf property through disaster or neglect. If the waqf did not have sufficient capital to repair the damage, the obvious person to restore the building was a tenant, but no tenant would be willing to make a significant investment in a leased property if he or she could not be assured of tenure after three years. In largely wood-built Istanbul, fire frequently devastated waqf holdings, and Ottoman Ḥanafī jurists developed the concept of *icāreteyn* (double rent) to deal with the problem. An icāreteyn contract involved a large, one-off payment known as the *icāre-yi muʿaccele* (advance rent), which secured an indefinite lease, followed by the payment of a smaller, annual *icāre-yi müʾeccele* (delayed rent). The offer of an indefinite lease could convince a potential tenant to bear the cost of restoring a building. The *icāre-yi müʾeccele* prevented the alienation of the property, which would violate the essential principle of waqf. Annual payment recognized the the waqf's ultimate ownership of the property, so a tenant paying it would not be able to claim ownership on the grounds of length of occupancy.[81]

The icāreteyn was the standard method for arranging long-term leases of waqf property in the European and Anatolian provinces, where only Ḥanafī doctrine was accepted. The same method was also used in transactions involving Egyptian awqāf;

particularly when people from the central regions of the empire were involved. A eunuch of the imperial harem called Beşīr Āğa leased a waqf-owned house in Cairo with an icāreteyn contract in early 1086 (early 1675).[82] However, the icāreteyn contained limitations that could be inconvenient to both parties to the contract. For the tenant, the chief restriction was that while the lease was inheritable, it could not otherwise be sold or transferred to third parties.[83] For the waqf supervisor, the icāreteyn still limited their freedom to negotiate, giving them only the choice between a standard three-year lease or an indefinite lease that would last until the tenant's descendants died out. It was a doctrine devised for a specific circumstance: to bring ruined buildings back into use. It was not intended to give greater flexibility to supervisors dealing with buildings in good condition. In Cairo, a simpler and more flexible approach based on Ḥanbalī and Mālikī doctrine was preferred. Both madhhabs allowed multiple, consecutive three-year leases to be arranged in a single contract: a transaction called *al-ijāra al-ṭawīla* (long lease).[84]

Long leases on waqf property were usually transacted by a Ḥanbalī nā'ib, and sometimes by a Mālikī. Similar to judicial divorce for abandoned wives, the parties to the lease first had to petition the Ḥanafī chief qāḍī for permission. An example is a sublease contract concluded by the Müteferrika officer ᶜĀbidīn ibn al-Amīr Muṣṭafā and al-Ḥājj Muḥammad ibn Salīm ibn Muḥammad, the headman (*shaykh al-nāḥiya*) of Bahramas district, before the Ḥanbalī nā'ib at Bāb al-Shaᶜriyya court on 15 Rabīᶜ al-Thānī 1078 (4 October 1667).[85] ᶜĀbidīn, who was acting as agent for his mother, Hibā Khātūn ibnat al-Amīr Bayram Çavuş, had submitted a petition to the Ḥanafī chief qāḍī, who gave permission to the Ḥanbalī nā'ib to oversee the transaction. The contract concerned a building close to the Shaᶜriyya gate and the Abū 'l-Wafā' market, which belonged to the waqf of al-Ḥājj Maḥfūẓ ibn Barakāt. Hibā held the *taṣarruf* (usufruct) of the property until the beginning of Rajab 1165 (15 May 1752), according to a document issued by the Mālikī nā'ib at the court of Bābay Saᶜāda wa 'l-Kharq on 23 Shaᶜbān 1077 (18 February 1667) and confirmed by the same court's Ḥanafī nā'ib. No further details of Hibā's acquisition of the property are given: presumably she had leased it herself directly from the waqf.

On Hibā's behalf, ᶜĀbidīn subleased the property to Muḥammad ibn Sālim, who assumed the taṣarruf for the full remaining period of Hibā's lease. In order to comply with the three-year limit on leases, the court record states that the property was sublet for twenty-nine successive contracts (*ᶜuqūd*, sing. *ᶜaqd*) of three years each, plus one further contract to run for two months and fifteen days. The total rent for the period was 6,740 silver niṣfs, of which Muḥammad handed over 5,000 in court, with the balance to be paid later. The Ḥanafī chief qāḍī then endorsed the contract, despite its illegitimacy from the perspective of Ḥanafī doctrine.

Another example is a contract concluded at the court of Bāb al-Shaᶜriyya on 1 Ramaḍān 1085 (29 November 1674). The lessor was a Coptic priest called Yaᶜqūb walad Yūsuf, who was supervisor of a waqf to benefit the Christian poor based at the Paromeos Monastery in Wādī al-Naṭrūn, Buḥayra. As in the previous example, Yaᶜqūb had petitioned the Ḥanafī chief qāḍī, who then referred the case to the

Ḥanbalī nā˒ib at Bāb al-Sha˓riyya. The waqf that Ya˓qūb supervised owned a small covered gallery (*riwāq*) in Darb al-Ibrāhīmī, which had been leased to a goldsmith called Tādrus walad Girgis until the end of 1098 (6 November 1687). Ya˓qūb and Tādrus came to the Bāb al-Sha˓riyya court to extend this period by signing a new lease, to begin immediately upon the expiry of the current one. The new lease was to last for twenty-five successive contracts of three years each; the rent was thirty silver niṣfs per year, to be paid annually. Documents issued by the Mālikī nā˒ib at the court of al-Ṣāliḥiyya al-Najmiyya, dated 21 Muḥarram and 23 Shawwāl 1084 (8 May 1673 and 31 January 1674) showed that Tādrus had already paid a lump sum of 2,400 niṣfs for the original lease.[86]

Madhhab-pluralism has often been presented as an example of forum-shopping, in which shrewd litigants, well-versed in the doctrinal differences between the madhhabs, could choose the madhhab that best suited their purposes.[87] The practice of judicial divorce and long-term leases within seventeenth-century Cairo's courts qualifies this image. It was not simply a free-for-all, or what legal theorists have called strong legal pluralism.[88] The state structured the options available, controlling access to non-Ḥanafī doctrines. The fact that women requiring a judicial divorce and people arranging long leases were required to petition the Ḥanafī chief qāḍī is also significant. Petitions were generally written by professional petition-writers, ˓arżuḥālcis, as described in Chapter 3. This additional bureaucratic procedure placed an intermediary between ordinary litigants and the exploitation of madhhab pluralism. It is not clear that most litigants were themselves well versed in legal doctrine: rather, the legal solutions for different problems were encoded within the bureaucratic procedures of the court system, and professional practitioners communicated the options available to ordinary Cairenes, mediating between them and the complex madhhab-plural legal system.

Renewed attempts at Ḥanafization in the late seventeenth and eighteenth centuries

For most of the seventeenth century, the system of madhhab pluralism established at the beginning of the century continued to operate. The courts were staffed by nā˒ibs of all four madhhabs, under the authority of the Ḥanafī chief qāḍī. Cairenes were generally free to choose any of the four madhhabs for their litigations and contracts. However, certain controversial non-Ḥanafī transactions, including judicial divorce for abandoned women and long-term leases for waqf-owned properties, could only be performed under the supervision of the chief qāḍī. This meant that a person wishing to perform such a transaction could not approach a Shāfi˓ī, Mālikī, or Ḥanbalī nā˒ib directly; rather, he or she had to petition the chief qāḍī for permission, who would then refer the case to the appropriate nā˒ib.

In the last decade of the seventeenth century, the Ottoman authorities decided to restrict access to these controversial doctrines further. Chief qāḍīs from this period sent frequent orders to nā˒ibs and other officials of Cairo's courts, instructing them that henceforth they were prohibited outright from performing the controversial transactions, and threatening them with dismissal if they disobeyed. An early example is an order dated 18 Shawwāl 1107 (21 May 1696), recorded in the register of Bāb al-Shaᶜriyya court. The chief qāḍī informed all qāḍīs, nāᵓibs, and court witnesses (ᶜudūl)[89] that henceforth they were not to perform transactions involving any of a list of controversial doctrines: long-term leases for waqf properties (*al-tawājir al-ṭawīl*), the sale of dilapidated waqf-owned buildings (*mubāyiᶜāt al-anqāḍ*), the sale of waqf-owned assets in order to reinvest the proceeds in other assets (istibdāl), judicial divorce (faskh), and passing judgment on an absent party (*al-ḥukm ᶜalā ᵓl-ghāyib*). They were also forbidden from performing any transactions that fell under the jurisdiction of the Qisma al-ᶜAskariyya or the Qisma al-ᶜArabiyya, the specialized courts that dealt with the inheritances of members of the ruling class and civilians respectively. The order warned that anyone who did perform such a transaction would be dismissed.[90]

Many similar orders appear in this and later registers of the Bāb al-Shaᶜriyya court.[91] This change did not entail a complete ban on these doctrines. Some of the orders clarified that these transactions now fell under the exclusive jurisdiction of al-Bāb al-ᶜĀlī, Cairo's main sharīᶜa court.[92] These transactions would now be performed by the Shāfiᶜī, Mālikī, and Ḥanbalī nāᵓibs of that court, under the direct supervision of the chief qāḍī who presided there.[93] Although the order did not mention the Dīwān al-ᶜĀlī, its records show that long leases and istibdāl transactions were conducted there in the 1740s.[94] This makes sense, as transactions at the Dīwān could also be supervised directly either by the chief qāḍī or by the Qāḍī al-Dīwān who was closely connected to the chief qāḍī and the governor.

It is possible that the tightening of the restrictions was a response to abuse of the previous system. It certainly appears that the requirement to petition the chief qāḍī for permission was not universally observed in the case of long leases on waqf properties. For example, on 2 Rabīᶜ al-Thānī 1085 (6 July 1674), al-Shaykh Muḥammad ibn Muḥammad al-Aṣīlī, the supervisor of a waqf founded by his ancestor the qāḍī ᶜAlā al-Dīn al-Aṣīlī, leased a building owned by the waqf located in the Bahā al-Dīn Qarāqūsh neighborhood in Cairo, to Sayyid Muḥammad of the Banī ᶜAbd Manāf family. The lease was for a total of nine years, expressed as three consecutive contracts of three years each. The contract was concluded before the Ḥanbalī and Mālikī nāᵓibs at the Bāb al-Shaᶜriyya court, but there is no indication in the record of permission having been sought from or granted by the chief qāḍī.[95] Another example is a lease signed before the Ḥanbalī nāᵓib at Bāb al-Shaᶜriyya on 2 Rajab 1085 (2 October 1674). A Christian called Ghaṭās walad Yūsuf rented from his co-religionist ᶜAbd Rabb al-Masīḥ walad Manṣūr six shares in a hall belonging to the waqf founded by ᶜAbd Rabb al-Masīḥ's father. The lease was for six consecutive contracts of three years each: eighteen years in total. Again, the document does not mention permission from the chief qāḍī.[96]

Nevertheless, the different profile of the users of al-Bāb al-ᶜĀlī and the Dīwān al-ᶜĀlī compared to the neighborhood courts such as Bāb al-Shaᶜriyya suggests another interpretation. The reform of the 1690s was not simply an attempt to remedy a deficiency in the existing system. It was an attempt to significantly reduce the use of the controversial non-Ḥanafī doctrines, possibly with the ultimate aim of eliminating them altogether. Such an attempt was no doubt resisted by Cairenes, particularly with regard to the waqf-related doctrines, and the Ottoman government would have predicted such resistance. The long lease and istibdāl were particularly important to the elites, for whom the waqf was the main legal structure used to manage, preserve, and pass on their wealth. As explained in Chapter 2, the clientele of al-Bāb al-ᶜĀlī and the Dīwān al-ᶜĀlī was disproportionately made up of members of the political and scholarly elites, while ordinary folk tended to use the neighborhood courts. Limiting the use of the controversial doctrines to al-Bāb al-ᶜĀlī and the Dīwān al-ᶜĀlī restricted the availability of these doctrines and so reduced the profile of the non-Ḥanafī madhhabs, while allowing the elites to continue using the long lease and istibdāl to manage their awqāf. This way, the government avoided a confrontation with the powerful and often assertive provincial elites. In other words, I suggest that the Ottomans wanted to prohibit these transactions entirely, but restricting them to al-Bāb al-ᶜĀlī and the Dīwān al-ᶜĀlī was the most that they could achieve politically at this time.

Parallels in Syria

The revitalized campaign to Ḥanafize the legal system in Egypt during the late seventeenth and early eighteenth centuries had parallels in Ottoman Syria. Brigitte Marino found orders from the chief qāḍī of Damascus to the city's nāᵓibs and scribes from the second half of the eighteenth century and the early nineteenth century, forbidding them from undertaking a list of transactions which involved non-Ḥanafī doctrines or were of particular interest to the authorities.[97] Marino's study begins in 1750, so it is not clear whether such orders had also been given by chief qāḍīs earlier in the eighteenth century. In the case of Cairo, although these orders were first made in the 1690s, similar orders were still being issued sporadically during the first half of the eighteenth century.[98] Marino's orders may similarly be restatements or modifications of previous orders.

There is reason to believe that these orders formed part of a wider campaign to assert Ḥanafī supremacy, as we have further evidence that the Ottomans were promoting the Ḥanafī madhhab in eighteenth-century Syria. John Voll noticed a significant shift in the madhhab affiliations of the Damascus ulema during this period. Traditionally, most of the ulema in Syria, as in Lower Egypt, had been Shāfiᶜī. Although some individual Syrians switched to the Ḥanafī madhhab early in the Ottoman period,[99] Voll demonstrates that there was a much bigger wave of madhhab-switching between the middle of the seventeenth century, when the notable ulema families in Damascus remained predominantly Shāfiᶜī, and the middle of the eighteenth century, when a clear majority of ulema families were Ḥanafī. Voll argues that this was due to an Ottoman policy of rewarding Ḥanafīs with official posts, which formed part of a wider strategy of promoting "cosmopolitan" scholars, who had connections outside Damascus and in particular in Istanbul, over scholars who were locally-rooted. Many of the ulema who switched to the Ḥanafī madhhab also made an effort to build networks in the capital.[100]

As with the story I have told about Cairo, Ḥanafization in eighteenth-century Syria should be placed into a longer narrative of contestation between the Ottoman ideal of Ḥanafī uniformity and the pluralistic legal culture of the Arab provinces. Immediately after the conquest of Damascus, Sultan Selim replaced the city's Ḥanafī chief qāḍī with his own candidate, and named him "Shaykh al-Islām," a title which had formerly been held by the preeminent jurist in the city, regardless of madhhab. This shocked Damascus's ulema, according to the chronicler Ibn Ṭulūn, and Selim's announcement that a Ḥanafī should give the Friday sermon at the Umayyad Mosque provoked a brawl between Ḥanafī and Shāfiʿī scholars. In 1590, the new governor of Damascus dismissed all the non-Ḥanafī qāḍīs in the city and declared that all cases should be heard by the Ḥanafī qāḍī. The court scribes and translators went on strike in response; the standoff continued until the mufti of Damascus spoke out against the reform, at which point the governor backed down and reinstated the dismissed qāḍīs.[101] This attempt to Ḥanafize Damascus's courts took place just ten years before the attempt to Ḥanafize Cairo's courts by the chief qāḍī ʿAbd al-Wahhāb ibn Ibrāhīm al-Rūmī, which I discussed above.

Both Egypt and Syria underwent similar struggles between Ḥanafī uniformity and madhhab pluralism under Ottoman rule. They were not exactly parallel, and during the seventeenth and eighteenth centuries the Ottomans' pursuit of Ḥanafization seems to have been more successful in Syria. But the general pattern of periods of attempted Ḥanafization followed by the reassertion of the local pluralistic legal culture was the same. There was also a rough correspondence in the chronology of this process in both regions: an initial push to Ḥanafize in the years after the conquest that petered out by the middle of the sixteenth century, a second brief period of Ḥanafizing pressure around the turn of the seventeenth century, and then a more sustained push that began towards the end of the seventeenth century and continued through the eighteenth. The tools used by the Ottomans were also similar in both regions: they included purging non-Ḥanafī qāḍīṣ and nāʾibs from the courts, restricting the availability of certain non-Ḥanafī doctrines, and favoring Ḥanafīs for senior appointments.[102] In both provinces, complete Ḥanafization had to wait until the nineteenth century, when new tools such as codification were employed.

While full Ḥanafization was never achieved in Egypt or Syria before the nineteenth century, the Ottomans' efforts in the earlier period were an extension of a campaign that had succeeded in Ḥanafizing the legal establishment in Anatolia during the fifteenth and early sixteenth centuries. The difference was partly due to resistance on the part of the Syrian and Egyptian scholarly elite, who had a particularly pluralistic intellectual culture and who maintained a greater distance from the ilmiye hierarchy than their Anatolian counterparts. It was also due to the entrenched attachment to madhhab pluralism and to useful non-Ḥanafī doctrines among the populations of Syria and Egypt, such that aggressive Ḥanafizing reform always risked alienating the public.

Madhhab pluralism and legal change

The Ottoman authorities' attempts to Ḥanafize Egypt, and the reactions by the Egyptian ulema, had an impact on what legal doctrines were available to users of the legal system in Cairo. This story has implications for our understanding of change in Islamic legal history. The extent to which post-classical Islamic law was capable of change has been one of the central controversies in Islamic legal historiography. The traditional narrative associated with Orientalist scholarship held that the replacement of *ijtihād* (independent reasoning) with *taqlīd* (following juristic precedent) as the guiding principle of Islamic jurisprudence in the tenth century CE signaled the end of innovation in Islamic law.[103] The "closing of the gates of ijtihād" was one component of what Orientalist scholarship perceived as the general stagnation and decline of Islamic civilization after the glory years of the ᶜAbbasid caliphate.

The question of innovation was closely intertwined with western scholarship's understanding of the relationship between Islamic jurisprudence and Muslim legal practice. If, as Joseph Schacht claimed, Islamic law suited "the social and economic conditions of the early ᶜAbbasid period,"[104] and had grown increasingly distant from social and political reality ever since, then it must have become increasingly irrelevant to the actual administration of justice. Its place was taken by the brute power of the Oriental despot and/or the arbitrary kadijustiz conceived by Weber, based on expediency rather than law.

The scholarship of the last few decades has effectively undermined the idea that post-classical Islamic law was an ossified relic with little relevance to real life. Scholars have challenged this idea from two main angles. Wael Hallaq has been the most prolific and authoritative voice questioning the central contention of the earlier Orientalists: the claim that ijtihād formally ended. Hallaq showed that, between the ninth and eleventh centuries CE, outright opponents of ijtihād were a minority who were eventually squeezed out of the Sunnī mainstream. Subsequently, while the question who was qualified to practice ijtihād remained a source of controversy, ijtihād was always accepted in principle as a legitimate tool of legal interpretation, alongside taqlīd.[105] Hallaq convincingly established that the pre-modern Muslim debate surrounding ijtihād was far richer and more complex than had previously been recognized. But his argument still implied that ijtihād, as a manifestation of human rationality, was superior to taqlīd as a method of legal reasoning.

Other scholars have questioned this assumption and have followed an alternative line of argument. They have accepted that taqlīd became the dominant mode of legal scholarship and that ijtihād was marginalized, if not prohibited, but they have denied that taqlīd was equivalent to intellectual stagnation. In other words, they have asked why the Orientalists routinely translated taqlīd as "slavish imitation," rather than as "following precedent." Mohammed Fadel argued that taqlīd was a response to a widely accepted need for predictability in the law.[106] Baber Johansen distinguished between different genres of legal writing, suggesting that while some genres served to transmit the madhhab's established doctrines for the purpose of education, the fatwā gave jurists the opportunity to respond creatively to new situations and was directly linked to court practice.[107] A detailed insight into what taqlīd as a method of legal interpretation involved was given by Sherman Jackson in his account of the sixteenth-century Mālikī jurist Badr al-Dīn al-Qarāfī's treatise on contested custody of children. Jackson presented Qarāfī's approach to the problem as a creative process conducted within the parameters of precedent: with the accumulated body of Mālikī doctrine as his primary frame of reference, rather than the Koran and ḥadīth.[108]

What unites the different approaches of Hallaq, Fadel, Johansen, and Jackson is their focus on doctrinal change: they investigate to what extent jurists were able to develop new or revised doctrines in response to current circumstances. This is an important project that is far from complete; Ottoman-era fiqh is particularly understudied. But if we are interested in the ability of legal systems to respond to changing social, economic, and political circumstances—in other words, if we are interested in changes in applied law—then we should recognize that doctrinal innovation was not necessary to effect legal change. Rather than looking for evidence of dynamism among jurists, we can look at how the main actors in historical legal systems—the governments that ran them and the private individuals who used them—were able to maneuver to advance their interests within a framework of juristic conservatism. Only if this framework were so rigid that it prevented these actors from pursuing their interests, so that they were forced to ignore the law, would we be able to conclude that Islamic law was immutable and therefore irrelevant to legal practice.

In fact, the legal framework was not anything like that rigid. Islamic law was a vast legal tradition that encompassed a huge variety of doctrines, interpretations, and opinions. Even within a single madhhab, the huge body of legal scholarship contained numerous, often mutually contradictory, opinions on any one issue. Change at the level of applied law could be effected without devising any new doctrines, but simply by choosing to follow different opinions drawn from the accumulated tradition. With the plurality of madhhabs, the flexibility of tradition was that much greater. While individual qāḍīs and jurists were bound to follow the precedents of their own madhhabs, a Muslim society had at its disposal the doctrines of all four.

Yossef Rapoport has demonstrated how the Mamluk Sultanate used madhhab pluralism to pick and choose particular doctrines that suited political and social preferences. The Mamluks softened the patriarchal strictures of Islamic family law, while toughening the position on heresy and apostasy. The authorities and private actors within Mamluk society were able to pursue their interests, and achieve changes in the applied law, without any doctrinal innovation on the part of jurists. The supposed rigidity of taqlīd turned out to be quite flexible, given the variety of different options the society could choose to follow.

Rapoport suggested that, for the most part, the views and interests of the judicial establishment were in harmony with those of the Mamluk government. The two collaborated to produce a plural legal system in which certain doctrines were systematically prioritized.[109] By contrast, in Ottoman Egypt there was a divergence of views between those judges who had built their careers in Egypt, who were largely in favor of pluralism, and the Ottoman authorities and ilmiye-trained qāḍīs, who preferred to move towards a uniform Ḥanafī court system. At several points during the Ottoman period in Egypt, the authorities made efforts to close down some of the options available to Cairenes, in order to bring Egyptian legal practice into line with that in the central lands of the empire. Unlike the Mamluks, whose pragmatic approach selected doctrines for their ability to solve particular problems, the Ottomans were driven by ideology and imperial legitimation. Many ilmiye jurists saw the Ḥanafī madhhab as superior, while the promotion of legal uniformity formed part of the government's imperial state-building strategy which, from the reign of Suleyman I, tied Ottoman legitimacy to law.

While the Ottoman authorities were able to control and limit the use of controversial non-Ḥanafī doctrines, they did not fully succeed in suppressing their use and imposing Ḥanafī uniformity on Cairo's legal system. However, their failure to achieve this was not due to any rigidity inherent in Islamic law. On the contrary, it was due to politics: Ḥanafization was opposed by the Cairene judicial establishment and the city's wider population, and the Ottomans recognized that they needed to balance their commitment to Ḥanafism with the need to avoid alienating their Egyptian subjects, in particular those who were wealthy and powerful. This political struggle took place within the accumulated legal tradition, which was large and diverse enough to accommodate both sides in this long-running conflict. As with the earlier Mamluk example, we can see that the law *as it was applied* could undergo significant change and development without any innovation in doctrine.

Conclusion

Students of nineteenth-century legal reform in the Ottoman Empire and Egypt have commented that one of the central effects of the reform process was to make what had been a highly flexible legal regime very rigid. Ḥanafization, along with its logical successor, the codification of Ḥanafī law, was the mechanism that made the legal system rigid. This new rigidity was particularly hard on women. The more flexible pre-modern Ottoman legal system—especially in the Arab provinces—gave women more opportunities to defend their interests within marriage and to end their marriages if necessary. Early modern Ottoman qāḍīs and nāʾibs took seriously their role to defend women against their husbands, albeit only so far as the patriarchal legal norms gave women defensible rights. In other words, the pre-modern legal system not only offered the potential for flexibility, but its judges were committed to exploiting that flexibility in order to secure the best possible deal for women. Nineteenth-century legal reform undermined the judges' commitment to this by insisting on the application of Ḥanafī law, which of the four madhhabs was the least favorable to women's marital rights.[110]

The essence of these arguments is that it is not Islamic law that is rigid and harmful to women, as is often supposed. Rather, it was the modernization of Islamic law, which involved the introduction of European concepts and ideals, that produced the rigidly patriarchal structure of Muslim family law observable in the modern world. The findings in this chapter do not undermine the first part of this argument: it is certainly true that the pre-modern Ottoman-Islamic legal system was flexible in many ways, that this flexibility was useful for women, and that much of this flexibility was lost during the period of reforms. What the observations in this chapter call into question is the association of the reformed legal system's rigidity with European influence: the claim that it was *European* ideals of uniformity, standardization, and codification that produced this outcome. I have argued in this chapter that a desire to Ḥanafize the Egyptian legal system, in the name of uniformity and standardization across Ottoman territories, was present from the beginning of Ottoman rule in Egypt. While not shared by everyone within the Ottoman administration, it was a prominent strand of thought that periodically came to the fore and led to attempts to restrict the non-Ḥanafī madhhabs in various ways. Attempts at Ḥanafization in Egypt had limited success, but this was due to the weakness of the early modern Ottoman state. The measures were unpopular among the Egyptian population, legal professionals, and laypeople, and the government's attempts at Ḥanafization met widespread opposition.

What changed in the nineteenth century was the power and ambition of the state in Egypt. Meḥmed ᶜAlī's regime and its successors achieved unprecedented levels of control over Egyptian society, largely thanks to military and bureaucratic reforms. The greater power of the nineteenth-century Egyptian state, and its greater determination to bring Egypt's institutions to heel, enabled it to pursue Ḥanafization much more aggressively and successfully. A very similar story can be told of the reformed Ottoman state and its control over the rest of the empire. Rather than describing the nineteenth-century Ḥanafization of Egypt's legal system as an example of European influence, we are better off seeing it as the culmination of Ottoman influence. This interpretation chimes with several revisionist works on nineteenth-century Egyptian history that stress the greater Ottomanization of Egyptian institutions, society, and cultural life, even as Egypt drifted away from Istanbul's control.[111]

CHAPTER

5

THE PRIVATIZATION OF JUSTICE: DISPUTE RESOLUTION AS A DOMAIN OF POLITICAL COMPETITION

In Jabartī's biography of ᶜUthmān Bey Dhū ᵓl-Faqār, a prominent figure in Cairo politics during the first half of the eighteenth century, there is the following intriguing passage:

> [ᶜUthmān Bey] held sessions in his house to hear cases involving the common people and to dispense justice to the oppressed against their oppressors. He established a special *dīwān* to hear cases involving women and to dispense sentences in strict accordance with *sharīᶜa* law (*wa lā yajrī aḥkāmuhu illā ᶜalā muqtaḍā ᵓl-sharīᶜa*). He refused bribes and punished those who gave them. He supervised matters of *ḥisba* in person. As a kindness to the poor, he fixed the price of bread and other items, including wax, coal, and similar commodities. He forbade the *muḥtasib* from taking bribes, and he chased false witnesses from the courts. He used to send his retainers to supervise the gathering of shares due (for pious purposes), even from the amīrs. He was never known to have confiscated anyone's property or to have taken any share of anyone's inheritance.[1]

This passage is fascinating on a number of levels; here I will draw out two aspects. First, ᶜUthmān Bey is said to have founded his own court to resolve disputes among Cairenes. ᶜUthmān Bey held a number of important positions in the administration of Ottoman Egypt: he was appointed *amīr al-ḥajj* for a total of four years, and was also appointed supervisor of three of the great blocs of *awqāf al-ḥaramayn* in Egypt: the Murādiyya, the Khāṣṣakiyya, and the Vālide Sulṭān.[2] He was one of the most important figures in Cairo during the late 1720s and 1730s; by the early 1740s he was, according to Damurdāshī, the most powerful man in the city.[3] But he was never appointed as either qāḍī or governor in Egypt, and so was never formally charged with operating a court. His establishment of his personal dīwān reflected the privatization of the provision of justice in eighteenth-century Egypt. It was an act of personal aggrandizement that sought to bolster ᶜUthmān Bey's power and his reputation among the Cairo populace; it was also a direct challenge to the authority of the governor.

Second, Jabartī describes this development positively: he is, in fact, gushing in his praise for the standards of justice achieved by ᶜUthmān Bey's forum. There are several reasons, connected with personal relationships and with the political circumstances of the early nineteenth-century context in which he wrote, why Jabartī might have taken this position. But the reason he offers is that ᶜUthmān Bey provided a clean alternative to the corrupt official legal system. Although Jabartī refrains from making any specific, direct accusations, he implies that prior to ᶜUthmān Bey's innovation, the muḥtasib was venal, the courts were riddled with false witnesses, the wealthy amīrs routinely evaded their contributions to the public purse, and property-owners were at constant risk of the seizure of their assets. The mid eighteenth-century chronicler Damurdāshī also reports ᶜUthmān Bey's creation of his own dīwān, and is similarly, though more succinctly, positive about the move, claiming that ᶜUthmān Bey "upheld justice and abolished wrong."[4]

It is interesting that both Damurdāshī and Jabartī approved of ᶜUthmān Bey's actions, as the two chroniclers were from very different backgrounds. Damurdāshī was a Cairene soldier of the mid eighteenth century, who was intimately involved in Cairo's factional politics, and who wrote only a decade and a half after ᶜUthmān Bey was at the pinnacle of his power. He did not have any scholarly training and his chronicle had no literary pretensions, often reading like a compendium of barracks gossip. Damurdāshī was sympathetic to ᶜUthmān Bey's faction and so, on partisan grounds, it is not surprising that he praised ᶜUthman Bey's dīwān. The position of Jabartī is more intriguing. Again, there were personal factors at work. Jabartī's family had been connected to ᶜUthmān Bey's household: Jabartī claims that his father had tutored and copied manuscripts for ᶜUthmān.[5] But Jabartī was a scholar who had received a traditional education in the religious sciences. He was well acquainted with the Islamic legal tradition, which insisted that the legitimacy of a judge rested on his appointment by the sovereign. ᶜUthmān Bey had not been appointed as a judge by the sovereign, and so the legitimacy of his judgments was doubtful according to legal theory. Yet Jabartī nevertheless described him as successfully implementing the sharīᶜa.

There are other interesting features of Jabartī's account: in particular, why was ᶜUthmān Bey particularly concerned with the rights of women? I will address this question briefly in what follows, although the answer is obscure. However, the focus of this chapter will be an exploration of the two issues outlined above. I will tell the history of the privatization of justice in the late seventeenth and early eighteenth centuries, and of the Ottoman authorities' response to this. I also ask what contemporary Egyptians thought about this process, and what they thought more generally about the standards of justice achieved by the various official and unofficial dispute resolution practices available in Ottoman Cairo.

Privatization in the seventeenth- and eighteenth-century Ottoman Empire

The privatization of justice described in this chapter occurred in the context of the long-term process of privatization of revenue-collection over the course of the seventeenth and eighteenth centuries, which has been discussed in Ottoman historiography following the classic article by Ariel Salzmann. The spread first of fixed-term, and later of life-term, tax-farming contracts, which by the mid eighteenth century had become the standard model for revenue collection throughout the empire, transferred control of revenue sources to private investors.[6]

The privatization of justice was loosely connected to the privatization of revenue-collection, but distinct from it. It was connected because the privatization of revenue-collection implied the privatization of political office itself and the various functions that derived from it. The rural tax-farmer was a figure of significant authority in the village; urban tax-farmers and customs-farmers wielded authority within the relevant trade. The tax-farmer had not only to collect the revenue, through coercion if necessary, but also to organize, or at least supervise, the underlying economic activity to ensure that it continued to produce sufficient revenue to ensure the government's due and the tax-farmer's profit. Tax-farming came with political obligations and political power.[7]

Categorizing an eighteenth-century political actor like ᶜUthmān Bey Dhū ᵓl-Faqār as either a public or a private figure is, therefore, problematic. ᶜUthmān's title of "bey" was granted to him by the Ottoman governor; he was also appointed by the governor to important administrative positions such as amīr al-ḥājj (commander of the pilgrimage) and supervisor of imperial awqāf. But his power and authority also derived from private sources. He owned the tax-farms of many villages: he held these positions as a private contractor, having purchased them with his master Dhū ᵓl-Faqār Bey's capital early in his career, and later with his own. Like other beys, ᶜUthmān maintained an extensive household that included a private militia composed of his own mamlūks and retainers. This militia was available to ᶜUthmān Bey for his own ends, such as the defense of his property and the pursuit of feuds, but was also used for his public functions, such as the protection of the pilgrimage caravan. The public and private aspects of ᶜUthmān Bey's power were very much intertwined: each could be used to bolster the other. It was the wealth and power of his household that made him a suitable candidate for high office. Conversely, his attainment of high office gave him further opportunities to build his household through patronage: for example, in 1740–1 (1153 AH) ᶜUthmān Bey's position as amīr al-ḥājj allowed him to reward his mamlūk Sulaymān Kāshif by subcontracting the pilgrimage to him.[8]

The privatization of revenue-collection via tax-farming therefore created a context in which an increasing number of government functions were being performed by private actors: provincial notables whose wealth and security was increasingly independent of the pleasure of the Sultan. It is not surprising that some of these private actors were encouraged to overreach, by seeking to add dispute resolution to their range of powers. Of the various functions of government, justice is one of the most useful in terms of its potential for securing respect, dependence, and loyalty. It was not the imperial government's intention, however, to devolve responsibility for justice onto provincial notables. Indeed, a court system independent of the notables who dominated tax-farming was essential for the smooth functioning of society, as the qāḍī was the main authority who could redress the grievances of taxpayers against abusive tax-farmers.[9]

Two important features of this private justice stand out. The first is that it was not licensed by the government and was offered as an alternative to the official court system. While ᶜUthmān Bey and others like him held administrative or military appointments, they were not charged with resolving disputes and so their judgments were illegitimate from the perspective of both Ottoman political theory and Islamic procedural law. In other words, this was not simply a case of the sovereign or the judge deputizing an agent to carry out the function on their behalf. It involved powerful men in a private capacity arrogating to themselves the right to resolve disputes.

The other feature is that the provision of private justice was deeply enmeshed in the politics of late seventeenth and early eighteenth-century Egypt, forming part of the strategies of men like ᶜUthmān Bey to build their political capital and their households. This meant that it followed two impulses: to reward clients as part of the exchange of favors and loyalties that was the currency of household-building, and to bolster one's reputation by demonstrating a commitment to justice.[10] These aims might seem mutually contradictory, but the tension between them is an example of the balancing of the interests of one's core support base and an appeal to wider society that is inherent in any political career. In practice, it meant that while justice was not dispensed for free, as payment in loyalty was expected, there was a limit to the protection that a bey's client could expect. The tension is evident in the narration of these activities by the chroniclers; narratives which probably derived from oral stories circulating in Egypt during the protagonists' careers. The fact that chroniclers prominently recorded these stories about justice points to the significance of justice in the legitimation of power; that the stories sometimes touch on the issue of patron–client relations show that private justice was not without controversy.

A concept similar to private justice has been used by social scientists seeking to explain the emergence of modern mafia groups. In his account of the Sicilian mafia, Diego Gambetta describes the mafia's core function as private protection.[11] This term denotes a phenomenon analogous to what I am describing: the provision of dispute resolution services by private actors.[12] Federico Varese makes a similar argument about the mafia in post-Soviet Russia.[13] Gambetta's model of the Sicilian mafia is complex and he argues that different mafiosi provide protection on different terms: lower-ranking mafiosi often accept cash payment, while the upper echelons and bosses prefer to build long-term relationships that secure the client's loyalty and embed him or her in a network of obligations that include providing favors and directing business to mafia-controlled companies. Either way, the mafia privatize what we assume to be a public function, and so subvert it to serve their own purposes.

Despite the ruthless violence of the Sicilian and Russian mafias, and the selective nature of their protection, Gambetta and Varese agree that in most individual cases the protection they provide is fair, in the sense that they enforce agreements and contracts.[14] As with Egypt's beys, mafia bosses are often keen to cultivate a reputation for justice and integrity, within a moral framework based on their domination. Moreover, the provision of private protection is far more effective at building a client base if people are attracted to the mafia's services and voluntarily use them, so that coercion is not necessary. This relies on the service being basically fair. Indeed, while the protection racket is clearly a feature of both mafias' activities, their core dispute resolution function is mostly used voluntarily by people who dislike or are excluded from the official courts in Italy and Russia. Another parallel between the dispute resolution activities of Egypt's beys and the Sicilian and Russian mafias is that they all emerged during periods when private ownership of property was expanding, in the sense of a growing number of property-owners, or a growing amount of property subject to private ownership, or both. The relevant historical contexts are the privatization of state revenues in the seventeenth and eighteenth-century Ottoman Empire, the break-up of the large rural estates in nineteenth-century Sicily, and the privatization of Russian state assets after the fall of communism. Gambetta and Varese argue that the expansion of property ownership created demand for protection from theft, fraud, and usurpation, and this rapidly expanding demand overwhelmed the capacities of the Italian and Russian courts, making the mafia's services attractive.

The privatization of justice has received little attention from previous Ottomanists. There are several reasons for this. First, because the privatization of justice was not an officially-endorsed process, it did not produce official documentation, and so is not very visible in the sources which historians rely upon. The recent generation of revisionist Ottoman historiography has for the most part been based on archival research; narrative sources, where privatized justice is observable, have been relatively under-scrutinized. This is particularly true of provincial Ottoman history.

Second, the privatization of justice sits uneasily with the emerging dominant paradigms of both Islamic legal history and Ottoman history. As discussed in this book's introduction, Islamic legal historiography has emphasized the qāḍī as the central figure in the administration of justice in the pre-modern period, and has marginalized the role of political authorities. A central argument of this book, however, is that Islamic law in Ottoman Egypt was never a pristine sphere uncontaminated by political involvement. The sharīʿa was always political: rulers and their officials were always involved in its definition and implementation, and so it is not surprising that it became an object of political contestation as the relationships among those political authorities changed over time.

Meanwhile, recent Ottoman historiography has stressed the continuing vitality of the seventeenth and eighteenth-century Ottoman Empire and dismantled the idea of "Ottoman decline." Historians have interpreted privatized revenue-collection, or tax-farming, as a creative adaptation to changing political and economic circumstances, rather than as a symptom of waning power. However, we instinctively see justice as the natural prerogative of the imperial government, and so its privatization is prima facie difficult to square with the new positive narrative of early modern Ottoman history. The assumption underlying this apparent disconnect is that the privatization of justice is illegitimate. This assumption is clear in a study of a similar phenomenon in an earlier period of Egyptian history. Robert Irwin described the privatization of justice in fifteenth-century Cairo under the Mamluk Sultanate; he claimed that the justice offered by the amīrs and junior mamlūks who began resolving disputes during this period "will not have differed very much from that offered by Don Corleone."[15] But while this assumption is instinctive for modern historians living in stable states with representative governments, the calculation of subjects in pre-modern societies as to who best protected their interests is not so obvious.[16] As we have seen, Jabartī, a leading scholar of late eighteenth and early nineteenth-century Egypt, held a different opinion, regarding the privatized justice of ʿUthmān Bey Dhū ʾl-Faqār as commendable, and even as superior to the official justice provided by the Ottoman state's courts. His outlook was not unusual, but was shared by other eighteenth-century Egyptian commentators.

Narrative sources and contemporary attitudes

In contrast to the rest of this book, this chapter is based largely on narrative sources: chronicles and biographical dictionaries written by Egyptians in the eighteenth and early nineteenth centuries. Stories of private justice appear in the chronicles as anecdotes, intruding into the narrative, and are used to highlight the qualities of prominent characters. My shift in focus to narrative sources reflects the fact that chronicles and biographical works contain the only evidence for the dispute resolution activities of personalities such as ʿUthmān Bey: their forums did not produce any documentation that has survived. It is also a productive approach, as these narrative sources provide a perspective on Ottoman legal practice which has not previously been explored by historians. Narrative sources give us insight into what contemporary Egyptians thought about Cairo's legal institutions and legal processes.

Historians have paid little attention to the question of what Ottomans thought about their legal system. Those who have addressed this issue have tended to assume that Ottomans thought the legal system fair, on the grounds that historians can observe it operating fairly in the court records, and that Ottomans were frequent and extensive users of the courts.[17] There are three problems with such an assumption. First, any corruption would not appear in the court records: the qāḍī and court officials would create a façade of fairness and would not admit corruption on paper. Second, even if corruption was minimal and the courts were generally fair, it does not necessarily follow that Ottomans would have approved of the system. There are things other than corruption which one might object to; modern Americans have a reasonable degree of faith in the fairness of the court process and the integrity of their judges, but they complain about the US legal system's expense and its encouragement of litigiousness. Third, use of the courts does not imply endorsement of them, but simply reflects a recognition that they are useful, which is compatible with them being flawed. An exploration of the attitudes of Ottomans to their legal system cannot rely on inferences from their participation in it, but must involve the investigation of contemporary commentary on the courts.[18]

The narrative sources of the period were partisan and polemical. Justice was an important component of political legitimation, and so it is not surprising that stories surrounding law and legal practice appear fairly often. The polemical nature of these stories, which serve to praise people the chronicler favors and to denigrate those he opposes, makes them problematic as sources of information on how courts and other dispute resolution forums actually functioned. But it makes them ideal for an investigation of attitudes. In the following sections I will investigate popular attitudes to the sharīᶜa courts and to the privatized justice of Cairo's beys and officers through an examination of several polemical stories.

The righteous soldier: Küçük Muḥammad

The first story I will discuss concerns Küçük Muḥammad, a soldier who was *başodabaşı* of the Janissaries at various points during the 1680s and 90s.[19] Küçük Muḥammad was feted by chroniclers as a just soldier who took the side of the common people against the corrupt and the powerful. As a senior Janissary officer, he exercised authority over aspects of marketplace trading and public morality, under the command of the Janissary Āghā, as detailed in Chapter 2. The chronicles detail his activities in these spheres: he was said to have clamped down on speculators who forced up the prices of staples during periods of drought, and abolished the extraordinary taxes levied on merchants and artisans by the regiments (the ḥimāyāt).[20]

The story discussed here, however, sees Küçük Muḥammad resolving a dispute between two subjects—a jeweler and his friend—over misappropriated property. The story is recounted in several chronicles including those by Jabartī and Qinalī, and an anonymous manuscript in Cambridge; its fullest rendition is given by Damurdāshī.[21] The dispute that Küçük Muḥammad resolves fell within the jurisdiction of the courts—indeed, the dispute is first heard by a nāᵓib—and lay outside the formal responsibility of a Janissary officer. The story is a legend and clearly not true: it is in fact a floating legend that was attached to other characters by other chroniclers.[22] Its interest to us here is two-fold. First, although we cannot take any of its details as empirical evidence, it does suggest that intervening in a property dispute between two private individuals was the kind of thing that Küçük Muḥammad did. The basic premise of the story must have been plausible for it to have served its purpose of bolstering Küçük Muḥammad's reputation. Second, the story is used by the chroniclers to praise Küçük Muḥammad's virtues. We can therefore learn what type of approach to dispute resolution the chroniclers thought praiseworthy. Their favored approach differed considerably from that taken by the sharīᶜa courts. Indeed, in Damurdāshī's rendition the two approaches are explicitly compared, to the disadvantage of the sharīᶜa court nāᵓib, making this account particularly fascinating.[23]

I am, therefore, interested less in the story of the jeweler and his friend than I am in the way it is told.

The jeweler had undertaken the pilgrimage to Mecca, and before he departed had left a trunk containing jewelry—both his stock and his wife's personal effects—with a friend of his called ᶜAlī al-Fayyūmī. He returned after having lived at Mecca for two years, and went to retrieve his trunk and to give ᶜAlī a gift for having looked after it. ᶜAlī, however, feigned ignorance of the trunk and claimed never to have met the jeweler. The jeweler first went to al-Bāb al-ᶜĀlī, Cairo's main sharīᶜa court, to plead his case. When ᶜAlī denied his claim, the nāʾib asked the jeweler for evidence. The jeweler was unable to provide any, and protested that he never imagined he would need proof, since he was leaving the trunk with a friend. The nāʾib, following correct procedure, told the jeweler that he could demand ᶜAlī's oath, but the jeweler declined. The nāʾib then found in favor of ᶜAlī, forbidding the jeweler from making his claim again, and issued a ḥujja (certificate) confirming this to ᶜAlī.

Later the jeweler, on the advice of an acquaintance, went to the house of Küçük Muḥammad and told him his story. Küçük Muḥammad told the jeweler to hide within the interior of the house, and dispatched a servant to fetch ᶜAlī. When ᶜAlī arrived, Küçük Muḥammad engaged him in conversation, at one point taking ᶜAlī's prayer beads and using them to say some prayers. He then excused himself, and sent his servant to ᶜAlī's house with instructions to say that ᶜAlī had confessed to Küçük Muḥammad and wanted the trunk sent to his house. The servant was to show the prayer beads as proof that he had been sent by ᶜAlī. While the servant was away, Küçük Muḥammad once more conversed with ᶜAlī, at one point raising the issue of the jeweler's trunk, of which ᶜAlī denied all knowledge, suggesting that the jeweler had mistaken him for someone else. Meanwhile, Küçük Muḥammad's ruse fooled ᶜAlī's wife, and the servant returned with the trunk, bringing it into the courtyard where they were sitting, at which ᶜAlī's face turned deathly pale. Küçük Muḥammad summoned the jeweler, checked that his key fit the trunk's lock and that his inventory matched its contents, and then returned the trunk to him. He decided not to punish ᶜAlī, thinking his fear and shame at being discovered to be sufficient.

What is particularly interesting about Damurdāshī's rendition of this legend is the way that he structures it: around a comparison between the nāʾib's failure to achieve justice and Küçük Muḥammad's success. As well as lionizing Küçük Muḥammad, Damurdāshī adopts a cynical attitude towards the nāʾib. Whereas Küçük Muḥammad acts decisively, investigates the case and uses his wit to prove ᶜAlī's wrongdoing, the nāʾib is passive, hidebound by legal procedures which prevent him from investigating. The nāʾib deals perfunctorily with the case because the jeweler has no proof, although the jeweler protests that he hadn't thought he would need any, as he was depositing the trunk with a friend. The sharīᶜa court, as presented by Damurdāshī, allows the unscrupulous to take advantage of the honest.

Damurdāshī's portrayal is a caricature, but it chimes with an underlying truth about the operation of Ottoman sharīᶜa courts, as effective satire should. Ottoman sharīᶜa courts were characterized by rigorous adherence to procedure. Islamic legal procedure was passive and adversarial rather than inquisitorial. Litigants themselves were responsible for prosecution and defense, and for the gathering and presentation of evidence. The evidentiary options were, for the most part, limited to eye-witness testimony, the defendant's confession, and the defendant's oath (or his or her refusal to take it). The qāḍī's job was to facilitate this process, and to assess the litigants' evidence according to the criteria laid down in the fiqh texts. These criteria were mechanical and related to the status of the witness and the formal qualities of the statement, rather than to the plausibility of what was said.[24]

This procedure-mindedness was informed by a certain conception of justice. Inherent in this conception was a reluctance to use the state's coercive power to inflict violence on an individual, whether by punishing, appropriating property, or compelling action. Only when strict procedural safeguards had been met could such violence be justified.[25] The appeal of this conception is clear, but the counter position is also compelling: rules are manipulable and their strict application can easily lead to travesties of common-sense justice. This tension between legality and justice is not unique to Islamic legal systems: it is the basis for the drama in countless police procedurals on TV. The tension is particularly acute in a pre-modern legal system with unsophisticated forms of evidence. Given the Ottoman system's overwhelming reliance on eye-witness testimony, two glaring problems are apparent. The first is that unless one was meticulous in arranging for witnesses to be present at all significant moments in one's life, it would be difficult to prove anything if one ended up in a legal dispute: this was the jeweler's problem.[26] The second is that those with dishonest associates had great opportunities for fraud: as long as a witness maintained his public status of ᶜadāla (integrity), anything he said in court would be considered proof. It is not surprising that some contemporaries were contemptuous of the courts' cautious procedures, seeing them as allowing the devious and the powerful to prevail over the honest and the weak, and preferring a strong leader who took matters into his own hands and used his intelligence and, if necessary, violence to uncover wrongdoing.

The corrupt retainer: Sayfī

Chroniclers did not always approve of the interventions of military officials in disputes. Damurdāshī rails against a corrupt and irreligious man called Sayfī, whom he accuses of intervening in disputes on behalf of his master's clients and allies and in return for bribes. Again, the stories surrounding Sayfī are probably exaggerated if not entirely fabricated. What is interesting is the way the stories are told, and what this can tell us about the chronicler's opinion of the legal system. It is striking that the sharīᶜa court appears again in a negative light. Whereas Küçük Muḥammad achieved justice by circumventing the sharīᶜa court and its methods, Sayfī pursues his nefarious ends through the courts, by exploiting and corrupting their vulnerable procedures.

Sayfī was a retainer of Çerkes Muḥammad Bey al-Kabīr, a powerful grandee of the early eighteenth century who was regarded as ruthless and unprincipled by most of the chroniclers of the period. Damurdāshī describes Sayfī as a corrupt and irreligious street urchin (*şehir oğlanı*), whom Çerkes Muḥammad Bey picked up in Gallipoli on his way back from the campaign against Venice in 1715. He would obtain favorable court judgments for his and Çerkes Muḥammad's clients by intimidating litigants, qāḍīs and court personnel, and by arranging false testimony. He allegedly maintained a *shāhid* (court witness) at the Ṭulūn sharīᶜa court permanently, who would protect false witnesses who appeared on behalf of Sayfī's clients.[27]

One story about Sayfī relates his intervention to secure the divorce of a woman against her husband's wishes. The woman was married to a money-changer but in love with another of Çerkes Muḥammad's retainers called Aḥmad. She asked Sayfī to arrange her divorce from her husband and marriage to her lover, offering him a share of her divorce settlement as an inducement. Sayfī summoned her husband and told him to divorce his wife. When he refused, Sayfī had him beaten until he complied. Sayfī then demanded that he pay the delayed dower, but the man insisted that he was not liable, having divorced his wife under duress.[28] Sayfī had him imprisoned until he paid the delayed dower and the *nafaqa* (maintenance) for her waiting period (*ᶜidda*).[29] The man's friends quickly raised the necessary money to secure his release. Sayfī then demanded that a shāhid marry the woman to her lover Aḥmad. The shāhid answered that it would be illegal to do so before the woman's waiting period had expired. Sayfī was not satisfied with this, and pressured the shāhid to marry the couple immediately. Damurdāshī does not specify what kind of pressure he exerted, but says that having married the couple the shāhid fled Cairo and did not return until Sayfī was no longer on the scene.[30]

This story has Sayfī subverting some of the basic principles of Islamic law on behalf of his clients, using violence and in return for money. To appreciate the shock value of this story in the context of eighteenth-century Egypt, we must bear in mind the patriarchal assumptions of the readers: that divorce was the absolute prerogative of men, and that, with a few exceptions, women could only obtain divorce by negotiating with their husbands. Damurdāshī portrays Sayfī as usurping this husband's control over his wife, forcing their divorce without his genuine consent and without his wife offering any concessions, and handing her to another man. Sayfī added insult to injury by compelling the husband to pay maintenance to his ex-wife for her waiting period, even though she had not waited but had, illegally, re-married immediately. The law conceived nafaqa as payment made to a wife in return for her submission to her husband in marriage: this man was effectively forced to subsidize his ex-wife's married life with her new husband. The case would have seemed outrageous to contemporary readers not only because it ignored Islamic legal doctrine but also because it violated their common-sense notions of justice in marital affairs.[31] While both the divorce settlement and the subsequent marriage made a mockery of the law and patriarchy, the sharīᶜa court official was supine before Sayfī's threats, a wholly ineffective guarantor of the husband's legal rights.

Another story concerning Sayfī sees him pitted against another notable, Ibrāhīm Efendī Katkhudā, as their respective clients, a forger and an honest cloth-dealer, litigate over a house owned by the cloth-dealer. Familiar aspects of sharīʿa court procedure—the production of documents, the examination of witnesses—appear in the story, but are portrayed as powerless and corruptible. The legal system, in this story, is prisoner to Cairo's factional politics. Indeed, the story is embedded in a longer narrative of a complicated feud between two of Cairo's major grandees: Sayfī's master, Çerkes Muḥammad Bey, of whom the chronicler Damurdāshī disapproved, and Ibrāhīm Efendī Katkhudā's ally, Dhū ʾl-Faqār Bey, with whom Damurdāshī sympathized.

The forger intended to use fake documents to seize a house owned by the cloth-dealer, and paid Sayfī a bribe to support him. Sayfī summoned the cloth-dealer, who attended with the documents proving his ownership of the house, the witnesses to those documents, and a group of fellow merchants from the Ṭulūn market where he traded. Of course, the justice of the cloth-dealer's claim meant nothing to the corrupt Sayfī. The cloth-dealer sought the protection of Ibrāhīm Efendī Katkhudā. Ibrāhīm Efendī is portrayed by Damurdāshī as having scruples: he took on the cloth-dealer's case only because it had merit. He examined the cloth-dealer's documents to make sure they were genuine, and investigated his witnesses' integrity, finding them to be of upright character.[32] On these grounds he confirmed the cloth-dealer's ownership of the house, and sent a message to Sayfī telling him to leave the cloth-dealer alone. Sayfī rudely dismissed the messenger and made it clear that he would continue to pursue the cloth-dealer. Ibrāhīm Efendī told the cloth-dealer to stay out of sight for a few days until he had dealt with Sayfī.

At this point, the chronicler Damurdāshī interrupts the story of the cloth-dealer and the forger to relate the next round in the ongoing feud between the factions of Çerkes Muḥammad Bey and Dhū ʾl-Faqār Bey. Ibrāhīm Efendī Katkhudā plots to arrange the return of Dhū ʾl-Faqār Bey from exile in order to balance Çerkes Muḥammad's influence in Cairo. Meanwhile, Çerkes Muḥammad and Sayfī set a trap for an ally of Dhū ʾl-Faqār and Ibrāhīm, luring him to a house in Miṣr al-Qadīma where he is murdered by Çerkes Muḥammad's retainers. The full details of these intrigues are not of interest here: the important point is that, for Damurdāshī, the dispute between the forger and the cloth-dealer is simply an episode in this wider factional conflict, its course entirely subject to the dynamics of elite politics. The dispute over the cloth-dealer's house is only settled when Çerkes Muḥammad Bey, for reasons that are obscure, decides that it is in his political interests to calm tension between Sayfī and Ibrāhīm Efendī. Çerkes Muḥammad arranges a meeting with three other beys at Ibrāhīm Efendī's house; the choice of location designed to flatter Ibrāhīm, as it involved the beys accepting the hospitality of their inferior. At the meeting Ibrāhīm Efendī is given the opportunity to hold forth on his own integrity, announcing that he only takes on just causes. Çerkes Muḥammad then prevails on Sayfī to drop his support of the forger, peace is established between him and Ibrāhīm, and the cloth-dealer is safe.[33]

This story presents the legal process as simply an extension of factional politics. The story, reflecting its teller's political sympathies, portrays one patron as law-abiding and one as corrupt. But the dynamics driving the progress of the dispute are those of political expediency rather than those of legal procedure. The fact that the cloth-dealer's claim is genuine and the forger's is based on fraudulent documents is irrelevant to the outcome of the case. It is actually a change of heart on the part of one of the story's bad guys—Çerkes Muḥammad Bey—that leads to the eventual just result; though that change of heart comes about not because of a new-found belief in justice on the part of Çerkes Muḥammad, but because of his pragmatic political calculations. The hierarchy of power in society at large is thus replicated in the legal process: the forger is able to swindle the cloth-dealer because he has Sayfī as his patron, but only so long as Sayfī's master Çerkes Muḥammad allows him to meddle in the case. Legal procedures—documents and witnesses—are present, but are essentially meaningless: the pursuit of one's rights depends not on these procedures but on the cultivation of the kind of patron-client relationships around which eighteenth-century Egyptian political life revolved. To the extent that courts and their procedures are involved in the narrative, they are presented as happening at the command of the story's key agents, Sayfī and Ibrāhīm Efendi. The impression given, then, is of legal personnel who were entirely under the sway of powerful individuals, or perhaps themselves members or allies of political households.

Justice in the eyes of the chroniclers

Eighteenth-century chroniclers portrayed Cairo's official legal system of sharīᶜa courts and qāḍīs as weak, corruptible, and hostage to the interests of the powerful. The stories they told were probably exaggerated for dramatic or comic effect. Nevertheless, they tell us something about contemporary popular attitudes to the courts. These were polemical texts written to bolster the reputations of some and to undermine others. The chroniclers intended to persuade, and to do so they told stories they hoped would resonate with the public consciousness. At least some eighteenth-century Egyptians clearly held a cynical attitude towards the courts and qāḍīs: they felt that the legal system often failed to live up to its ideals, and that its procedures were hopelessly inadequate to protect the honest and innocent from determined crooks. The chroniclers saw the potential for justice in eighteenth-century Cairo, but they saw it as lying with powerful just men rather than with impersonal procedures and institutions.

But what constituted just dispute resolution in the opinion of the chroniclers? We saw earlier, in the story of Küçük Muḥammad, that his outwitting of ᶜAlī al-Fayyūmī was praised by Damurdāshī, Jabartī, Qinalī, and the anonymous chronicler; Damurdāshī explicitly contrasted this with the sharīᶜa court's pedantic procedures. Further stories about other celebrated power-brokers also suggest that what these chroniclers valued in a dispute resolver was the intelligence and cunning of a detective. He should not simply mechanically apply procedures that would result in an artificial, legal "truth"; rather, he should figure out how to uncover the real truth.

Another story about ᶜUthmān Bey Dhū ᵓl-Faqār, who introduced this chapter, illustrates this. Related by Jabartī, it tells how ᶜUthmān Bey solved a murder committed by a member of his own household. In sharīᶜa court procedure, homicide was treated as a claim of the victim's heirs against the perpetrator. The heirs had to sue the perpetrator, having identified him or her themselves; they had to provide evidence and, if successful, could either claim blood money or demand retaliation.[34] This is indeed how homicide was handled in its relatively infrequent appearances in the court records.[35] ᶜUthmān Bey, however, took the lead and investigated the case himself, discovering the murderer's identity through an examination of circumstantial evidence.

A man whose wife had been missing for several days approached ᶜUthmān Bey and asked for his help. ᶜUthmān told the man to search through his wife's possessions for anything unfamiliar. The man went away and returned with a man's vest that he had found among his wife's clothes. ᶜUthmān summoned the shaykh of the tailors' guild, who determined which of the guild's members had made the vest. ᶜUthmān interrogated the tailor in question, who claimed that he had made it for one of ᶜUthmān's retainers. ᶜUthmān had the retainer's house searched, and the missing woman's body was discovered hidden in the bathroom. ᶜUthmān arranged for her burial and had his retainer beheaded.[36]

Ismāᶜīl Bey ibn ᶜIwaḍ, another leading figure of the early eighteenth century who was the principal enemy of Çerkes Muḥammad Bey and was generally liked by the chroniclers, was also lauded for his detective work. Jabartī described him as having an extraordinary ability to predict the behavior of criminals. Having discerned who the likely culprit was, he would then prove their guilt by extracting a confession.

In one story, a woman from Sharqiyya province in the Nile Delta whose cow had been stolen traveled to Cairo to report this to Ismāᶜīl Bey. Ismāᶜīl sent one of his guards to her village, with instructions to arrest the first person who approached him and inquired about his purpose. The guard was to assume that this would be the person who had taken the cow, presumably on the grounds that his guilt made him anxious about any newcomers to the village. The guard was to take the person to the qāᵓimmaqām (the agent of the village's tax-collector) for questioning. Sure enough, when the guard arrived at the village, a man came down to ask him his business. The guard arrested him and took him to the qāᵓimmaqām, who beat him until he confessed that the cow was at his house; the animal was then returned to its rightful owner.[37]

In another story, Ismāᶜīl Bey deduced the culprit from among a group of suspects for an undefined crime. Ismāᶜīl Bey repeatedly called the group into his presence, questioned them, dismissed them, called them in again, and so on. After repeating this procedure several times, he selected one of the men for interrogation. After suffering only mild torture, the man quickly confessed. Those present were amazed and asked Ismāᶜīl Bey how he had discerned the identity of the criminal. He replied that the man had always been the first to leave the room when the group was dismissed, and the last to enter when they were summoned. Ismāᶜīl Bey had inferred from his nervousness that he was the guilty party.[38]

Our chroniclers wanted dispute resolvers to use their intelligence and cunning to uncover criminality, not simply to rely on the mechanical procedures of the sharīᶜa courts. Another striking feature of the two stories concerning Ismāᶜīl Bey ibn ᶜIwaḍ is the resort to torture. Jabartī is sanguine, if not openly approving, about the use of torture to secure confession; he describes the torture endured by the criminal in the second story as only "mild." Sharīᶜa court procedure frowned upon the use of torture, and a confession extracted in this way was not admissible as evidence. Cairenes knew this, and some attempted to retract confessions they had previously made on the grounds that they had been tortured or had feared torture.[39] It is particularly interesting that Jabartī was willing to tolerate torture as means of extracting confession: as mentioned at the beginning of the chapter, he was a scholar who had received an education in Islamic law, and so was fully aware of the illegitimacy of torture in legal theory.[40]

In these stories, however, torture is seen as justified because Ismāᶜīl Bey had determined the identity of the criminal, but had no proof. Again, what was important to the chroniclers was the righteousness of Ismāᶜīl Bey's cause: they relied on the integrity and justice of an individual, rather than on the procedural safeguards of an impersonal system. The stories contain an implied critique of the inadequacy of the sharīᶜa courts' evidentiary requirements. Violence was accepted, if not applauded, if it led to a just outcome.

This acceptance of torture to secure the confessions of criminals fits with a wider celebration of violence in the legal system that is observable in these chronicles. The accounts of the Janissary commander ᶜAlī Āghā's campaign against market corruption and public immorality given by Damurdāshī, Aḥmad Çelebi, and Jabartī, which I discussed in Chapter 2, describe approvingly extreme summary violence meted out against persons and property. ᶜAlī Āghā is said to have beaten crooked oil-merchants and corrupt public weighers to death in the street, and to have demolished brothels and bars.[41] In his biographies of Cairene notables, Jabartī quotes at length from many panegyric poems composed upon their deaths: praise for their ferocity and violence is a recurring theme.[42] Violent epithets are also frequently granted to figures of whom the chroniclers approve: Aḥmad Çelebi described the governor Silaḥdār ᶜAlī Pasha as a "shedder of the blood of the corrupt."[43]

The chroniclers examined in the preceding sections favored decisive action over cautious procedure, and they looked for these virtues in members of Cairo's military elite rather than in the official legal system. They sometimes praised these figures by explicitly contrasting them to the sharīᶜa courts, which they criticized. The chroniclers were also willing to tolerate, or even applaud, the use of violence in the pursuit of justice. This popular conception of justice is at odds with the approach to justice developed in Islamic legal theory, which has received the overwhelming bulk of attention from historians of Islamic law. Alternative conceptions of justice such as those detailed in this chapter, which can be found by broadening the scope of Islamic legal history to include non-legal sources, deserve more attention if we are to understand fully the place of Islamic law in historical societies.

Dispute resolution as a domain of political competition

The fact that justice was such a prominent theme in the polemical chronicles of the eighteenth century points to another issue: that justice was an object of political competition during this period. Beys and regimental officers intervened in disputes on behalf of their clients and others, and attempted to build reputations as protectors of the honest and providers of justice. Partisan chroniclers repeated tales of heroic and scandalous interventions in disputes in order to bolster the reputations of the political figures they supported and malign their opponents.

The stories discussed above focused on a few individuals who achieved particular fame or notoriety. Other passages in the chronicles indicate that such involvement in dispute resolution was widespread. Jabartī, writing nostalgically about the Cairo of the mid eighteenth century, under the duumvirate of Ibrāhīm Katkhudā al-Qāzdughlī and Riḍwān Katkhudā al-Jalfī, describes the receipt of petitions as a key virtue of the great notables of the period, along with their hospitality. The two practices were linked. According to Jabartī, every grandee's house had a public kitchen that provided meals for all comers at noon and in the evening. Guests were fed at long tables, with the bey sitting at the head. The fact that the public area of the house was open to everyone at mealtimes made them the conventional occasion for the submission of grievances. Petitioners would attend the meal and then wait behind afterwards, at which point the host would attend to their requests.[44]

The provision of justice was not only a factor in the factional struggles among the Egyptian elite. It necessarily involved some tension with the Ottoman imperial government and its representative in Cairo, the governor, because the imperial government, as sovereign, assumed ultimate responsibility for justice and put great effort into the maintenance of an empire-wide judiciary and network of legal institutions. The privatization of justice by Cairo's beys and officers encroached on the jurisdiction of the empire's qāḍīs. The provision of justice was a function that the imperial government guarded jealously: it was a critical component of Ottoman legitimation strategies and of the Ottoman conception of sovereignty. It is striking that the two offices in Ottoman Egypt most closely connected with justice—the chief qāḍī ship and the governorship—were almost never devolved to Egypt's elite households. The chief qāḍī was always appointed by the imperial government from among the empire's senior judges. The Ottoman governors of Egypt were also always outside appointees, with the exception of the five years immediately following the Ottoman conquest.

During the early eighteenth century this tension over the provision of justice became particularly manifest. This is apparent in the accounts of ᶜUthmān Bey Dhū ᵓl-Faqār's creation of his own dīwān. Whereas the stories concerning Küçük Muḥammad, Sayfī, and Ismāᶜīl Bey ibn ᶜIwaḍ relate isolated instances in which they intervened in disputes, ᶜUthmān Bey is credited with creating an institution.[45] Moreover, the name given to ᶜUthmān Bey's institution by both Damurdāshī and Jabartī—the dīwān—mirrored the name of the Ottoman governor's tribunal—the

Dīwān al-ᶜĀlī. ᶜUthmān Bey sought to create a dispute resolution forum: this was a greater affront to the governor's authority than simply intervening in disputes on an ad hoc basis. ᶜUthmān Bey's move was one of intelligent ambition rather than one of simple arrogance. Both Damurdāshī and Jabartī claim that ᶜUthmān Bey's dīwān specialized in hearing cases involving women.[46] The reason behind this focus is obscure in their brief accounts, but it is clear that ᶜUthmān Bey identified a weakness in the existing legal system and attempted to solve it. He did not simply emulate the governor by setting up a rival dīwān, but he sought to do it better than the governor.

ᶜUthmān Bey's dīwān was short-lived, as ᶜUthmān Bey was forced into exile by a rival faction a few years after its creation.[47] During the years of its operation, however, it posed a genuine challenge to the authority of the governor. The dīwān was not ᶜUthmān Bey's only provocation. He built an extravagant palace near Suwayqat al-Aṣfūr.[48] In 1742–3 (1155 AH), he threw a banquet at his palace and invited the Ottoman governor, Yaḥyā Pasha.[49] This was, according to Jabartī, the first time that a governor had ever visited the house of an Egyptian bey. Hospitality was hierarchical, and ᶜUthmān Bey violated protocol by inviting a supposed superior to be his guest. Nevertheless, Yaḥyā Pasha was unable to refuse.

There is evidence that the Ottoman governors of the early 1740s responded to the threat posed to their authority by ᶜUthmān Bey by attempting to bolster the appeal of their own Dīwān al-ᶜĀlī. It is striking that the earliest extant register of the Dīwān al-ᶜĀlī dates from the tenure of Ḥekīmoğlu ᶜAlī Pasha and his successor Yaḥyā Pasha: precisely the moment that ᶜUthmān Bey created his rival dīwān. The keeping of detailed registers of the Dīwān al-ᶜĀlī's judicial activity may have been an innovation of Ḥekīmoğlu ᶜAlī Pasha.

Of course, the absence of extant prior registers cannot prove that registers were not kept at an earlier date. There are many reasons why even the most meticulously-kept records can disappear. They can be lost or discarded by subsequent generations who no longer regard them as important, they can rot or burn, and they can be intentionally destroyed during political upheavals. But none of these suggestions is compelling in this case, because there is an almost complete lack of surviving documentation from before the nineteenth century for provincial governors' tribunals throughout the entire Ottoman Empire. This compares with very high rates of survival for sharīᶜa court records in most large and medium-sized Ottoman cities. It seems unlikely that the records of every provincial governor's tribunal suffered some mishap, while very few sets of sharīᶜa court records did. It is much more likely that the different rates of survival are explained by differences in the contemporary practices surrounding the different sets of records. Sharīᶜa courts kept records of proceedings in bound volumes, preserved within the institution. Provincial governors' tribunals either did not make records, or they made records but preserved them elsewhere. Scattered collections of documents belonging to late seventeenth-century governors of Egypt located in German libraries suggest that the practice may have been that Ottoman governors took their records with them when they took up new posts. The documents in question were in the possession of former governors of

Egypt who led armies in eastern Europe during the Ottoman–Habsburg wars of the late seventeenth century: the documents were captured along with other booty by German nobles fighting for the Habsburgs.[50] If Ottoman governors carried the records of their tribunals with them from posting to posting, and even to the frontline during wars, then their absence today is not surprising: lacking an institutional infrastructure to preserve them, these records were far more likely to perish or disappear.[51]

In 1741, however, the practice changed, and bound registers of the proceedings of the Dīwān al-ᶜĀlī were preserved at the citadel in Cairo, where the Dīwān was held. These registers were identified with the institution of the Dīwān al-ᶜĀlī rather than with the person of the governor: the first register covered the regimes of both Ḥekīmoğlu ᶜAlī Pasha and Yaḥyā Pasha. It is certainly plausible that this reform was a response to the challenge posed by ᶜUthmān Bey's dīwān. The privatization of justice represented by ᶜUthmān Bey's dīwān threatened to undermine one of the governor's key roles, and therefore his legitimacy. By creating a public archive of its records, the governors sought to give the official Dīwān al-ᶜĀlī an air of permanence and institutional security that ᶜUthmān Bey's new creation would have lacked. The governors tried to suggest to the population that, while ᶜUthmān Bey's political influence and military strength might be able to force a solution to a dispute in the short term, there was no guarantee that that solution would endure beyond ᶜUthmān Bey's death or fall from power. By contrast, a judgment of the Dīwān al-ᶜĀlī would be recorded and preserved in perpetuity, safe within the walls of the citadel, whatever might happen to the particular governor who issued it. The governors tried to shore up popular trust in the Dīwān al-ᶜĀlī by emphasizing that it was a public institution that transcended any particular, private personality.[52]

Conclusion

Powerful individuals similar to ᶜUthmān Bey Dhū ʾl-Faqār, Ismāᶜīl Bey ibn ᶜIwaḍ, and Çerkes Muḥammad Bey al-Kabīr and their households continued to dominate Cairo in the latter half of the eighteenth century. The Qāzdughlī household that gained supremacy during the middle of the century would, for a period, successfully marginalize the Ottoman governor to an unprecedented extent.[53] In the early nineteenth century, however, all centers of power that rivaled and threatened the state were crushed, in brutal fashion, by the reforming Ottoman governor Meḥmed ᶜAlī Pasha, paving the way for the highly centralized governments that have ruled Egypt since. As well as strengthening the state by reorganizing the legal, educational, and medical systems, reforming land tenure, and creating a conscript army, Meḥmed ᶜAlī literally eliminated the beys and the leaders of the great households at the infamous "Massacre of the Mamlūks" in 1811.[54]

Nationalist Egyptian historiography has generally sided with the centralized state, seeing the power of the great eighteenth-century households as the decadence of the Ottoman Empire, and celebrating Meḥmed ᶜAlī for neutralizing this threat and for unifying and modernizing the nation.[55] ᶜUthmān Bey Dhū ʾl-Faqār and his peers lost their public relations campaign in the very long run. But the chronicles surveyed in this chapter show that earlier opinion had been rather different. Jabartī wrote his biographical dictionary at the time of Meḥmed ᶜAlī's reforms. His support for ᶜUthmān Bey's dīwān, along with his celebration of the grace and generosity of eighteenth-century Cairene notables, reveal his nostalgic view of a more personal form of power that was being replaced by the impersonal structures of a modern state during his lifetime. The chroniclers of the mid eighteenth century, who were contemporaries of ᶜUthmān Bey, also sympathized with this personal form of power; perhaps they could imagine no other model of state-society relations. The adoption of dispute resolution functions by beys and officers won admiration so long as it was undertaken with the intention of securing a just outcome. This was the case even though such activities infringed on the jurisdiction of the long-established sharīᶜa courts and deviated from the courts' methods. The chroniclers were in fact inclined to cynicism about the value of the sharīᶜa courts' strict adherence to procedure. It was the very idiosyncratic methods of the beys and officers—aggressive, individualistic, and violent—that the chroniclers appreciated. This has significant implications for our understanding of Islamic legal history. Islamic law cannot be understood solely by reference to fiqh texts and the sharīᶜa court records. The sharīᶜa was a flexible concept that was interpreted differently by different constituencies, and many of these interpretations accommodated actors and institutions other than jurists and sharīᶜa courts. It is noteworthy that in praising ᶜUthmān Bey, Jabartī did not describe his dīwān as an alternative system of law: he described it as an implementation of the sharīᶜa. This was also how ᶜUthmān Bey himself saw his initiative, or at least how he marketed it to the Cairo populace: as an attempt to reform a corrupt system by correctly implementing sharīᶜa. The question of what sharīᶜa meant, and who was entitled to interpret and implement it, was debated and contested in Cairo's politics long before the legal reforms of the nineteenth century, let alone the acrimonious debates about Islamization in the late twentieth century.

CHAPTER

6

A CULTURE OF DISPUTING: HOW DID CAIRENES USE THE LEGAL SYSTEM?

In this chapter I turn my focus away from the institutions and authorities that structured Ottoman Cairo's legal system to take in the perspective of the litigants who used it. How did Cairenes navigate the pluralism of their city's judicial infrastructure? What strategies did they employ? What did they expect to gain from their engagement with the legal system? Approaching our subject from the perspective of the litigant, or the legal consumer, helps us to understand how Cairo's legal system actually functioned, rather than how its creators and administrators wanted it to work. In all societies, litigants and other court users manipulate the legal process for their own ends, often in ways not intended by the rulers, jurists, and judges who create and manage the legal system.

As this book has demonstrated, Cairenes had a number of options available when they wanted to resolve a dispute. The default institution was the network of sharīᶜa courts dispersed throughout the city and its suburbs. Cairenes could also send a petition to the Sultan or approach the governor's Dīwān. As described in Chapter 3, procedurally there was not a great deal to choose between these different institutions. All ultimately relied on the same understanding of evidence, which held the eye-witness testimony of two Muslim men to be the paradigm of proof, presented and assessed according to the same set of procedures overseen by a qāḍī. The bureaucratic procedures of the Dīvān-i Hümāyūn, described in Chapter 3, were only used to produce a judgment when they could reliably stand in for testimony: when the case rested on a document that could be verified by the palace's archives or by the authentication mechanisms embedded in a ḥujja physically presented to the Dīvān. There was also no formal hierarchy between the sharīᶜa court, the Dīwān al-ᶜĀlī and the Dīvān-i Hümāyūn, and no recognized system of appeal. Despite the similar functioning of these institutions, litigants saw them as offering different possibilities: how this worked is one theme of this chapter.

Cairenes could avoid adjudication by opting for mediation. Ṣulḥ had a close relationship with the sharīᶜa court and the Dīwān al-ᶜĀlī. The practice of ṣulḥ was almost the opposite of formal adjudication—unstructured rather than procedural, relying on persuasion rather than formal evidence, aiming to extract concessions from both parties rather than to decide a winner—and it could produce strikingly different results. But it was encouraged by the qāḍī and may sometimes have taken place within the court. The resulting agreements were often ratified by the sharīᶜa court or Dīwān, which made them enforceable in future lawsuits.

Cairenes were also, particularly during the eighteenth century, able to approach other powerful men who brokered resolutions to disputes, despite having no formal appointment to do so. In some cases, such as that of ᶜUthmān Bey Dhū ᵓl-Faqār's dīwān, these men adopted some kind of formal procedure and took on the pretensions of a court. Lastly, as with people in any society, Cairenes could also try to resolve disputes completely informally, by negotiating, persuading, harassing, and pressuring by whatever means were at hand.

While legal history tends to focus on the state institutions that produce and implement law, scholars using the concept of legal pluralism have emphasized the litigant's perspective. If there are multiple spheres of law, and if there is no overall authority channeling particular litigants into particular spheres, then clearly the initiative of the litigant plays a role in how he or she maneuvers between these overlapping spheres. The concept most frequently used to explain litigant behavior in a situation of legal pluralism is "forum-shopping." Put simply, forum-shopping means that the litigant shops around and chooses the forum which offers the best resolution to his or her claim.[1]

In Chapter 4, I considered the applicability of forum-shopping to the madhhab pluralism within Ottoman Cairo's sharīᶜa courts. In this chapter I consider its usefulness in understanding the institutional plurality of Ottoman Cairo's legal system: should we see Cairenes as forum-shopping between the sharīᶜa court, the Dīwān al-ᶜĀlī, the Dīvān-i Hümāyūn, and so on? Forum-shopping, however, is a limited approach to the dynamics of legal plurality. It assumes that the litigants act rationally in order to secure their interests, on the basis of accurate knowledge of the doctrinal and procedural differences between the various forums. Embedded within this is a further assumption that litigants hope that the legal process will itself resolve the dispute: in other words, that the litigant's desired outcome is a judicial ruling in his or her favor.

A more complex approach recognizes that for the litigant, the lawsuit is not an isolated event. Rather, it is embedded within a broader dispute that has been going on for some time beforehand, and will often continue after the court case has concluded. This broader dispute will likely involve other, extra-judicial attempts at resolution. In other words, the lawsuit is only one stage in a dispute: never the first stage, rarely the last stage, and often concurrent with other dispute resolution activities taking place outside the court. Bearing this in mind, we can think more creatively about the intentions and motivations of litigants in Ottoman Cairo. Of course, in some cases the litigant simply sought a favorable judgment, and was justifiably confident of obtaining it. There are plenty of examples, however, of litigants bringing legally weak cases to court. Attention to the place of a lawsuit within the broader culture of disputing can help us to understand these.

One possible explanation of weak cases is that the litigant was misinformed about the law or about the capability of the court. This is rarely considered by Ottomanists, and some have made the positive claim that most litigants were highly knowledgeable and savvy users of the legal system.[2] However, in her study of working-class litigants in the courts of 1980s New England—a society with far wider literacy than the early modern Ottoman Empire—Sally Engle Merry found a great disparity between litigants' expectations of the law and what the courts could actually provide. Despite the generally high level of education and the wide availability of legal advice in the modern United States, many litigants only gained an accurate understanding of their exercisable legal rights after they had commenced legal proceedings.[3] In Ottoman Cairo too, it is likely that in some cases litigants had unrealistic expectations and ended up disappointed and disillusioned. This disillusionment is captured in Damurdāshī's rendition of the legend of Küçük Muḥammad and the jeweler, discussed in Chapter 5, which mocks the impotence of the sharīᶜa court nāᵓib when faced with outright mendacity.[4]

However, ignorance is not a satisfactory answer in itself. Even when well-informed, people did not litigate only when they could be confident of victory in court. Some litigants brought cases not because they hoped to win, but because they hoped to achieve an outcome in a different legal or social sphere. Legal historians must try to understand the role a particular lawsuit played in the broader dispute of which it formed a part; in other words, the relationship of the lawsuit to its wider social context. This involves thinking not only of a plurality of formal legal forums, but about a broader plurality of dispute resolution practices and strategies.

Often, although the lawsuit did not exist in isolation, the extant record of it does. Even when a dispute involved several formal hearings in different forums, it is rarely possible to trace the records of all of them because the extant court records are not only incomplete, but also exist only in manuscripts with often difficult handwriting. Most lack even an index, let alone the text-search facilities available in the digitized collections available for some European legal archives.[5] Trying to follow up a reference to a lawsuit is like searching a haystack for a needle that might not be there. Moreover, if we include informal dispute resolution practices in our inquiry, we confront the fact that in many cases records were never made in the first place. For these reasons, awareness of the broader plural context usually comes from glimpses found through close reading of a court or petition record. More rarely, we can find traces of the same dispute within the records of different institutions.

There are a number of ways in which a litigant or petitioner might hope that the lawsuit or petition had an impact outside the forum that he or she approached. A litigant might start action in one forum in the hope of influencing a case in another forum. A litigant might also use litigation to force the opponent into a confrontation, from where he or she might be pressured into negotiation or compromise. In other words, a legal action could be initiated in order to produce a social solution. The Ottoman courts' emphasis on ṣulḥ encouraged this tactic. As discussed in Chapter 2, there are many cases in the court registers that begin as adjudication but end with a result obtained through ṣulḥ. In some cases, this might have been the result of the qāḍī encouraging two litigants bent on confrontation to compromise, as he was enjoined to do by manuals of judicial practice. But this pattern was so common and well-known that it seems certain that many litigants would have anticipated achieving a result through ṣulḥ at the time they first issued their lawsuits.[6] This explains why some litigants brought lawsuits that were weak or even hopeless. We can imagine why this tactic was effective. The lawsuit acted as a summons, compelling the defendant, or his or her agent, to attend court, where pressure could be applied by the plaintiff, the qāḍī, or any member of the public to enter negotiations. If nothing else, it forced a confrontation which the defendant could not avoid or stonewall.

The publicity of court action is key to thinking about a much broader range of impacts that the litigant might hope to achieve. Leslie Peirce's description of how the court in sixteenth-century ᶜAyntāb gave voice to women litigants in particular is a suggestive example of this. Court procedure was disadvantageous to women. But Peirce shows that despite these procedural handicaps women in ᶜAyntāb engaged with the court assertively, often in ways that suggest that they hoped to achieve a social rather than a legal solution. In one particularly striking case, Peirce describes an Aleppine woman called Hadīce bīnt Bilāl who traveled to ᶜAyntāb to accuse a local man of rape. Predictably, due to a lack of witnesses, she lost the lawsuit when the man took an oath of innocence. Unusually, Hadīce did not subsequently withdraw or tone down her accusation, leaving her legally liable to punishment for qadhf (sexual slander).[7] Peirce suggests that her goal was to publicize the rape in front of the man's own community, so as to create doubts about his character, and that Hadīce willingly risked the qadhf penalty in order to do this.[8] The idea of the court as a public stage on which people acted out their disputes, humiliating or shaming their opponents and redeeming their own moral characters in the process, has been explored by scholars studying other societies. Daniel Lord Smail showed how in medieval Marseille litigants used the court, which was located outdoors near the city's central marketplace, to mount verbal attacks on their enemies in an ongoing contest over honor and reputation. In the case of Marseille, the court was not only a stage but also a sanctuary, where people could make allegations without fearing prosecution for slander.[9] In classical Athens, the court was a stage on which the city's elites sought to demonstrate their rhetorical abilities while attacking their enemies. Court oratory was such a highly regarded art that the speeches were preserved in literary collections, enabling David Cohen's fascinating study of Athenian litigation.[10]

The aim of this chapter is to try to understand litigants' strategies in the context of both the plural, formal legal system and the wider culture of disputing. In what follows I will describe a number of disputing strategies and explain how these connected different institutions and practices, formal and informal.

The multi-pronged attack

Some Cairenes pursued their adversaries through several different forums, petitioning the Sultan before or after suing in a sharīᶜa court. Some petitioned the Sultan more than once, and some also approached the Şeyhulislām or another mufti to obtain a fatwā bolstering their case. Such litigants clearly intended that the actions in different forums would complement and support one another, although the legal basis for this was often dubious.

An example is Aḥmad Nūr al-Dīn, who sent a petition around the end of 1674 concerning a waqf he had founded.[11] The waqf supported a mosque and two madrasas in Cairo. Aḥmad had stipulated in the endowment deed that the waqf's supervisor should be appointed from his male line (*evlād ü evlādı*). The position had been held by Aḥmad's father, ᶜAlīm, but when he died, a replacement had been appointed from outside his family, contravening the stipulations of the endowment deed. The petition Aḥmad sent at the end of 1674 was not the first action he took. Aḥmad stated in the petition that he had previously taken the case to the sharīᶜa court, where he had obtained a ḥujja in his favor from the qāḍī. He had also previously approached the Dīvān-i Hümāyūn, and received an imperial order. And he had obtained a fatwā in his favor from a mufti.

This raises the question why Aḥmad went to the trouble of approaching several legal authorities. Strictly from the perspective of legal procedure, there was little value in this strategy. The sharīᶜa court case should have been sufficient on its own, since a qāḍī's ruling was final and binding. The purpose of the additional step of petitioning the Sultan is not clear. Aḥmad's case rested on previous documents issued by the imperial government, so the Dīvān-i Hümāyūn made a decision in his favor rather than simply referring the case to the local qāḍī. But the Dīvān's order simply repeated the qāḍī's judgment that Aḥmad had already obtained. It is possible, given that Aḥmad ended up petitioning the Sultan twice, that this was a matter of enforcement, as I discussed in Chapter 3. Perhaps Aḥmad had failed to dislodge the supervisor despite the qāḍī's ruling, and that is why he appealed for the Dīvān-i Hümāyūn's support.

His decision to procure a fatwā is more curious. A fatwā is the mufti's opinion on a hypothetical case presented to him by the questioner. The mufti conducts no adjudication; indeed he is not even interested in whether the facts told to him are true or not. His job is simply to explain the legal consequences of the facts as presented. Therefore, while a fatwā could be binding with regard to a point of law, it could never be binding on a question of fact, by definition. It is strange, therefore, that a questioner would request a fatwā for a case where the legal basis was obvious and uncontroversial, as Aḥmad did. The crucial element of this case was not the law's position on whether endowment deeds were binding, but rather the factual question whether Aḥmad's claim about the stipulations in his endowment deed was true or not. The crucial document was the endowment deed, and there was no legal value in a fatwā that simply reiterated the obvious point that endowment deed stipulations should be followed.

There are other examples of litigants acquiring apparently pointless fatwās in this way. In 1742 (1155 AH), a man called al-Ḥājj Muṣṭafā petitioned the Sultan to complain about his Christian neighbor, Banūb, who had built a house taller than those of the Muslims in the delta town of Ziftā, roughly fifty miles north of Cairo.[12] Muṣṭafā requested an imperial order that Banūb should either lower the height of his house to that of the neighboring Muslim-owned houses, or that he should sell the house to a Muslim. Muṣṭafā had also obtained a fatwā from the Şeyhulislām. Again, the legal value of this fatwā is questionable. The legal basis for Muṣṭafā's claim—that non-Muslims should not own houses taller than those of the neighboring Muslims—was clear, and no one needed the Şeyhulislām to confirm this. While this particular restriction was inconsistently (and perhaps rarely) enforced, its legal validity was not in doubt.[13] Again, the crucial element in this case was a question of fact: was Banūb's house really taller than those of his Muslim neighbors? A fatwā could not answer this question.

Another persistent litigant was Shaykh Muṣṭafā ibn Aḥmad Muḥammad Abbār, whose efforts to fend off several unnamed enemies who were seeking his position as supervisor of a waqf are revealed in a particularly detailed petition surviving from 1676.[14] Muṣṭafā was the supervisor of the waqf of Sīdī Muḥammad Abū ʾl-Saʿūd al-Jāriḥī. He had been granted the hereditary right to this position by the Sultan in recognition of his efforts to restore the mosque and other buildings owned by the waqf. His petition seems to have been prompted by the resurrection of a dispute over the supervisorship of this waqf that had previously been resolved in Shaykh Muṣṭafā's favor. Muṣṭafā asked the Dīvān-i Hümāyūn to confirm again that he had been granted the hereditary right to this position, and the Dīvān complied. In support of his petition, Muṣṭafā referred to several documents he had been awarded when the dispute was last aired nine years previously. In addition to obtaining an imperial order from the Dīvān-i Hümāyūn, Muṣṭafā had also appealed to the Dīwān al-ʿĀlī, which had issued a *buyuruldu* in his favor, and he had registered a *temessük* (title-deed) at the sharīʿa court.[15] He had also obtained four separate berāts (appointment deeds) from the imperial government certifying his position.

Again, Shaykh Muṣṭafā's dogged pursuit of further authoritative documents to bolster his claim to the supervisorship strikes us as over the top. From a technical procedural perspective, each additional document added no further value: any of these documents on its own should have guaranteed Muṣṭafā's position. Clearly, however, Muṣṭafā felt it was important to cover every base and have his right to the position confirmed by every relevant authority. Historians have noted similar behavior by litigants in other parts of the empire. Leslie Peirce described litigants in sixteenth-century ʿAyntāb supporting their cases with assortments of fatwās, orders from the Dīvān-i Hümāyūn and from the provincial governor in Marʿaş, imperial *ʿadāletnāme*s, and rulings from the qāḍī in Istanbul; she labeled this behavior "redundancy in documentation."[16] Richard Wittman's study of the legal activities of Istanbul's non-Muslim population showed around one third of litigants obtaining both a fatwā and an order from the Dīvān-i Hümāyūn.[17] Michael Ursinus found that several of the Christian clerics in his sample similarly paired a fatwā with an order from the Dīvān-i Hümāyūn.[18]

This suggests a number of mutually compatible conclusions. First, people did not always trust the different legal authorities to cooperate with one another and work together. They took their case to all relevant authorities at the same time, to preempt their opponent from trying to reverse the outcome by going to a different authority. Returning to Shaykh Muṣṭafā's case, he possibly feared that if he simply relied on his berāt and the imperial order, his opponent would go to the governor of Egypt, or to the qāḍī, and obtain an order or judgment that contradicted Muṣṭafā's documents. I have not seen any evidence that such a strategy would have been successful, and indeed it is difficult to imagine that it could work before a qāḍī, whose procedure was adversarial and who would have called Muṣṭafā to give his side of the story. On the other hand, Boğaç Ergene found several examples of litigants taking disputes to different authorities in the hope of obtaining a different result, and in some cases doing so.[19] In any case, even if this situation was unlikely, litigants could nonetheless have feared it. Perhaps litigants did not see a legal "system" in Cairo, the different elements of which worked in unison, but rather a series of separate authorities that worked in different ways that were not always transparent and may sometimes have been corruptible. They thought the safest course of action was to secure the support of all relevant authorities as quickly as possible, before an opponent was able to approach them.

Second, people who amassed multiple documents did so not because the documents were legally effective, but as part of a performative strategy of intimidation. The rapid accumulation of documents demonstrated a litigant's tenacity, capability, and knowledge of the legal system: he or she had the determination and the resources to pursue the case aggressively. The litigant saw each individual document not as a decisive judgment but as another tool with which to wear his or her opponent down. In sharīᶜa court procedure, litigants bore the responsibility for the progress of adjudication. The qāḍī was not an inquisitor; he simply provided the procedural framework within which the two litigants could conduct their dispute. One route to victory in the sharīᶜa court, therefore, was to intimidate one's opponent into conceding defeat. Meanwhile, a court ruling was only one stage in concluding a dispute. Enforcing the court ruling was potentially another battle, since in many cases the qāḍī's enforcement powers were weak or non-existent. The easiest way to enforce a ruling was to persuade one's opponent to comply with it voluntarily. Again, a demonstration of aggressive determination could be an effective way of convincing one's opponent to obey the ruling rather than continue resistance. Equally, this strategy of intimidation could be effective in achieving an outcome in an extra-judicial forum, through informal negotiation.

The behavior observed here does not fit the concept of forum-shopping, because the litigants did not choose a particular forum based on the more advantageous solution it offered. Rather, they used all of the forums at the same time, aiming not to outwit their opponents but to wear them down through sheer persistence.

Interestingly, Nathan Brown made a similar observation about the strategies of litigants in late twentieth-century Cairo. Brown described litigants involved in marital and family disputes issuing multiple suits and counter-suits—both civil claims and criminal charges—in the hope of either bullying their spouse into submission or horse-trading the dropping of claims and charges for concessions.[20] The similarity between these two accounts derives not from the legal-institutional context, which is wholly different, but from the fact that Brown also adopted the perspective of the litigants and studied court cases as embedded in broader disputes. We might expect to find litigants using legal action instrumentally, as one strategy within a wider dispute, in most societies.

The lawsuit as a springboard to ṣulḥ

Another strategy was to issue a lawsuit with the intention of pressuring one's opponent into ṣulḥ negotiations. Ergene observed this in Kastamonu, and it was also common in Cairo.[21] This was an effective strategy since the lawsuit forced the defendant to confront the plaintiff in public, where he or she could be subjected to pressure by the qāḍī or by people from the local community. The lawsuit could also serve as a bargaining chip: the plaintiff could offer to drop the claim if the other party agreed to ṣulḥ.[22] A weak lawsuit could still be an effective bargaining chip, because even if the defendant could be confident of winning it would cost him or her time, money and public exposure.[23]

The following dispute is an example of this strategy in action. It also provides a rare opportunity to trace the progress of a single dispute from one Ottoman legal institution to another: the dispute led to hearings at both al-Bāb al-ᶜĀlī sharīᶜa court and the Dīwān al-ᶜĀlī during 1742, and the records of both hearings survive. The dispute shows how the existence of multiple judicial forums, which lacked clearly-defined jurisdictional boundaries and hierarchies, opened possibilities for determined litigants. When the dispute was litigated for a second time at the Dīwān al-ᶜĀlī, the Dīwān respected the previous sharīᶜa court judgment. Nevertheless, the loser managed to negotiate an improved outcome through ṣulḥ.

The dispute was first brought before the Ḥanafī nāᵓib at al-Bāb al-ᶜĀlī on the last day of Muḥarram 1155 (6 April 1742), when Muḥammad Efendī al-Shaᶜrāwī, who held the second rank in the Çavuşān regiment, sued Fāṭima bint al-Ḥājj Aḥmad al-Maghribī.[24] Fāṭima was a wealthy woman from a merchant family. Her late father had been a successful trader in the copperware souk, and Fāṭima owned and controlled a significant amount of real estate. Fāṭima also had connections within political society; she was represented at the hearing by the Janissary officer al-Amīr Aḥmad al-Malāṭyalī. Muḥammad claimed that Fāṭima had sold him a number of properties in three separate transactions, for a total of 2,100 gold funduqlī dīnārs. The first two transactions were registered in certificates of purchase (*ḥujjat al-tabāyuᶜ*) issued by the sharīᶜa court of al-Zāhid on 24 Rajab 1152 (27 October 1739) and by the sharīᶜa court of Bābay Saᶜāda wa ᵓl-Kharq on 10 Shaᶜbān 1152 (12 November

1739). The third transaction concerned a property owned by a waqf that Fāṭima controlled, and was registered in a certificate of istibdāl issued by al-Bāb al-ᶜĀlī, also on 10 Shaᶜbān 1152 (12 November 1739).[25] Muḥammad claimed that he had paid the 2,100 dīnārs in full, but that Fāṭima was now trying to prevent him taking possession of the properties.

At the hearing, Fāṭima acknowledged most of Muḥammad's claim, including her receipt of the 2,100 dīnārs, but she argued that she had not sold the properties, but had mortgaged them as security against a loan, a transaction called *rahn*. Muḥammad insisted that the transactions had been final sales (*shiran battan*), and produced the three ḥujjas, which were read in court. They confirmed the finality of the sales (*inbitāt al-bayᶜ*). Fāṭima continued to deny this, and demanded proof in the form of testimony, as was her right according to sharīᶜa procedure.[26] Muḥammad produced three witnesses—al-Ḥājj Ḥusayn ibn ᶜAlī al-Sukrī, Muḥammad ibn ᶜAlī al-Qudsī, and al-Ḥājj ᶜAbdullāh ibn Muḥammad al-Ziftāwī—all of whom had been present at the conclusion of the transactions and had signed, as court witnesses, Muḥammad's ḥujjas. Only at that point did Fāṭima concede, offering no defense. The nāᵓib informed her that in light of Muḥammad's evidence, her claim that the transactions were mortgages was baseless, and he forbade her from claiming it in future. The nāᵓib confirmed Muḥammad's ownership of the properties, the finality of the sales, and the validity of the ḥujjas he possessed.

This appears to be a decisive victory for Muḥammad. But despite the fact that the nāᵓib had forbidden Fāṭima from pursuing Muḥammad, she did exactly that in a lawsuit she brought against Muḥammad four and a half months later, at the Dīwān al-ᶜĀlī on 20 Jumādā ᵓl-Thānī 1155 (22 August 1742).[27] The case was heard by the Qāḍī al-Dīwān and the governor Yaḥyā Pasha. Again, Fāṭima was represented by a Janissary officer, this time al-Sayyid Ismāᶜīl ibn ᶜAlī, who was a member of the household of al-Amīr Ibrāhīm al-Qāzdughlī. Fāṭima claimed that Muḥammad had illegally seized properties belonging to her: the same properties that had been contested in the previous lawsuit. Muḥammad produced the same three documents, and also the ḥujja that al-Bāb al-ᶜĀlī issued in his favor (a *ḥujjat al-daᶜwā*). The crucial elements of the previous case were explained to the court: Fāṭima's claim that the transactions were mortgages and Muḥammad's success in proving that they were in fact final sales. The four ḥujjas were read in court, and this time Fāṭima did not insist on confirmation by oral testimony.

Within the confines of adjudication, there was nowhere further to go. Muḥammad had proved his ownership of the properties, and Fāṭima had no grounds on which to challenge the previous judgment. However, at this point the formal adjudication process ended, and Muḥammad and Fāṭima entered ṣulḥ. The mediation took place before a group of military officers, some from Muḥammad's regiment and some close to Fāṭima's agent al-Sayyid Ismāᶜīl ibn ᶜAlī.[28] The ṣulḥ process concluded with Fāṭima acknowledging Muḥammad's ownership of the properties, her receipt of 2,100 dīnārs in payment, and the finality of the sales. However, Muḥammad also agreed to make a further payment to Fāṭima of 160 zinjirlī dīnārs. Fāṭima had effectively managed to renegotiate the terms of the sale, almost three years after the fact.

This example demonstrates how litigation could be merely one part of a broader strategy in a dispute. We can only guess why Fāṭima pursued this case so aggressively. Perhaps she felt she had been cheated in some way, perhaps she had a change of heart and genuinely wanted to reverse the sales, or perhaps she was simply ruthless and unscrupulous in all her business dealings. But regardless of her motives, we can see that her determination produced a result for her—a significant further payment—despite the overwhelming evidence against her claim. As well as issuing a second lawsuit at the Dīwān, she also mobilized her impressive social connections. The influence she could bring to bear through her agent in the Dīwān lawsuit—a Janissary officer and member of the powerful Qāzdughlī household—may have helped to sway the ṣulḥ negotiations in her favor.

Fāṭima used the lawsuit at the Dīwān as a means of applying pressure, rather than as a claim she believed she could win. In other words, Fāṭima used the lawsuit as an instrument in her strategy of intimidation, rather than as a means of redress in itself. The lawsuit may have pushed Muḥammad towards compromise by costing him time and money. If Muḥammad had been avoiding Fāṭima's requests for negotiation outside the court, the lawsuit, which compelled him to attend the Dīwān, forced him into a public confrontation where he faced social pressure to enter mediation. The prominence of the Dīwān, as a forum where influential and powerful people were often in attendance, could have been significant in this respect: Muḥammad was forced to air the dispute before an audience of notables. The existence of several legal forums that did not have any fixed procedural relationship to each other gave disputants opportunities to use a lawsuit as a means of exerting pressure in this way.

Seeking ṣulḥ: the court, publicity, and social pressure

Fāṭima's case against Muḥammad is particularly interesting as it reveals the movement of a dispute from one court to another, allowing us to trace the formal relationships between legal institutions as well as a dogged litigant's attempts to maneuver around their edges. While the ability to document the separate stages of a dispute is rare, this is only due to the huge volume of documents, their incomplete survival, and their haphazard organization. It is likely that there were many other disputes that traveled from forum to forum as determined litigants refused to back down.

There are certainly further examples of the strategy employed by Fāṭima in the second lawsuit at the Dīwān: that is, using a lawsuit as a way to push the opponent into ṣulḥ. The court hearing publicized a dispute before officials and other prominent figures—bearers of formal and informal authority—whose influence could help push a reluctant defendant into accepting mediation. This mediation often resulted in the defendant waiving some of his or her legal rights, and accepting a resolution less favorable than what was obtainable through adjudication.

Plaintiffs could employ this strategy successfully when they wanted to obtain specific objectives that fell short of complete victory, but which were still better than what they were entitled to under adjudication. In other words, plaintiffs could hope to receive specific, limited concessions. The court records often reveal intelligent, strategic planning by litigants who, while in a legally weak position, were able to identify and then exploit these limited opportunities. An example is a dispute between Baraka bint Aḥmad and her son-in-law, al-Ḥājj Muḥammad ibn ᶜAbd al-Jawād al-Jammāl, which was heard at Bāb al-Shaᶜriyya on 8 Dhū ᵓl-Ḥijja 1077 (1 June 1667). Baraka was acting as the guardian for her daughter, Sitayta bint Ghānim, who was a minor and Muḥammad's wife. Baraka claimed that Muḥammad had not provided Sitayta with sufficient clothing, and that both Muḥammad and his mother, Fāṭima, who lived with the couple, had been beating her. Muḥammad admitted liability for the clothing, but he denied the allegation of beating. The nāᵓib ordered Muḥammad to pay Sitayta the value of the clothing she was entitled to. At this point Muḥammad, his mother, father, sister, and a group of women who were accompanying them caused a disturbance in the court, yelling and shouting.

We can only imagine how the nāᵓib handled the breakdown of order in his court. Perhaps the *muḥḍir* (court bailiff) restrained Muḥammad and his family, or perhaps the nāᵓib relied on his moral authority and that of any assembled notables to quiet them. The terse court record moves directly on to the next legally significant event, which was most likely some hours or even days later. A group of people from Muḥammad's neighborhood attended and made a statement before the nāᵓib that Muḥammad and his family were evil people who had repeatedly committed wicked acts (*min ahl al-shirra taqaddama lahum al-shirra mirāran*). Mediators then intervened. The agreement reached through ṣulḥ was that Sitayta would go to live with her mother Baraka until she reached the age of maturity.[29] Meanwhile, Muḥammad would pay Baraka one silver niṣf per day for her maintenance.

Although Muḥammad and his mother were not punished for beating Sitayta, this was a good outcome for Baraka. Punishment would have been difficult to obtain: although their neighbors gave Muḥammad's family a damning character reference, Baraka could not provide witnesses to the beatings. This was hardly surprising, as they took place within a private home. What Baraka did gain was custody of Sitayta, removing her from immediate danger, with the expenses this entailed covered by Muḥammad. This was only a temporary solution, as Baraka's custody was to last only until Sitayta reached maturity. However, Baraka's custody would have allowed her to help Sitayta to dissolve the marriage at that point. A minor girl who had been married by her guardian was allowed to repudiate her marriage upon reaching maturity, according to the doctrine known as *khiyār al-bulūgh*. Successful exercise of this right required careful planning. The girl had to renounce her marriage immediately: as soon as she first menstruated.[30] In order to prove that she had done this, Sitayta would have to arrange for suitable witnesses to be present when she made her renunciation. As long as she was isolated in Muḥammad's abusive household, Muḥammad could prevent this from happening. By contrast, at her mother Baraka's house this would be easy to arrange. Baraka's custody of Sitayta created the circumstances in which Sitayta could eventually escape from her marriage.

It seems likely that resolving the dispute through ṣulḥ was Baraka's intention from the beginning. While she could establish that Muḥammad owed Sitayta her clothing allowance and so obtain a judgment ordering payment, she knew she could not prove the more serious allegation of beating and so had no legal grounds to obtain either the punishment of Muḥammad or the removal of Sitayta. But the court case provided a context in which Muḥammad could be pressured to enter ṣulḥ negotiations. Sympathetic mediators, persuaded to support Baraka by Muḥammad and his family's performance in court and by their neighbors' poor opinion of them, pushed Muḥammad towards accepting a compromise that went beyond what the nāʾib could impose. The court's location in a wider socio-cultural context was crucial for the resolution of this dispute, even though the law itself played a limited role in deciding the settlement. The court provided a context in which Baraka could elicit the support of influential local people, perhaps including the nāʾib, who then used their influence to pressure Muḥammad into making significant concessions. The court also provided a very public stage on which Muḥammad and his family's failings were displayed. Their atrocious behavior in court, which was entirely counter-productive, suggests that the family was chaotic and incapable of strategizing to procure sympathy or create a good impression. Perhaps Baraka anticipated that they would embarrass themselves: knowing that this would help her cause, this was a further incentive for Baraka to bring them to court despite her lack of evidence. And finally, the court's notarization of the ṣulḥ agreement turned it into an enforceable contract: once Muḥammad had handed Sitayta over to Baraka's custody, he could not renege and demand her back.

Courts and extra-judicial dispute resolution

The prevalence of disputes resolved through ṣulḥ illustrates the fact that Ottoman Cairo's legal institutions were embedded in a wider culture of disputing. Although legal doctrine provided answers to most situations that would come before the courts, these were not the only answers, and litigants were free to pursue other solutions through the less prescriptive route of ṣulḥ. These solutions would then be stamped with the authority of the legal system when they were ratified by a qāḍī or nāʾib. Ṣulḥ, which lacked formal procedures and was only loosely circumscribed by legal doctrines, was a process that was necessarily influenced by other factors such as social prestige and community norms. Ṣulḥ was a key interface between a normative law, that saw itself as universal, and local Cairene culture. It limited the scope for the law's demands to conflict egregiously with local expectations, and it allowed Cairene communities to place the law's authority behind communal solutions.

Beyond the practice of ṣulḥ, which was formally sanctioned by both the Ottoman legal system and Islamic jurisprudence, the culture of disputing was wider still. Disputants looked to employ any dispute resolution technique that might work in their favor. Many disputes would have been resolved without any input from the courts or even from such an informal but officially recognized practice as ṣulḥ. As in other societies, seventeenth and eighteenth-century Cairenes in disputes asked influential contacts to have words in ears, they used emotional blackmail against their families and spouses, they cajoled, harassed, and threatened, and sometimes they intimidated, attacked, or even murdered their adversaries.

These types of informal dispute resolution were beyond the domain of law as normally conceived. But it is important to pay attention to them if we are to understand the place of law in Cairene society. Legal action was undertaken within the context of this wider culture of disputing: to disputants, legal action was one tool among many at their disposal. In order to understand the meaning of law to ordinary Cairene disputants, we must attempt to understand why they chose legal action over other dispute resolution methods, or why they did not. These other informal dispute resolution mechanisms also interacted with the legal system in interesting ways. Inasmuch as these mechanisms emerged from a culture specific to late seventeenth and early eighteenth-century Cairo, they again offer insight into how the Ottoman-Islamic legal system accommodated other normative orders.

Unlike ṣulḥ, dispute resolutions that were entirely informal were never formally recorded, and so are difficult for the historian to grasp. Yet there are glimpses of such acts both in narrative sources and, obliquely, in the court records. In what follows I look at incidents in which disputants used violence, either to coerce their opponents into submission or simply as revenge. As is clear from narrative sources, many Cairenes saw violence as a legitimate means of dispute resolution. Ottoman Cairo shared this aspect of disputing culture with many other societies, pre-modern and modern: particularly those where a concept of honor was prominent.[31] The Islamic legal tradition was rather more hesitant to endorse violence carried out by individuals. Although it allowed the patriarch a limited amount of violence as a tool of discipline within his household, Islamic law did not generally permit revenge attacks, vigilantism, or coercive violence within the public sphere.[32] Ottoman Cairo's courts, however, showed a greater willingness to accommodate a local culture of honor and revenge. They did not routinely tolerate violence, but they did in certain circumstances. Three contrasting cases can help us examine the contours of this accommodation.

One course of action open to disputants was to physically intimidate their opponents into concessions. Some employed local strongmen to help them do this. An example can be seen in a case that came before the court of Bāb al-Shaᶜriyya on 2 Ṣafar 1078 (24 July 1667).[33] The dispute was between Muḥammad ibn ᶜAlī and ᶜAbd al-Rāziq ibn ᶜAbd al-Karīm. Muḥammad claimed that earlier that day, ᶜAbd al-Rāziq had visited him accompanied by al-Ḥājj Yūsuf, who was a *qawāṣṣ* (guard) and retainer of the Amīr Shahīn, the multazim of the Khurda tax-farm. Muḥammad claimed that they attempted to extort from him fifteen silver niṣfs per month.

ᶜAbd al-Rāziq admitted that he had visited Muḥammad and asked for money. He claimed that he, Muḥammad, and another man called al-Ḥājj ᶜAbd al-Ḥāfiẓ were partners in a lamp-making business, and were collectively obliged to pay two ghurūsh per month in taxes.[34] The fifteen silver niṣfs were Muḥammad's share. Muḥammad denied owing any money, saying that he already paid ᶜAbd al-Hāfiẓ two niṣfs per day, which was supposed to cover the taxes. He demanded proof from ᶜAbd al-Rāziq, but ᶜAbd al-Rāziq failed to provide any. The qāḍī therefore forbade ᶜAbd al-Rāziq from pursuing any claims against Muḥammad, unless he was able to prove the debt.

The court record gives us no concrete information about why this dispute arose. We can guess, however, that whatever the basis was for ᶜAbd al-Rāziq's demand of fifteen extra silver niṣfs per month, it was not something which had been formally agreed between the partners. If it had been, we would expect ᶜAbd al-Rāziq to be able to prove it, as business agreements were usually documented, or at least made orally before witnesses who could be called upon in any subsequent disputes. It seems likely that ᶜAbd al-Rāziq was attempting to renegotiate a previous agreement: perhaps in response to a tax hike, or perhaps due to a change in his perception of Muḥammad's contribution of capital or labor to the enterprise. He turned to al-Ḥājj Yūsuf to help him convince Muḥammad to accept the extra obligation. It is not clear why al-Ḥājj Yūsuf helped him: perhaps he was a relative or friend, perhaps ᶜAbd al-Rāziq paid him, or perhaps this was one of the series of reciprocal favors and services that made up a patron–client relationship. But as a qawāṣṣ, al-Ḥājj Yūsuf would have been armed and fearsome: his role was to intimidate Muḥammad.

The nāʾib in this case had nothing to say about al-Ḥājj Yūsuf's involvement: whatever his opinion was, there was no room within legal procedure for him to express it, as the lawsuit was brought by Muḥammad against ᶜAbd al-Rāziq only, and because the subject of the lawsuit was the legality of ᶜAbd al-Rāziq's demand itself, rather than the means by which he made it. Nevertheless, the court offered Muḥammad the opportunity to resist ᶜAbd al-Rāziq's attempted intimidation. He was able to secure a nāʾib's judgment, which was made in public and which also produced a ḥujja which Muḥammad could use as proof, stating that ᶜAbd al-Rāziq's demand was illegitimate. This may not have prevented future intimidation from ᶜAbd al-Rāziq. But through the court case, Muḥammad shifted the dispute back into the territory of law where he had the upper hand. It might also have served to publicize the attempted intimidation and so embarrass ᶜAbd al-Rāziq.

In a similar case involving intimidation, heard at Bāb al-Shaᶜriyya on 20 Muḥarram 1078 (12 July 1667), the nāʾib did respond to the intimidation and punish the person behind it.[35] In this case, a shopkeeper called Ḥamūda ibn Ramaḍān sued a woman called Fāṭima ibnat Sarrāj, claiming that the previous night she had complained to al-Zaynī Khalīl Çorbacı, an officer of the ᶜAzabān regiment and guard of the tower at the Shaᶜriyya gate from which the neighborhood took its name, about him and his family. She had led Khalīl to Ḥamūda's house, where he had forced his way in, arrested, and then imprisoned Ḥamūda's brother Zayn. In court, Fāṭima denied the incident outright and demanded that Ḥamūda prove his allegation. Ḥamūda produced three witnesses who confirmed his story. The qāḍī sentenced Fāṭima to taᶜzīr: the court record states that she was punished immediately in court, probably by lashing.

In this case the court record gives no indication as to what the underlying dispute between Fāṭima and Ḥamūda's family was. But whatever it was, Fāṭima attempted to resolve it through intimidation, by having a local strongman arrest and imprison Zayn. We can only speculate about why Fāṭima decided to enlist Khalīl Çorbacı in her support. As the guard of the local city gate, Khalīl was responsible for the night watch and street patrols, and had the authority to detain petty criminals and troublemakers. From the limited information in the court record it is not certain, but it seems that Khalīl was the unwitting victim of Fāṭima's deception. Ḥamūda's plaint states that Fāṭima "complained" (*shakat*) about him and his family to Khalīl: it seems likely that Fāṭima made a false accusation to the local police official in order to provoke Zayn's detention. She used Khalīl to intimidate Ḥamūda's family, either to coerce them into conceding on some issue or to take revenge for an earlier slight. The nāʾib considered this violent tactic totally illegitimate, and punished Fāṭima for her actions. Perhaps the nāʾib was particularly incensed by Fāṭima's misuse of official authority and subversion of the police system for her own ends. As the next case I will discuss shows, the same nāʾib could be remarkably tolerant of violence in the form of a revenge attack, when it was carried out by the disputant himself.

It is hardly surprising that vengeance formed part of Ottoman Cairo's culture of disputing. Revenge has held a significant place in most moral worlds throughout history, and is central to cultures of honor.[36] The Islamic law of injuries and homicide was based on the principle of retaliation: when both perpetrator and victim were of equal status, killing was punished with death, and injuries were punished with the infliction of an equivalent injury.[37] But although Islamic law incorporated the eye-for-an-eye equivalence of revenge, it did not tolerate revenge carried out by individuals.[38] Indeed, the incorporation of retaliation into the Islamic legal tradition was an attempt to channel the instinct for revenge into a controlled and fairly-administered penal system, and so to prevent the chaos of vigilantism.[39] Nevertheless, the urge to revenge was something with which Ottoman-Egyptian society sympathized, and acts of revenge could be accommodated by the courts. Again, ṣulḥ was the conduit which allowed the community's values and norms to be accommodated.

A fascinating case heard at the court of Bāb al-Shaʿriyya on 12 Ṣafar 1078 (3 August 1667), by the very same nāʾib who sentenced Fāṭima ibnat Sarrāj to lashing the previous month, illustrates this. The case concerned a dispute between al-Sayyid Shukur ibn ʿĀmir and his former servant Shaʿbān ibn Nāfiʿ. The case actually conflated what were, legally, two separate claims, both of which related to the same underlying dispute. Shukur claimed that during the previous year, when Shaʿbān was still his servant, they had traveled together to Edirne; during the trip Shaʿbān had stolen from him goods worth a total of sixteen and one-sixth ghurūsh. Shaʿbān denied the allegation; Shukur failed to prove it and declined to demand Shaʿbān's oath. Meanwhile, Shaʿbān claimed that Shukur had attacked him earlier on the day of the court hearing, hitting him, drawing his weapon, and threatening to kill him. Shaʿbān produced two witnesses who corroborated his claim.[40]

The immediate prompt for the court case was Shukur's attack on Shaᶜbān. It seems likely that Shukur, having not seen Shaᶜbān since the trip to Edirne, encountered him in the street and, enraged, took his revenge on the spot by attempting to kill him. Bystanders intervened, learned the background to the dispute, and brought the pair to the court. The interesting part of this case is the result. Whatever the actual truth of Shukur's allegation of theft, in terms of legal procedure he had no leg to stand on. He lacked any evidence, and he did not demand Shaᶜbān's oath. Had he done so, Shaᶜbān could have established his innocence by taking the oath. Shaᶜbān, meanwhile, produced two witnesses who testified that Shukur attacked him flagrantly in the street. Shukur had no grounds on which to claim recompense from Shaᶜbān, while Shaᶜbān could have demanded that Shukur be punished for the attack. If Shaᶜbān had suffered an injury, he could also have demanded compensation or retaliation in kind.

However, the case was not resolved by adjudication, but by ṣulḥ. According to the ṣulḥ settlement agreed to by both parties, Shaᶜbān paid Shukur 30 niṣfs, and both parties renounced all future claims connected with the dispute. Shukur thus gained doubly from this settlement. He not only received 30 niṣfs to which he had no legal claim,[41] but he was also absolved of the attack and so avoided punishment. We can only speculate as to why Shaᶜbān agreed to this settlement, which conflicted with both his interests and his legal rights. It seems likely that the implicit threat of further violence hung over the negotiations. It also seems probable that the mediators sympathized with Shukur. His inability to prove the theft was not surprising: it had taken place a year ago in distant Edirne. Shukur was of higher status than Shaᶜbān: not only was Shaᶜbān a former employee of Shukur, but Shukur bore the title sayyid, indicating descent from the Prophet, while Shaᶜbān used no title. The mediators were likely of similarly high status. While fully aware that the attack was illegal, they also understood that in their social world the ability to take revenge was central to the defense of one's honor. In particular, they recognized that if Shukur had not responded to such an affront from his social inferior, he would surely have lost face. The mechanism of ṣulḥ allowed the court to ignore, and so tacitly condone, a revenge attack carried out in broad daylight in front of witnesses. A dispute resolution method that was not only extra-judicial but actually illegal was nevertheless accommodated within the judicial sphere.

Ṣulḥ and arbitrariness

The resolution to the case of *Shukur* vs. *Shaᶜbān* was at significant variance from what should have occurred according to the legal procedure of the sharīᶜa. The case of Baraka and her abusive son-in-law Muḥammad also ended in a resolution at odds with the judgment that would have emerged from procedurally-correct adjudication. In both cases, although the ṣulḥ agreements deviated from the law, they were fair according to the ethical and cultural standards of late seventeenth-century Cairo. Indeed, in both cases adjudication would have produced an outcome that was widely seen as *unfair*. Shukur would have been punished for what seemed, to Cairenes of the higher social classes, a perfectly understandable defense of his honor against an insubordinate, while Shaᶜbān walked away scot free having robbed his employer. Sitayta, a vulnerable underage girl, would have been left in the care of her husband and his family, who were widely known to be abusive and immoral.

The fact that ṣulḥ agreements could diverge so significantly from the result that would be obtained through adjudication suggests an explanation for the dissonance between the views of Ottoman legal historians of the past few decades, who describe the Ottoman legal system as characterized by a rigorous adherence to legal doctrines and procedure, and the views of contemporary western travelers in the Ottoman legal process, who saw it as arbitrary, incoherent, and corrupt.[42] These latter views are connected with the stereotype of "kadijustiz," in which the qāḍī dispenses judgments based on his capricious assessment of right and wrong rather than a settled body of law. Ottomanists, and historians of Islamic law more generally, have tended to view adjudication as the core function of the courts.[43] Focusing on records of adjudications, they have found that procedures were followed closely and that the judgments of qāḍīs always followed what fiqh texts prescribed. The present study is no exception in this regard: in the vast majority of adjudications, Ottoman Cairo's qāḍīs followed legal procedures faithfully and based their judgments on the doctrines propounded by their particular madhhabs. Ottomanists and Islamic legal historians have therefore been very uncomfortable with the views of European travelers and with the kadijustiz paradigm; some have devoted studies to disproving it.[44] But despite the predictability and rationality of adjudication in Ottoman Cairo's courts, ṣulḥ was inherently non-procedural, with the litigants being guided to mutual compromise through social pressure and moral exhortation, and it could lead to settlements that diverged significantly from accepted legal doctrine. These settlements were then approved and made binding by the qāḍī, who may also have been involved in guiding the ṣulḥ negotiation itself.[45] It was perhaps this role of the qāḍī, or rather the fact that the qāḍī played different roles in different cases, sometimes mediating and sometimes adjudicating, that looked like incoherence and arbitrariness to European travelers.[46] While the source of their confusion is understandable, their conclusion was technically incorrect. Ṣulḥ agreements were voluntary contracts that in no way contradicted the legal doctrine on the relevant issues, because the parties to the contract were permitted to waive their legal rights; moreover, the practice of ṣulḥ was regulated (loosely, but intentionally so) by legal doctrine.[47] Nevertheless, the flexibility introduced by ṣulḥ opened the door to various means of applying pressure. As the case of *Shukur* vs. *Shaᶜbān* demonstrates, there were no doubt many litigants who were coerced into waiving their rights in dubious circumstances.

Conclusion

In the courts of Ottoman Cairo, lawsuits almost always represented the initiative of private litigants.[48] Legal action only occurred when a disputant thought it would serve his or her interest. Whatever the high-minded aspirations of those who created and administered it, an adversarial, reactive court system like Ottoman Cairo's was driven not by a commitment to an abstract justice, but by thousands of self-interested litigants looking out for themselves. The litigant's perspective, then, is as crucial as the formal design of the legal system if we want to figure out how it actually worked.

In this chapter I have outlined some of the strategies employed by litigants when navigating this complex, plural court system. Although there was no system of appeal or court hierarchy, some litigants took their disputes to multiple forums. In fact, the lack of formal definitions of jurisdiction may have helped them to do this. For example, Fāṭima bint al-Ḥājj Aḥmad al-Maghribī was able to have her lawsuit against Muḥammad Efendī al-Shaᶜrāwī heard at the Dīwān al-ᶜĀlī, even though the judgment against her was a foregone conclusion due to the previous verdict in favor of Muḥammad at al-Bāb al-ᶜĀlī. In modern legal systems with a formal hierarchy of courts, such a lawsuit would never make it to the judge's desk because it would not meet the criteria for appeal.

When they approached multiple legal forums with their disputes, Cairenes were engaging in a strategy of intimidation, as well as creating bargaining chips. The resolute determination displayed by aggressively pursuing a dispute, even with authorities as far away as Istanbul, pressured the opponent to concede. If the opponent was inexperienced with the law, it might create an impression of inevitable defeat: he or she might think, "this person has access to the highest levers of power, he knows how to work the system, everyone is on his side, so how can I resist?" If the opponent was experienced with the law but recalcitrant, the barrage of suits and documents served as harassment. Court hearings represented a cost of time, money, and possibly pride or social standing; the persistent plaintiff told the defendant, "I will relieve you of this burden if you settle the dispute."

As demonstrated by the numerous ṣulḥ agreements in the court records, disputes were frequently settled without adjudication. Mediation allowed litigants to waive their rights, voluntarily but often under considerable social pressure, and so settlements could diverge considerably from the outcome that legal procedure would arrive at. This is where we see how deeply enmeshed the court system was in broader, communal dispute resolution practices and values. The court was often the venue in which a defendant was persuaded to undergo ṣulḥ. Whether it was the qāḍī or local notables present at court who did the persuading, we have seen that people often agreed to mediation even when they would win an adjudication hands down. In some cases, such people may have been weak willed and easily bullied; in many others, they simply saw that it was in their interest to preserve or improve their relations with their neighbors by making concessions. Ṣulḥ was a mechanism that enabled the courts, with their formalistic procedures, to be brought into line with community understandings of justice and equity. It was widely accepted that strict adherence to procedure could, in some cases, lead to unfair outcomes. Ṣulḥ allowed settlements that were endorsed by the community as fair to also receive the backing of the law.

While the court records, structured by legal procedure, tend to present adjudication and mediation as distinct processes, in reality litigation and mediation were not alternative options but ran concurrently. It was expected that people would attempt resolution in multiple forums, formal and informal, at the same time. Even if two parties were not actively engaging in mediation, the possibility of mediation was always held in front of them at every stage of a lawsuit. Litigation provided a spur to engage in mediation, and also a fall-back position if mediation failed. But even after the litigation had concluded and a judgment had been issued, the parties could still agree to mediation and were encouraged to do so.

Given that informal processes of mediation and negotiation, embedded in the community, were accepted and endorsed by the courts of Ottoman Cairo, the social hierarchies of the community were reproduced in the justice the courts produced. The courts were not neutral arbiters between social groups, nor were they champions of the oppressed. They embodied a society that was highly inegalitarian. This is not to say that the courts were simply a tool for the strong to dominate the weak. The concept of justice held by the courts and wider society took seriously the obligations of the powerful, and so the courts defended the poor against abusive landlords or rapacious officials, and they forced husbands to honor their commitments to their wives. But their fundamental respect for existing social hierarchies was reflected in the tolerance they could show to the misdeeds of the elite Muslim man: such as when Shukur the sayyid's armed attack on a servant in broad daylight was glossed over in a ṣulḥ agreement that saw his victim withdraw the charge and pay compensation.

CONCLUSION: OTTOMAN CAIRO'S LEGAL SYSTEM AND GRAND NARRATIVES

Ottoman Cairo's legal system was a complex mesh of institutions, produced by the combination of the long evolution of the fiqh juristic tradition and the Ottoman variant of the Turco–Persian imperial tradition. As a mix of sometimes antagonistic traditions, the Ottoman legal system was typical of early modern empires, which accumulated traditions as they grew over centuries, and used different idioms of legitimation for different constituencies.[1] Searching for neat order in such polities is anachronistic. This was a plural legal system; exhibiting pluralism both in the bodies of legal doctrine on which judgments could be based, and in the judicial forums which litigants could approach. The doctrinal pluralism consisted of the plurality of madhhabs. The four madhhabs had coexisted in Cairo's courts since 1265, but under Ottoman rule this was not a straightforward case of legal pluralism where litigants could choose freely: the Ottoman government shaped and restricted the choices available. The pluralism of judicial forums—the main ones being the sharīᶜa courts, the Dīwān al-ᶜĀlī, and the Dīvān-i Hümāyūn—was more open. This was due to the lack of clear jurisdictional boundaries between these institutions, itself a result of the amalgamation of the sharīᶜa and the Persianate imperial tradition, which both claimed universal sovereignty.

While the Ottoman legal system drew on several elements, it was produced and practiced by a society that saw itself, its government, and its law as Islamic. This study has followed recent literature in Islamic legal studies by expanding the scope of the subject beyond fiqh. While fiqh, and the ulema who produced it and studied it, were very closely identified with Islamic law, elements from outside this tradition were incorporated and indigenized throughout Islamic legal history. The authority of fiqh never stood alone, but was always in dialogue with other sources of authority, in particular the authority of kings and emperors. This dialogue and incorporation was not seen as problematic, in principle, by most of the people who produced, enforced, and lived under pre-modern Islamic legal regimes. Certainly, we as historians should accept all these elements as part of the Islamic legal tradition that we study. This does not mean that there is no room in the narrative for tension. In fact, there was lots of tension, over the precise ranges and limits of different authorities, which often competed with one another. Decentering fiqh restores these tensions to their right place, which is as one of the main storylines in the narrative of Islamic legal history, rather than dismissing them as aberrations or as peripheral phenomena.

Islamic legal history

Works on other periods of Islamic legal history have made comparable arguments to mine. Based on recent work, I think we can start to construct a new grand narrative of Islamic legal history. This is not the place to attempt such a project, but I will conclude by offering a rough sketch of what it might look like.

While the distinct post of qāḍī first emerged in the late seventh century, we know very little about the administration of justice in the Umayyad caliphate due to a lack of contemporary documentation.[2] It is in the ᶜAbbāsid caliphate that we first see the theorists carving out a distinct jurisdiction for the qāḍī, and making claims for judicial independence. Mathieu Tillier has shown how in the second half of the ninth century and the early tenth century CE, writers began to assert that the qāḍī exercised authority not on the caliph's behalf, but on God's or the Muslim community's behalf, and that the early caliphs and even the Prophet had submitted to the judgments of impartial arbiters.[3] Claims for judicial supremacy notwithstanding, alternative jurisdictions associated with the ruler continued to exist alongside the courts of the qāḍīs. In particular, the maẓālim tribunal, nominally presided over by the ruler, was a common feature of legal systems during this period. In places where relations between qāḍīs and the ruler deteriorated, it became a direct competitor to the qāḍī. However, for most of the time qāḍīs were closely involved in maẓālim tribunals; it was a qāḍī who heard the cases at the maẓālim tribunal, and only rarely did the ruler preside in person.[4] The situation was very similar in the contemporary period in Spain, under the Umayyad caliphate of Cordoba.[5]

After the turbulence caused by the decline of ᶜAbbāsid power, by the eleventh century a rough accord had been reached between the qāḍī's court and the ruler's maẓālim, and their coexistence became the norm. Indeed, while the tenth century saw the emergence of a theory of judicial independence, the eleventh saw Māwardī elaborate his theory of the maẓālim jurisdiction.[6] While Māwardī's theory delineated a specific jurisdiction for the maẓālim tribunal, and a specific set of circumstances in which the strict procedural law used by qāḍīs could be relaxed, the limited historical evidence we have for the operation of maẓālim tribunals after Māwardī, which mostly comes from the Mamluk Sultanate, indicates that the maẓālim jurisdiction overlapped considerably with that of the qāḍī's court. Moreover, qāḍīs often, though not always, sat in judgment at the Mamluk maẓālim tribunal as well as those of ᶜAbbāsid caliphate and Umayyad Spain.[7] In other words, it is misleading to think of this tribunal as "extra-judicial." Although it is very common to do so, we should not base our understanding of medieval maẓālim on Māwardī, who was theorizing an ideal rather than reporting actual practice.

Yossef Rapoport has recently proposed a new narrative of Mamluk legal history. In Rapoport's narrative, executive authorities play an increasingly prominent role in the legal system over the course of the Mamluk period. This includes both increasing government intervention in the application of fiqh, and figures such as Sultans, amīrs, and chamberlains playing an increasingly central role in dispute resolution. Rapoport rejects the interpretation of previous scholars, who saw such close involvement by the government in the justice system as corruption and as the decay of the sharīᶜa. Instead, he argues positively that this was a state-building project that made correct implementation of sharīᶜa one of the key goals and attributes of the ruler.[8]

Rapoport's trajectory is reflected in another recent work on Mamluk legal history: Kristen Stilt's book on the muḥtasib. Stilt portrays a change in the holders of this post: early in the Mamluk period, a high proportion of the muḥtasibs were members of the ulema, but by the end of the period they were almost all administrators or military men.[9] Like Rapoport, however, Stilt does not see this as a decline in the institution's standards. Whether the holder of the post came from the ulema or not, Stilt sees the muḥtasibs as effective agents of governance, who drew on both fiqh and siyāsa for their authority.[10]

By the time the Ottomans arrived in the Arab Middle East, there was already an established trajectory of the executive authorities increasingly involving themselves in the administration of justice; not by displacing the sharīᶜa, but by incorporating the sharīᶜa into the institutions of government. The development of the early modern Ottoman legal system, in both the central lands and the Arab provinces, fits well into this trajectory, pushing state intervention further but also in new directions. In terms of the judicial infrastructure, while some of the nomenclature changed, the key jurisdictions remained fairly similar to earlier polities. The sharīᶜa court, of course, remained vital. In addition, the ruler, or rather his representative the Grand Vizier, held court and received complaints from any subject, although the word "maẓālim" was no longer used for this tribunal. In the provinces, the same role was played by the Sultan's local representative, the governor. Market inspection remained in the hands of individuals distinct from the qāḍī, as did public morality and public order. In Ottoman Cairo, rather than these tasks being amalgamated in the single jurisdiction of the muḥtasib, they were shared between the Janissary Āghā, the police chief, the muḥtasib, and the multazim of al-Khurda. As in medieval polities, qāḍīs played an important role beyond the sharīᶜa courts in governors' and Grand Viziers' tribunals. Another element of continuity was the lack of clear jurisdictional boundaries, leaving a great deal of choice to individual litigants.

Perhaps the most distinctive aspect of the Ottoman legal system was the ilmiye hierarchy: the deep integration of the ulema into the political and social fabric of the Ottoman ruling class. This involved the creation of a network of madrasas, a hierarchy of professorial and judicial posts with a clear system of promotion, the position of Şeyhulislām, the chief mufti of the empire, and the creation of official muftiships in provincial cities.[11] While the creation of the ilmiye must be counted as an extraordinary success, it did not incorporate everyone. Particularly after the conquest of the Arab provinces, the Ottomans had as their subjects a large community of ulema who were not members of the ilmiye. Although the boundaries between the two groups were often traversed by individuals, there remained two distinct groups throughout the early modern period, and relations between them were often marked by tension.[12]

Connected with the ilmiye project was the adoption of Ḥanafism as the empire's official madhhab. The creation of the "state madhhab," involving not only its recognition and support but the cultivation of a specific branch within the wider Ḥanafī madhhab, is the most distinctive and original aspect of the Ottoman legal system.[13] The case of Ottoman Cairo illustrates the limits of this project. As discussed in Chapter 4, various attempts to Ḥanafize Cairo's legal system were made between the early sixteenth and early eighteenth centuries. The very different legal culture of Cairo meant that these attempts met with resistance. While the state madhhab idea and the Ḥanafizing instinct remained alive throughout this period, the limited capabilities of the early modern state meant that the Ottomans were not in a position to eradicate the non-Ḥanafī madhhabs from Cairo's courts; they had to settle for a Ḥanafī monopoly on the top judicial posts, and the gradual restriction and marginalization of the most controversial non-Ḥanafī doctrines.

The legal reforms of the nineteenth century, in the Ottoman Empire, Egypt, and across the Muslim world, also look different in our new grand narrative. Ḥanafization was one key element of continuity. In Egypt, complete Ḥanafization of the legal system was achieved through a series of administrative reforms over the course of the nineteenth century. This had significant consequences, in particular on women's rights within family law.[14] However great the impact on people's lives, the Ḥanafizing project was not new. What was new was the centralized state created in Cairo by the reforming governor, Meḥmed ᶜAlī. Autonomous from Istanbul, the state controlled by Meḥmed ᶜAlī and the dynasty he founded achieved a far deeper reach into Egyptian institutions and Egyptians' lives than anything the early modern Ottomans could have hoped for.

Ḥanafization also accelerated in the rest of the Ottoman Empire under the legal reforms of the Tanzimat. Perhaps the pinnacle of what Sami Zubaida calls the "étatization" of Islamic law was the *Mecelle-yi Aḥkam-i ᶜAdliye*, the Ottoman civil code introduced in 1877.[15] The Mecelle codified the Ḥanafī law of contract and procedure, and was implemented in both the sharīᶜa courts and the new *Niẓāmiye* courts, staffed by graduates of new European-style law schools. In much previous scholarship the Mecelle has represented a fundamental rupture in the history of Islamic law: the state's seizure of the jurists' authority to make law.[16] I would suggest that from the perspective of Islamic legal history, codification's novelty lay in its systematic nature and in the determination and success with which it was implemented, rather than in the usurpation of legislative authority by the state. As discussed in Chapter 4, early modern Ottoman history provided many precedents for the government intervening to tell qāḍīs how the fiqh tradition should be applied in the courts.

As well as the assertion of government control over substantive law via codification and Ḥanafization, the nineteenth century also saw an expansion of the role of government officials in the adjudication of disputes and administration of justice. In Egypt, a succession of new tribunals was established: the *Majlis al-tujjār* in the 1830s, the *Cemᶜiyet-i Ḥakḳāniye* in 1842, and the *Majlis al-aḥkām* in 1849.[17] These new tribunals were presided over not by a qāḍī, but by bureaucrats or, in the case of the majlis al-tujjār, a bench containing both Egyptian and foreign merchants. They also made use of new legal procedure based on forensic medicine.[18] In 1876, at a time when Egypt was succumbing to the heavy weight of European pressure due to its indebtedness, the Prime Minister, Nubar Pasha, established the Mixed Courts to hear disputes between Ottoman subjects and foreigners; the Mixed Courts were then used as a template to create the National Courts, which completed the modernization and centralization of Egypt's judicial system.[19] Again, similar reforms took place contemporaneously in the rest of the Ottoman Empire, with the establishment of the Niẓāmiye court system.[20]

The reformed judicial institutions of the nineteenth-century Ottoman Empire and Egypt replicated European models to an even greater extent than the Mecelle. Certainly, many people complained that the sharīᶜa was being sidelined; particularly the traditionally-educated ulema who, with the rise of secular law schools, had lost their monopoly on judicial and teaching posts. But it is a mistake to assume that this sentiment was shared by the reformers. They did not wish to destroy the sharīᶜa, and they did not think that they were undermining it. Aḥmed Cevdet Pasha, architect of both the Mecelle and the Niẓamiye courts, had also had a traditional jurist's education. He believed strongly that he was saving the sharīᶜa by making it more usable and more compatible with the modern state. And he found ample support for his reforms in the Islamic legal tradition. To justify the establishment of the Dīvān-i Aḥkām-i ᶜAdliye, the upper tier of the Niẓāmiye court system, he cited the jurisdiction of maẓālim, and in particular a treatise penned by the Persian scholar, Jamāl al-Dīn Davānī, in the late fifteenth century, at exactly the moment when the classical Ottoman-Islamic legal system was being formed. Translating the treatise from Persian to Turkish, he used it to demonstrate an indigenous Islamic precedent for his new tribunal.[21]

Avi Rubin commented that Ottoman borrowing of French law during the nineteenth century was a "typical case" of legal borrowing.[22] In other words, legal borrowing is a normal mechanism of legal change, common in almost all legal cultures and systems. The Ottoman adoption of aspects of French law during the Tanzimat should not, in itself, be seen as unusual or inauthentic. Rather, it was the natural result of the encounter between the Ottoman Empire and modern French intellectual culture, and it was merely the latest in a series of borrowings that shaped Islamic law: from Mongol law, Byzantine law, Turkish customary law, and so on. To many Ottomans, the legal system as a whole remained recognizably Islamic, despite the French accretions.

During this period, most of the rest of the Muslim world was under European colonial domination. Colonial legal reforms tended to progressively marginalize the sharīᶜa, eventually restricting it to the domain of family law only. This colonial model would ultimately become the norm across the twentieth-century Muslim world, at least until the re-Islamization programs that began in several countries in the 1970s. The Republic of Turkey was one of the handful of exceptions: it abolished sharīᶜa entirely, even for marriage and divorce. In the twentieth century, then, the idiom of religious and secular—religious referring to the sharīᶜa-derived family law, secular referring to the rest of the legal system—became almost universal. It is, however, teleological to project this far back into the nineteenth-century reforms. The change should be located not in the increasing intervention of the government into the law, which began in the early nineteenth century, and for which there were many Islamic precedents. The change should be located in the explicit jettisoning of sharīᶜa doctrines, which began in the mid nineteenth century but only came to its conclusion over the course of the twentieth. It was only at this point that Islamic law became seen as a separate, limited jurisdiction.

Ottoman provincial history

This book has also engaged with models of center–province relations in the Ottoman Empire; in particular, with the model of decentralization during the seventeenth and eighteenth centuries. There is no doubt that, in many ways, the Ottoman Empire's ability to project its power in distant Egypt diminished between the mid sixteenth and the mid eighteenth centuries. Istanbul lost control of Egypt twice in the second half of the eighteenth century, to ᶜAlī Bey al-Kabīr in the 1760s, and to Napoleon in 1798. Again, we must be careful not to project backwards the exceptional weakness of the late eighteenth century. I wish to challenge the decentralization model on two grounds.

The first argument is that the deterioration of central power in Egypt was not a linear decline from the late sixteenth century until 1798, as previous narratives have suggested.[23] Rather, there were different stages of assertion and retreat. The early seventeenth century was a time of particular weakness, but the Köprülü period of the late seventeenth century saw a vigorous reassertion of central power and serious attempts at reform, as it did across the empire. Little has been written about the implementation of the Köprülü reforms in Egypt, but it is clear that it upsets a model based on linear decline.

Within the legal system, the oscillation of assertion and retreat can be seen in the periodic attempts to Ḥanafize the legal system. Ḥanafization was not only an issue in the decades immediately after the conquest. It remained an ideal throughout Ottoman rule, but was pursued with varying degrees of vigor. After the initial aggressive attempts at Ḥanafization by purging the judiciary in the 1520s, there was a further bout of similar pressure at the turn of the seventeenth century. After that an accord was reached that lasted most of the century: non-Ḥanafī doctrines offensive to ilmiye-trained Ḥanafī qāḍīs were tolerated, but supervised. The supremacy of the Ḥanafī chief qāḍī was clearly expressed in the need for his permission to use controversial doctrines. From the 1690s, however, Ḥanafizing pressure was stepped up. The supremacy of the Ḥanafī chief qāḍī was augmented, by insisting that not only was his permission necessary, but use of controversial non-Ḥanafī doctrines had to take place under his direct supervision at his court. This had the effect of significantly reducing access to these doctrines, by eliminating them from most of the courts in the city.

The second argument is a call to rethink the nature of the central government's authority in Egypt. Previous scholarship has tended to focus on top-down power projected by Istanbul onto Egypt's political elites. But much of Istanbul's authority in Egypt was not imposed, but invited. Egyptian subjects of all social strata sought out, or even demanded, the involvement of the central government in their personal affairs. They sent petitions to the Dīvān-i Hümāyūn in Istanbul, and they took their cases to the governor's Dīwān al-ᶜĀlī in Cairo. The first sijill of the Dīwān al-ᶜĀlī is an excellent example of the possible disconnection between the raw power and the authority of the Istanbul government in Cairo. Dating from the early 1740s, it covers a period when, according to the narrative sources we have, the Ottoman governors in Egypt appear to have been relatively weak. The Qāzdughlī household was ascending to dominance. Beys and regimental officers had become fabulously wealthy from their monopolization of what was the key bottleneck in the international coffee trade before the French Caribbean plantations began to offer serious competition. The power of the provincial political elite had been symbolized by the creation of the new honorary title of shaykh al-balad, "master of the country," which carried no particular responsibility but essentially indicated that its holder was the most powerful man in Cairo. One particular holder of this title, ᶜUthmān Bey Dhū ᵓl-Faqār, created his own tribunal to rival the governor's, and he goaded the governor by inviting him to accept his hospitality, and therefore recognize his equal status.

Nevertheless, the governor's Dīwān al-ᶜĀlī was a busy tribunal resolving a constant flow of disputes involving real estate, trade, and other matters. Many of the litigants bringing their cases to the governor's Dīwān were members of the very elite that the governor struggled to control in his political activities. This is not necessarily surprising: the combination of disdain for government control and eager use of government services is familiar in our own society. The important point here is that the governor's authority over this aspect of Cairene social life was not imposed, but demanded. The Dīwān was an authoritative institution despite the governor's relative weakness, because Egyptian litigants made it so.

APPENDIX

EXAMPLES OF DOCUMENTS USED IN THIS STUDY

The letter *hamza* was rarely used in the Arabic writing of the period: almost never in the court records. I have followed this in my transcriptions: for example, the phrase "he was questioned" is written *suyila* rather than *suʾila.* The use of diacritics in the Arabic and Turkish documents was more or less arbitrary, depending on the scribe, and I have regularized this.

Bāb al-Shaʿriyya register 623, entry 333

(Discussed above at p. 88.)
This is an example of a judicial divorce (faskh) at the request of the wife, conducted according to the standard procedure in Cairo in the seventeenth century. The woman requesting the divorce, Hibā bint Muḥammad al-Ḥāyik, had been abandoned by her husband. She petitioned the Ḥanafī chief qāḍī, who then referred the case to the Mālikī nāʾib at Bāb al-Shaʿriyya and gave him permission to issue a judicial divorce according to Mālikī doctrine. Also of note is the document's attention to Hibā's behavior after abandonment, and the care taken by the court to establish that there were no alternative means of relief for Hibā.

١. لدى الحاكم المالكي بعد الاذن الكريم الواجب القبول
والتكريم الوارد من حضرة سيدنا ومولانا شيخ مشايخ الاسلام
ملك العلما والاعلام اشرف الموالي العظام قاموس
٢. البلاغة ونبراس الافهام المفتخر بوجوده مذهب النعمان
الفخام مويد شريعة المصطفى عليه افضل الصلاة واشرف
السلام الناظر في الاحكام الشرعية والامور الدينية
٣. يوميذ بمصر المحمية ابده الله تعالى واسبغ عليه فضله

وانعامه امين بدلالة عرض الحال المرفوع لحضرته العلية في
خصوص ما سيذكر فيه على يدي [...] الحرمة
٤. هبا المراة ابنة المرحوم محمد الحايك المتوجه عرض الحال
المذكور بما قراته بنظر القاضي المالكي بالمحمكة المزبورة هو
سيدنا ومولانا الشيخ الامام العلامة الهمام
٥. نور الدين علي الرفاعي الحاكم الشرعي المالكي الموقع خطه
الكريم باعلا اصله وعرض ذلك عليه فقابله بمزيد الامتثال
مضمونه ثبت لدى مولانا الحاكم المالكي
٦. المومى اليه اعلاه بشهادة المحترم الحاج علي بن شرف
الدين الكعكي وسليمان بن محمد الصواف المعدلين لديه
بشهادة الحاج محمد بن محمد والحاج قنديل بن منتصر
٧. التعديل الشرعي معرفة الحرمة هبا المذكورة ومعرفة زوجها
محمد بن محمد الصواف وغيبته عن مصر المحروسة وضواحيها
الغيبة الشرعية مدة سنة كاملة وشهرين
٨. متواليين سابقين على تاريخه وهي بلا نفقة ولا منفق
شرعيين ولا ترك عندها شيا تبيعه وتنفقه علي نفسها ولا ارسل
لها شيا فوصل ولا وجدت من يتبرع
٩. لها عنه بالانفاق وليس له حرارا[؟] ولا عقارا وانها مقيمة في
محل طاعتها الذي غاب وتركها فيه لم يخرج منه الا لضرورة
شرعية ولتعاطي الفسخ المذكور ثبوتا
١٠. شرعيا وثبت ايضا لديه جريان حلف الزوجة المذكورة بالله
العظيم الذي لا اله الا هو الرحمن الرحيم منزل القران على قلب
النبي صلى الله عليه وسلم ان
١١. زوجها محمد المذكور سافر وتركها المدة المذكورة على
الصفات المشروحة الحلف الشرعي الموجه بالطريق الشرعي
ومن شهد لها صادق في شهادته محق [...]
١٢. وباطن الامر في ذلك كظاهره وظاهره كباطنه وانها
مستحق العمل بما قامت به البينة المذكورة بشهادتها لديه
وطلبت هبا المذكورة من مولانا الحاكم
١٣. المشار اليه اعلاه ان يمكنها من فسخ نكاحها من عصمة
زوجها محمد المذكور فوعظها وصبرها ولومها المدة بعد المدة
والكرة بعد الكرة فابت والحت الا الفسخ
١٤. المذكور فاجابها لذلك ومكنها من فسخ نكاحها من عصمة
زوجها محمد المذكور فقالت بصريح لفظها فسخت نكاحي من
عصمة زوجي محمد المذكور فسخا شرعيا ملكت

١٥. به نفسي واخبرت فراقه وبعده عني وطلبت من مولانا
الحاكم المشار اليه اعلاه ان يحكم لها بما اوقعته على نفسها
فاجابها الى مطلوبها وحكم لها بموجب ذلك
١٦. ومن موجبه عنده على قاعدة مذهبه الشريف ببينونة
الحرمة هبا المذكورة من عصمة زوجها محمد المذكور البينونة
الشرعية للمقتضى المشروح حكما
١٧. شرعيا وامرها بالاعتداد من تاريخه تحريرا في تاسع
عشر صفر الخير سنة ثمان وسبعين والف وحسبنا الله ونعم
الوكيل
١٨. الشيخ فايد البحيري والفقير عبد الباقي البحيري
والشيخ عبد العظيم الوارسي والشيخ عبد الرحمن القصبي

Translation:

Before the Mālikī judge, after receiving noble permission, which must be accepted and honored, from His Excellency, our leader and teacher, shaykh of the Muslim shaykhs, the king of the distinguished scholars, the most noble of the great lords, the dictionary of eloquence and the lamp of intellect, in whose presence the eminent madhhab of [Abū Ḥanīfa] al-Nu^c^mān takes pride, the supporter of the law of al-Muṣṭafā [i.e. the Prophet Muḥammad], the most excellent prayers and the most noble peace be upon him, the supervisor of legal rulings and religious affairs, currently in the protected city of Cairo, may God almighty perpetuate [his life] and bestow upon him benefits and kindnesses, amen. [This was] marked on a petition sent to His Sublime Excellency on the matter mentioned below, by the honorable woman Hibā, daughter of the late Muḥammad al-Ḥāyik. The aforementioned petition, and what he read [in it], was directed to the attention of the Mālikī judge of the aforementioned [sic] court, who is our leader and teacher, the distinguished and virtuous shaykh and imam Nūr al-Dīn ^c^Alī al-Rifā^c^ī, the sharī^c^a judge of the Mālikī madhhab, who has signed with his noble hand at the top of the original [document].

[The petition] was presented to [the Mālikī judge] and he received it with the utmost obedience. Its contents were established to our teacher the aforementioned Mālikī judge, by the testimony of the respected al-Ḥājj ^c^Alī ibn Sharaf al-Dīn al-Ka^c^kī and Sulaymān ibn Muḥammad al-Ṣawwāf, whose integrity was proved to [the judge] by the testimony of al-Ḥājj Muḥammad ibn Muḥammad and al-Ḥājj Qandīl ibn Muntaṣir, through an investigation (*ta^c^dīl*) in accordance with the law, and [given with] the knowledge of the aforementioned honorable Hibā and the knowledge of her husband, Muḥammad ibn Muḥammad al-Ṣawwāf, and his absence from the protected city of Cairo and its hinterland, a legally-relevant absence for a period of a full year and two months, consecutive and immediately prior to the present date. [Hibā] has been without legally-valid maintenance payments and without an alternative source of support, and [her husband] did not leave her anything that she could sell in order to support herself with the proceeds, and he has not sent her anything that arrived. She has not found anyone who can donate anything for her support, and he has no property [that could provide her an income]. She has remained in the marital home, which [her husband] left and where he abandoned her, and she has not gone out except for legally-valid necessities, and to transact the aforementioned judicial divorce. This was established in accordance with the law.

It was also established before [the judge] that the aforementioned wife had taken an oath by the almighty, compassionate, merciful God, apart from whom there is no other god, the revealer of the Koran to the heart of the Prophet, peace and blessings of God be upon him, that her husband the aforementioned Muḥammad had traveled and left her for the aforementioned period and with the aforementioned details. This was a legally-valid testimony, delivered in accordance with the law, and the witness who testified to this was truthful.

The essence of the matter is as the apparent, and the apparent is as the essence, and [Hibā] is entitled to the execution of that which has been established by the proof of her testimony to [the judge]. The aforementioned Hibā requested that our teacher the aforementioned judge allow her to dissolve her marriage and her bond to her aforementioned husband Muḥammad. [The judge] cautioned her, urged patience, and reprimanded her time after time, but she refused and insisted on the aforementioned dissolution. [The judge] responded by giving her permission to dissolve her marriage and her bond to her aforementioned husband Muḥammad. [Hibā] said, in a clear voice, "I dissolve my marriage and my bond to my husband the aforementioned Muḥammad, in accordance with the law, and by this I take possession of myself. I report his separation and distance from me." Then [Hibā] requested a judgment from our teacher the aforementioned judge [confirming] what she had brought into effect regarding herself. [The judge] answered her request with a legally-binding judgment in accordance with this and in accordance with the doctrines of his noble madhhab, confirming the severance of the aforementioned Hibā's marital bond to her aforementioned husband Muḥammad, in accordance with the law and on the basis of the aforementioned details. [The judge] ordered [Hibā] to observe her waiting period beginning from that day. This was issued on the nineteenth of the excellent Ṣafar in the year 1078. God is sufficient for us and the best guide.

[Witnessed by] al-Shaykh Fāyid al-Buḥayrī and al-Faqīr ᶜAbd al-Bāqī al-Buḥayrī and al-Shaykh ᶜAbd al-ᶜAẓīm al-Wārisī and al-Shaykh ᶜAbd al-Raḥmān al-Qaṣabī.

Bāb al-Sha^c^riyya register 623, entry 309

(Discussed above at pp. 131–2.)
This is an intriguing case that demonstrates how far an agreement reached through ṣulḥ could deviate from the resolution that would be reached through adjudication. The case concerned a notable man called Shukur ibn ^c^Āmir and his former servant, Sha^c^bān ibn Nāfi^c^. Legally, it consists of two separate claims: Shukur claimed that Sha^c^bān had stolen from him during the previous year, and Sha^c^bān claimed that Shukur attacked him on the day of the court case. Shukur failed to substantiate his claim, while Sha^c^bān proved his with eye-witnesses, yet the ṣulḥ agreement saw Sha^c^bān compensate Shukur and drop his claim concerning the attack.

١. لدي الحاكم الحنفي بعد ان صدر التخاصم والتداعي بين السيد
الشريف شكر بن السيد عامر السايس وبين شعبان بن نافع المتسبب
بسبب ما ادعاه
٢. السيد شكر المذكور على شعبان المذكور بانه كان خادما عنده في
صناعة السياسة وتوجه معه الى ادرنه في سنة سبع وسبعين والف وان
شعبان
٣. المذكور اختلس منه جميع زبون جوخ تمر هندي قيمته خمسة
غروش وشاش قيمته غرشا واحدا وطربوش احمر قيمته غرشا واحدا
وقميص رومي
٤. قيمته غرشا واحدا وتقميطة قيمتها ثلاثة غروش وقيمتها (sic) ثلثي
غرش وبارجه[؟] بيضا قيمتها غرشان اثنان ونصف غرش وزبون
صغير ابيض
٥. قيمته غرشا واحدا ولباس [...] ابيض قيمته غرش واحد وطالبه
باحضار ذلك ان كان موجودا او بقيمته ان كان معدوما وسال سواله
عن ذلك
٦. فسيل المدعى عليه المذكور اجاب بالانكار في ذلك فطلب من المدعي
المذكور البيان على ذلك فخرج وعاد ولم يحضر بينة لتشهد له بذلك
٧. ولم يلتمس يمينه على ذلك وبعد ما ادعاه شعبان المذكور على
السيد شكر المذكور بانه تعدي عليه في يوم تاريخه وضربه واشهر عليه
السلاح
٨. ليقتله واذاه بذلك فسيل المدعى عليه المذكور اجاب بالانكار في ذلك
فطلب من المدعي المذكور البيان على ذلك فخدج وعاد واحضر كل من
٩. المحترم محمد بن يوسف الغيطاني والمحترم احمد بن محمد الحمار
المعدلين لديه بشهادة المحترم سلامة بن سلامة وخاطر بن شحادة
النجار النجار (sic)

١٠. واستشهدهما عما يعلمانه من ذلك فاقاما شهادتهما لدى مولانا الحاكم المشار اليه اعلاه بمعرفة المتداعيين المذكورين اعلاه وان السيد شكر

١١. المذكور تعدي على شعبان المذكور وضربه واشهر عليه السلاح ليقتله في يوم تاريخه شهادة شرعية مقبولة تكلم بينهما متكلم في الصلح فاصطلحا

١٢. على ان السيد شكر المذكور قبض من شعبان المذكور ثلاثون نصفا فضة القبض الشرعي بالمجلس وصدر بينهما اقرار بعدم الاستحقاق وتباري[؟]

١٣. عام مطلق موسع[؟] الاسقاط من الجابنين ومن جملة ذلك ولا اسبابا ولا قيمة لها ولا تعديا ولا ضربا ولا علقة ولا [...] لا حقا من ساير الحقوق

١٤. ولا يمينا باسمه سبحانه وتعالى ولا شي قل ولا جل لما سلف من الزمان والى تاريخه وتصادقا على ذلك كله وثبت الاشهاد بذلك الى مولانا

١٥. الحاكم المشار اليه اعلاه بشهادة شهوده ثبوتا شرعيا وحكم بموجب ذلك الحكم الشرعي واشهد على نفسه ذلك وبه شهد في ثاني عشر صفر

١٦. الخير سنة ثمان وسبعين والف وحسبنا الله ونعم الوكيل الفقير عبد الباقي البحيري والشيخ عبد العظيم الوارسي والشيخ شرف الدين الفقري

Translation:

Before the Ḥanafī judge:
A dispute and claim arose between al-Sayyid al-Sharīf Shukur ibn al-Sayyid ᶜĀmir al-Sāyis and Shaᶜbān ibn Nāfiᶜ, a shopkeeper. The aforementioned al-Sayyid Shukur claimed that the aforementioned Shaᶜbān used to be employed by him in his work as a stable groom, and that he traveled with him to Edirne in the year 1077, and that [during that trip] the aforementioned Shaᶜbān stole from him all of the following: a broadcloth undergarment of tamarind color[?], worth five ghurūsh, a muslin worth one ghirsh, a red hat worth one ghirsh, a Rūmī shirt worth one ghirsh, a girdle worth three and two-thirds ghurush, a white piece of cloth[?] worth two and a half ghurūsh, a small white undergarment worth one ghirsh, and white […] underpants, worth one ghirsh. [Shukur] demanded that [Shaᶜbān] return these items if he had them, or [pay] their value if he did not.

Shukur asked this [in court], and the aforementioned defendant was questioned. He replied by denying [Shukur's claim], and he demanded proof from the aforementioned plaintiff. The plaintiff left [to gather evidence], then he returned and failed to produce proof to corroborate [his claim], and he did not demand an oath [from Shaᶜbān].

After that, the aforementioned Shaᶜbān claimed that the aforementioned al-

Sayyid Shukur had, on that day, attacked him, hit him, and drawn his weapon in order to kill him and injure him. The aforementioned defendant [this now refers to Shukur] was questioned and he replied by denying the claim, and demanded proof from the aforementioned plaintiff [this now refers to Shaᶜbān]. [Shaᶜbān] left [to gather evidence], then he returned and brought the respected Muḥammad ibn Yūsuf al-Ghīṭānī and the respected Aḥmad ibn Muḥammad al-Ḥammār, whose integrity was established to [the judge] by the testimony of the respected Salāma ibn Salāma and Khāṭir ibn Shaḥāda al-Naggār. [Shaᶜbān] asked them to testify on what they knew about the matter. They undertook their testimony before our teacher the aforementioned judge, with the knowledge of the aforementioned litigants. [They testified] that, on that day, the aforementioned al-Sayyid Shukur attacked the aforementioned Shaᶜbān, hit him, and drew his weapon to kill him; [their] testimony was in accordance with the law and was accepted.

Then a mediator conducted mediation with the two, and they agreed the following: the aforementioned al-Sayyid Shukur received thirty niṣf fiḍḍa from the aforementioned Shaᶜbān; this was received in court in accordance with the law. Then the two declared that neither had any claim against the other, and a general, complete absence of debts, and the dropping by each side of all claims: no [claim for] goods, nor for the value of them, nor claim of attack, nor hitting nor beating, nor [....], no claim for any other right, no claim for an oath in the name of God almighty, may he be praised, and no thing great or small, from any time in the past until today. [Shukur and Shaᶜbān] mutually agreed on all of this. Their testimony to this, before our teacher the aforementioned judge, was established by the testimony of [the court] witnesses, in accordance with the law. [The judge] ruled in accordance with this and in accordance with the law. [The judge] testified to this, and it was witnessed, on the twelfth of the excellent Ṣafar, in the year 1078. God is sufficient for us and he is the best guide. [Witnessed by] al-Faqīr ᶜAbd al-Bāqī al-Buḥayrī, and al-Shaykh ᶜAbd al-ᶜAẓīm al-Wārisī, and al-Shaykh Sharaf al-Dīn al-Faqarī.

al-Dīwān al-ᶜĀlī register 1, entry 331

(Discussed above at p. 65.)

This is an example of litigation from the Dīwān al-ᶜĀlī. It demonstrates how the Dīwān's procedure was overseen by a qāḍī and was the same as that in sharīᶜa courts, as discussed in Chapter 3. In this case, a slave called Fāṭima bint ᶜAlī al-Qalāyjī, who was owned by the notable al-Azhar professor, Aḥmad ibn ᶜAbd al-Munᶜim al-Damanhūrī, sued for her freedom and won the case after proving that she was of free Muslim origin. The case reveals corruption in the Ottoman slave trade: as a Muslim living in Kilīs in Ottoman-ruled southern Anatolia, Fāṭima's enslavement was unambiguously illegal, yet she had apparently been sold openly in Cairo to a prominent member of the ulema. The document raises interesting questions about how such cases were resolved. As a slave in Cairo, how was Fāṭima able to find suitable witnesses from distant Kilīs, and were the witnesses in Cairo on a specific mission to rescue her?

١. سبب تحرير حروفه هو انه بالديوان العالي بمصر المحروسة بحضرة مولانا الوزير المعظم والدستور المكرم المشير المفخم ممهد
٢. بنيان الدولة والاقبال مسند اركان العادة والاجلال مولانا يحيى باشا يسر الله له من الخيرات ما يريد وما يشا محافظ
٣. مصر المحمية دامت سعادته السنية بين يدي سيدنا ومولانا جمال العلما والمدرسين كمال البلغا معدن الفضل واليقين
٤. معتمد الموالي المعظمين الناظر في الاحكام الشرعية يوميذ بديوان مصر المحمية الموقع خطه الكريم اعلاه دام علاه
٥. حضر الشيخ الامام العمدة الهمام مفيد الطالبين الكرام الشيخ شهاب الدين احمد بن المرحوم عبد المنعم الدمنهوري
٦. الشافعي من اهل الافادة والتدريس بالجامع الازهر وبصحبته فاطمة المراة الثابت معرفتها بشهادة من ياتي ذكره
٧. فيه الثبوت الشرعي وادعت فاطمة المذكورة على مولانا الشيخ شهاب الدين احمد المذكور بان فاطمة المذكورة حرة
٨. الاصل بمقتضى انها بنتا لعلي القلايجي وامها امنة وان مسقط راسها بمدينة كليس بمحلة اسكي حمام بولاية
٩. اناضول وان المدعى عليه المذكور واضع اليد عليها بطريق الرق ويطالبه برفع يده عنها وتخليه سبيلها بالوجه
١٠. الشرعي فسيل من المدعى عليه المومى اليه عن ذلك فاجاب بالاعتراف بوضع يده عليها بطريق الرق بمقتضى انه
١١. اشتراها من شخص يدعى محبي ابو فادن المغربي في شهر رجب سنة اربعة وخمسين ومائة والف بسبعة
١٢. وستين فندقليا وبالانكار في كون المدعية المذكورة حرة الاصل على الوجه المشروح وكلف المدعية المذكورة
١٣. ثبوت دعواه بالوجه الشرعي وطلب من المدعية المذكورة البيان على ذلك فاحضرت فخر اقرانه السيد
١٤. محمد بن الشريف قاسم والسيد احمد بن محمد من ولاية كليس المذكورة واستشهدتهما عنما يعلمانه من ذلك
١٥. فاقام كل واحد منهما شهادته على انفراده بمعرفة فاطمة المدعية المذكورة وانها حرة الاصل والدها
١٦. علي المذكور وامها امنة المذكورة وان مسقط راسها مدينة كليس المذكورة بمحلة اسكي حمام المذكورة
١٧. يعلمان ذلك ويشهدان به كذلك شهادة شرعية واقعة في وجه المدعى عليه المذكور المومى اليه اعلاه
١٨. مقبولة بعد رعاية شرايط القبول ولما تم الحال على هذا المنوال طلب كل من المتداعيين المذكورين

١٩. من حضرة مولانا افندي المومى اليه اعلاه اجرا ما يقتضيه الشرع الشريف في شان ذلك اجابهما لذلك

٢٠. وعرف الشيخ احمد المدعى عليه المرقوم انه حيث ثبت بشهادة البينة المذكورة اعلاه ان فاطمة

٢١. المدعية المذكورة حرة الاصل وانها بنتا لعلي المذكور وامها امنة المذكورة وان مسقط راسها

٢٢. مدينة كليس المذكورة فلا معارضة له عليها واللازم عليه رفع يده عنها وتخليه سبيلها

٢٣. ومنعه من المعارضة بسبب ذلك وحكم بحرية فاطمة المذكورة على الوجه المذكور وامره مولانا افندي

٢٤. المومى اليه بان يرجع بثمنها على بايعها المذكور تعريفا والزاما ومنعا وحكما وامرا شرعيات تحريرا

٢٥. في خامس شهر ربيعي الاخر سنة خمس وخمسين وماية والف والحمد لله الجليل وحسبنا الله ونعم الوكيل

Translation:

The cause of the writing of these letters is as follows:
At the Dīwān al-ᶜĀlī in the protected city of Cairo, in the presence of our teacher the esteemed vizier, the venerated minister, the honored facilitator of fortune and prosperity, support of the pillars of custom and honor, our teacher Yaḥyā Pasha, may God ease his attainment of the blessings he desires, the governor of protected Cairo, may his sublime happiness endure. And before our leader and teacher, the beauty of the scholars and professors, the perfection of eloquence, the source of erudition and certitude, the support of the revered lords, currently the supervisor of legal affairs in the Dīwān of the protected city of Cairo, who has signed above with his noble hand, may his sublimity endure:

The virtuous shaykh, imam and leader, the benefit of the distinguished students, Shaykh Shihāb al-Dīn Aḥmad, son of the late ᶜAbd al-Munᶜim, al-Damanhūrī, of the Shāfiᶜī madhhab, of the knowledgeable teachers of the mosque of al-Azhar, attended [the Dīwān]. He was accompanied by the woman Fāṭima, whose competence was established, in accordance with the law, by the testimony of those mentioned below.

The aforementioned Fāṭima made a claim against our teacher the aforementioned Shaykh Shihāb al-Dīn Aḥmad. [The claim was] that the aforementioned Fāṭima is of free origin, by virtue of the fact that she was the daughter of ᶜAlī al-Qalāyjī, and her mother was Āmina, and that her birthplace was the city of Kilīs, in the neighborhood of Eski Ḥammām, in the province of Anatolia. [She further claimed that] the aforementioned defendant had taken possession of her as a slave. She demanded that he relinquish possession of her and release her, in accordance with the law.

The aforementioned defendant was questioned about this. He replied by acknowledging that he had taken possession of her as a slave, having purchased her from a person called Muḥibbī Abū Fādin al-Maghribī, in the month of Rajab of the year 1154, for sixty-seven funduqlī [dīnārs]. He denied that the aforementioned plaintiff was of free origin as described above, and charged the aforementioned plaintiff with establishing her claim in accordance with the law, demanding from the aforementioned plaintiff proof of [her free origin]. She brought to the Dīwān the pride of his peers, al-Sayyid Muḥammad ibn al-Sharīf Qāsim and al-Sayyid Aḥmad ibn Muḥammad, from the aforementioned province [sic] of Kilīs, and she asked them to give testimony on what they knew about the matter.

Each of the two testified individually, with the knowledge of the aforementioned Fāṭima, that she was of free origin, that her father was the aforementioned ᶜAlī and her mother was the aforementioned Āmina, and that her birthplace was the city of Kilīs, in the aforementioned neighborhood of Eski Ḥammām. [They declared that] they knew this and testified to it in accordance with the law and in front of the aforementioned defendant, and this was accepted after consideration of the conditions of acceptance.

When the question was concluded in this way, the litigants requested His Excellency, our teacher, the gentleman [qāḍī], to implement what the noble law commanded in this matter. He responded by informing the aforementioned defendant, Shaykh Aḥmad, that whereas it had been established by testimony in accordance with the law that the aforementioned plaintiff Fāṭima was of free origin, and that she was the daughter of the aforementioned ᶜAlī and that her mother was the aforementioned Āmina, and that her birthplace was the aforementioned city of Kilīs, [it followed] that [Aḥmad] had no recourse against her and must relinquish possession of her and release her. [The qāḍī] forbade [Aḥmad] from challenging this, and issued a judgment that the aforementioned Fāṭima was free, by virtue of the aforementioned reasons. Our aforementioned teacher, the gentleman [qāḍī], ordered [Aḥmad] to seek to recover the aforementioned purchase price from the aforementioned seller. This is a legal statement, commandment, prohibition, judgment, and order, issued on the fifth of the month of Rabīᶜ al-Thānī in the year 1155. Thanks be to the glorious God. God is sufficient for us and the best guide.

[NB: Unusually, no court witnesses are named in this entry. Most of the entries in the Dīwān register name the court witnesses just as the sharīᶜa court records transcribed above do].

Divan Kalemi 77/64[1]

(Discussed above at pp. 60–1 and 122–3.)
This document is an example of an original petition, sent from Cairo to the Dīvān-i Hümāyūn in 1676. It is a particularly interesting example because the petition has been annotated by several officials, illustrating how the Dīvān handled the case. The petitioner, Muṣṭafā ibn Aḥmad Abbār, claimed the right to the supervisorship of a waqf in Cairo on the basis of several documents including a fermān issued by the Sultan. A Dīvān bureaucrat verified Muṣṭafā's claim by looking up the palace's copy of this fermān in the archives, and copied it onto the petition. A senior official then annotated the Dīvān's decision onto the petition, instructing a scribe to issue an imperial order to the governor and qāḍī in Cairo to guarantee Muṣṭafā's control of the waqf.

A: Petition (lower left of paper):

١. دركاه فلك مدار وبركاه كردون اقتدار لا زال عاليا الى يوم القرار ترابنه عرض داعى

٢. بودر كه بو داعيلرى اوقات خمسه لرى وقرأت قرآن عظيم الشان وذكر وتوحيد وحضرت سيدنا محمد مصطفي

٣. صلي الله عليه وسلم حضرتلرينه صلوات شريف كتوردكده ودام ايام عمر ودولت پادشاهى ادعيه سنه مداومت

٤. اوزره اولوب حق تعالى قبول ايدوب مهابتلو پادشاهمز پادشاه كردون خلدت خلافته الى يوم يبعثون حضرتلرينه

٥. عمرني ودولتني زياد بر زياد ايدوب اعداى دين ودولت اوزرينه منصور ومظفر ايليه والطاف خفيهٔ

٦. الهيه وعنايت جليلهٔ ربانيه ايله عالم ظهور وبطونده محروس ومحفوظ اوله امين يا رب العالمين حاليا

٧. مصر اوقافلرندن حضرت قطب الوجود سيدي محمد ابو السعود الجارحي قدس الله سره العزيزك

٨. وقفي فقير واون بش سنه دن برو خراب ايكن تبركا مقام شريفك خذمتي ايله مشرف وجامعك ووقف

٩. يرلرينك عماريله مقيد اولمامز ايچون نظارت وتوليتي بو داعيلرينه توجيه اولمغين بحسب الاركان جامعك

١٠. اكثر يرلري وعقاراتلري عمار واحيا ايليوب وبوندن اقدم صدقات پادشاهيدن بو دايلري واوندن صكره

١١. اولادي واولادينك اولادي عزيز مشار اليهك [وقفينك] نظارت وتوليتنده قيد حياتله ابقا ومقرر اولمق بابنده

١٢. تواريخ مختلفه ايله دورت دفعا برات شريف همايون وبر دفعا فرمان عاليشان صدقه وعنايت بيوريلوب

١٣. وموجبلرنجه ديوان مصردن بيورلديلر ويريلوب ومحروسهٔ مصرده تمسكات شرعيه ايله سجل محفوظه قيد اولنوب

١٤. وبو انعام بيوريلان فرمان پادشاهينك بري بيك يتمش يدي سنه نك ماه ربيع الاول اواسطنده مورخ وتواريخ

١٥. مختلفه ايله اولان تقرير حجتلرينك بري بيك يتمش يدي سنه نك ماه شوال اوايلي ايله مورخه وضبط تصرفمده

١٦. ايكن حاليا بعض غرض وبغض صاحبلري هر بار بو داعيلرينه معارضه ايدوب نظارتي المق صدديله رنجيده دن

١٧. خالي المدوقلري اجلدن عواطف عليهٔ شاهانه دن رجا اولنور كه يدمده اولان برات همايون وامر شريف

١٨. عاليشان موجبنجه بو داعيلري واوندن صكره اولادي واولادينك اولادي قيد حيات ايله عزيز مشار اليهك وقفي

١٩. نظارت وتوليتنده كما كان ابقا ومقرر اولمق بابنده فرمان همايون ايله خط شريف عاليشان صدقه وعنايت بيورلمق

٢٠. رجاسنه در دولت مداره عرض اولندي باقي امر [و] فرمان دركاه معلانكدر والصلاه والسلام على سيد المرسلين سيدنا محمد وعلى اله وصحبه الطاهرين وعلى عباد الله الصالحين والحمد لله العالمين
٢١. من الحقير الفقير الى ربه العلى الكبير
٢٢. الداعى مصطفى بن الشيخ احمد محمد
٢٣. ابار

B: Note of date of arrival (bottom right corner):
فى اواخر ر سنه ٨٧

C: Previous *fermān* cited by petitioner, checked and copied on to petition by Dīvān bureaucrat (top right of paper):
١. نظارت اوقاف سيد محمد ابو السعود جارحى در محروسهٔ مصر
٢. مصر پاشاسنه ومنلاسنه حكم كه مشايخ كرامدن شيخ احمد محمد ابار اوغلى [...] شيخ مصطفى كلوب
٣. محروسهٔ مصرده واقع اجدادينك زاويه سنده زاويه دار اولوب دوام عمر ودولتم ادعيه سنه مداومت
٤. اوزره اولمغله مصرده واقع سيد محمد ابو السعود جارحى قدس سره العزيزك اوقافى نظارتى برات
٥. برات (sic) شريفله اوزره اولوب بعد اليوم كندو قيد حيات ايله متصرف ووفاتندن صكره اولاد اولادى
٦. متصرف اولمق اوزره نظارت مزبور مومى اليهه النده اولان برات وتمسكاته موجبنجه ابقا ومقرر
٧. قلنوب اخردن مداخله اولنمامق بابنده عنايت رجا ايتمكده وجه مشروح اوزره النده اولان
٨. برات وتمسكاته موجبنجه ابقا ومقرر قلنوب يازلمشدر فى اواسط را سنه ٧٧

D: Annotation immediately below the *fermān* (possibly, this phrase was accidentally omitted from the previous line):

قيد حيات

E: Annotation by senior Dīvān official, above the *fermān*:
صحيحدر

F: Dīvān's instruction (top left of paper):
قيدى موجبنجه ضبطيجون صورت حكم بيورلدى

Translation:

A: Petition (lower left of paper)
The petition of the claimant, to the dust at the throne that revolves the heavens, the court that has power over fortune, may it remain exalted, is as follows:

This petitioner has given prayers for the five prayer times, for the glorious Koran, for the remembrance of God, for God's unity, and for our leader Muḥammad, may the peace and prayers of God be upon him. May God accept the prayers for the continuation of the life and the rule of the Sultan. May the caliphate of our majestic Sultan last until the day of judgment, may his life and rule be extended, and may he be victorious over the enemies of religion and the state. May both the apparent and the hidden worlds be protected by God's imperceptible mercies and his great grace. Amen, oh lord of the worlds.

One of the awqāf of Egypt is the waqf of the chief of existence, Sīdī Muḥammad Abū ʾl-Saʿūd al-Jāriḥī, may God sanctify his secret. This waqf is poor, and since it fell into ruin fifteen years ago, because I have diligently undertaken repairs of the mosque and the waqf's buildings as an act of piety and in service of the holy places, I have been appointed supervisor of the waqf. I have restored other parts of the mosque, and earlier the Sultan confirmed the assignation of the position of supervisor with life tenure to myself and then to my sons and their sons. At various times, four noble imperial berāts and one exalted fermān have kindly been issued, and in accordance with these the Dīwān of Egypt has given a *buyuruldu*, and in Cairo a title-deed has been recorded in the official register. The fermān with which the Sultan bestowed this favour was dated mid Rabīʿ al-Awwal 1077 (11–20 September 1666), and of the variously-dated ḥujjas,[2] one was dated early Shawwāl 1077 (27 March–5 April 1667).

However, while this waqf has been under my control, various people who bear grudges and ill-will towards me have been constantly interfering. Because I cannot be free of the injuries these people are doing to me with the intention of taking my position, I request from your exalted imperial kindnesses that, in accordance with the imperial berāt and the exalted, noble order[3] in my possession, an imperial fermān signed by your exalted, noble hand kindly be issued confirming my, and after me, my sons' and their sons' right to life tenure in the position of supervisor of the aforementioned waqf. This petition has been submitted to he who is the center of greatness. The decision rests with the exalted throne. Prayers and peace be upon the leader of the prophets, our leader Muḥammad, and on his family and his pure companions, and on the righteous worshippers of God. Thanks be to God, the lord of the worlds.

From he who is wretched and poor before his great and exalted Lord, Muṣṭafā, son of al-Shaykh Aḥmad Muḥammad Abbār.

B: Date of arrival (bottom right corner)
Late Rabīʿ al-Thānī of the year [10]87 (3–11 July 1676).

C: Previous fermān cited by petitioner, checked and copied on to petition by Dīvān bureaucrat (top right of paper)
The position of supervisor of the waqf of Sayyid Muḥammad Abū ᵓl-Saᶜūd al-Jāriḥī in Egypt.

This order is to the governor and the judge of Egypt:

Shaykh Muṣṭafā, the son of Shaykh Aḥmad Muḥammad Abbār of the illustrious shaykhs, came [to the palace to petition the Sultan]. He is the guardian of a *zāwiya* (Sufi lodge) founded by his forefathers in Egypt, in which prayers are said for the continuation of my life and rule. According to a noble berāt, Muṣṭafā has been granted the position of supervisor of the waqf of Sayyid Muḥammad Abū ᵓl-Saᶜūd al-Jāriḥī, may God sanctify his secret, located in Egypt, with life tenure, and after his death his sons' sons will have the right to this position. In order that no one interfere with his position, he has requested my favor, to confirm his supervision of the waqf in accordance with the berāt and the title-deed that he holds. With respect to the above, I have ordered that [his supervision of the waqf] be confirmed in accordance with the berāt and title-deed that he holds.

Mid-Rabīᶜ al-Awwal of the year [10]77 (11–20 September 1666).

D: Annotation immediately below the fermān (possibly, this phrase was accidentally omitted from the previous line)
Life tenure.

E: Annotation by senior Dīvān official, above the fermān
Correct.

F: Dīvān's instruction (top left of paper)
In accordance with the record, it is commanded that an order be issued to guarantee his possession.

Şikayet Kalemi 1/93

(Discussed above at pp. 63 and 122.)
This document is a petition sent by al-Ḥājj Muṣṭafā, a resident of the town of Ziftā near Cairo, in 1742. Muṣṭafā claimed that a Christian called Banūb had built a house in the Muslim quarter of Ziftā that was taller than the houses of the neighboring Muslims, and requested that he be forced to reduce the house's height or sell it to a Muslim. A Dīvān official annotated onto the petition the generic decision that many petitioners received, instructing a scribe to issue an imperial order to the governor and qāḍī of Cairo to hear the case according to the sharīᶜa.

A: Petition:

١. دولتلو مرحمتلو سلطانم حضرتلری صاغ اولسون

٢. عرضحال قوللری مصر قاهره ساکنلرندن زفته قصبه سنده واقع
بنوب نام

۳. نصرانی مسلمین محله سنده اولان منزلنی مسلمین منزللرندن
زیاده ترفیع ووضع
٤. قدیمنی تغییر ایلیوب اطراف اربعه سنده واقع مسلمین وجوهله
اذا
٥. وتعجیزدن خالی اولمامکله مراحم علیه لرندن مرجودر که یدمزده
اولان
٦. شیخ الاسلام فتوای شریفه سی موجبنجه ترفیع ایلدیکی بناسنی
مسلمین منزللرینه
۷. مساوی اولنجه هدم اولنوب ویاخود قبل شرعده منزل مزبوری
۸. بر مسلمینه بیع ایتدرلک بابنده حالا مصر والیسینه خطاباً فرمان
شریفه
۹. رجا اولنور امر [و] فرمان سلطانمکدر بنده الحاج مصطفی

B: Dīvān-i Hümāyūn's instruction (annotated above petition):

محلنده شرعله حکم بیورولدی

Translation:

A: Petition

Long live His Excellency, my Sultan, the illustrious and merciful!

The petition of the slave [is as follows]: Among the inhabitants of Victorious Cairo, living in the town of Ziftā,[4] is a Christian named Banūb. His house, which is in the Muslim quarter [of Ziftā], is taller than the houses of the Muslims, contravening established tradition. Because the Muslims living on all four sides [of Banūb] cannot be free of harm and trouble [due to this], I request from your august mercies that, in accordance with the noble fatwā of the Şeyhulislām that we possess, the building that has been raised [higher than the Muslims'] should be brought down to the level of the Muslims' houses, or the aforementioned house should be legally sold to one of the Muslims. A noble fermān to that effect, addressed to the current governor of Egypt, is requested. The order and fermān is my Sultan's [prerogative]. [From] the slave, al-Ḥājj Muṣṭafā.

B: Dīvān-i Hümāyūn's instruction

[Issue an] order that this should be judged according to the law in the relevant locality.

***Registerbuch*, fo. 123b, 6th entry**

(Discussed above at pp. 61–2.)

This is an example of a copy of an outgoing imperial order issued in response to a petition, entered in a stray Şikayet Defteri that has ended up in the Austrian National

Library. This order responded to a petition from Beşīr Āghā, the head āghā of the Ottoman princess, Gevher Cān Sulṭān, who had purchased a long lease on a house in Cairo (with an *icāreteyn* contract), presumably in anticipation of retiring there, as most African eunuchs working at the imperial palace did. Beşīr's agent in Cairo had been prevented from taking possession of the house by some unnamed antagonists, and the Dīvān ordered the governor and qāḍī in Cairo to ensure he was able to secure it.

١. مصر واليسينه ومنلاسنه حكم كى
٢. كوهرجان سلطان دامت عصمتهانك باش اغاسى بشير اغا دام علوه
عرض حال ايدوب محروسۀ مصرده واقع متوفى ادريس اغا اوقافندن باب
٣. زويله خارجنده بركة الفيل جوارنده [...] قربنده حياتيه ديمكله معروف
معلومة الحدود منزلى وقف مزبور متوليسى مصطفى نام كمسنه دن اوچ
٤. بيك غروش اجاره معجله ايله اشترى وجانب وقفه ادا ايدوب حجت
شرعيه وممهور تمسك ويريلوب طرفنده وكيلى [...] نام كمسنه
٥. ضبط مراد ايلدكده اصحاب اغراضدن تعرض كمسنه لر ضبطنه مانع
اولدقلرى وفتواى شريفه سى اولدوغنى بلدروب خلاف شرع مداخله
٦. ايتدرلمامك بابنده امر شريفم رجا ايدر خلاف شرع مداخله اولنمامغى
ايچون حكم يازلشدر فى اواسط را سنه ٨٦

Translation:

The order to the governor and judge of Egypt is as follows:

Beşīr Āghā, may his greatness endure, the head āghā of Gevher Cān Sulṭān, may her virtue endure, sent a petition. In the protected city of Cairo, belonging to the endowments of the late İdrīs Āghā, outside of Bāb Zuwayla, in the vicinity of al-Fīl lake, next to [...], is a house known as Ḥayātiyya, the boundaries of which are known. [Beşīr Āghā] bought [this house] from the supervisor of the aforementioned endowment, a person called Muṣṭafā, for an advance rent of 3,000 ghurūsh.[6] [Beşīr Āghā] paid [this sum] to the endowment, and a legal certificate and a sealed title-deed were issued. When Beşīr Āghā's agent in [Cairo], a person called [...][7] attempted to take possession [of the house], interfering people who bore grudges prevented him. Beşīr Āghā has informed [me] that he has a noble fatwā [supporting him] and he has requested my noble order in order to prevent interference contrary to the law. In order that there not be interference contrary to the law, I issue this order.[8] In the middle of Rabīᶜ al-Awwal, [in the] year 86.

NOTES

Introduction

1. Even in so-called secular states in the Muslim world, fiqh remains relevant. Oussama Arabi has described as "neo-Shāfiᶜī" the approach of contemporary Egyptian jurists, products of a westernized legal education designing law that will be passed as legislation by the Egyptian government, who engage with the fiqh tradition in those areas of Egyptian law which are based on sharīᶜa. See Arabi, "Dawning of the Third Millennium."
2. For an overview of traditional Islamic legal education and its place in Muslim society see Hallaq, *Sharīᶜa*, 125–58. For detailed studies of education in the medieval Muslim world, see Berkey, *Transmission of Knowledge*; Chamberlain, *Knowledge and Social Practice*. For an example of the survival of traditional forms of education into the modern world, see Messick, *Calligraphic State*, 75–99.
3. For an extensive critique of this paradigm see Shalakany, "Islamic Legal Histories." Although the Orientalist approach looms largest in western-language scholarship, Shalakany points out that a similar understanding of Islamic law emerged within Muslim societies during the late nineteenth and twentieth centuries. Here, the scriptural bias that became central to reformed, modern Islamic thought tended to define Islamic law as that which was derived from the Koran and Sunna, which also led to the reduction of the field of Islamic law to fiqh.
4. Indeed, some jurists served as qāḍīs, especially in the senior posts. The average qāḍī, however, had a similar but less distinguished education: being a jurist was the more prestigious career.
5. Hallaq, *Sharīᶜa*, 549.
6. Hallaq, *Sharīᶜa*, 200. Even Hallaq's own list of exemptions suggests that the scope of siyāsa was far from limited. Indeed, his assertion here that jurisdiction over land and crime was of little consequence sits uneasily with later sections of the book where

he highlights the nineteenth-century Ottoman land and penal codes as milestones of Europeanizing legal reform; see Hallaq, *Sharīʿa*, 401–9.

7. Hallaq, *Sharīʿa*, 208.
8. Hallaq, *Sharīʿa*, 355–499. In a more recent book, Hallaq has argued at length that the modern state is fundamentally antithetical to Islamic traditions of law and governance, such that the very concept of an "Islamic state" is an oxymoron: see Hallaq, *Impossible State*.
9. Jennings, "Office of Vekil"; Jennings, "Women"; Jennings, "Kadi, Court"; Jennings, "Zimmis"; Jennings, "Limitations of the Judicial Powers." In later work, Jennings explored similar themes in the context of Cyprus. See Jennings, *Christians and Muslims*; Jennings, "Divorce." Jennings' articles are collected in his *Studies on Ottoman Social History*.
10. See Jennings, "Kadi, Court"; Jennings, "Limitations of the Judicial Powers."
11. Gerber, *State, Society and Law*; Gerber, *Islamic Law and Culture*; Gerber, "Social and Economic Position"; Gerber, "Muslim Law of Partnerships"; Gerber, "Public Sphere."
12. Gerber, *Islamic Law and Culture*.
13. Gerber, *State, Society and Law*, 69; Gerber "Public Sphere," 70–1.
14. Gerber was not the only scholar of Islamic law to engage with the kadijustiz idea around this time. See also Sonbol, "Women in Shariʿah Courts"; Powers, "Kadijustiz"; Powers, *Law, Society and Culture*.
15. See in particular Barkey, *Bandits and Bureaucrats*; İslamoğlu-İnan, *State and Peasant*.
16. For critiques, see Ze'evi, "Use of Ottoman Sharīʿa Court Records"; Ergene, *Local Court*, 125–41; Agmon, "Women's History."
17. For example: Peirce, *Morality Tales*; Ergene, *Local Court*; Ginio, "Administration of Criminal Justice." The main exceptions are Başak Tuğ, who studied petitions sent from central Anatolia to the Dīvān-i Hümāyūn, and Michael Ursinus, who studied a single register of petitions sent to the Kaymakam of Rumelia in the 1780s. See Tuğ, "Politics of Honor"; Ursinus, *Grievance Administration*.
18. For example: Zarinebaf, *Crime and Punishment*; Wittman, "Before Qadi and Grand Vizier"; Akarlı, "Law in the Marketplace."
19. For example: Salzmann, *Tocqueville*; Khoury, *State and Provincial Society*; Canbakal, *Society and Politics*; Ze'evi, *Ottoman Century*; Wilkins, *Forging Urban Solidarities*; Greene, *Shared World*.
20. On nationalism and Arabic-language Egyptian historiography, see Di-Capua, *Gatekeepers*.
21. For example: Shaw, *Financial and Administrative Organization*; Holt, *Egypt and the Fertile Crescent*, 33–101; Winter, *Egyptian Society*; Marsot, *History of Egypt*, 48–64.
22. The most prolific writers in this group have been André Raymond and Nelly Hanna. For example, see Raymond, *Artisans et commerçants*; Hanna, *Artisan Entrepreneurs*.
23. Hathaway, *Politics of Households*. For further analysis of the culture of Egypt's political elite see Hathaway, *Tale of Two Factions*.
24. Mikhail, *Nature and Empire*. See also Mikhail, "Irrigated Empire."
25. In this respect, the integration of Egypt into the Ottoman legal system was similar to the various colonial situations described by Benton in *Law and Colonial Cultures*.

26. Holt, *Egypt and the Fertile Crescent*, 33–57; Winter, *Egyptian Society*, 7–75; Behrens-Abouseif, *Egypt's Adjustment*.
27. Faraḥāt, *al-Tārīkh al-ijtimāʿī*, 191.
28. Hanna, "Administration of Courts"; Winter, *Egyptian Society*, 108–11, quotation from 110.
29. Meshal, *Sharia*, see especially 69–102; Meshal, "Antagonistic Sharīʿas."
30. I discuss ʿUthmān Bey's tribunal in Chapter 5.
31. For an overview of legal pluralism, see Griffiths, "What is Legal Pluralism?" For a recent reformulation of the concept from a global perspective, see Berman, *Global Legal Pluralism*. For a defense of the concept's application to Muslim societies, see Shahar, "Legal Pluralism." For studies of legal pluralism in a range of modern Arab societies, see Dupret et al, *Legal Pluralism*.
32. Griffiths, "What is Legal Pluralism?"
33. Shahar, "Legal Pluralism," 123.
34. Berman, *Global Legal Pluralism*, 23–57.
35. Burak, *Second Formation*; Ibrahim, *Pragmatism*; Meshal, *Sharia*.
36. For example, Barkey, "Aspects of Legal Pluralism."
37. On non-Muslims using the sharīʿa courts, see: Jennings, "Zimmis"; Gradeva, "Orthodox Christians"; al-Qattan, "Dhimmīs"; Ivanova, "Muslim and Christian Women"; Gerber, *Crossing Borders*; Wittman, "Before Qadi and Grand Vizier." For a study that takes a legal-pluralist perspective, exploring how Christians moved between sharīʿa, ecclesiastical and communal courts, see Kermeli, "Right to Choice."
38. To my knowledge, the only historian writing in English who has studied non-Muslim legal institutions using their own records is Eugenia Kermeli, who has pioneered scholarship on Orthodox ecclesiastical courts: see Kermeli, "Right to Choice." There is some work on Jewish law in the Ottoman Empire based on the responsa (legal opinions issued by rabbis, similar to Islamic law's *fatwās*), but it is not clear to what extent the responsa reflected actual legal and social practices. For an overview of early modern responsa across the Mediterranean, see Goldish, *Jewish Questions*. For Ottoman Egypt, Syria, and Palestine see Lamdan, *Separate People*.
39. For example: Tucker, *In the House*; Hanna, "Administration of Courts"; Peters, "What Does it Mean"; Rafeq, "Application of Islamic Law"; Ibrahim, *Pragmatism*, 129–63; Ibrahim, "Al-Shaʿrānī's Response."
40. The recent exceptions are Tuğ, "Politics of Honor"; Wittman, "Before Qadi and Grand Vizier."
41. Tyan, *Histoire de l'organisation judiciaire*; Nielsen, *Secular Justice*; Darling, *History of Social Justice*, 67–125; Rapoport, "Royal Justice"; Petry, "Royal Justice"; Irwin, "Privatization of Justice"; Müller, "Redressing Injustice"; Tillier, "Qāḍīs of Fusṭāṭ-Miṣr"; Tillier, "Qāḍīs and the Political Use."
42. For the characterization of sharīʿa courts and maẓālim tribunals as distinct jurisdictions, see Tyan *Histoire de l'organisation judiciaire*, 433–525; Darling, *History of Social Justice*, 78–81, 120–3; Hallaq, *Sharīʿa*, 55, 200–10. For empirical studies that suggest that the lines between the two were blurred, see Nielsen, *Secular Justice*, 93–121; Müller, "Redressing Injustice."

43. See Tillier, *Pluralisme judiciaire*; Tillier, "Pluralisme judiciaire." These came out of a very productive conference Tillier organized at the Institut français du Proche-Orient in Beirut in 2012.
44. I describe the structure of Cairo's courts in more detail in Chapter 2. See also Mīlād, *al-Wathāʾiq al-ʿUthmāniyya*, I: 91–137; el-Nahal, *Judicial Administration*, 74.
45. Ze'evi, "Use of Ottoman Sharīʿa Court Records"; Ergene, *Local Court*, 125–41; Agmon, "Women's History."
46. Beshara Doumani and Judith Tucker consulted the sijills of Ottoman Nablūs in the modern sharīʿa court of Nablus. See Doumani, *Rediscovering Palestine*; Tucker, *In the House*.
47. For a contemporary description of the bombardment, see Shādhilī, "Dhikr ma waqaʿa," 354ff. For a broader account of the 1711 war, see Raymond, "Revolution."
48. *Awḍaḥ*, 170.
49. For a reflection on the lack of surviving archives from the medieval Middle East, see el-Leithy, "Living Documents."
50. The only other example of a complete register from such an institution that I know of is a "book of complaints" belonging to the Kaymakam of Rumelia dating from 1781–3, which was published by Michael Ursinus. See Ursinus, *Grievance Administration*.
51. ENA, Ḥujaj sharʿiyya ṣādira min maḥkamat al-Dīwān al-ʿĀlī sana 1030 ilā 1272, document 1, 23 Dhū ʾl-Ḥijja 1030 (8 November 1621); document 2, 14 Muḥarram 1103 (7 October 1691); document 3, 18 Jumādā ʾl-Thānī 1124 (23 July 1712); document 4, 24 Ṣafar 1127 (1 March 1715); document 5, 11 Dhū ʾl-Qaʿda 1127 (8 November 1715); document 6, 8 Shaʿbān 1150 (1 December 1737); document 7, 9 Ramaḍān 1150 (31 December 1737). PMA, Cevdet Maliye 26058, 18 Rajab 1081 (1 December 1670); DK 65/34, 28 Jumādā ʾl-Ūlā 1083 (21 September 1672); DK 76/29, 20 Dhū ʾl-Ḥijja 1086 (6 March 1676); MK 1/18, 3 Rajab 1134 (19 April 1722); İbnülemin Adliye 846, 7 Dhū ʾl-Ḥijja 1139 (26 July 1727). The ḥujjas I found in the Prime Ministry Archive were scattered across several collections, two of which (DK and MK) are not cataloged, so further ḥujjas may well exist there.
52. These records are located at the Prime Ministry Archive in Istanbul. Original petitions are found in a series of boxes dedicated to petitions labeled Şikayet Kalemi, and also in various other archival units including Divan Kalemi, Mısır Kalemi, Cevdet, İbnülemin and Ali Emiri where they are mixed up with other types of document including drafts and copies of imperial orders, accounts and *tezkeres* (notes used for internal communication by different departments of the bureaucracy). The registers containing responses to petitions are called Şikayet Defterleri: in the Prime Ministry Archive today, there are two series of these, the main series is labeled Atik Şikayet Defterleri and listed in catalog 989, and the second series is labeled Şikayet Defterleri and listed in catalog 980. The second series is much smaller and some of its defters are fragments. There doesn't appear to be any systematic basis for this division and I assume it is the result of records having been mislaid and then re-filed in the wrong place at some point during the archive's history. For the period from 1742 there is a parallel series labeled Vilayet Ahkam Defterleri which contains responses to petitions organized by the province of the

petitioner. Some responses are also found in the Mühimme Defterleri series. For more on these documents see Baldwin, "Petitioning the Sultan," 503–6.

53. Studies using these registers include: Faroqhi, "Political Activity"; Gerber, *State, Society and Law*, 127–73; İnalcık, "Şikayet Hakkı"; Ursinus, "Petitions"; Wittman, "Before Qadi and Grand Vizier," 129–223; Zarinebaf-Shahr, "Women, Law and Imperial Justice."
54. An exception is Tuğ, "Politics of Honor," see especially 26–30, 97–172.
55. The petitions are arranged in the archive by date. Most of the dates have been added by later archivists, and it is not clear how they determined the dates; perhaps they were copied from the files where the petitions were put when they were first processed. In some cases only a year is given, in others a month and year.
56. For example: ŞK 1/93, in which the petitioner identifies himself simply as al-Ḥājj Muṣṭafā from Ziftā (a town 45 miles north of Cairo); DK 394/43, in which the petitioners sign off simply as Fāṭima and Zeyneb; they identify their father in the text of the petition as Ömer Efendi, but they do not say where in the empire they live. Given the relatively narrow range of first names used by Arabic-speaking Muslims in this period, how the petitions and responses were ultimately matched to individuals is something of a mystery. My assumption is that either they were carried in envelopes on which identifying details were written, or that petitioners informed the local qāḍī or governor, to whom the response would be addressed, that they were expecting it. Clearly the system must have worked somehow, but it is a striking and curious contrast to the care with which individuals were identified in most Ottoman legal records.
57. For details of the production of these documents, see Baldwin, "Petitioning the Sultan," 505–6.
58. For examples, see Peirce, *Morality Tales*; Ergene, *Local Court*; Ergene, "Why did Ümmü Gülsüm go to Court?"; Ghazzal, *Grammars of Adjudication*; Peters, "Administrator's Nightmare." For a similar approach to records from the reformed legal system of nineteenth-century Egypt, see Fahmy, "Anatomy of Justice"; Fahmy, "Police and the People"; Fahmy, *Bodies of Law*.
59. Ergene, "Social Identity." Ergene used the micro-historical approach in previous work: he is suggesting that quantification should accompany rather than replace it. Quantitative approaches to Ottoman sijills were popular between the 1970s and 1990s, but this body of research was criticized for its naïve understanding of how the courts functioned and how the records were produced; see especially Ze'evi, "Use of Ottoman Sharīᶜa Court Records."
60. Ergene, "Social Identity"; Coşgel and Ergene, "Selection Bias"; Coşgel and Ergene, "Law and Economics." Timur Kuran is another scholar who has recently applied a quantitative method to Ottoman sharīᶜa court records, though he has used this research to build an argument about economic rather than legal history; see Kuran, *Long Divergence*.
61. Ergene's dataset consists of 1293 disputes that cover the period from 1684 to 1790 (it does not include notarized contracts). A similar-sized set of disputes from all Cairo's courts might stretch to five years or so. Of course, this is hardly surprising: Kastamonu was a small, remote town of 10–12,000 people, while Cairo was a metropolis of a quarter million located on major international trade routes.

62. Of course, quantitative study could be a way to answer these questions, but that does not make it feasible to undertake.
63. Even in the context of Kastamonu, where there was only one official court, there are still some such unknowns. Coşgel and Ergene note that only 3% of disputes involved non-Muslims, whereas non-Muslims constituted up to 15% of the town's population: this clearly suggests that Kastamonu's non-Muslims preferred to use a different forum, whether that was a communal court or an informal dispute resolution mechanism. See Coşgel and Ergene, "Selection Bias," 526.
64. The Egyptian National Archive has an ongoing project to index the records of al-Bāb al-ᶜĀlī. This was in its infancy when I was conducting my archival research in Cairo. Somewhat later, the index was completed and put online. The searchable index included basic data, including names of litigants/parties to contracts, the subject of the dispute/contract and dates, for every entry in every register: a major resource with few counterparts. However, the index was taken offline in 2012 and it remains offline at the time of writing.
65. By "executive authorities" I refer to the Ottoman Sultan, viziers, provincial governors, and other officials who represented the authority of the imperial government, excluding qāḍīs. I recognize that it is an imperfect term, resonating of the modern separation of powers in a potentially anachronistic way. But I think it is least problematic of the English terms available. The direct English translation of the relevant Ottoman term is "military" (from *ᶜaskerī*), but this is misleading, because many of these people were not involved in actual military activities, or were so only occasionally: this became more true in the eighteenth century, as the bureaucracy rather than the army provided an increasing proportion of the candidates for high office. "Political" is too vague, as it could include almost anyone who wielded power. While I use the term "political" when referring to political authority in a more abstract sense, I use "executive" when referring to the specific agents of the imperial government active in Ottoman Cairo, and in my analytical framework that distinguishes between juristic, judicial, and executive spheres of power involved in the administration of Ottoman justice. I explain these categories in more detail below at pp. 71–4.

Chapter 1

1. For examples, see: Abu-Lughod, *Cairo*, 50–5; AlSayyad, *Cairo*, 149–71. Of all the writers to have attempted a synthetic treatment of Cairo's long history, André Raymond is the most positive about the Ottoman period; unsurprisingly, given his pioneering role in creating the field of Ottoman-Egyptian economic and social history in the 1960s. Susan Jane Staffa also stands out from most others by paying serious attention to the Ottoman era, although her overall evaluation of the period is of stagnation prior to the French occupation; see Staffa, *Conquest and Fusion*, 227–385.
2. On the coffee trade in early modern Cairo and the wider Ottoman Empire, see Tuchscherer, *Commerce du café*, in particular the essays by Nelly Hanna and André Raymond: Hanna, "Coffee and Coffee-Merchants"; Raymond, "Famille."

3. Raymond, *Artisans et commerçants*, II: 477–81, 483–91; Sāmir, *al-Shawām*.
4. Raymond, *Artisans et commerçants*, II: 459–64, 497–501; Trivellato, *Familiarity of Strangers*, 61, 118.
5. Irfana Hashmi provides a list of riwāqs at al-Azhar during the Ottoman period (I put the groups supported in parentheses where it is not self-evident): Yamanī (Yemenis & Hejazis); ᶜAjamī (Persians, Kurds, and Turks from Anatolia and Azerbaijan); Sulaymāniyya (Central Asians); Turkumān (Turkic-speakers from Anatolia and Iraq); Rūmī (Turks from Ottoman Anatolia and Rumelia); ᶜIrāqī; Maghribī; Barbarī (people from the Nile region south of Aswan); Jabartī (Somalis); Takrūrī (people from the bilād al-Sūdān, i.e. modern Sudan to Senegal); Riyāfa (Egyptians); Banū Muᶜammar (open to students of various backgrounds); Fayyūmiyya (people from the Fayyūm region in middle Egypt); Fuwwāt (people from the region of Fuwwa in the western Nile delta). See Hashmi, "Patronage," 53.
6. On Sufism in Ottoman Egypt see Winter, *Society and Religion*; Chih & Mayeur-Jaouen, *Soufisme*. On Rūmī Sufis visiting Cairo, see Ballanfat, "Nîyâzî Mısrî." The most famous Syrian Sufi to spend time in Cairo was ᶜAbd al-Ghanī al-Nābulsī, who wrote a well-known travelogue covering Egypt called *al-Ḥaqīqa wa ʾl-majāz*; see Sirriyeh, *Sufi Visionary*, 84–128. Murtaḍā al-Zabīdī, who settled in Cairo in 1753, shortly after the period I study here, was from Lucknow, India and came to Egypt via Yemen and the Hejaz. See Reichmuth, *World of Murtaḍā al-Zabīdī*.
7. On harem eunuchs in Cairo, see Hathaway, "Role of the Kızlar Ağası"; Hathaway, "Wealth and Influence"; Hathaway, *Beshir Agha*.
8. For the management of agriculture in Ottoman Egypt, see Mikhail, *Nature and Empire*.
9. On tax-farming in Ottoman Egypt see Cuno, *Pasha's Peasants*. On the awqāf see ᶜAfīfī, *al-Awqāf*.
10. Raymond, *Cairo*, 208–10.
11. On Egypt's role in the spice trade see Casale, "Ottoman Administration." On the coffee trade, see Tuchscherer, *Commerce du café*. On sugar, see Hanna, *Making Big Money*, 81–4.
12. "Bey" was the highest rank in Egyptian political society; see p. 28.
13. Jabartī B, I: 204–5; Jabartī P, I: 333–5.
14. Raymond, "Famille," 119–20. The sabīl-kuttāb was a two-story structure with a public water fountain on the ground and an elementary school, where children were taught Koran-recitation, above. This was one of the most popular types of philanthropic foundation among Cairo's elites in the seventeenth and eighteenth centuries.
15. Hathaway, *Politics of Households*, 134–6.
16. Only a few of these houses remain standing today. The best-preserved is Bayt al-Suḥaymī, located on al-Muᶜizz li dīn Allāh street, built in 1648 and restored in the 1990s.
17. On the rabᶜ and other forms of middle-class housing in Ottoman Cairo see Hanna, *Habiter au Caire*.
18. On the career of the oil-presser Aḥmad al-Jalfī and the household he founded, see Hanna, *Artisan Entrepreneurs*, 104–27.

19. Raymond, *Cairo*, 255–64.
20. The rich used endowments for both philanthropy and intergenerational wealth management. The law recognized a distinction between a *waqf khayrī*, supporting a charitable activity, and a *waqf ahlī*, where the beneficiaries were the founder's family, with the income only reverting to a charitable cause once the family line had died out. However, the two purposes could happily coexist within a single endowment, if the income was directed to charity but the endowment deed awarded the post of administrator, with salary, to a family member.
21. The classic accounts of pre-modern Muslim education are Berkey, *Transmission of Knowledge*; Chamberlain, *Knowledge and Social Practice.* By remaining in line with this model, al-Azhar differed from the madrasas founded by the Ottomans as part of the *ilmiye* hierarchy, which did have prescribed curricula; I discuss this further in Chapter 4.
22. On science in eighteenth-century Cairo see Murphy, "Improving the Mind."
23. On history-writing in Ottoman Egypt, see Hanna, "Chronicles"; Crecelius, *Eighteenth-Century Egypt.*
24. On Sufism in Ottoman Egypt, see Winter, *Society and Religion*; Chih and Mayeur-Jaouen, *Soufisme.*
25. On this incident see Peters, "Battered Dervishes."
26. Hanna, *In Praise of Books.*
27. Ibid., 104–71.
28. Raymond, "Opuscule."
29. On Egypt's role in provisioning Istanbul, the holy cities and other regions of the empire with foodstuffs, see Mikhail, *Nature and Empire*, 82–123.
30. On land tenure and agricultural taxation see Cuno, *Pasha's Peasants*; Shaw, *Financial and Administrative Organization*, 12–97. On the awqāf in Egypt see ᶜAfīfī, *al-Awqāf.*
31. Built as part of the Vālide Sulṭān mosque complex in the 1660s, this bazaar was initially known as the Vālide Çarşısı (the Queen Mother's Bazaar) and then as the Yeni Çarşı (New Bazaar). It acquired the name Mısır Çarşısı in the mid eighteenth century. Eldem, *French Trade*, 71, n. 15.
32. On Cairo's role in the coffee trade see: Raymond, "Famille des grands négociants"; Raymond, *Artisans et commerçants*, I: 107–202; Hanna, *Making Big Money*, 70–99; Hathaway, *Politics of Households*, 132–8. On the spice trade see Casale, "Ottoman Administration." On the trade with sub-Saharan Africa see Walz, *Trade between Egypt and Bilād al-Sūdān.* On the trade in African eunuchs, see Hathaway, *Beshir Agha*, 17–23.
33. The anonymous author of the chronicle *Zubdat ikhtiṣār tārīkh mulūk Miṣr* reports that on 13 Ramaḍān 1079 (14 February 1669), an imperial order arrived in Cairo demanding 1,000 soldiers for the final stages of the siege of Candia: *Zubdat ikhtiṣār*, 148. Damurdāshī reports that during the Ottoman–Venetian war of 1714–18, 3,000 Egyptian troops were sent to Gallipoli for the defense of the straits. Damurdāshī claims that the Egyptian beys Muḥammad Bey al-Kabīr and Aḥmad Bey played such a crucial role in the Ottoman victory that the Sultan personally recognized their efforts: Damurdāshī C, 204–6; Damurdāshī A, 125–6. During the Polish–Ottoman War of 1672–6, 3,000 Egyptian soldiers were sent to Kamaniçe in Shawwāl 1084 (January–February 1674),

and a further 2,000 in Dhū ᵓl-Ḥijja 1086 (February 1676): *Zubdat ikhtiṣār*, 154, 156. In Dhū ᵓl-Qaᶜda 1093 (November 1682) 3,000 Egyptian troops were sent to the Hungarian front, and a further 3,000 were sent on 1 Shawwāl 1095 (11 September 1684): *Zubdat ikhtiṣār*, 163–4.

34. Faroqhi, *Pilgrims and Sultans*, 37–40.
35. ᶜAlī Bey al-Kabīr established a brief period of autonomy in Egypt in the 1760s and 1770s but even he did not secure the position of governor for himself; rather, he refused to accept an Ottoman governor in Egypt, and exercised power as *qāᵓimmaqām* (acting governor). On his rule see Crecelius, *Roots of Modern Egypt.*
36. Bayram Pasha served as governor of Egypt from 1626–8, and then as Grand Vizier from 1637–8. Tarhoncu Aḥmed Pasha served as governor of Egypt from 1649–51 and went on to serve as Grand Vizier from 1652–3. Ḥekīmoğlu ᶜAlī Pasha served as governor of Egypt from 1740–41, in between his first and second terms as Grand Vizier, and again from 1755–7, after his third term as Grand Vizier. Rāgib Meḥmed Pasha served as governor of Egypt from 1746–8 and went on to serve as Grand Vizier from 1757–63.
37. For an analysis of the household political culture in Ottoman Egypt, see Hathaway, *Politics of Households*. For a narrative political history of seventeenth and eighteenth-century Egypt, see Holt, *Egypt and the Fertile Crescent*, 61–101.
38. In Egypt, the Janissaries were often called Mustaḥfiẓān in Arabic, meaning "guards," rather than the Turkish Yeniçeri. The other five regiments were the Tüfekçiyān, Gönüllüyān, Çerākise, Müteferriḳa and the Çavuşān.
39. For a study of this process in the context of Cairo, see Raymond, "Soldiers in Trade." For other regions of the Ottoman Empire, see Kafadar, "Yeniçeri–Esnaf Relations"; Wilkins, *Forging Urban Solidarities*; Yılmaz, "Economic and Social Roles." For a stimulating recent interpretation of this development, see Tezcan, *Second Ottoman Empire.*
40. Of course, this competition remained a factor after 1805, but the political dynamics changed significantly after this, as the reforming regime of governor Meḥmed ᶜAlī introduced a radically new understanding of the aims and capacities of government.
41. Readers interested in a narrative history can refer to Volume 2 of the *Cambridge History of Egypt*; and to Holt, *Egypt and the Fertile Crescent*, 33–101.
42. For examples of the rise and decline model, see Holt, *Egypt and the Fertile Crescent*; Winter, *Egyptian Society*; Marsot, *History of Egypt.*
43. On the Ottoman conquest of Egypt and its aftermath, see Lellouch & Michel, *Conquête ottomane*. The ḳānūnnāme of Egypt has been published: see Barkan (ed.), "Mısır Kanunnamesi."
44. In much of the older literature the beys are identified as the "Mamlūks," and are assumed to be the socio-cultural, if not the genealogical, descendants of the ruling class in the Mamluk Sultanate. Jane Hathaway has debunked this interpretation, demonstrating that Ottoman Egypt's political households resembled the households that constituted the basic unit of political activity across the seventeenth and eighteenth-century Ottoman Empire. For examples of the "neo-Mamluk" interpretation see Ayalon, "Studies in al-Jabartī"; Holt, "Exalted Lineage." For Hathaway's argument see Hathaway, *Politics of Households.*

45. At least, not until Meḥmed ᶜAlī, but he used his great power to grant himself autonomy, not to enhance Istanbul's control over Egypt.
46. For an account of one such deposition, and the articulation of grievances in legal terms, see Baldwin, "Deposition."
47. On the 1711 war see Raymond, "Une revolution au Caire."
48. The rise of the Qāzdughlī household is the central narrative of Hathaway, *Politics of Households*.
49. For ᶜAlī Bey al-Kabīr, see Crecelius, *Roots of Modern Egypt*.
50. For a preliminary exploration of the impact of political violence on the city and urban life, see Baldwin, "Factional Conflict."
51. On the role of the Dīvān-i Hümāyūn in mediating a dispute between Egyptian merchants and the States-General of Holland over losses suffered to Dutch privateers, see Van den Boogert, "Redress for Ottoman Victims."
52. On the *iltizām* system in Egypt see Cuno, *Pasha's Peasants*, 33–47; ᶜĀmir, "Niẓām al-iltizām."
53. For example, a contract between the governor Nişāncı Meḥmed Pasha and a group of beys and senior regimental officers, in which the latter undertook to subdue the bedouin who had been attacking traffic on the Suez road, and recover the boats and goods that they had seized. See MK, 1/18, 3 Rajab 1134 (19 April 1722).
54. This function of the legal system in the Ottoman provinces has been commented on by several scholars. See, for example: Darling, *Revenue-Raising*, 246–80; Singer, *Palestinian Peasants*; İnalcık, "Şikayet Hakkı"; Gerber, *State, Society and Law*, 127–73.
55. On the importance of justice in Ottoman strategies of legitimation, see Darling, *History of Social Justice*, 127–54.

Chapter 2

1. The exceptions are a small cache of court records from fourteenth-century Jerusalem known as the Ḥaram al-Sharīf documents, a number of endowment deeds held mainly at the national archives of Egypt and Syria, and scattered documents in the various Cairo Geniza collections. The reason for the lack of surviving Mamluk court records is probably that they were not preserved within an institutional framework, instead being held in the personal archives of individual qāḍīs, and so were dispersed and largely lost. See Hallaq, "Qāḍī's Dīwān."
2. For example, see Rapoport, "Royal Justice"; Stilt, *Islamic Law*; Fuess, "Ẓulm by Maẓālim?"; Irwin, "Privatization of Justice"; Nielsen, *Secular Justice*; Tyan, *Histoire de l'organisation judiciaire*, 433–525.
3. Of course, the survival of sharīᶜa court records in the Ottoman Empire is not an accident, but is the result of conscious Ottoman policy, and so is in itself evidence for the importance of sharīᶜa courts. However, while the introduction of court registers by the Ottomans indicates a significant milestone in the conception of judgeship and in the institutional development of courts in the Muslim world, it was essentially a reform of archiving practices, not of the general function of the courts. It does not indicate that

other Ottoman legal institutions which lacked institutional registers were insignificant; nor does it show that pre-Ottoman sharīʿa courts were unimportant.

4. Within Cairo, the neighborhood courts were: Qanāṭir al-Sibāʿ, al-Ṭulūn, al-Quṣūn, al-Jāmiʿ al-Ṣāliḥ, Bābay Saʿāda wa ʾl-Kharq, al-Ṣāliḥiyya al-Najmiyya, al-Jāmiʿ al-Ḥākim, Bāb al-Shaʿriyya, al-Zāhid, al-Baramshiyya and al-Azbakiyya. Registers survive for all of these courts except al-Azbakiyya, the existence of which we know of through a handful of loose documents. See Mīlād, *al-Wathāʾiq al-ʿUthmāniyya*, I: 141–73.
5. Mīlād, *al-Wathāʾiq al-ʿUthmāniyya*, I: 96–100, 115–17, 113–14. For a description of the Ḥākim mosque see Behrens-Abouseif, *Islamic Architecture*, 63–5. The Nāṣirī al-Jadīd mosque no longer survives, while only the gate of the Quṣūn mosque stands today. The precise location of the court of Bāb al-Shaʿriyya court, one of the three whose sijillāt I used, is not known. It would have been somewhere in the neighborhood called Bāb al-Shaʿriyya, which was in the northwest of the walled city.
6. Mīlād, *al-Wathāʾiq al-ʿUthmāniyya*, I: 104–13. The Kāmiliyya madrasa was founded in the Ayyubid period, but most of what stands today is an Ottoman restoration. The Ẓāhiriyya madrasa was demolished in the late nineteenth century.
7. Scholars of other Ottoman provinces have also described the sharīʿa courts as a key meeting point of the imperial and the local. See, for example, Singer, *Palestinian Peasants*; Ze'evi, *Ottoman Century*; Peirce, *Morality Tales*; Tuğ, "Politics of Honor." For a portrayal of the sharīʿa court as a tool of Ottomanization following the conquest of Aleppo in the sixteenth century, see Fitzgerald, "Ottoman Methods of Conquest," 207–31.
8. Uzunçarşılı, *Osmanlı Devletinin İlmiye Teşkilatı*, 99–100. In 1135/1722 the new category of *Ḥarameyn* judgeships was created, consisting of Mecca and Medina; these ranked above the *Bilād-i Erbāʿa* category, in which Mecca was replaced by Damascus; later Filibe was added to this category, which made it the *Bilād-i Hamse*. On the incorporation of the qāḍīship of Cairo and other Arab cities into the imperial hierarchy, see Atçıl, "Route to the Top," 502–9.
9. For a list of chief qāḍīs of Cairo in the seventeenth century, see el-Nahal, *Judicial Administration*, 78–9.
10. Because Miṣr al-Qadīma and Būlāq were administratively separate cities, the Ḥanafī judge in their courts had the rank of qāḍī rather than nāʾib.
11. The difference between a qāḍī and a nāʾib was one of rank. Within the day-to-day operation of the sharīʿa court, qāḍīs and nāʾibs operated in exactly the same way and had the same powers. In this book, when I use the word qāḍī in a generic sense, it can be taken to mean qāḍī or nāʾib: to always use both terms would be tedious. By contrast, when I am referring to a specific qāḍī or nāʾib, for example when I am discussing a particular court case, I will use the appropriate term. The chief qāḍī of Cairo, and all other qāḍīs holding senior administrative posts, will always be identified precisely.
12. The ilmiye referred to the Ottoman legal profession, including professors, jurists, muftis and qāḍīs, and to the madrasas that trained them. Consisting of a network of madrasas and a hierarchical professional structure with specified paths of promotion, the ilmiye

represented the Ottomans' attempt to integrate the ulema into the fabric of the state. Not all scholars and judges were part of the ilmiye, especially in the Arab provinces where large and prestigious educational institutions predated the Ottomans and continued to operate outside the ilmiye framework. On the development of the ilmiye see Atçıl, "Formation of the Ottoman Learned Class" and "Route to the Top."

13. Abū ʾl-Saʿūd ibn ʿAbd al-Raḥīm ibn ʿAbd al-Muḥsin al-Shaʿrānī left Egypt for Istanbul with his father when young. After training in various medreses in the capital, including the Süleymāniye, he served as qāḍī in Damascus, Jerusalem, Bursa, Edirne, and Istanbul before being appointed ḳāżʿasker of Anatolia. See Muḥibbī, *Khulāṣat al-athar*, I: 144–6. Abū Bakr Efendī al-Bakrī al-Ṣadīqī al-Ashʿarī served as qāḍī in Aleppo; see ʿĪsā, *Tārīkh al-qaḍāʾ*, 236. Muḥammad ibn ʿUmar ibn Muḥammad Taqī al-Dīn al-Faraskūrī entered the service of Şeyhulislām Yaḥyā Zakariyyāʾ while he was qāḍī of Cairo and returned with him to Istanbul; after studying there he later became qāḍī of Jerusalem. See Muḥibbī, *Khulāṣat al-athar*, IV: 82–9.
14. Muḥibbī, *Khulāṣat al-athar*, IV: 77.
15. Van Gelder, "Shihāb al-Dīn al-Khafājī"; Muḥibbī, *Khulāṣat al-athar*, I: 371–84; Brockelmann, *Geschichte der arabischen Litteratur*, II: 285–6.
16. Records of contracts in the court registers always say that the contract was concluded before (*ladā*) the presiding qāḍī or nāʾib. However, orders sent by the chief qāḍī to the neighborhood courts giving instructions about whether and how certain types of contract should be drawn up are often addressed directly to the scribes, suggesting that they carried out this function independently. I discuss several such orders in Chapter 4.
17. On the role of the shuhūd ʿudūl, see ʿĪsā, *Tārīkh al-qaḍāʾ*, 301–10.
18. Compared with sharīʿa court registers, individual ḥujjas issued by courts are relatively rare, and so have not been much studied. For examples of ḥujjas issued by al-Bāb al-ʿĀlī see: DK 64/38, 22 Dhū ʾl-Qaʿda 1083 (11 March 1673); British Library, MS Or. 15259/b, Jumādā ʾl-Ūlā 1207 (8 January 1793); Cambridge University Library, MS T-S Ar.38.116, Rajab 925 (June–July 1519); MS T-S Ar.42.184, 21 Rajab 1023 (27 August 1614); Leiden University Library, MS Or. 22324, 27 Rabīʿ al-Awwal 1217 (28 July 1802). An example of a ḥujja issued by the court of Fayyūm: DK 65/35, 10 Jumādā ʾl-Thānī 1083 (3 October 1672). A ḥujja issued by the court of Manṣūra: DK 65/44, 23 Shaʿbān 1083 (14 December 1672). A ḥujja issued by the court of Rosetta: PMA, İbnülemin Dahiliye 415, 9 Ṣafar 1081 (28 June 1670).
19. This concurs with what Boğaç Ergene found for seventeenth and eighteenth-century Kastamonu and Hülya Canbakal found for seventeenth-century ʿAyntāb. See Ergene, *Local Court*, 29; Canbakal, *Society and Politics*, 134.
20. Fāyid al-Buḥayrī appears regularly throughout the registers BS 623 and BS 624. Muḥammad al-Buḥayrī appears regularly throughout register BS 629; he is identified as Muḥammad ibn Fāyid al-Buḥayrī in BS 629, entry 1125, 17 Rajab 1111 (8 January 1700).
21. ʿAbd al-Bāqī al-Buḥayrī appears regularly throughout the registers BS 623 and BS 624. He also appears infrequently in BS 625, e.g. entry 63, 10 Rabīʿ al-Thānī 1085 (14 July 1674). Muḥammad al-Buḥayrī appears in entries in the register BS 625, e.g. entry 6, 2

Rabī[c] al-Awwal 1085 (6 June 1674), entry 48, 21 Rabī[c] al-Awwal 1085 (25 June 1674), entry 61, 10 Rabī[c] al-Thānī 1085 (14 July 1675), entry 105, 10 Jumādā [ᵓ]l-Ūlā 1085 (12 August 1674), and in some entries in the register BA 159, e.g. entry 135, 8 Muḥarram 1086 (4 April 1675).

22. In this respect, Cairo differed from seventeenth-century Kayseri and sixteenth-century [c]Ayntāb, where court witnesses were a diverse group consisting of people who happened to be at court that day or people who had a personal interest in the case or the litigants. See Ronald Jennings, "Limitations of the Judicial Powers," 162–3; Peirce, *Morality Tales*, 97–8. It also differed from seventeenth-century [c]Ayntab, where the court witnesses constituted a clique representing the local urban elite. See Canbakal, *Society and Politics*, 123–49.
23. BS 629, entries 2 and 3, both dated 12 Sha[c]bān 1110 (13 February 1699).
24. For example: BS 629, entry 387, 18 Shawwāl 1107 (21 May 1696); BS 629, entry 404, 2 Dhū [ᵓ]l-Ḥijja 1107 (3 July 1696). These orders are discussed at length in Chapter 4.
25. Damurdāshī A, 127–8; Damurdāshī C, 207–8. This story is discussed at greater length in Chapter 5.
26. *Awḍaḥ*, 200–1. The sixteenth-century Ottoman criminal ḳānūnnāme, published by Uriel Heyd, prescribes exposure to public scorn (*teşhīr*) for false witnesses, but the generic "severe punishment" (*haḳḳından geleler*) for the specific offense of providing a fraudulent legal document. See Ottoman Criminal Code, clause 98, in Heyd, *Studies*, 83 (Turkish text), 121 (English translation). The teşhīr punishment has not been widely studied in the Ottoman context; for an analysis of teşhīr punishments in Abbasid Baghdad, see Lange, "Legal and Cultural Aspects."
27. Cases heard by [c]Alī al-Rifā[c]ī as Mālikī nā[ᵓ]ib include BS 623, entry 333, 19 Ṣafar 1078 (10 August 1667) and BS 624, entry 301, 13 Ramaḍān 1078 (26 February 1668). Meanwhile, [c]Alī al-Rifā[c]ī was among the court witnesses listed in several other cases from the same period: BS 623, entry 413, 18 Rabī[c] al-Awwal 1078 (7 September 1667); BS 624, entry 18, 24 Rabī[c] al-Thānī 1078 (13 October 1667); BS 625, entry 280, 14 Shawwāl 1085 (11 January 1675).
28. Court witnesses were described as imāms in the following entries. Fāyīd al-Buḥayrī: BS 623, entry 339, 11 Ṣafar 1078 (2 August 1667); BS 624, entry 74, 14 Jumādā [ᵓ]l-Ūlā 1078 (1 November 1667). Muḥammad al-Buḥayrī: BS 625, entry 6, 2 Rabī[c] al-Awwal 1085 (6 June 1674); BS 625, entry 48, 21 Rabī[c] al-Awwal 1085 (25 June 1674); BS 625, entry 61, 10 Rabī[c] al-Thānī 1085 (14 July 1674); BS 625, entry 105, 10 Jumādā [ᵓ]l-Ūlā (12 August 1674). Another Muḥammad al-Buḥayrī: BS 629, entry 417, 21 Dhū [ᵓ]l-Ḥijja 1107 (22 July 1696); BS 629, entry 714, 16 Jumādā [ᵓ]l-Thānī 1109 (30 December 1697).
29. Barkan, "Mısır Kanunnamesi," 378, clause 32.
30. Damurdāshī A, 260–1; Damurdāshī C, 388.
31. Faraḥāt, *al-Tārīkh al-ijtimā[c]ī*, 189–92.
32. Works discussing the Dīwān as a consultative body include: Shaw, *Financial and Administrative Organization*, 2 and passim; el-Nahal, *Judicial Administration*, 91, n. 90; Faraḥāt, *al-Tārīkh al-ijtimā[c]ī*, 189–92; Behrens-Abouseif, *Egypt's Adjustment*, 60–3; Marsot, "Power and Authority," 43–7.

33. Gerber, *State, Society and Law*, 69; Gerber, "Public Sphere," 70–1; Hallaq, *Sharīᶜa*, 208–12. A few Ottomanists have addressed the role of provincial governors' councils and described them as a manifestation of the maẓālim tradition: see Ursinus, *Grievance Administration*; Gradeva, "On Judicial Hierarchy."
34. The only comparable pre-nineteenth-century source I am aware of is a register belonging to the kaymakam of Rumelia and dating from the 1780s, which has been published by Michael Ursinus. See Ursinus, *Grievance Administration*. The few other scholars who have discussed the judicial role of provincial governors' councils have done so on the basis of evidence in sharīᶜa court registers or the records of the imperial bureaucracy in Istanbul, or on the basis of narrative sources, rather than documents produced by the provincial councils themselves. For example, Gradeva, "On Judicial Hierarchy"; Ginio, "Administration"; Marcus, *Middle East*, 114–20.
35. ENA, Ḥujaj ṣādira min maḥkamat al-Dīwān al-ᶜĀlī min sana 1030 ilā 1272; PMA, Cevdet Maliye 26058, 18 Rajab 1081 (1 December 1670); DK 65/34, 28 Jumādā ᵓl-Ūlā 1083 (21 September 1672); DK 76/29, 20 Dhū ᵓl-Ḥijja 1086 (6 March 1676); MK 1/18, 3 Rajab 1134 (19 April 1722); İbnülemin Adliye 846, 7 Dhū ᵓl-Ḥijja 1139 (26 July 1727).
36. On the citadel, see Behrens-Abouseif, *Islamic Architecture*, 78–85; Rabbat, *Citadel of Cairo*.
37. Damurdāshī A, 78–9; Damurdāshī C, 139–42.
38. Damurdāshī A, 40–1; Damurdāshī C, 79–81.
39. These records contain copies of imperial orders issued in response to petitions. The orders begin by declaring that a person had petitioned: this is described either as *ᶜarżuḥāl idüb* (so and so sent a petition) or as *gelüb ᶜarżuḥāl idüb* (so and so came to submit a petition). For examples where an Egyptian had traveled to the imperial palace to submit his or her petition, see: AŞD 20, entry 1257, mid Shawwāl 1106 (25 May–3 June 1695); AŞD 28, entry 45, late Jumādā ᵓl-Ūlā 1109 (5–14 December 1697); AŞD 170, entry 1445, early Ramaḍān 1154 (10–19 November 1741); ŞD 992, p. 43, 4th entry, early Jumādā ᵓl-Thānī 1131 (21–30 April 1719); DK 77/64, mid Rabīᶜ al-Awwal 1077 (11–20 September 1666)—the document cited here is a petition dated 1087/1676, but the order I refer to has been annotated onto the top right corner.
40. Imber, *Ottoman Empire*, 153.
41. For example: İnalcık, "Şikayet Hakkı"; Gerber, *State, Society and Law*, 127–73.
42. Ottoman-Islamic legal theory contained no category equivalent to the modern Anglo-American concept of criminal law. While a handful of offenses were categorized as "claims of God," which the ruling authorities had a duty to prosecute and which were punished with fixed penalties (the *ḥadd* offenses), most acts that are considered crimes today, including murder, assault, vandalism, and most thefts, were treated as private disputes between the offender and the victim or the victim's heirs. The ḥadd offenses were drinking alcohol (*sharb al-khamr*), fornication (*zināᵓ*), false accusation of fornication (*qadhf*), theft (*sariqa*), highway robbery (*qaṭᶜ al-ṭarīq*) and, according to some jurists, apostasy from Islam (*ridda*). Although sariqa was a ḥadd offense, jurists defined the concept very narrowly so that it excluded many petty thefts, shoplifting, and pickpocketing; these were instead treated as private claims of usurpation (*ightiṣāb* or *ghaṣb*), for

which the fixed penalty of amputation did not apply. For an overview of Islamic criminal law, and its application in the Ottoman Empire, see Peters, *Crime and Punishment in Islamic Law*, 6–102.

43. For example, the petition sent by the villagers of Banī Suwayf and Bahnasā described above.
44. For examples of cases of theft, see BS 624, entry 179, 5 Rajab 1078 (21 December 1667); BS 625, entry 367, 5 Dhū ʾl-Ḥijja 1085 (2 March 1675); BS 629, entry 91, 4 Dhū ʾl-Ḥijja 1106 (16 July 1695); BS 629, entry 1105, 10 Jumādā ʾl-Thānī 1111 (3 December 1699); BS 638, entry 225, 27 Ṣafar 1151 (16 June 1738). In all of these cases the act was described as taking (*akhdh*) or usurpation (ghaṣb), thereby rendering the offense ineligible for the ḥadd penalty of amputation. For examples of cases of verbal abuse, see BS 624, entry 51, 6 Jumādā ʾl-Ūlā 1078 (24 October 1667); BS 624, entry 295, 10 Ramaḍān 1078 (23 February 1668); BS 625, entry 259, 10 Ramaḍān 1085 (8 December 1674); BS 625, entry 320, 29 Shawwāl 1085 (26 January 1675). For examples of cases of assault, see BS 625, entry 146, 15 Jumādā ʾl-Thānī 1085 (16 September 1674); MQ 105, entry 13, 14 Dhū ʾl-Qaᶜda 1091 (6 December 1680); BS 629, entry 601, 14 Dhū ʾl-Ḥijja 1108 (4 July 1697). See also an example of an attack made on a house while its owner was out which was made, according to the owner, in order to humiliate him: BS 625, entry 264, 24 Ramaḍān 1085 (22 December 1674). For examples of cases of homicide, see DA 1, entry 283, 14 Muḥarram 1155 (21 March 1742); DA 1, entry 472, 29 Shawwāl 1155 (27 December 1742).
45. Damurdāshī C, 356–7; Damurdāshī A, 238–9.
46. Barkan, "Mısır Kanunnamesi," 378, clause 32.
47. Gerber, "Public Sphere," 70–1.
48. On Zaynī Barakāt see Stilt, *Islamic Law*, 69–71. Zaynī Barakāt was the subject of a historical novel by the modern Egyptian writer Gamal al-Ghitani: see al-Ghitani, *Zayni Barakat*.
49. Two copies of Ibn Ukhuwwa's *Maᶜālim al-qurba fī aḥkām al-ḥisba* were made in 968 (1560–1) and 987 (1579–80); they are now held at the Arab League Manuscript Institute in Cairo (MS siyāsa 26 and MS siyāsa 25, respectively). A copy of ᶜAbd al-Raḥmān ibn Naṣr al-Shayzarī's *Nihāyat al-rutba fī ṭalab al-ḥisba*, now held in the Egyptian National Library (MS ṣināᶜat 72), was made in 1079 (1668). A copy of Aḥmad Ibn Rifᶜa's *Badhl al-naṣāʾiḥ al-sharᶜiyya*, now held in the Bibliothèque nationale de France (MS arabe 2451), was made in 1056 (1646–7). A copy of Ibn Bassām's *Nihāyat al-rutba fī ṭalab al-ḥisba*, now held at the Egyptian National Library (MS ijtimāᶜ ṭalaᶜat 614), was copied in 1195 (1780–1). See Stilt, *Islamic Law*, 215.
50. Although in the Ottoman Empire the term *wālī* (or in Turkish, *vālī*) usually referred to a provincial governor, in Ottoman Egypt it was used to refer to the police chief. This was true in Arabic and Turkish; the ḳānūnnāme of Egypt refers to the police chief as the *vālī-i şehir* (the vālī of the city) and the governor as the *beylerbeyi*; see Barkan, "Mısır Kanunnamesi," 378–83. Arabic sources typically refer to the governor as the *wazīr* (vizier) or the *bāshā* (Pasha).
51. On this process see Raymond, *Artisans et commerçants*, II: 601–6.
52. Shaw, *Financial and Administrative Organization*, 118–20.

53. Ibid., 120–3.
54. Raymond, *Artisans et commerçants*, II: 608–9. Both André Raymond and Michael Winter, following the account of the Ottoman traveler Evliyā Çelebi, claim that the police chief was also responsible for regulating and taxing Cairo's thieves. Evliyā Çelebi gives a list of "guilds" (*eṣnāf*) that the police chief regulated, including a guild of pickpockets (*eṣnāf-i neşşaller yaʿnī hemyānkesiciler*). Rather than take this literally to mean that thieving was formally recognized and taxed by the authorities, which seems implausible, I think it is better to read this as a satirical comment on police corruption: it may have been true that the police chief "taxed" the thieves, but this was a protection racket, not a formal or officially sanctioned arrangement. See Evliyā Çelebi, *Evliyā Çelebi Seyahatnamesi*, 204–6; Winter, *Egyptian Society*, 229. On the other hand there is sufficient evidence that, despite its illegality, prostitution was, for much of the time, formally tolerated and regulated under the authority of the police chief with the consent of the highest levels of provincial government. For example, when the governor ʿAbdullāh Pasha Köprülü decided to close the city's brothels in 1731, the fact that the police chief and military regiments received payments from the brothels was openly discussed by military officers and the governor at a session of the Dīwān; the governor agreed to compensate them with an alternative revenue stream; *Awḍah*, 574–5. Formal toleration of prostitution is not particularly surprising, as it is in line with the approach to prostitution taken by many pre-modern societies. See Baldwin, "Prostitution," 142–6.
55. Damurdāshī A, 233–4; Damurdāshī C, 350.
56. *Awḍah*, 220–2; Jabartī B, I: 208–9; Jabartī P, I: 341–2. I discuss this incident in Baldwin, "Elite Conflict."
57. Damurdāshī A, 23; Damurdāshī C, 51–3.
58. Damurdāshī A, 169; Damurdāshī C, 266.
59. Damurdāshī A, 15, 35, 41, 57, 62, 123, 125, 200, 214, 238, 256; Damurdāshī C, 39, 70, 81, 104, 112, 202, 204, 305, 324, 356, 382.
60. Damurdāshī A, 32; Damurdāshī C, 65.
61. Damurdāshī A, 225–6; Damurdāshī C, 340.
62. Damurdāshī C, 298; Damurdāshī A, 195–6. We might doubt Damurdāshī's interpretation of both events. His narrative tends to emphasize the agency of individuals from among Egypt's regiments and military households: Damurdāshī was himself a lower-ranking officer, and his chronicle reads like a compendium of gossip from the barracks. Furthermore, the regularity with which a dynamic soldier cracks down on prostitution and alcohol, in many chronicles, suggests that this is a trope. In Aḥmad Çelebi's version of the ʿAlī Āghā story, the initiative comes from a meeting of the Dīwān. Similarly, Aḥmad Çelebi recounts a campaign against vice in 1731, but in his story the campaign is undertaken by the governor ʿAbdullāh Pasha Köprülü, on the order of the Sultan. In this account, the police chief and other soldiers attempt to block the campaign, as they are accustomed to taxing the brothels and are not inclined to give up that income; ʿAbdullāh Pasha compensates them with an alternative revenue stream. *Awḍah*, 207–9, 574–5.
63. The ardabb is a dry measure; its size varied considerably, from 75 liters in 1665 to 184 liters in 1798.

64. *Awḍaḥ*, 189–90. See also Holt, "Career of Küçük Muḥammad."
65. *Awḍaḥ*, 207–9; Damurdāshī A, 65–8; Damurdāshī C, 117–23; Jabartī B, I: 102–4; Jabartī P, I: 168–70.
66. According to Aḥmad Çelebi, this meeting was held at the Dīwān. Damurdāshī claims that it was held, on the governor's instruction, at the house of Ḥasan Āghā al-Balfiyya.
67. Damurdāshī A, 65; Damurdashi C, 117. For the role of the Janissaries in policing the Ottoman capital, see Zarinebaf, *Crime and Punishment*, 125–40.
68. This detail is added by Damurdāshī; Aḥmad Çelebi does not mention any action against bar-keeping or prostitution.
69. The çavuş was the third highest ranking officer in the regiment.
70. The naqīb al-ashrāf was the communal head of the descendants of the Prophet Muḥammad (ashrāf, sing. sharīf), who enjoyed certain privileges. Here, çavuş refers to the naqīb's attendant.
71. The list of people I give here is an amalgamation of the lists given by Damurdāshī and Aḥmad Çelebi. See Damurdāshī A, 66; Damurdāshī C, 119; *Awḍaḥ*, 208. A çavuş from each regiment and the çavuş of the naqīb al-ashrāf joined the procession in order to punish regimental soldiers and descendants of the Prophet respectively, in recognition of their immunity from prosecution by the police.
72. Damurdāshī A, 67–8; Damurdāshī C, 121–2. Damurdāshī explains that the women singers performed at the weddings of Cairo's wealthier families, which he declares an immoral practice in itself. But this detail comes in the middle of his account of ᶜAlī Āghā's crackdown on prostitution. It seems likely that there was some overlap between women singers and prostitutes, and that al-ᶜAnza had some role in the organization of prostitution in Cairo.
73. *Awḍaḥ*, 214.
74. Damurdāshī A, 225–6; Damurdāshī C, 340.
75. Jabartī B, I: 104; Jabartī P, I: 170 (translation from Jabartī P).
76. It is interesting that Aḥmad Çelebi uses virtually the same Arabic word to describe both ᶜAlī Āghā and Ibrāhīm Āghā—describing the former as tyrannical (*jabbār*) and referring to the latter's tyranny (*tajabbur*)—yet the implication is positive in the first instance and negative in the second.
77. *Awḍaḥ*, 287–8.
78. Raymond, *Artisans et commerçants*, II: 594.
79. Barkan, "Mısır Kanunnamesi," 382, clause 41.
80. Perhaps, if Aḥmad Çelebi's account is accurate, during ᶜAlī Āghā's procession this nāʾib presided over hurried trials of offenders before they were punished. But the evidence strongly suggests that this was not always the case, and that trial before a qāḍī or nāʾib was not considered necessary when offenders were caught in the act, or in possession of false weights.
81. ᶜAlī Āghā's procession is not the only example of a qāḍī sanctioning such action. When the governor ᶜAbdullāh Pasha Köprülü had the bars and brothels of Cairo demolished in 1731 on the order of a haṭṭ-i şerīf, the qāḍī wrote up a ḥujja sanctioning the action in advance. Aḥmad Çelebi does not specify who carried out the demolitions, but it would most likely have been either the Janissary Āghā or the police chief. *Awḍaḥ*, 574–5.

82. This is the way we should read Evliyā Çelebi's claim that there was a "guild of pickpockets" regulated by the police chief: see p. 174, note 54.
83. For example, Aḥmad Çelebi reports the arrival of a haṭṭ-i şerīf deposing Riḍwān Āghā and appointing Aḥmad Āghā ibn Bākīr Efendī on 12 Jumādā ʾl-Thānī 1119 (10 September 1707); and the arrival of another deposing Ibrāhīm Āghā and appointing Muḥammad Āghā ibn al-Jīʿān on 22 Ṣafar 1128 (16 February 1716). *Awḍaḥ*, 213, 287.
84. Raymond, *Artisans et commerçants*, II: 600–1; Ḥuseyn Efendî, *Ottoman Egypt*, 40, 91–2.
85. Damurdāshī A, 145; Damurdāshī C, 230. The original text uses the verb *ʿamala*, meaning "to make." Crecelius and Bakr translate this as "appointed," but I think the author's meaning was not that specific.
86. Damurdāshī A, 194–6; Damurdāshī C, 296–8.
87. During the Mamluk period, some of Cairo's muḥtasibs were qāḍīs or jurists, while some had an administrative or military background. In a similar trajectory to that of Ottoman Cairo, qādīs/jurists dominated the post during the early period of Mamluk rule, while soldiers/administrators dominated in later years. See Stilt, *Islamic Law*, 62–72.
88. Damurdāshī A, 225–6; Damurdāshī C, 340.
89. Damurdāshī A, 189; Damurdāshī C, 289. The ḥulvān tax was payable upon the acquisition or transfer of an iltizām. See Shaw, *Financial and Administrative Organization*, 35–8.
90. Damurdāshī A, 68; Damurdāshī C, 122.
91. Damurdāshī A, 247; Damurdāshī C, 368–9.
92. Jabartī B, I: 192; Jabartī P, I: 314 (translations from Jabartī P).
93. A significant body of scholarship explores the use of the Ottoman sharīʿa courts by non-Muslims. See, for example, Jennings, "Zimmis"; Jennings, *Christians and Muslims*, 69–106, 132–72; Gradeva, "Orthodox Christians"; Ivanova, "Muslim and Christian Women"; al-Qattan, "Dhimmīs"; Wittman, "Before Qadi and Grand Vizier." For the specific case of Ottoman Egypt, see Shūmān, *al-Yāhūd fī Miṣr*, II: 36–43.
94. Ottomanists once held that under the "millet system" the Ottoman Sultans granted the leaders of the various non-Muslims communities formal jurisdiction over their flocks during the fifteenth century. But Benjamin Braude has shown that the millet concept was projected back from the nineteenth century in order to legitimize the authority that non-Muslim leaders gained during the reform period. See Braude, "Foundation Myths."
95. On Christian awqāf in the Ottoman period, see Laiou, "Diverging Realities"; Kermeli, "Ebūʾs-Suʿūd's Definitions."
96. On non-Muslims taking advantage of Islamic law's more generous provisions for divorce, see Gradeva, "Orthodox Christians," 55–62; al-Qattan, "Dhimmīs," 433–5.
97. For recent exceptions, see Kermeli, "Right to Choice"; Wittman, "Before Qadi and Grand Vizier," 51–67; Shūmān, *al-Yāhūd fī Miṣr*, II: 30–6.
98. Shūmān's account of Jewish legal practices in Ottoman Cairo is based on scattered references to Jewish legal officials in the sharīʿa court records.
99. These records consist of several loose documents held at the Center for Advanced Judaic Studies, University of Pennsylvania, and a register held at the British Library. The details given here are drawn from the relevant catalogs. From the University of Pennsylvania: an affidavit of a widow confirming that she received money specified in her marriage

contract, dated 1626 (Halper 362); a document in which witnesses testify that Eleazer Fureikh intends to coerce Jacob Eliakim into selling land at a loss, 1609 (Halper 370); a deed of trusteeship over property, 1624 (Halper 371). According to the catalog, all three documents were written by the same scribe, suggesting institutional continuity between 1609 and 1626. See the Penn–Cambridge Genizah Fragment Project, http://sceti.library.upenn.edu/genizah. From the British Library: a register of the Cairo Jewish community, dated 1683 (MS Or. 6356). See Margoliouth, *Catalogue*, III: 572.

100. Magdi Guirguis gives a brief account of the Coptic legal system under Ottoman rule before the nineteenth century, based largely on narrative sources but also a couple of official orders to sharīᶜa court qāḍīs ordering them not to intervene in certain matters involving Christians. See Girgis, *al-Qaḍāʾ al-Qibṭī*, 54–6.
101. Abraham Marcus is working on a book on Jews in Ottoman Aleppo, based on the Jewish courts' records.
102. For fiqh's position on ṣulḥ see Othman, "And Amicable Settlement is Best."
103. On sixteenth-century ᶜAyntāb, see Peirce, *Morality Tales*, 120–1, 185–6. On sixteenth-century Istanbul see Othman, "And Ṣulḥ is Best," 230–43. On seventeenth-century Kayseri, see Jennings, "Limitations of the Judicial Powers," 179–80; Jennings, "Kadi, Court," 147–8. On seventeenth-century Sofia, see Gradeva, "Orthodox Christians," 53–4. On seventeenth-century Bursa, see Abacı, *Bursa Şehri'nde Osmanlı Hukuku*, 104–5. On seventeenth and eighteenth-century Çankırı and Kastamonu, see Ergene, *Local Court*, 62–3, 183–5, 201. On eighteenth-century Salonica, see Ginio, "Administration," 204–8. On eighteenth-century Esna, see Michel, "Paysans," 141–3. On eighteenth-century Üsküdar and Adana, see Tamdoğan, "*Sulh*," 55–83.
104. Ergene, "Why did Ümmü Gülsüm go to Court?"
105. The phrase is almost always in the plural, so if the qāḍī was acting as mediator, he was not the only one.
106. The mediators in this case are identified as al-Ḥājj Manṣūr ibn Shaᶜbān, Jādullāh ibn Sālim, known as Ibn Qamar, al-Ḥājj ᶜUmar ibn Muḥammad and al-Shaykh Sālim al-Fālimī. The only identifying detail beyond titles and names given by the record is that Manṣūr ibn Shaᶜbān was a local *mudawlab* (warehouse-keeper). This suggests that mediators were often local people who lived or worked in the neighborhood where the dispute took place. Two carried the title al-Ḥājj, which does not give any definite information beyond the fact of having been on pilgrimage, but does suggest that they were at least moderately wealthy, as they were able to afford it. The fourth mediator carried the title al-Shaykh, which is not specific but does indicate some standing in the local community: it could be held by a learned man, a leader of a Sufi group, a leader of a trade guild, or a community elder. MQ 105, entry 13, 14 Dhū ʾl-Qaᶜda 1091 (6 December 1680). The details of this case are discussed below.
107. BS 625, entry 2, 29 Ṣafar 1085 (4 June 1675).
108. The delayed dower was the portion of the dower retained by the husband and paid to the wife upon his death or upon divorce. For a summary of marriage, divorce, and their associated financial obligations in Islamic law, see Tucker, *Women, Family and Gender*, 38–132.

109. The phrase is: *ba^cd an ṣadara al-takhāṣum wa ʾl-tanāzuᶜ wa ʾl-tadāᶜī bayna [fulān wa fulān]... fa ṭāla ʾl-khiṣām wa ʾl-nizāᶜ baynahuma... fa kallama baynahuma mutakallim fī ʾl-ṣulḥ.*
110. BS 624, entry 295, 10 Ramaḍān 1078 (23 February 1668).
111. On litigants' decisions to opt for either ṣulḥ or adjudication, see Coşgel and Ergene, "Selection Bias."
112. On cultural attitudes towards privacy and their legal consequences in eighteenth-century Aleppo, see Marcus, "Privacy."
113. MQ 105, entry 13, 14 Dhū ʾl-Qaᶜda 1091 (6 December 1680).
114. Shaham, "Women as Expert Witnesses," 54–6.
115. The offense of qadhf (false accusation of zināʾ) carried a fixed penalty of eighty lashes. While this penalty is rarely found in the court records, Cairo's courts routinely sentenced people to taᶜzīr (discretionary corporal punishment) for insults which were sexual in nature, and for minor assaults. For example, Aḥmad al-Barāzaᶜī received taᶜzīr for hitting Ramaḍān ibn Muḥammad in the face, pulling his beard, and calling him a pimp: BS 625, entry 259, 10 Ramaḍān 1085 (8 December 1674). ᶜAlī ibn Ḥarāz was sentenced to taᶜzīr for claiming that Yūnus ibn Marᶜī and Sharāya bint Muḥammad had sexual relations before their marriage: BS 625, entry 320, 29 Shawwāl 1085 (26 January 1675). When physical assaults caused injury, the offender could also be liable to retaliation on an eye-for-an-eye basis. See Peters, *Crime and Punishment*, 38–53.
116. Ibn Khalīl need not have feared that Muḥammad and Sālima would later pursue him for the return of the money, because they had renounced all claims against him as part of the ṣulḥ agreement. The agreement included not just the renunciation of the specific claims that Ibn Khalīl had made against them, but also a generic mutual renunciation of all financial claims that either party had against the other: "no silver, no gold, no copper" (*lā fiḍḍatan wa lā dhahaban wa lā fulūsan*).
117. For example: BS 623, entry 301, 9 Ṣafar 1078 (31 July 1667); BS 624, entry 202, 22 Rajab 1078 (7 January 1668). Hallaq emphasizes that pre-modern Islamic law as a working system cannot be understood without its moral-religious context. See *Sharīᶜa*, 164–76. No doubt there were people in Ottoman Cairo who were irreligious and cynically self-interested. But there were many more who were not.
118. Ergene argues that the woman in the case at the center of his article, Ümmü Gülsüm, who also had no evidence to support her claim of rape, issued her apparently hopeless lawsuit with the intention of forcing her assailant into ṣulḥ negotiations. Ergene, "Why did Ümmü Gülsüm go to Court?" 237–43.
119. I discuss this phenomenon in more detail in Chapter 6, pp. 126–8.

Chapter 3

1. Hallaq, *Sharīᶜa*, 208; Gerber, *State, Society and Law*, 69; Gerber, "Public Sphere," 70–1.
2. On ᶜAbbāsid Iraq, see Tillier, "Qāḍīs and the Political Uses." On Umayyad Spain, see Müller, "Redressing Injustice." On Mamluk Egypt, see Nielsen, *Secular Justice*, 74–77, 81–90. Each of these cases is different. In Umayyad Spain, the *ṣāḥib al-maẓālim* and the

qāḍī were distinct positions, but candidates for both were drawn from the same social group and many people served as qāḍī and as ṣāḥib al-maẓālim at different points in their careers. In ᶜAbbāsid Iraq, qāḍīs served the maẓālim tribunal as qāḍīs. In Mamluk Egypt, both of these were true.

3. See Müller, "Redressing Injustice"; Nielsen, *Secular Justice*, 43–7; Rapoport, "Royal Justice."
4. In addition to Hallaq, Coulson and Schacht portray maẓālim in terms familiar from Māwardī. Even though much of the empirical data in Nielsen's *Secular Justice* demonstrates that practice was very different from Māwardī's model, Nielsen still describes the maẓālim system in Mamluk Egypt in Māwardian terms when he is summing up.
5. For a revisionist narrative of Mamluk legal history that takes this perspective, see Rapoport, "Royal Justice."
6. The Ottomans themselves certainly claimed to be reforming Mamluk legal institutions. The ḳānūnnāme for Egypt issued in 1524 included several criticisms of Mamluk legal practice, and enjoined Ottoman officials not to imitate their predecessors' misdeeds. For example, the Ottomans claimed that in the past illegal and immoral activities had been permitted and treated as a source of government revenue, and that people had been punished without a trial before a qāḍī. See Barkan, "Mısır Kanunnamesi," 378, clause 33 and 382, clause 41. At the same time, the Ottomans also sought to anchor their legitimacy in the Mamluk past by claiming to reinstate the ḳānūn of the illustrious Sultan Qāytbāy: see Burak, "Between the Kānūn of Qāytbāy." For an analysis of political rhetoric in the Egyptian ḳānūnnāme, see Buzov, "Lawgiver," 19–45.
7. I explore this in more detail in Chapter 4.
8. That the activities of the Dīvān-i Hümāyūn, including the receiving and processing of petitions, were transferred to the Ottoman camp during war is attested to by the recovery of a Şikayet Defteri (a register containing responses to petitions) from the battlefields of the late seventeenth-century Ottoman–Habsburg wars. Now held at the Austrian National Library, this register has been published in facsimile; see *Registerbuch*. There is a gap in the holdings of Şikayet Defters in the Prime Ministry Archive in Istanbul, totaling around ten years' worth of records, roughly covering the 1670s. The other volumes from this period were presumably carried with the camp and lost.
9. For the development of the Dīvān see Imber, *Ottoman Empire,* 141–63.
10. See p. 162, note 52, for details of the relevant archival units.
11. For examples of petitions to do with employment, pensions and stipends, see DK 74/10; DK 74/24; DK 75/62; DK 76/7; DK 76/41; DK 576/1; Ali Emiri IV. Mehmed 4241. On petitions complaining about taxation, see Darling, *Revenue-Raising*, 246–80. An Egyptian example of a petition to request a new governor following the deposition of Defterdar Aḥmed Pasha in 1676 is described in *Awḍaḥ*, 174–5; for a detailed analysis of this incident and its fallout, see Baldwin, "Deposition." For further examples see Damurdāshī A, 37, 155–6, 222–3; Damurdāshī C, 75, 244, 335–6.
12. On these *kisve bahası* petitions, see Minkov, *Conversion*, 110–92.
13. İnalcık, "Şikayet Hakkı"; Gerber, *State, Society and Law*, 127–73; Faroqhi, "Political Activity"; Faroqhi, "Political Initiatives."

14. DK 394/43, 21 Ṣafar 1120 (12 May 1708).
15. *Registerbuch*, fo. 199b, 4th entry, early Jumādā ʾl-Thānī 1086 (23 August–1 September 1675).
16. *Registerbuch*, fo. 140b, 2nd entry, early Rabīʿ al-Thānī 1086 (25 June–4 July 1675).
17. Indeed, Gerber recognized that only around half of the petitions in his sample concerned complaints against officials. His focus on them was motivated by his argument about Ottoman governance. See Gerber, *State, Society and Law*, 155.
18. The range of issues covered contradicts Fariba Zarinebaf's argument that the Dīvān-i Hümāyūn handled matters of ḳānūn (dynastic law) while qāḍīs handled matters of sharīʿa; in any case, it is difficult to delineate precisely between these two spheres. See Zarinebaf-Shahr, "Women, Law and Imperial Justice."
19. The Dīvān-i Hümāyūn's broad and undefined competence was not specific to Egypt. For descriptions of the Dīvān responding to a similarly broad range of issues raised by petitioners in Anatolia and Istanbul, see Tuğ, "Politics of Honor," 97–172; Wittman, "Before Qāḍī and Grand Vizier," 129–223.
20. For a brief global perspective, see Kracke, "Early Visions of Justice." For an exploration of justice and legitimacy in the Middle East from antiquity to the end of the twentieth century, see Darling, *History of Social Justice*.
21. Wittman, "Before Qāḍī and Grand Vizier," 129–30.
22. Contemporary chronicles cite numerous instances of Egyptians traveling to Istanbul to submit petitions. For example: Damurdāshī C, 139ff., 325–7, 335–6; *Awḍaḥ*, 175, 222–4; Bibliothéque nationale de France, MS arabe 1855, fos. 57v-58v.
23. Necipoğlu, *Architecture, Ceremonial and Power*, 19.
24. Imber, *Ottoman Empire*, 153.
25. There is no literature on postal communications between Egypt and Istanbul. On the Ottoman Empire's official postal system in Rumelia, see Heywood, "Via Egnatia." On private couriers operating between the Ottoman Empire and India, see Sood, "Informational Fabric." On European consuls' use of private couriers to transport mail within the Ottoman Empire, and on postal communication between Istanbul and Europe, see Ghobrial, "World of Stories," 91–134.
26. Yerasimos, *Voyageurs*, 67.
27. Aḥmad Çelebi reports that news of the accession of Sultan Aḥmed III on 27 Rabīʿ al-Awwal 1115 (10 August 1703) arrived in Cairo during Rabīʿ al-Thānī: *Awḍaḥ*, 209.
28. Imperial orders were often copied into the registers of al-Bāb al-ʿĀlī in Cairo. Unfortunately these copies do not often include the date of arrival, but some do, and these suggest a journey time of around two months. For example: BA 139, p. 4 (order dated 5 Jumādā ʾl-Ūlā 1075 / 24 November 1664, date of arrival 19 Rajab 1075 / 5 February 1665); BA 167 *mukarrar*, unnumbered page before p. 1, first entry (order dated late Shawwāl 1092 / 3–11 November 1681, date of arrival 23 Dhū ʾl-Ḥijja 1092 / 3 January 1682).
29. For an example of a particularly elaborate opening prayer see DK 77/64, transcribed and translated at pp. 152–6.
30. This particular phrase is from DK 77/64.

31. I discuss these issues further and provide examples at p. 163, notes 55 and 56.
32. Evliyā Çelebi counted the ᶜarżuḥālcis operating in Cairo and noted that some of them were Rūmīs (*Ervām'dan*), i.e. Turks from the central regions of the empire. Evliyā Çelebi, *Evliyā Çelebi Seyahatnamesi*, 202.
33. Damurdāshī A, 78–9; Damurdāshī C, 139–42.
34. DK 77/64. The petition itself is not dated, but the date of its arrival is noted: late Rabīᶜ al-Thānī 1087 (3–11 July 1676). See pp. 152–6 for a transcription and translation of this document.
35. *Registerbuch*, fo. 23a, 3rd entry, early Dhū ᵓl-Qaᶜda 1085 (27 January–5 February 1675).
36. AŞD 28, entry 45, late Jumādā ᵓl-Ūlā 1109 (5–14 December 1697).
37. On the role of harem eunuchs in Cairo see Hathaway, *Politics of Households*, 139–64; Hathaway, "Role of the Kızlar Ağası"; Hathaway, "Wealth and Influence"; Hathaway, "Exiled Harem Eunuchs"; Hathaway, *Beshir Agha*. The Beşīr Āghā I discuss here is not the subject of Hathaway's biography.
38. This transaction was an *icāreteyn* contract: for details of this type of lease see below, pp. 89–90, and Barnes, *Introduction to Religious Foundations*, 51–9.
39. *Registerbuch*, fo. 123b, 6th entry, mid Rabīᶜ al-Awwal 1086 (5–14 June 1675). See pp. 157–8 for a transcription and translation of this document.
40. *Registerbuch*, fo. 165b, 6th entry, early Jumādā ᵓl-Ūlā 1086 (24 July–2 August 1675).
41. AŞD 28, entry 3, late Jumādā ᵓl- Ūlā 1109 (5–14 December 1697). Another noteworthy feature of this case is that the chief qāḍī of Cairo is senior to the qāḍī of Rosetta, taking on the dispute that the latter has not successfully resolved. This hierarchy, with the qāḍī of a major city supervising the qāḍīs of smaller towns in the same province, is similar to that described by Rossitsa Gradeva in the context of Sofia. See Gradeva, "On Judicial Hierarchy."
42. The phrase used by Muṣṭafā is *vażᶜ-ı ḳadīmini tağyīr eyleyüb*. It is interesting that he framed Banūb's action as an offence against custom, as it was also a violation of a well-known principle of Islamic law, that the houses of non-Muslims should be smaller than those of their Muslim neighbors. On the importance of appeals to established custom in petitions see Faroqhi, "Political Activity," 5–6.
43. Expert witnesses (*ahl al-khibra*) were employed where specialist knowledge of fields such as medicine, engineering, weights and measures, or the established customs of a particular trade, were crucial to evaluating a litigant's claim. See Shaham, *Expert Witness*, 27–98; Abacı, *Bursa Şehri'nde Osmanlı Hukuku*, 120–2; ᶜĪsā, *Tārīkh al-qaḍāᵓ*, 317–19. On the role of architects and builders as expert witnesses in cases involving buildings, see Hanna, *Construction Work*.
44. ŞK 1/93. This document is the original petition sent by al-Ḥājj Muṣṭafā, not the imperial order sent in response. However, an annotation made at the top of the paper by the Dīvān-i Hümāyūn provides the instruction to the scribe who would write the imperial order, and so tells us what the Dīvān's response was. The petition is dated only with the year 1155 (March 1742–February 1743). The date has been added by an archivist; no date is mentioned within the text of the petition itself. See pp. 156–7 for a transcription and translation of this document.

45. For a more detailed discussion of what petitioners gained from petitioning, see Baldwin, "Petitioning the Sultan," 511–20. Enforcement of judicial decisions seems to have been a particular concern of petitioners: some petitions mention that the dispute had already been decided in favor of the petitioner by a qāḍī, but that his or her opponent had ignored the decision. Ottoman qāḍīs' lack of enforcement powers has been noted by other scholars. See Ergene, *Local Court*, 52; Ginio, "Patronage," 125–8.
46. Barkan, "Mısır Kanunnamesi," 378.
47. For example, Shaw, *Financial and Administrative Organization*, 2, passim; Faraḥāt, *al-Tārīkh al-ijtimāᶜī*, 189–92; Behrens-Abouseif, *Egypt's Adjustment*, 60–3; Marsot, "Power and Authority," 43–7; el-Nahal, *Judicial Administration*, 91, n. 90. For descriptions of the Dīwān in contemporary chronicles, see Damurdāshī A, 260–1; Damurdāshī C, 388; *Awḍah*, 574–5. Damurdāshī specifies the composition of the Dīwān at a meeting in 1755: the shaykhs of the Sādāt and Bakrī clans (who claimed descent from the fourth caliph ᶜAlī and from the first caliph Abū Bakr respectively), the shaykhs of the Sufi orders, the heads of the guilds, the "four imāms" (meaning the senior muftis of the Ḥanafī, Shāfiᶜī, Mālikī, and Ḥanbalī madhhabs), the ulema (he does not specify which particular ulema attended, but presumably it was those holding senior offices such as the shaykh of al-Azhar), the beys, the commanders of the seven regiments, and the lieutenants of the Janissary and ᶜAzabān regiments.
48. ᶜĪsā briefly discusses the judicial role of the Dīwān, but does not use any archival sources, relying solely on narrative accounts. See ᶜĪsā, *Tārīkh al-qaḍāʾ*, 136–8.
49. DA 1.
50. ENA, Ḥujaj sharᶜiyya ṣādira min maḥkamat al-Dīwān al-ᶜĀlī sana 1030 ilā 1272; PMA, Cevdet Maliye 26058, 18 Rajab 1081 (1 December 1670); DK 65/34, 28 Jumādā ʾl-Ūlā 1083 (21 September 1672); DK 76/29, 20 Dhū ʾl-Ḥijja 1086 (6 March 1676); MK 1/18, 3 Rajab 1134 (19 April 1722); İbnülemin Adliye 846, 7 Dhū ʾl-Ḥijja 1139 (26 July 1727).
51. On Sofia, see Gradeva, "On Judicial Hierarchy." On Salonica, see Ginio, "Administration of Criminal Justice." On Aleppo, see Marcus, *Middle East*, 114–20.
52. Ursinus, *Grievance Administration.*
53. The procedures surrounding changes of governor are documented by Damurdāshī for every handover during the period he covers. His chronicle is arranged around governorships, and so an account of the handover can be found at the beginning of every chapter.
54. DK 65/34, 28 Jumādā ʾl-Ūlā 1083 (21 September 1672).
55. DK 76/29, 20 Dhū ʾl-Ḥijja 1086 (6 March 1676). For an analysis of this case see Baldwin, "Deposition."
56. DA 1, entry 283, 14 Muḥarram 1155 (21 March 1742).
57. DA 1, entry 472, 29 Shawwāl 1155 (27 December 1742).
58. There was no legal barrier to owning Muslim slaves: indeed there were many in Ottoman Cairo, and they formed the power base of many political households. But such slaves had converted after enslavement: it was illegal to enslave somebody who was already a Muslim. Legally, only non-Muslims in the *dār al-ḥarb* (the "abode of war," i.e. beyond the jurisdiction of a Muslim sovereign) could be enslaved.
59. DA 1, entry 66, 25 Jumadā ʾl-Ūlā 1154 (8 August 1741).

60. Damanhūrī was a celebrated and versatile scholar who became the shaykh al-Azhar. See Murādī, *Silk al-durar*, I: 117; Jabartī B, II: 25–7; Jabartī P, II: 37–40; for a modern study see Murphy, "Aḥmad al-Damanhūrī." I discuss him briefly at p. 80.
61. DA 1, entry 331, 5 Rabīᶜ al-Thānī 1155 (9 June 1742). See pp. 149–52 for a transcription and translation of this document.
62. Any litigant could appoint a wakīl to appear in court on his or her behalf, either to enter into a contract or to instigate or defend a lawsuit. In many cases, the wakīl may have had superior legal knowledge, and so have played the role of a lawyer. For women, and especially elite women, using a wakīl also offered the opportunity to conduct legal business without appearing in public and so violating social norms of female seclusion. Thus these norms, which were especially important to elite families, did not prevent women from amassing and managing large portfolios of property.
63. DA 1, entry 118, 15 Rajab 1154 (26 September 1741).
64. DA 1, entry 222, 8 Dhū ᵓl-Qaᶜda 1154 (15 January 1742).
65. For examples of cases resolved by an oath, see DA 1, entry 7, 22 Rabīᶜ al-Awwal 1154 (7 June 1741); DA 1, entry 467, 15 Shawwāl 1155 (13 December 1742).
66. Interestingly, the Dīwān al-ᶜĀlī's procedures were different from those of the only other provincial governor's tribunal we have documentary evidence for. The Kaymakam of Rumelia between 1781 and 1783 dealt with complaints using a petition-based procedure similar to that of the Dīvān-i Hümāyūn; see Ursinus, *Grievance Administration*.
67. For example, İnalcık, "Şikayet Hakkı"; Gerber, *State, Society and Law*, 127–73.
68. Gerber, *State, Society and Law*, 158–61; Akarlı, "Law in the Marketplace," 247–8; Zarinebaf, *Crime and Punishment*, 141–56.
69. On the hierarchies of judicial and scholarly positions in the Ottoman Empire, see Uzunçarşılı, *Osmanlı Devletinin İlmiye Teşkilatı*, 91–103.
70. For example: *Registerbuch*, fo. 23a, 3rd entry, early Dhū ᵓl-Qaᶜda 1085 (27 January–5 February 1675); AŞD 28, entry 3, late Jumādā ᵓl-Ūlā 1109 (5–14 December 1697); AŞD 28, entry 45, late Jumādā ᵓl-Ūlā 1109 (5–14 December 1697).
71. I have not attempted a quantitative study of the court records, for the reasons outlined above at p. 17. The difference between the clientele of the Dīwān al-ᶜĀlī and the neighborhood sharīᶜa courts is obvious with just a casual observation. For the purposes of illustration, I analyzed the cases in the first six months of the year 1155 AH (8 March–31 August 1742), in register 1 of the Dīwān al-ᶜĀlī and register 639 of the Bāb al-Shaᶜriyya sharīᶜa court, counting the number in which both parties were of elite status, the number in which one party was elite, and the number in which neither party was. I categorized court users as elite or non-elite based on the titles they were given by the scribe. I did not treat simple titles like al-Muḥtaram, al-Ḥurma, al-Ḥājj, and al-Shaykh as evidence of elite status, as they were used by a wide section of society. I categorized people as elite on the basis of higher titles such as bey, āghā, and amīr, or superlative honorifics such as *fakhr aqrānihi* (the pride of his peers) along with officer rank in one of the military regiments, evidence of distinction in commerce or scholarship and/or sayyid status. This is not a watertight method—there were quite a few judgment calls—but it need not be, as the differences are stark. Furthermore, my method makes it easier for

someone with a military/political background than for someone with a commercial or scholarly background to qualify as elite: this does not matter too much, as it suits my claim that it was the political elite in particular who were over-represented at the Dīwān. Far fewer titles were used for women. I categorized women as elite based on the status of their fathers (patronyms were always recorded) and/or husbands, and based on the use of the prestigious titles al-Muṣawwana or al-Khātūn rather than the generic al-Ḥurma. When disputants were represented by agents, I counted the status of the disputant rather than that of the agent. When a group of litigants acted jointly as a single party to a case, the elite status of any one of them qualified the party as elite. There were a handful of cases involving the foundation of awqāf: these had only one party (the founder), and I categorized these cases as "both parties" having the founder's status. In register 639 of Bāb al-Shaᶜriyya, out of 120 cases, both parties were elite in six cases (5%), one party was elite and one non-elite in twenty-three cases (19%), and neither party was elite in ninety-one cases (76%). In register 1 of al-Dīwān al-ᶜĀlī, out of 126 cases, both parties were elite in ninety-two cases (73%), one party was elite and one non-elite in twenty-five cases (20%) and neither party was elite in nine cases (7%).

72. On the antiquity of the "circle of justice" see Darling, *History of Social Justice*.
73. Nielsen, *Secular Justice*; Tillier, "Qāḍīs and the Political Uses"; Müller, "Redressing Injustice."
74. An example is Mollā Hüsrev, the author of the important Ḥanafī text *Durar al-ḥukkām sharḥ Ghurar al-aḥkām*, who served in various qāḍīships. See Reinhart, "Molla Hüsrev."
75. Most significantly, the great sixteenth-century Şeyhulislām Ebūʾs-suᶜūd, who had previously served as qāḍī of Istanbul, Bursa, and Rumelia. See Imber, *Ebūʾs-suᶜūd*.
76. This is true of most courts in all societies. On the boring caseloads of modern sharīᶜa courts in Lebanon, see Clarke, "Judge as Tragic Hero," 109.
77. For example: BS 629, entry 235, 22 Rabīᶜ al-Thānī 1107 (30 November 1695); the Shāfiᶜī qāḍī hearing this case referred the question of the right of a woman to override her guardian's wishes regarding her re-marriage to the Shāfiᶜī professor of iftāʾ at al-Azhar.
78. Miriam Hoexter has shown how, collectively, Ottoman qāḍīs contributed to the development of Islamic legal doctrine through judicial practice. New types of contract emerged in particular areas, through mechanisms that are often obscure: people used these contracts and had them notarized by local qāḍīs. Eventually, jurists would legitimize a new contract on the basis that it was in common use. This is compatible with my argument, because Hoexter is describing how the collective but uncoordinated actions of many qāḍīs could ultimately produce a change in legal doctrine: she does not say that individual qāḍīs would explicitly resolve contentious legal questions by themselves. See Hoexter, "Qāḍī, Muftī and Ruler."
79. On the development of this division of labor across the long sweep of Islamic legal history, see Ibrahim, "Codification Episteme."
80. Technically, it was the creditor who took the initiative: the creditor would request that the qāḍī imprison the debtor, and the qāḍī would then carry this out. The creditor could also choose to free the debtor at any point, as part of a negotiated settlement or out of

good will. Again, the initiative came from the creditor, but the qāḍī was the agent who carried out the freeing. Imprisonment for debt was routine and there are numerous cases throughout the court registers. Here are a few representative examples: a woman had her husband imprisoned for failure to pay the clothing allowance specified in their marriage contract, BS 623, entry 257, 6 Muḥarram 1078 (28 June 1667); a merchant had a weaver imprisoned when he failed to deliver a consignment of cotton the merchant had already paid for, BS 624, entry 201, 22 Rajab 1078 (7 January 1668); a soldier in the ᶜAzabān regiment had a Jewish woman imprisoned for failure to pay for a quantity of fabric he had sold her, BS 625, entry 127, 4 Jumādā ʾl-Thānī 1085 (5 September 1674); an ᶜAzabān officer had another man imprisoned for failure to repay a loan, BS 629, entry 473, 6 Rabīᶜ al-Thānī 1108 (2 November 1696); a Janissary officer had a Christian man imprisoned when his father, for whom he had stood as guarantor, failed to pay for the coffee beans he had bought, BS 632, entry 192, 23 Dhū ʾl-Ḥijja 1124 (21 January 1713).

81. ᶜĪsā, *Tārīkh al-qaḍāʾ*, 321–4.
82. Most records simply state that the qāḍī ordered taᶜzīr, but in some the record also says that the taᶜzīr was carried out, suggesting that the punishment was carried out soon and within the court. This is always stated in the passive voice, so we do not know which court official administered the punishment. For example: BS 623, entry 381, 8 Rabīᶜ al-Awwal 1078 (28 August 1667); BS 624, entry 51, 6 Jumādā ʾl-Ūlā 1078 (24 October 1667); BS 625, entry 320, 29 Shawwāl 1085 (26 January 1675).
83. Ibn Nujaym, the most prolific Egyptian jurist of the sixteenth century, and Shaykhzādah, the author of a commentary on the Ḥanafī manual *Multaqa ʾl-abḥur*, which was widely used in the Ottoman Empire, agreed that taᶜzīr could include anything from lashing through slapping, rubbing the ears, and public admonishment, to an angry look from the judge. See Ibn Nujaym, *al-Baḥr al-rāʾiq*, V: 68; Shaykhzāda, *Majmaᶜ al-anhur*, I: 609.

Chapter 4

1. Important works addressing the issue of change in Islamic law via doctrinal development include: Hallaq, "Was the Gate of Ijtihād Closed?"; Fadel, "Social Logic of Taqlīd"; Johansen, *Islamic Law on Land Tax*; Gerber, *Islamic Law and Culture*; Jackson, "Kramer versus Kramer."
2. The same is true of the *ḳażᶜaskers* of Anatolia and Rumelia, who were of limited relevance to the legal administration of Cairo.
3. This is not meant to suggest that the Şeyhulislām abandoned the normal practices and references of the mufti. The point of the post of chief mufti was, after all, to grant legal legitimacy to the government. But in such cases the Şeyhulislām was guided by imperial interests and the public good as well as fiqh, and the function of these fatwās within the Ottoman legal system was to impose an official definition of doctrine on the empire's courts. Colin Imber's study of Ebūʾs-suᶜūd shows how the Şeyhulislām worked to promote the interests of the imperial government while reconciling them with fiqh; see Imber, *Ebuʾs-suᶜud*.

4. The secondary literature usually describes this issue as the relationship between sharīᶜa and ḳānūn. This formulation has the virtue of reflecting Ottoman usage: a common phrase found in Ottoman documents is *şerᶜ ü ḳānūn üzere* (according to sharīᶜa and ḳānūn). But the subject of this discussion is the relationship between ḳānūn and the body of positive law produced by the jurists, for which a better term is fiqh, or even more precisely, *furūᶜ al-fiqh*. For this debate see: Heyd, *Studies*, 167–207; Repp, "Qanun and Sharīᶜa"; Imber, *Ebu'ˀs-suᶜud*, 24–62; Tezcan, *Second Ottoman Empire*, 14–45; Ergene, "Qanun and Sharia."
5. Although jurists were involved in the production of ḳānūn, the initiative came from the government and the ḳānūn's authority rested on its promulgation by the Sultan, not on the expertise of the jurists.
6. On the fatwās of the Şeyhulislām see Heyd, "Some Aspects."
7. Imber, *Ebuˀs-suᶜud*, 107–8. For the original text of the petition and emr, see Horster, *Zur Anwendung des Islamischen Rechts*, 56.
8. While Suleyman's order imposed the fifteen-year limit throughout the empire, he did not conjure the number out of thin air. Leslie Peirce mentions a case in ᶜAyntāb in December 1540, in which ownership of a vineyard was successfully defended against the claim of a former owner by reference to a fifteen-year statute of limitations: Peirce, *Morality Tales*, 30. According to Peirce, the court record cites no authority for this rule (private communication). Possibly the fifteen-year limit was a local custom, or was part of the formal legal practice of the Mamluk Sultanate or the Dulkadir Beylik, the polities which had formerly ruled ᶜAyntāb. Clearly, the idea of a time limit on claims was not new; indeed Ebūˀs-suᶜūd's petition states that people frequently came to him asking for a fatwā on what the limit should be. Suleyman's intervention was to set a uniform limit for the entire empire; when doing so he probably chose from a number of different traditional limits observed in different regions.
9. For example, seventeenth-century Kayseri: Jennings, "Limitations," 153–4, 159, 170; seventeenth-century Bursa: Gerber, *State, Society and Law*, 81; eighteenth-century Salonica: Ginio, "Living on the Margins," 176.
10. DA 1, entry 95, 18 Jumādā ˀl-Thānī 1154 (31 August 1741).
11. DA 1, entry 121, 17 Rajab 1154 (28 September 1741). It is striking that the nāˀib still went through the usual legal procedure, granting Riḍwān a delay in order to gather evidence (a *muhla*), when his claim was inadmissible due to the lapse of time. It is also interesting that Ibrāhīm went to the trouble of gathering a large group of neighbors to state in court the reputation of Riḍwān and his family for fraudulent claims. Again, this seems unnecessary: Riḍwān's claim was inadmissible, and in any case he failed to produce evidence. This may have been motivated not by legal necessity, but by the desire to publicly humiliate Riḍwān and his family and to put their misdeeds on the public record.
12. Ramlī, *al-Fatāwā*, II: 48; Ibn ᶜĀbidīn, *al-ᶜUqūd al-durriyya*, II: 5. See Gerber's discussion of jurists' reaction to the statute of limitations: Gerber, *Islamic Law and Culture*, 63–4.
13. Tyser et al, *Mejelle*, 289.

14. Hallaq, *Sharī^ca*, 401–20; Messick, *Calligraphic State*, 54–72; Peters, "From Jurists' Law to Statute Law."
15. The classic account of the cash waqf controversy is Mandaville, "Usurious Piety"; see also Tezcan, *Second Ottoman Empire*, 31–4.
16. Rapoport, "Legal Diversity."
17. Rapoport, "Legal Diversity," 219–20, 222–3.
18. Tucker, *In the House of the Law*, 78–112.
19. Cuno, *Modernizing Marriage*, 136–41. I thank Ken for sharing his typescript with me prior to publication.
20. See Burak, *Second Formation*, for an account of the Ottomans' cultivation of a particular strand within Ḥanafism as a "state madhhab."
21. This question has now received sustained attention in the work of Guy Burak, cited above. Ruud Peters also addressed this question more briefly in "What Does it Mean?"
22. Peters, "What Does it Mean," 158.
23. Rafeq, "Application of Islamic Law," 414.
24. Jackson, "Kramer versus Kramer," 28.
25. Heller, "The Shaykh and the Community."
26. Ahmed Ibrahim's statistical analysis of a large sample of cases confirms this, demonstrating that the default preference in Cairo's courts was for the Ḥanafī qāḍī or nā^ᵓib, and that the choice of a different madhhab was almost always dictated by the need for a particular doctrine. See Ibrahim, *Pragmatism*, 135–51.
27. To a certain extent, Ḥanafism was institutionalized under Ottoman rule. But this only applies to a subset of the Ḥanafī community that was Turkish-speaking and associated with the Ottoman state. Plenty of Ḥanafī scholars studied in the empire's Arabic-speaking provinces outside of the Ottoman *ilmiye* network of madrasas. Pre-existing madrasas continued to function and, while they were to some extent under the influence of the Ottoman dynasty due to its unmatched capacity for patronage, they were not fully integrated into the ilmiye system. Egypt's historic mosque-university al-Azhar is a case in point; for a recent study of this institution under Ottoman rule see Hashmi, "Patronage." Ḥanafism was also, of course, a global phenomenon that transcended the borders of the Ottoman Empire; Ḥanafī scholarship was written across much of the early modern Muslim world, in India and Central Asia in particular. On Ḥanafī scholarship in Mughal India, see Guenther, "Hanafi Fiqh."
28. See, for example, the note of the appointment of Shaykh Abū ᵓl-Ḥasan as Mālikī nāᵓib at the Bāb al-Shaᶜriyya court, which states that "he must assist with hearing lawsuits according to the Mālikī madhhab when necessary," BS 625, unnumbered entry before 842, Rabīᶜ al-Awwal 1087 (May-June 1676).
29. Muḥibbī, *Khulāṣat al-athar*, II: 282–9.
30. Jabartī B, II: 60; Jabartī P, II, 95–6.
31. Jabartī B, II: 15–16; Jabartī P, II: 21–2.
32. Jabartī B, II: 100–1; Jabartī P, II: 169–70.
33. For example: Shāhīn ibn Manṣūr al-Armanāwī (d. 1101/1689–90) was a Ḥanafī but studied under the Shāfiᶜī Ibrāhīm al-Maymūnī and the Mālikī ᶜAbd al-Salām

al-Laqānī. Muḥammad ibn Qāsim al-Baqarī (d. 1111/1699) was a Shāfiᶜī but studied under the Ḥanafī Aḥmad al-Shawbarī. Meanwhile, Baqarī taught Muḥammad ibn Muḥammad al-Bulaydī (d. 1176/1763), a Mālikī; the latter also studied under the Ḥanafī ᶜAlī ibn ᶜAlī Iskandār al-Ḍarīr (d. 1146/1733–4). Another of Ḍarīr's students was the distinguished Shāfiᶜī professor and rector of al-Azhar, Shams al-Dīn al-Ḥifnī (d. 1181/1767), who also studied under another Ḥānafī, Muḥammad ᶜAbd al-ᶜAzīz al-Ziyādī (d. 1148/1735). This is drawn from the following biographies: Armanāwī: Jabartī B, I: 68; Jabartī P, I: 112–13. Baqarī: Jabartī B, I: 66; Jabartī P, I: 109. Bulaydī: Jabartī B, I: 259; Jabartī P, I: 429. Ḍarīr: Jabartī B, I: 156; Jabartī P, I: 256. Ḥifnī: Jabartī B, I: 289–304; Jabartī P, I: 479–505. Ziyādī: Jabartī B, I: 156–7; Jabartī P, I: 256.

34. Murādī, *Silk al-durar*, I: 117; Jabartī B, II: 25–7; Jabartī P, II: 37–40. For Damanhūrī's wider intellectual activities, see Murphy, "Aḥmad al-Damanhūrī."
35. Jabartī B, II: 53–4; Jabartī P, II: 83–5.
36. BS 629, entry 109, 16 Dhū ᵓl-Ḥijja 1106 (28 July 1695).
37. BS 624, entry 15, 24 Rabīᶜ al-Thānī 1078 (13 October 1667).
38. BS 629, entry 417, 21 Dhū ᵓl-Ḥijja 1107 (22 July 1696).
39. Ibrahim, *Pragmatism*, 63–104.
40. Ibrahim, "Al-Shaᶜrānī's Response"; see also Winter, *Society and Religion*, 181–5.
41. Ibrahim, *Pragmatism*, 105–25.
42. Like Cairo, Syria was historically a center of Shāfiᶜī scholarship, which also had a large community of Ḥanafī scholars and a smaller community of Ḥanbalīs. The Mālikī madhhab had less of a presence there than in Egypt. As another former Mamluk territory, Syria also had a tradition of pluralism in its sharīᶜa courts, which was retained under Ottoman rule. In contrast to Cairo, Damascus saw Ḥanafism become dominant among its jurists, in terms of prestige and influence if not numerically, during the eighteenth century; see Voll, "Old ᶜUlamāᵓ Families."
43. On the development of the ilmiye system see Atçıl, "Formation of the Ottoman Learned Class"; Atçıl, "Route to the Top."
44. Jonathan Berkey and Michael Chamberlain described this model for medieval Cairo and Damascus respectively: see Berkey, *Transmission of Knowledge*; Chamberlain, *Knowledge and Social Practice*.
45. The document has been summarized and analyzed by Ahmed and Filipovic, "Sultan's Syllabus."
46. İzgi, *Osmanlı Medreselerinde İlim*, I: 69–77, 163–7.
47. There is evidence that an education within Ottoman imperial circles bestowed a narrow, Ḥanafī-centric outlook on people other than scholars. Jane Hathaway has demonstrated, through studies of their endowment deeds, that two prominent chief eunuchs of the seventeenth and eighteenth centuries, ᶜAbbās Ağa and Beşīr Ağa, collected mainly Ḥanafī books; Beşīr Ağa also stipulated that the fiqh teacher in the primary school he founded in Cairo should be a Ḥanafī. See Hathaway, "Wealth and Influence"; Hathaway, "Exiled Chief Harem Eunuchs."
48. Düzdağ, *Şeyhulislam Ebussuud*, 44, fatwā no. 79.

49. Due to the limited secondary literature on Ottoman Iraq, I do not know to what degree Ḥanafization was pursued there. In Libya, the Ottomans faced a rather different situation: instead of a pluralistic legal culture, in Libya the Mālikī madhhab was dominant and, at least initially, the Ottomans allowed it to continue to predominate. See İnalcık, "Maḥkama."
50. Hanna, "Administration of Courts"; Winter, *Egyptian Society*, 108–11.
51. Meshal, "Antagonistic Sharīʿas," 194–6; Lellouch, *Les ottomans en Égypte*, 93–8.
52. Ibn Iyās, *Badāʾiʿ al-zuhūr*, V: 165.
53. Many Arabic sources referred to the chief qāḍī as the Qāḍī ʾl-ʿAskar rather than the Qāḍī ʾl-Quḍā throughout the sixteenth, seventeenth, and eighteenth centuries: we can consider the two terms as equivalent.
54. Ibn Iyās, *Badāʾīʿ al-zuhūr*, V: 453–4.
55. Diyārbekrī, *Tercüme-yi en-Nüzhe es-seniyye*, fo. 346a.
56. Damīrī, *Quḍāt Miṣr*, 214–8. A decade earlier another newly-appointed chief qāḍī, ʿAzmīzāde, sent an order dismissing all the nāʾibs and shuhūd before he even set sail for Cairo. Damīrī does not specify that this was aimed at non-Ḥanafīs in particular, though this seems likely given the context. ʿAzmīzāde died on the journey to Cairo, so the order was never implemented; *Quḍāt Miṣr*, 132–3. On these campaigns see Meshal, "Antagonistic Sharīʿas," 196–200.
57. The others included *mubāyiʿāt al-anqāḍ* (the sale of dilapidated waqf holdings), *istibdāl* (the sale of waqf-owned assets in order to reinvest the proceeds in other assets), and *al-ḥukm ʿalā ʾl-ghāyib* (passing judgment on an absent party).
58. This type of divorce was also known as *tafrīq*, but in the documents I studied it was always called faskh.
59. For an overview of divorce in Islamic law, see Tucker, *Women, Family and Gender*, 86–104.
60. The Ḥanafī reply to this argument was that impotence was incurable, and so permanently prevented sexual relations, whereas husbands sometimes returned even from lengthy absences. Tucker, *Women, Family and Gender*, 92–5.
61. As numerous studies based on the sharīʿa court records have shown, many women did work, particularly in small-scale artisanal production. However, the law's concept of marriage assumed they did not; therefore the abandoned wife who no longer received maintenance from her husband presented a significant legal problem. Furthermore, while it was not unusual for women to undertake paid work, there were many families, particular those who had or aspired to high social status, who believed strongly that work dishonored a woman, and for whom the abandonment of a woman by her husband would therefore present a difficult financial problem. Lastly, women often worked for their husbands. This was treated as wage labor by the law, which reflected its assumption that married women did not work: husbands could not expect labor other than child-rearing and household management from their wives, so if such labor was performed, the husband was obliged to pay a wage on top of her maintenance payments. For women in this kind of arrangement, the disappearance of the husband would clearly disrupt her ability to earn. Women with significant capital were much better placed to look after themselves: the law protected

women's property from their husbands and other male relatives, and wealthy women were investors in real estate and business ventures throughout the Ottoman Empire. Examples of court cases involving Cairene women who worked for male relatives in the textile industry (which had a significant presence in the Bāb al-Shaᶜriyya neighborhood) include: BS 623, entry 238; BS 625, entry 62, 10 Rabīᶜ al-Thānī 1085 (14 July 1674); BS 625, entry 63, 10 Rabīᶜ al-Thānī 1085 (14 July 1674); BS 625, entry 65, 12 Rabīᶜ al-Thānī 1085 (16 July 1674); BS 625, entry 128, 7 Jumādā ᵓl-Thānī 1085 (8 September 1674). For women in the textile industry in nineteenth-century Egypt, see Tucker, *Women in Nineteenth-Century Egypt*, 64–91. On women as property owners and investors in eighteenth-century Egypt, see Fay, "From Concubines to Capitalists"; Fay, "Women and Waqf."

62. Tucker, *In the House*, 81–7.
63. Rapoport, "Legal Diversity," 218.
64. Zaman, *Ulama*, 26–9. It is not clear from Zaman's account whether women in India were able to have such a dissolution recognized by the colonial authorities. At this point courts within British-ruled territory were staffed by British judges implementing codified Anglo-Muhammadan law. Some of the muftis cited by Zaman insisted that a judicial divorce be performed by a properly-appointed qāḍī, which meant that a women would have to travel to one of the Muslim-ruled princely states to obtain the dissolution.
65. Imber, *Ebuᵓs-suᶜud*, 186–7.
66. This imperial decree is mentioned by Ebūᵓs-suᶜūd in an annotation he made on a fatwā issued by his predecessor Kemālpaşazāde. See Düzdağ, *Şeyhulislam Ebussuud*, 44, fatwā no. 79.
67. Tuğ, "Politics of Honor," 345–64.
68. Zečević, "Missing Husbands," 346–7.
69. Ivanova, "Divorce," 120.
70. Ibn Nujaym, *Fatāwā*, fo. 11b.
71. Tucker, *In the House of the Law*, 78.
72. Ibid., 83.
73. ENA, Sijillāt maḥkamat al-Qanāṭir al-sibāᶜ 126, p. 645, 17 Rabīᶜ al-Thānī 1015 (22 August 1606) and Sijillāt maḥkamat al-Ṣāliḥiyya al-najmiyya 429, p. 1, 9 Ramaḍān 1015 (8 January 1607); both reproduced in Faraḥāt, *al-Qaḍāᵓ al-sharᶜī*, 35–6.
74. The marital home is referred to in the court document as *maḥall al-ṭāᶜa*: the place of obedience.
75. Tucker, *In the House*, 51–9.
76. Ṣawwāf indicates an occupation (wool trader), and so Sulaymān's sharing the name with Hiba's absent husband does not demonstrate a family relationship between the two, although neither does it preclude one.
77. BS 623, entry 333, 19 Ṣafar 1078 (10 August 1667). See pp. 143–6 for a transcription and translation of this document.
78. Again, the suffix Ḥāyik indicates a profession (weaver)—in the case of Ḥalīma it refers to her father's profession—and so it neither implies nor excludes the possibility that the two were from the same family.
79. BS 624, entry 301, 13 Ramaḍān 1078 (26 February 1668).

80. In fact, awqāf frequently did sell properties using the doctrine istibdāl, meaning substitution. This transaction required the waqf to use the proceeds of the sale to purchase another property of equal or greater utility, and so enabled the waqf to trade individual properties for its benefit, while preserving the principle that the sum total of the waqf's property was inalienable.
81. Barnes, *Religious Foundations*, 50–6.
82. I have not seen the contract itself, but it is referred to in an imperial order recorded in a Şikāyet Defteri, which responded to a petition from Beşīr in which he claimed that, although he had paid the icāre-yi muᶜaccele, his agent had been prevented from taking possession of the house. *Registerbuch*, fo. 123b, 6th entry, mid Rabīᶜ al-Thānī 1086 (5–14 July 1675).
83. Barnes, *Religious Foundations*, 53.
84. In Damascus, long leases were usually contracted before a Shāfiᶜī judge; Shāfiᶜī doctrine was also more generous than Ḥanafī doctrine on this subject. See van Leeuwen, *Waqfs and Urban Structures*, 163–4; Rafeq, "Relations between the Syrian ᶜUlamāʾ and the Ottoman State," 70–2; Rafeq, "City and Countryside in a Traditional Setting," 312–23.
85. BS 624, entry 17, 15 Rabīᶜ al-Thānī 1078 (4 October 1667).
86. BS 625, entry 245, 1 Ramaḍān 1085 (29 November 1674).
87. For example: Hanna, "Administration of Courts," 53–4.
88. On the concept of legal pluralism see Griffiths, "What is Legal Pluralism?" For a useful analysis of how this concept can be applied to sharīᶜa courts, see Shahar, "Legal Pluralism." Griffiths distinguished between weak legal pluralism, in which different bodies of law were applied to different sections of the population, and strong legal pluralism, in which more than one legal order existed within the same social field, at least one of which was outside the control of the state. Shahar proposed instead that the distinction between strong and weak legal pluralism is better formulated in terms of choice: strong pluralism exists when litigants can forum-shop, having a genuine choice of forums offering different outcomes, while weak pluralism exists when litigants are directed to a particular forum by the governing authorities. Madhhab pluralism in Ottoman Cairo seems to belong somewhere in between strong and weak pluralism according to Shahar's definition. The government controlled litigants' access to certain non-Ḥanafī doctrines, but in areas not seen by the authorities as controversial, litigants did have the freedom to choose the madhhab.
89. The ᶜudūl, called in full the shuhūd ᶜudūl (just witnesses; sing. *shāhid ᶜadl*) were the professional witnesses employed by the court, discussed in Chapter 2. It seems that many of the ᶜudūl had a legal training: some ᶜudūl also served as nāʾibs. Their inclusion in this and other similar orders suggests that they sometimes presided over legal transactions themselves, without the presence of a nāʾib or qāḍī.
90. BS 629, entry 387, 18 Shawwāl 1107 (21 May 1696).
91. BS 629, entry 316, 4 Rajab 1107 (8 February 1696); BS 629, entry 387, 18 Shawwāl 1107 (21 May 1696); BS 629, entry 598, 4 Dhū ʾl-Ḥijja 1108 (24 June 1697); BS 629, entry 876, 12 Rabīᶜ al-Awwal 1110 (18 September 1698); BS 629, entry 1135, 7 Shaᶜbān 1111 (28 January 1700); BS 632, entry 115; BS 632, entry 136; BS 632, entry 168; BS 633, entry

1, 5 Shawwāl 1130 (1 September 1718); BS 638, entry 94, 1 Rabīᶜ al-Thānī 1151 (19 June 1738); BS 638, entry 223, 15 Ṣafar 1152 (24 May 1739); BS 638, entry 340, 1 Muḥarram 1153 (29 March 1740); BS 639, entry 547, 13 Jumādā ᵓl-Ūlā 1155 (16 July 1742).

92. BS 629, entry 598, 4 Dhū ᵓl-Ḥijja 1108 (24 June 1697).

93. The doctrines related to waqf were the most frequently used, and there are numerous examples of long leases and istibdāl transactions in eighteenth-century records from al-Bāb al-ᶜĀlī. I did not see any examples of judicial divorce for abandoned wives in the eighteenth century; however the disappearance of a husband was a far less common event, so the lack of such a case in my sample does not indicate that judicial divorces did not take place. For long leases see BA 201, entry 269, 25 Shaᶜbān 1131 (13 July 1719); BA 214, entry 690, 5 Shawwāl 1144 (1 April 1732); BA 225, entry 2, 28 Dhū ᵓl-Ḥijja 1154 (6 March 1742). For istibdāl see BA 225, entry 23, 26 Dhū ᵓl-Ḥijja 1154 (4 March 1742); entry 38, 1 Dhū ᵓl-Ḥijja 1154 (7 February 1742); entry 41, 1 Dhū ᵓl-Ḥijja 1154 (7 February 1742); entry 51, 1 Muḥarram 1155 (8 March 1742); entry 70, 1 Muḥarram 1155 (8 March 1742); entry 94, 3 Muḥarram 1155 (10 March 1742); entry 95, 4 Muḥarram 1155 (11 March 1742); entry 96, 3 Muḥarram 1155 (10 March 1742); entry 102, 5 Muḥarram 1155 (12 March 1742); entry 107, 7 Muḥarram 1155 (14 March 1742); entry 222, 30 Muḥarram 1155 (6 April 1742); entry 224, 25 Muḥarram 1155 (1 April 1742).

94. For long leases, see DA 1, entry 74, 20 Jumādā ᵓl-Thānī 1154 (2 September 1741). For istibdāl, see DA 1, entry 14, 25 Rabīᶜ al-Awwal 1154 (10 June 1741); entry 269, 8 Dhū ᵓl-Ḥijja 1154 (14 February 1742); entry 270, 20 Dhū ᵓl-Ḥijja 1154 (26 February 1742); entry 299, 27 Muḥarram 1155 (3 April 1742); entry 305, 8 Ṣafar 1155 (14 April 1742); entry 330, 30 Rabīᶜ al-Awwal 1155 (4 June 1742).

95. BS 625, entry 52, 2 Rabīᶜ al-Thānī 1085 (6 July 1674).

96. BS 625, entry 186, 2 Rajab 1085 (2 October 1674).

97. Marino, "Les correspondances," see especially 93, 96–7. The list of transactions is not identical with those in Cairo, but they overlap; in particular, the Damascus orders prohibited faskh. Interestingly, the Damascus orders also prohibited nāᵓibs from registering marriages, suggesting that the marriage contract itself was being subjected to Ḥanafī law. Apart from marriage, the main areas of concern for Damascus's chief qāḍī were transactions involving land, major awqāf, and the division of inheritances.

98. For example, the chief qāḍī issued an order to the scribes of Cairo's courts in July 1738, prohibiting them from writing ḥujjas for a similar list of controversial non-Ḥanafī transactions including the dissolution of an absent husband's marriage and long-term rental contracts. See BS 638, entry 94, 1 Rabīᶜ al-Thānī 1151 (19 July 1738). This suggests that at least some of the lower officials in the courts had ignored the ban, perhaps drawing up the documents for such transactions privately, outside the purview of the sharīᶜa court and the qāḍī or nāᵓib.

99. The seventeenth-century Aleppine biographer Raḍī al-Dīn Muḥammad ibn Ḥanbalī wrote that his grandfather changed from the Ḥanbalī to the Ḥanafī madhhab to indicate his devotion to the Ottoman dynasty; see Masters, *Arabs*, 64. The father of the famous Damascene Sufi and scholar ᶜAbd al-Ghanī al-Nābulūsī switched from the Shāfiᶜī to the Ḥanafī madhhab in the early seventeenth century; see Voll, "Old ᶜUlamāᵓ Families," 58–9.

100. Voll, "Old ᶜUlamāᵓ Families." See also Barbir, *Ottoman Rule*, 81–3. Abdul-Karim Rafeq, looking at all the ulema from Palestinian cities mentioned in the major Syrian biographical dictionaries of the sixteenth through eighteenth centuries, tells a slightly different story: he argues that the major wave of conversion from Shāfiᶜism to Ḥanafism took place in the seventeenth century, with the momentum tailing off during the eighteenth. Rafeq also points to the issue of long leases on waqf properties as evidence of the enduring popularity of Shāfiᶜism. He argues that the proportion of waqf leases made according to Shāfiᶜī law increased during the first quarter of the eighteenth century. However, the number of Ḥanafī leases in his samples is very low, so it is not clear that we can discern a trend in them. There are two Ḥanafī leases in each of his two samples, as opposed to sixteen Shāfiᶜī leases in the 1700–1 sample and twenty-five in the larger 1724–5 sample: the increased number of Shāfiᶜī leases is mostly accounted for by the larger size of the sample. What these figures certainly do show is that Shāfiᶜism remained by far the most popular madhhab for arranging waqf leases. See Rafeq, "Relations," 67–74.
101. Masters, *Arabs*, 64–5.
102. Jane Hathaway also argues that the endowment of libraries and *kuttāb* (elementary schools) by the chief harem eunuchs was an attempt by Ottoman elites to promote Ḥanafism in Cairo. Hathaway overstates the impact of such awqāf when she suggests that such libraries represented the "importation of seminal works of Ḥanafī fiqh into Cairo." Cairo had been a center of Ḥanafī scholarship long before the Ottoman conquest, and readers there did not lack access to Ḥanafī books. Nonetheless, the awqāf's creation of posts for Ḥanafī teachers was an effort to support the madhhab by providing employment for Ḥanafī graduates and educating potential Ḥanafī scholars of the future. See Hathaway, "Exiled Chief Harem Eunuchs"; Hathaway, "Wealth and Influence."
103. See, for example: Schacht, *Introduction to Islamic Law*, 69–75; Coulson, *History of Islamic Law*, 80–2.
104. Schacht, *Introduction to Islamic Law*, 75.
105. Hallaq, "Was the Gate of Ijtihād Closed?"
106. Fadel, "Social Logic," see especially 196–200.
107. For a summary of this argument, see Johansen, "Legal Literature." For an extended version see Johansen, *Islamic Law on Land Tax*.
108. Jackson, "Kramer versus Kramer."
109. Rapoport, "Legal Diversity"; Rapoport, "Royal Justice," 76–9.
110. Cuno, *Modernizing Marriage*, 136–41.
111. For example: Fahmy, *All the Pasha's Men*; Toledano, *State and Society*.

Chapter 5

1. Jabartī B, I: 179; Jabartī P, I: 292 (translation from Jabartī P).
2. For his appointments as amīr al-ḥājj see: Jabartī B, I: 179; Jabarti P, I: 291–2; Aḥmad al-Rashīdī, *Ḥusn al-ṣafā*, 215–6. For his awqāf appointments, see Hathaway, *Politics of Households*, 89.
3. Damurdāshī A, 170; Damurdāshī C, 266.

4. Damurdāshī A, 227, 229; Damurdāshī C, 342, 345.
5. Jabartī B, I: 179; Jabartī P, I: 292–3.
6. Salzmann, "Ancien Régime." See also Salzmann, *Tocqueville*; Khoury, *State and Provincial Society*; Tezcan, *Second Ottoman Empire*. In the case of Egypt, the classic account of the privatization of agricultural revenue collection is Cuno, "Origins." See also ᶜĀmir, "Niẓām al-iltizām." For the operation of rural tax-farming in Egypt in the eighteenth century, see Cuno, *Pasha's Peasants*.
7. What made the political office of a tax-farmer "private" was the fact that it was purchased and contractual. This distinguished tax-farming from the broader phenomenon of venality: the payment of bribes to obtain appointment to an office. The aspiring tax-farmer did not bribe anyone: there was no hint of illegitimacy about his purchase. And what he bought was not an appointment, from which he could later be dismissed, but a contractual right to the office, for a specified term in the case of an iltizām, or for life under a malikāne. Of course, in many cases the tax-farming contract was owned by a consortium of investors based far away in Istanbul or another major city, who employed an agent to deal with affairs on the ground. But that agent worked for the investors, not for the government.
8. Jabartī B, I: 178; Jabartī P, I: 292.
9. This, of course, is another reason why tax-farming notables were tempted to muscle in on the qāḍī's jurisdiction.
10. It is possible that we could also see privatized justice straightforwardly as another privatization of revenue. The Ottoman sharīᶜa court system was, after all, a revenue source: fees were charged for litigation and notarization of contracts, and these constituted the qāḍī's income. If ᶜUthmān Bey had charged fees for the use of his dīwān, it would likely have attracted little comment, being consistent with what Cairene litigants were used to. Whether or not fees were charged, however, I think that private justice was more useful as a tool of patronage than a source of enrichment.
11. Gambetta does not deny that the mafia are involved in many criminal activities: drug-trafficking, smuggling, fraud, extortion, robbery, etc. But he claims that these activities are carried out independently by small gangs, which may or may not be affiliated to the mafia, who operate under the mafia's protective umbrella. In other words it is the provision of protection, to people involved in illicit and licit activities, that constitutes "organized" crime.
12. Gambetta, *Sicilian Mafia*.
13. Varese, *Russian Mafia*.
14. Or to be more precise: the underlying judgments they make are fair, although we may balk at their ultimate methods of enforcement. Of course, in most cases, violent enforcement is not necessary, as people voluntarily comply. But the violence must remain a genuine threat in order to achieve high levels of compliance.
15. Irwin, "Privatization of Justice," 70.
16. And, indeed, in some modern societies with poor governance, as Gambetta and Varese argue. Irwin is, perhaps, too quick to dismiss Don Corleone's justice.
17. Gerber, *State, Society and Law*, 157–9.

18. Boğaç Ergene explored the commentary of European travelers on Ottoman legal affairs, but not that of Ottoman subjects. See Ergene, *Local Court*, 115–23.
19. For an overview of Küçük Muḥammad's career see Holt, "Career of Küçük Muḥammad."
20. *Awḍāḥ*, 189ff.; Damurdāshī A, 17; Damurdāshī C, 42; Jabartī B, I: 92; Jabartī P, I: 150.
21. See Damurdāshī A, 18–21; Damurdāshī C, 43–7; Jabartī B, I: 92; Jabartī P, I: 150–1; al-Qinalī, *Tārīkh Miṣr*, fos. 6b–8a; Anon., *al-Durra al-munṣāna*, fos. 36b–39b.
22. Meḥmed ibn Yūsuf al-Ḥallāḳ, in his chronicle *Tārīh-i Mıṣr-ı Ḳāhire*, tells the same story with the governor of Egypt Ḥusayn Pasha in the lead role instead of Küçük Muḥammad. See Jane Hathaway, "Sultans, Pashas, Taqwīms and Mühimmes," 65, n. 50.
23. This extra part of the story is included only by Damurdāshī; it is his version of the story that I recount below.
24. In brief: the witness should be an adult, free, Muslim man, although the testimony of non-Muslims and women was admissible in certain circumstances. The witness should be publicly acknowledged to have integrity (*ᶜadāla*). His testimony should relate to a specific event and he should specify the date and place where it occurred; these details should agree with those given by the other witnesses. And he should use specific formulae when giving his testimony: the *lafẓ al-shahāda*. See the manual of al-Ḥalabī, which was the standard reference work for Ottoman qāḍīṣ, and the commentary on it by Shaykhzāda; Shaykhzāda, *Majmaᶜ al-anhur*, III: 256–67. As discussed in Chapter 2, the evidentiary procedures could be dispensed with when disputes were resolved through the freer process of mediation (ṣulḥ). This could only happen with the consent of both parties, however.
25. The jurists' hesitance about the use of the state's coercive power against individuals is clearest in the case of the offenses meriting severe corporal and capital punishments, for which they impose much tighter evidentiary requirements. See Peters, *Crime and Punishment*, 6–68.
26. The court records show that many Ottomans did take care to have witnesses present at all their business and personal transactions, who would then testify to the transaction before a qāḍī in order to produce a notarized document.
27. The court witnesses (*shuhūd ᶜudūl*, sing. *shāhid ᶜadl*, or simply *shāhid*) were employees of the court; for their role see above, pp. 36–7.
28. The dower owed by a husband to his wife was divided into two parts. The first part was paid upon marriage; the second, "delayed" part (*al-mahr al-muʾakhkhar*) was retained by the husband and paid upon divorce or after his death. However, while men had the right of unilateral divorce, women did not, and could generally only obtain divorce with the husband's consent. The negotiation over a divorce requested by a wife usually involved her waiving her right to the delayed dower in return for her husband's consent. See Tucker, *Women, Family and Gender*, 84–111.
29. The ᶜidda was a waiting period of three menstrual cycles after a divorce, during which a woman was forbidden from re-marrying, in order that the paternity of any child she might be carrying would be known. A husband owed his wife nafaqa (maintenance) during marriage and for the ᶜidda after divorce.
30. Damurdāshī A, 127–8; Damurdāshī C, 207–8.

31. Damurdāshī seems to have written his chronicle for the entertainment of his colleagues at the barracks of the ᶜAzabān regiment, so I think we are justified in assuming that most of his readers were men.
32. Interestingly, given the contempt for the sharīᶜa courts he displayed earlier in the Küçük Muḥammad story, here Damurdāshī uses Ibrāhīm Efendī's adherence to sharᶜī procedure to illustrate his integrity.
33. Damurdāshī A, 157–61; Damurdāshī C, 246–51.
34. See Peters, *Crime and Punishment*, 38–53. The exception was highway robbery (*qaṭᶜ al-ṭarīq*) involving homicide. This was treated as a claim of God, which the state authorities had a duty to prosecute.
35. For examples of homicide lawsuits heard according to sharīᶜa court procedure see DA 1, entry 283, 14 Muḥarram 1155 (21 March 1742); DA 1, entry 472, 29 Shawwāl 1155 (27 December 1742).
36. Jabartī B, I: 180; Jabartī P, I: 294.
37. Jabartī B, I: 120; Jabartī P, I: 195–6.
38. Jabartī B, I: 120; Jabartī P, I: 196.
39. In a theft case heard at the sharīᶜa court of Bāb al-Shaᶜriyya in 1739, a man called Bilāl ibn ᶜAbdullāh was accused of stealing a knife from the house of Ḥusayn ibn Muḥammad al-Sakākīnī. Ḥusayn produced witnesses who testified that Bilāl had confessed to taking the knife. Bilāl claimed that he had only confessed because he feared torture at the hands of the police (the *ḥukkām al-siyāsa*). Bilāl's defense failed, but it failed because he could not show that he had a genuine fear of torture. Had he been able to establish that he had reason to fear torture, his confession would have been inadmissible. See BS 638, entry 225, 27 Ṣafar 1152 (5 June 1739).
40. There is some support in post-classical fiqh for torture as a means of extracting a confession. The medieval Ḥanbalī jurists Ibn Taymiyya and Ibn Qayyim al-Jawziyya argued that when the qāḍī had certain knowledge that the accused was guilty but no legally-acceptable proof, he could coerce a confession through torture. In other words, this was a roundabout way of admitting circumstantial evidence into sharīᶜa procedure; see Johansen, "Signs as Evidence." Johansen, in "Verité et torture," 166–7, n. 110, suggests that these ideas were influential in Ottoman Ḥanafī fiqh, but he cites the nineteenth-century Damascene jurist Ibn ᶜĀbidīn, who was writing in the very different context of the Tanzimat and state centralization. It is not clear that that these ideas influenced Ottoman sharīᶜa court practice during the early modern period: certainly, there is no evidence in the court records that torture was used as a formal part of legal procedure. That does not mean, of course, that there was no torture: the stories I am discussing here strongly suggest that torture was practiced. But I think it happened outside the sharīᶜa courts, and if torture-tainted evidence was ever accepted in sharīᶜa court litigation, the qāḍī would either have been ignorant of the torture, or he would have pretended to be. Indeed, as the case in the note shows, claiming that a confession was the result of torture could be used as a defense.

41. Damurdāshī A, 65–8; Damurdāshī C, 117–23; *Awḍah*, 207–9; Jabartī B, I: 102–5; Jabartī P, I: 168–71.
42. See the poem in Jabartī's biography of ᶜAlī Āghā (previous citation) and also the poems in his biography of Riḍwān Katkhudā al-Jalfī: Jabartī B, I: 193–8; Jabartī P, I: 315–23.
43. *Awḍāḥ*, 127.
44. Jabartī B, I: 203; Jabartī P, I: 332.
45. Jabartī's reference to the petition-receiving rituals of the notables in the mid eighteenth century, mentioned above, suggests that ᶜUthmān Bey was not alone in institutionalizing his private dispute resolution practices at this time.
46. Damurdāshī A, 227, 229; Damurdāshī C, 342, 345; Jabartī B, I: 179; Jabartī P, I: 292.
47. For the events leading to ᶜUthmān Bey's exile, see Damurdāshī A, 227–40; Damurdāshī C, 342–59; Jabartī B, I: 180–5; Jabartī P, I: 294–302; Hathaway, *Politics of Households*, 81–3, 89–95.
48. Hanna, *Habiter au Caire*, 74–5; Raymond, "Essai de geographie," 78.
49. Damurdāshī C, 345; Damurdāshī A, 229; Jabartī B, I: 179; Jabartī P, I: 292.
50. These documents belonged to ᶜAbdurraḥmān Pasha, who governed Egypt from 1676 to 1681, and Boşnak ᶜOsmān Pasha, who governed Egypt from 1681 to 1683. The collections do not include registers of these governors' tribunals, so this evidence is only suggestive. However, they do include some petitions, which formed part of legal proceedings. The collections are housed at the Badische Landesbibliothek in Karlsruhe and the Bayerische Staatsbibliothek in Munich. A selection of the Karlsruhe collection was published by Franz Babinger: *Archiv*. An item from the Munich collection was published by Colin Heywood: "Red Sea Trade."
51. Cf. Wael Hallaq's arguments concerning the lack of extant pre-Ottoman sharīᶜa court records; Hallaq, "Qāḍī's Dīwān."
52. It may not be a coincidence that archives relating to dispute resolution in the imperial center were reformed at almost the same time. A new series of registers recording responses to petitions, the Vilayet Ahkam Defterleri, was created in 1742; these were subdivided by province, unlike the old "complaints registers" (Şikayet Defterleri). Simultaneously, the palace began archiving the incoming petitions themselves systematically, in their own archival unit, the Şikayet Kalemi; extant original petitions are only plentiful from 1742 on. I discuss the Şikayet Kalemi unit in the introduction; for more on the creation of the Vilayet Ahkam Defterleri see Başak Tuğ, "Politics of Honor," 102–7. Taken together, these reforms suggest a greater concern for documenting the dispute resolution activities of the executive authorities at this time.
53. On the rise of the Qāzdughlī household see Hathaway, *Politics of Households*. For the supremacy of the household and its bid for autonomy under ᶜAlī Bey al-Kabīr, see Crecelius, *Roots of Modern Egypt*.
54. For Meḥmed ᶜAlī's reforms, see Fahmy, *All the Pasha's Men*.
55. For the nationalist narrative of Meḥmed ᶜAlī's regime, see Marsot, *Egypt in the Reign of Muhammad Ali*.

Chapter 6

1. On forum-shopping between different tribunals in the Ottoman Empire, see Gradeva, "Kadi Court," 58–61; Ergene, *Local Court*, 174–7; Rubin, *Ottoman Nizamiye Courts*, 61–71; Barakat, "Regulating Land Rights"; On forum-shopping in modern Egypt, see Shaham, "Shopping for Legal Forums."
2. Hanna, "Administration," 53–4; Ergene, *Local Court*, 143–9.
3. Merry, *Getting Justice and Getting Even.*
4. Damurdāshī A, 18–21; Damurdāshī C, 43–7; for my discussion see above, pp. 105–7.
5. While many of Cairo's courts appear to have continuous series of sijills over long periods, the individual sijills themselves are often fragmentary. This is particularly true of the records of the neighborhood courts, which are poorly bound and in a few cases seriously damaged; the records of al-Bāb al-ᶜĀlī are in much better condition. The ENA has a unit, labeled *Maḥāfiẓ al-dasht*, containing boxes of loose leaves that have fallen out of assorted sijills. The ENA had a project to digitize the sijills of al-Bāb al-ᶜĀlī and to create a digital catalog of every individual entry within them, providing the basic information such as identity of litigants, madhhab of judge, subject of dispute, and so on. This project was just beginning when I was studying in the archive in 2007. Subsequently, the catalog was completed and briefly made available online, but at the time of writing this it has been offline for more than two years. If made accessible, this resource would be unique in its size across the post-Ottoman world. There are several projects to index Istanbul court records, including those run by Cemal Kafadar, Timur Kuran, and the İslam Araştırma Merkezi, but they are all on a much smaller scale. Collectively, these projects promise to open up new possibilities in sijill-based research. The Old Bailey Proceedings Online at the University of Sheffield shows what is possible with sufficient funding and expertise.
6. Ergene has argued that Ottoman qāḍīs often led ṣulḥ negotiations, and that this explains why some litigants brought apparently hopeless cases to court; see "Why did Ümmü Gülsüm go to Court?" I am not sure that qāḍīs and nāᵓibs led ṣulḥ negotiations, at least in the case of Cairo, as I discussed in Chapter 2. But for the purposes of answering the hopeless case conundrum, this does not necessarily matter. The qāḍī may well have—indeed should have, according to the jurists—encouraged the litigants to enter ṣulḥ, even if he did not lead the process himself. Moreover, the court was a busy, public venue, where anyone with an interest in a case could turn up, and where a litigant could expect to find in attendance numerous people of standing in the community as a matter of routine. Bringing a lawsuit with the hope of achieving resolution through ṣulḥ rather than adjudication was a viable strategy regardless of the precise role of the qāḍī.
7. Qadhf was false accusation of zināᵓ (fornication) and was one of the ḥadd offenses with penalties specified in the Koran; in the case of qadhf, the penalty was eighty lashes. Most jurists agreed that even a witness who testified in a zināᵓ prosecution should be punished for qadhf if the prosecution failed. This was one of several rules jurists used to effectively make the horrendous penalty for zināᵓ—stoning to death in the case of married Muslim culprits—unenforceable. These rules had the additional effect of making it very

difficult to prosecute rape. For a summary of the jurists' attempts to make the zināʾ penalty unenforceable, see Baldwin, "Prostitution," 121–4; on the difficulty of proving rape in Ottoman courts, see Sonbol, "Rape and Law," 219–23.

8. Peirce, *Morality Tales*, 203.
9. Smail, *Consumption of Justice.*
10. Cohen, *Law, Violence and Community.*
11. *Registerbuch*, fo. 23a, 3rd entry, early Dhū ʾl-Qaᶜda 1085 (27 January–5 February 1675). This is the imperial order issued in response to Aḥmad's petition, not the petition itself. I discussed Aḥmad's case from the perspective of the Dīvān's procedure above, p. 61.
12. ŞK 1/93. The petition is undated, but the year 1155 (March 1742–February 1743) has been added by an archivist. See pp. 156–7 for a transcription and translation of this document.
13. On the inconsistent enforcement of the "Pact of ᶜUmar" regulations on non-Muslims in the Ottoman Empire, see Masters, *Christians and Jews*, 42–4, 72–3, 106–7. While non-enforcement of most of the regulations other than the poll-tax seems to have been the norm, there were sporadic incidents of unrest in various parts of the empire in which the protestors' complaints included the widespread flouting of the rules by non-Muslims.
14. DK 77/64. The petition is undated but its date of arrival at the palace is noted as late Rabīᶜ al-Thānī 1087 (3–11 July 1676). For a transcription and translation see pp. 152–6.
15. The petition does not explicitly mention the sharīᶜa court, it simply states that the temessük was recorded in the sijill (register) in Cairo, but such documents were usually recorded in the sijills of the sharīᶜa court.
16. Peirce, *Morality Tales*, 282–5.
17. Wittman, "Before Qadi and Grand Vizier," 146.
18. Ursinus, "Petitions."
19. Ergene, *Local Court*, 105–8, 170–7.
20. Brown, *Rule of Law*, 187–220.
21. Ergene, "Why did Ümmü Gülsüm go to Court?"
22. The dropping of all claims connected with a dispute was also a necessary, integral component of any agreement resulting from ṣulḥ.
23. We see a similar dynamic today, when lawsuits against corporations, government agencies, and public bodies are frequently dropped after out-of-court settlements with gagging clauses attached.
24. BA 225, entry 226, 30 Muḥarram 1155 (6 April 1742).
25. It is noteworthy that, although they contracted the sale at Bābay Saᶜāda wa ʾl-Kharq on the same day, Fāṭima and Muḥammad went to al-Bāb al-ᶜĀlī to transact the istibdāl. This suggests that the prohibition on controversial non-Ḥanafī transactions being conducted within the neighborhood sharīᶜa courts, discussed in Chapter 4, was being observed.
26. On the role of documents in Islamic law, see Wakin, *Function of Documents.* For the specific case of the Ottoman Empire, see Ergene, "Document Use."
27. DA 1, entry 380, 20 Jumādā ʾl-Thānī 1155 (22 August 1742).
28. It is not clear whether the people in this group were formally the mediators, because the record follows most others in referring to the mediators by the generic term *al-muslimūn*

(the Muslims). The record states that the agreement was formalized in the presence of the group, so it seems highly likely that they were involved in the mediation.

29. Girls attained legal majority when they reached puberty.
30. Ergene, *Local Court*, 146–9.
31. The relationships between violent and legal methods of dispute resolution have been explored in a range of historical societies. On classical Athens, see Cohen, *Law, Violence and Community*. On early modern Spain, see Taylor, *Honor and Violence*, 65–99. On early modern France, see Carroll, *Blood and Violence*, 185–213. On modern Lebanon, see Gilsenan, "Law, Arbitrariness."
32. For an analysis of pre-modern legal opinion on a husband's right to discipline his wife with violence, see Chaudhry, *Domestic Violence*, 95–132.
33. BS 623, entry 295, 2 Ṣafar 1078 (24 July 1667).
34. *Ḥimāyāt*—i.e. the unofficial "protection" dues levied on artisans and merchants by the regiments. While technically illegal, the regiments' levying of them was only sporadically suppressed. As this case indicates, while people may have complained about them, they were generally treated by both artisans and the courts as a cost of doing business in Cairo.
35. BS 623, entry 276, 20 Muḥarram 1078 (12 July 1667).
36. In many societies, revenge is expressed most clearly through feud or vendetta: structures of formalized enmity and patterns of reciprocal violence. On feud and vendetta cultures in the early modern world, see Black-Michaud, *Feuding Societies*; Zmora, *Feud*; Taylor, *Honor and Violence*; Carroll, *Blood and Violence*; Kaminsky, "Noble Feud." For a classic study of the integration of feud and revenge into a legal system, see Miller, *Bloodtaking and Peacemaking*. In classical Athens, judges saw revenge as a legitimate motive for bringing a legal action that reflected well on the plaintiff's character, as opposed to envy, which reflected badly and so rendered the suit unreliable; see Cohen, *Law, Violence and Community*, 82–5.
37. On retaliation (*qiṣāṣ*) and the Islamic law of injuries, see Peters, *Crime and Punishment*, 38–53.
38. There was one important exception: some Ḥanafī jurists, including the sixteenth-century Egyptian Ibn Nujaym, held that a man who caught his wife in the act of adultery could legitimately kill both her and her lover. This was an extreme extension of the generally wide latitude the Ḥanafīs were willing to grant husbands to discipline their wives. See Chaudhry, *Domestic Violence*, 108, n. 45. This was reflected in Ottoman ḳānūn: the criminal ḳānūnnāme of the sixteenth century absolves the husband who kills his adulterous wife and her lover after catching them red-handed, as long as he immediately calls people to bear witness to the circumstances. See Ottoman Criminal Code, clause 13, in Heyd, *Studies*, 59 (Turkish text), 98 (English translation).
39. The same could be said of all legal systems that employ corporal punishment in their criminal laws. Historically, the rise of civil litigation also served as an alternative to violent revenge. While this has often been understood as displacing the urge to take vengeance, some historians have argued that in the early modern period litigation

was incorporated into the vendetta framework, with the lawsuit itself seen as an act of violence; for France, see Carroll, *Blood and Violence*, 185–213.

40. BS 623, entry 309, 12 Ṣafar 1078 (3 August 1667). See pp. 147–9 for a transcription and translation of this document.
41. This sum did not cover anything like the full value of the goods that Shukur claimed Sha^cbān had stolen. According to Shukur, these goods had been worth 16 and one-sixth ghurūsh, which at the usual exchange rate of 30 niṣfs to one ghirsh, totaled just over 485 niṣfs. But the important point is that, legally, Shukur had no claim to anything.
42. On early modern European visitors' critical opinions of the Ottoman legal system, see Ergene, *Local Court*, 108–24.
43. Ergene criticizes Ottoman legal historiography for this focus, arguing that it has produced a narrow and misleading view of Ottoman legal practice: "Why did Ümmü Gülsüm go to Court?," 216–20 and passim.
44. Gerber, *State, Society and Law*; Powers, *Law, Society and Culture.*
45. Anthropological studies of modern Muslim courts have portrayed the judge primarily as a mediator rather than an adjudicator. For example: Rosen, *Anthropology of Justice*; Clarke, "Judge as Tragic Hero."
46. Aida Othman also suggests that ṣulḥ may have been responsible for the kadijustiz concept: Othman, "And Amicable Settlement is Best," 70.
47. For the parameters of legitimate ṣulḥ according to the jurists, see Othman, "And Amicable Settlement is Best."
48. Cases such as that of *Shukur* vs. *Sha^cbān*, when the parties were brought to court by bystanders or by police officials, were exceptions to the norm.

Conclusion

1. For a comparative study of law in early modern empires, see Benton, *Law and Colonial Cultures.*
2. For a recent account of Umayyad justice, necessarily based largely on later sources, see Judd, *Religious Scholars*, 91–141.
3. Tillier, "Judicial Authority"; Tillier, *Les cadis d'Iraq*. Judd argues that Umayyad qāḍīs also had a degree of independence, but he admits that as his information comes from ^cAbbāsid-era biographical dictionaries, this could be a back-projection seeking precedents for ^cAbbāsid practices. See Judd, *Religious Scholars*, 93–103.
4. Tillier, "Qāḍīs of Fusṭāṭ-Miṣr"; Tillier, "Qāḍīs and the Political Uses of the Maẓālim."
5. Müller, "Redressing Injustice."
6. For Māwardī's theory see Nielsen, *Secular Justice*, 17–33.
7. On the maẓālim's personnel and procedure, see Nielsen, *Secular Justice*, 63–92.
8. Rapoport, "Royal Justice and Religious Law." For the government's interest in determining how fiqh was applied, see Rapoport, "Legal Diversity."
9. In the earlier Seljuk period, a majority of muḥtasibs were drawn from the ulema. See Lange, "Changes in the Office of Ḥisba."
10. Stilt, *Islamic Law in Action.*

11. On the ilmiye system see Uzunçarşılı, *Osmanlı Devletinde İlmiye Teşkilatı*; Atçıl, "Formation of the Ottoman Learned Class." On the integration of the education system see Ahmed and Filipovic, "Sultan's Syllabus." On the system of promotion see Atçıl, "Route to the Top." On the position of Şeyhulislām, see Repp, *Müfti of Istanbul*. On the official muftis in the provinces see Burak, *Second Formation of Islamic Law*, 21–64.
12. On relations between non-ilmiye scholars, ilmiye members, and the Ottoman government in Egypt see Meshal, *Sharia*; Meshal, "Antagonistic Sharīᶜas." For Syria see Burak, *Second Formation of Islamic Law*; Rafeq, "Syrian ᶜUlamāʾ."
13. Surprisingly poorly understood for many years, the Ottoman "state madhhab" now has a definitive study in Burak, *Second Formation of Islamic Law*. See also Peters, "What Does it Mean?"
14. Cuno, *Modernizing Marriage*, 136–41. I am grateful to Prof. Cuno for providing me with his typescript before the book was published.
15. For Zubaida's account of the Ottoman legal reforms, see *Law and Power*, 121–46.
16. Hallaq, *Sharīᶜa*, 411–20; Messick, *Calligraphic State*, 54–72; Zubaida, *Law and Power*, 132–5.
17. On the majlis al-tujjār see Cheta, "Rule of Merchants." On the Cemᶜiyet-i Ḥaḳḳāniye and the Majlis al-aḥkām see Peters, "Administrators and Magistrates"; Fahmy, *Bodies of Law*.
18. Fahmy, "Anatomy of Justice."
19. On Egyptian legal reform in the late nineteenth century, see Brown, *Rule of Law*, 23–60.
20. Rubin, *Ottoman Nizamiye Courts*.
21. Burak and Brown, "Justice."
22. Rubin, *Ottoman Nizamiye Courts*, 20–1. See also Rubin, "Legal Borrowing."
23. For example: Holt, *Egypt and the Fertile Crescent*, 33–101; Winter, *Egyptian Society*.

Appendix

1. For a photograph of this document, see Baldwin, "Petitioning the Sultan," 520.
2. Ḥujja usually refers to a deed issued by a qāḍī confirming a transaction or litigation. Here, however, the petitioner seems to be referring back to the four berāts he has just mentioned.
3. The word used here is *emr*, which means order and was often used interchangeably with fermān. Here, the petitioner is referring to the fermān he cited previously.
4. The petitioner's spelling ends with a *tāʾ marbūṭa* (Zifta), but the spelling used today ends with *alif* (Ziftā).
5. In the document a blank space has been left for the name of Beşīr Āghā's agent.
6. The advance rent (icāre-yi muᶜaccale) was the upfront payment in an icāreteyn contract, which secured a lifetime lease on a property owned by a waqf. See above, pp. 89–90, for details.
7. In the document a blank space has been left for the name of Beşīr Āghā's agent.
8. The original Turkish puts this in the passive voice—"an order was written"—but the sense is active.

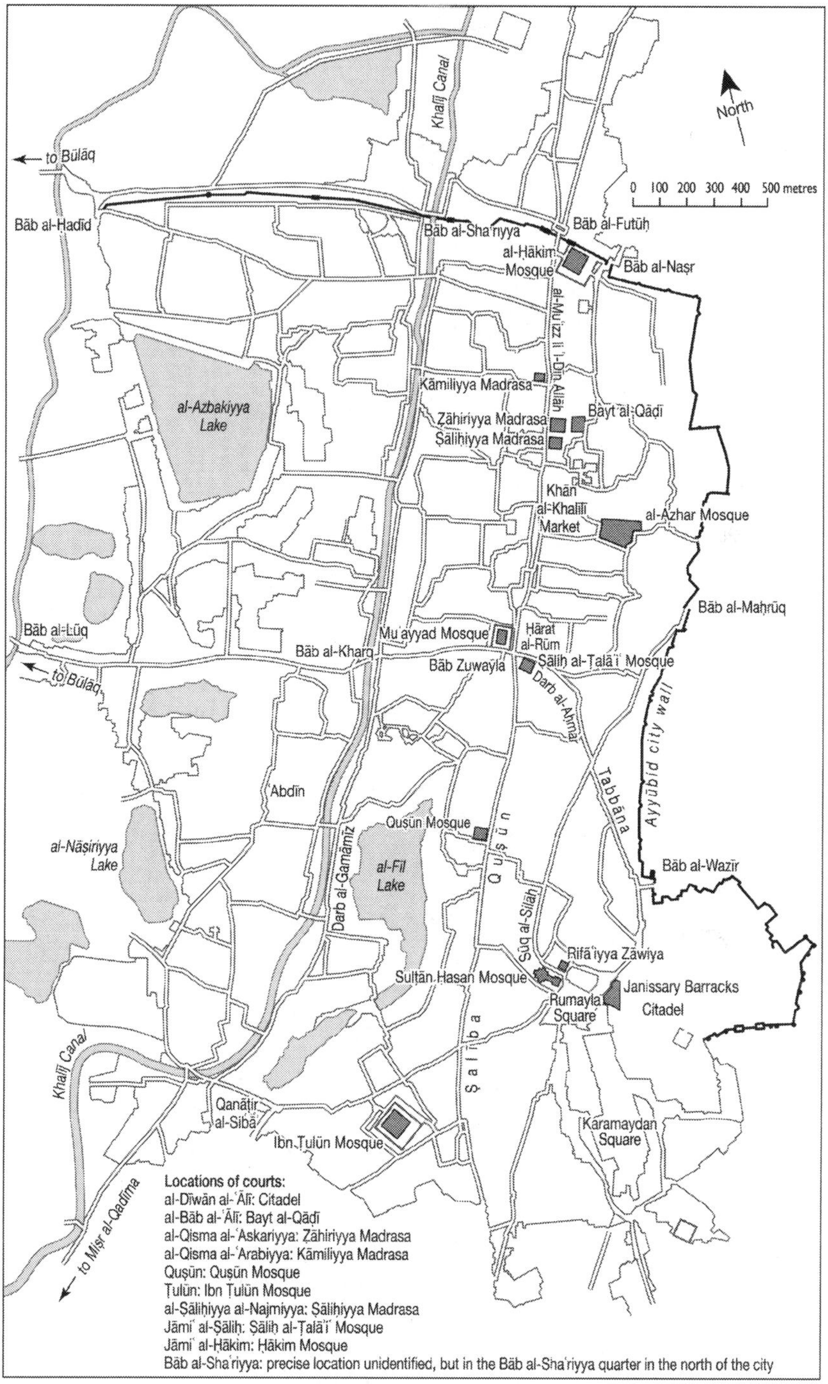

Map of Cairo in the Eighteenth Century

GLOSSARY

āghā (Tr. ağa)	A title used by various senior military and political officials in the Ottoman Empire, including the commanders of regiments and the eunuchs who guarded the imperial palace and harem.
amīn al-iḥtisāb	*see* muḥtasib
amīr	A title used in Ottoman-Egyptian political society.
amīr al-ḥajj	Commander of the pilgrimage. In Egypt, this was the title of the official who organized the pilgrimage caravan departing from Cairo, one of two major caravans in the Ottoman Empire (the other departed from Damascus).
arżuḥāl (Ar. arḍ al-ḥāl)	A petition.
arżuḥālci	A professional petition-writer.
Awqāf	*see* waqf
ᶜAzabān	One of the seven military regiments in Ottoman Cairo. The ᶜAzabān and the Janissaries were the two biggest.
al-Azhar	The mosque-madrasa complex in Cairo. Founded in the tenth century, during the Ottoman period it was the largest religious institution in Cairo and the center of intellectual life.
başodabaşı	A senior officer in a military regiment.
berāt	A certificate appointing a person to an office or granting them a status, issued by the Sultan.
buyuruldu	An order issued by a senior government official. In Egypt, it typically designated an order issued by the Ottoman governor.
bey	The shorter and more common form of the title sancaḳbeyi, bey was one of the highest-ranking titles in use in Ottoman Egypt's political society. In most of the empire, a sancaḳbeyi

	was in charge of a sancak, a unit of territory. In Egypt, the title had no territorial connotations, but the number of beys in Egypt at any one time was limited to twenty-four.
çavuş (Ar. jāwīsh)	An attendant or guard of an important person, also a military rank. Furthermore, in Ottoman Cairo, it could refer to a member of the Çavuşān regiment.
defter	A register containing official records. Similar to a court's sijill; the registers of institutions other than the courts were usually called defters.
defterdār	Treasurer: the title was used for the official in charge of the imperial treasury in Istanbul and also for the officials in charge of the various provincial treasuries, such as Cairo's.
dīnār	A gold coin used in Ottoman Egypt.
Dīvān-i Hümāyūn	The Ottoman imperial council, presided over by the Grand Vizier.
al-Dīwān al-ᶜĀlī	The high council of the Ottoman governor in Egypt.
emr-i şerīf	An imperial order issued by the Sultan.
faqīh (pl. fuqahāᵓ)	A Muslim jurist, trained in fiqh.
fatwā (pl. fatāwā)	A legal opinion given by a mufti.
fermān	An imperial order issued by the Sultan.
fiqh	Muslim jurisprudence, consisting of uṣūl al-fiqh (legal theory) and furūᶜ al-fiqh (positive law).
ghirsh (pl. ghurūsh)	A silver coin in circulation in Ottoman Egypt. Also spelled qirsh / qurūsh.
Grand Vizier	The prime minister of the Ottoman Empire.
Ḥanafī	One of the four madhhabs in Sunni Islamic law, named after the eighth-century jurist Abū Ḥanīfa. The Ḥanafī madhhab was the preferred madhhab of the Ottoman dynasty.
Ḥanbalī	One of the four madhhabs in Sunni Islamic law, named after the ninth-century jurist Ibn Ḥanbal.
haṭṭ-i şerif (Ar. khaṭṭ sharīf)	A document in the Sultan's own hand, usually containing an imperial order.
ḥisba	A jurisdiction originating in medieval Muslim societies, encompassing marketplace trading and public morality. The official in charge of ḥisba was usually called the muḥtasib; or sometimes, in Ottoman Egypt, the amīn al-iḥtisāb.
ḥujja (pl. ḥujaj, Tr. ḥuccet)	A certificate issued by a court recording a hearing that took place there. A ḥujja was issued to each of the parties to the dispute or contract, while a copy was made in the sijill.
iftāᵓ	The practice of giving fatwās.
ilmiye	The hierarchical scholarly profession in the Ottoman Empire. The word ilmiye designated the hierarchy of

	professorial and judicial posts, and the network of madrasas that trained its incumbents. Not all scholars were members of the ilmiye, and not all madrasas were incorporated within it.
iltizām	A tax-farm: leased to a revenue contractor by the government for a fixed period.
Janissaries	One of the seven military regiments in Ottoman Cairo. The Janissaries and the ᶜAzabān were the two biggest. Known as the Yeniçeri in Turkish, in Egypt the Janissaries were also known as the Mustaḥfiẓān (guards), as they guarded the citadel.
ḳānūn (Ar. qānūn)	In an Ottoman context, it usually referred to Ottoman dynastic law, though the word also meant custom or tradition. The two meanings are connected, as one of the justifications for dynastic law was that it formalized customary law.
ḳānūnnāme	A text containing ḳānūn. Typically, a ḳānūnnāme was issued for a particular province, and covered landholding, taxation and administration. The Ottoman government also issued ḳānūnnāmes covering criminal law.
katkhudā (Tr. kethuda)	Lieutenant. As well as regimental katkhudās, prominent officials and political grandees also had a katkhudā.
ḳāżᶜasker	*see* qāḍī ʾl-quḍāh
al-Khurda	An iltizām in Ottoman Cairo, covering various urban activities. Because it covered the disreputable end of the entertainment business, including dancers, snake-charmers, and hashish-merchants, the multazim of al-Khurda played a significant role in policing.
madhhab (pl. madhāhib, Tr. mezheb)	A school of interpretation in Islamic law: each madhhab consisted of an interpretive method and a body of accumulated doctrine. Before the modernist movement of the late nineteenth century, almost all jurists and judges adhered to a madhhab.
madrasa (Tr. medrese)	A school or college, typically a place for advanced instruction in fiqh and other religious sciences.
Mālikī	One of the four madhhabs in Sunni Islamic law, named after the eighth-century jurist Mālik ibn Anas.
mamlūk	A male slave from the Caucasus who was employed in the military or administrative service of his master.
maẓālim	A court of grievances, presided over by the ruler or his agent. Unlike in a sharīᶜa court, a qāḍī did not necessarily preside over a maẓālim tribunal. Nonetheless, qāḍīs were involved in the maẓālim institution in most societies. The word maẓālim was rarely used in the Ottoman Empire, but

	one of the contentions of this book is that the practice survived under different names.
muḥḍir (Tr. muḥżır)	Court bailiff, responsible for summoning defendants to court.
muḥtasib	The official in charge of the ḥisba jurisdiction, also called the amīn al-iḥtisāb.
mufti	A Muslim jurist qualified to give a fatwā.
multazim	The revenue contractor who holds an iltizām.
nāᵓib (pl. nuwwāb)	The deputy of a qāḍī. In Ottoman Egypt, the distinction between nāᵓib and qāḍī was largely one of rank. Nāᵓibs heard cases independently and could exercise most of the powers of a qāḍī; indeed most of the courts in Cairo were staffed exclusively by nāᵓibs.
naqīb al-ashrāf	*see* sayyid
niṣf fiḍḍa	A silver coin in use in Ottoman Egypt; sometimes called simply the niṣf.
odabaşı	An officer in a military regiment.
qāḍī (pl. quḍāh, Tr. ḳaḍı)	A sharīᶜa judge. In the Ottoman Empire, qāḍīs were mostly based in sharīᶜa courts, although they also acted for other institutions. Various other officials within the empire performed tasks that we might associate with the Anglo-American concept of a judge. The distinctive attribute of the qāḍī was that he performed qaḍāᵓ: the task of evaluating evidence, establishing facts and awarding rights, as defined in fiqh.
qāḍī ᵓl-quḍāh	The chief qāḍī of a major city. In Egypt, the chief qāḍī was also called the qāḍī ᶜaskar by locals. In the wider Ottoman Empire, the term qāḍī ᶜaskar, more recognizable in its Turkish form ḳāżᶜasker, was reserved for the chief qāḍīs of Rumelia and Anatolia, the two highest positions in the judicial hierarchy after the Şeyhulislām.
qānūn	*see* ḳānūn
qirsh (pl. qurūsh)	*see* ghirsh
sayyid (pl. sādāt)	A descendant of the Prophet Muḥammad. Also known as sharīf (pl. ashrāf); the two words were often combined as the title al-sayyid al-sharīf. The naqīb al-ashrāf was the leader of the community of sayyids in an Ottoman city.
sancaḳbeyi	*see* bey
Şeyhulislām	The chief mufti of Istanbul, the highest position in the Ottoman judicial profession.
Shāfiᶜī	One of the four madhhabs in Sunni Islamic law, named after the eighth / ninth-century jurist al-Shāfiᶜī. The Shāfiᶜī

	madhhab was historically the most prominent in Cairo and Lower Egypt.
shāhid (shuhūd)	A witness. *See* separate entry for shuhūd al-ḥāl / shuhūd ᶜudūl.
sharīf (pl. ashrāf)	*see* sayyid
shaykh	A title used by people in various positions of authority within Ottoman society: scholars, Sufi leaders and other religious authorities; neighborhood headmen (shaykh al-ḥāra); and the leaders of artisanal or trade guilds (shaykh al-ṭāʾifa).
shaykh al-balad	A prestigious title used by the political elite in eighteenth-century Cairo. It was connected to no particular office, but indicated recognition by peers as the most powerful member of elite society.
shuhūd al-ḥāl	*see* shuhūd ᶜudūl
shuhūd ᶜudūl (sing. shāhid ᶜadl)	Court witnesses, who witnessed court hearings and testified to the validity of the proceedings and the accuracy of the record. This role is distinct from that of circumstantial witnesses, who gave testimony on behalf of a litigant concerning something that happened outside of the court.
sijill (pl. sijillāt, Tr. sicil)	The register in which records of court proceedings were kept.
siyāsa	The exercise of power by the ruler. The concept of siyāsa sharᶜiyya meant the exercise of such power in accordance with sharīᶜa law.
ṣulḥ	Mediation: the negotiation of a mutually acceptable resolution to a dispute, as an alternative to adjudication.
taᶜdīl	Also known as tazkiyya, the process by which the qāḍī determined whether a witness was reliable, by investigating his or her character.
tamassuk (Tr. temessük)	A receipt or deed, confirming that a transaction has taken place and/or that a person has a title to property or another right.
Tanzimat	A process of reform undertaken by the Ottoman government in the nineteenth century, encompassing military, fiscal, political, legal, educational and medical reform. Typically, the Tanzimat refers to the reforms carried out between the Edict of Gülhāne in 1839 and the suspension of the Ottoman constitution in 1878. This was one phase in a longer process of reform that began in the late eighteenth century and continued until the empire's demise.
taᶜzīr	Punishment at the discretion of the qāḍī.
tazkiyya, *see* taᶜdīl	
ulema (Ar. ᶜulamāʾ, sing. ᶜālim)	Scholars. The ulema were an important social group in most historical Muslim societies. The category encompasses the

fuqahāʾ but is broader, including all religious and natural sciences.

waqf (pl. awqāf) — An endowment. A waqf could fund a public service such as a mosque, madrasa or soup kitchen, but it could also be a trust paying benefits to the founder's family; the latter type had to have an ultimate charitable purpose, once the founder's line was extinct. Awqāf founded by the Sultans, other members of the dynasty and prominent officials supported major religious and educational institutions in the empire. The awqāf al-ḥaramayn were a large block of imperial awqāf that benefited the poor of Mecca and Medina.

SOURCES AND WORKS CITED

Archival and manuscript sources

Egyptian National Archive, Cairo

Sijillāt al-Dīwān al-ᶜĀlī
Sijillāt maḥkamat al-Bāb al-ᶜĀlī
Sijillāt maḥkamat Bāb al-Shaᶜriyya
Sijillāt maḥkamat Miṣr al-Qadīma
Ḥujaj ṣādira min maḥkamat al-Dīwān al-ᶜĀlī

Prime Ministry Ottoman Archive, Istanbul

Atik Şikayet Defterleri (listed in catalog 989)
Şikayet Defterleri (listed in catalog 980)
Mühimme Defterleri
Divan Kalemi
Mısır Kalemi
Şikayet Kalemi
Cevdet Tasnifi
İbnülemin Tasnifi
Ali Emiri Tasnifi

British Library, London

MS Add. 7846 ᶜAbduʾṣ-ṣamed ed-Diyārbekrī, *Tercüme-yi en-Nüzhe es-seniyye fī zikr el-hulafā ve ʾl-mülūk el-Mıṣriyye.*

MS Or. 14277	Zayn al-Dīn Ibrāhīm Ibn Nujaym, *Fatāwā Ibn Nujaym.*
MS Or. 15259	Miscellaneous legal documents from Ottoman Egypt.

Bibliothèque nationale de France, Paris

MS arabe 1855	Untitled, anonymous history of Ottoman Egypt.

Cambridge University Library

MS Add. 278/7	Anon., *Kitāb majmū*ᶜ *al-Durra al-munṣāna fi waqāyi*ᶜ *Kināna min sanat alf tis*ᶜ*a wa tis*ᶜ*īn.*
MS T-S Ar.38.116	Two ḥujjas, one issued by al-Bāb al-ᶜĀlī and one issued by an unidentified court.
MS T-S Ar.42.184	Ḥujja issued by al-Bāb al-ᶜĀlī.

Leiden University Library

MS Or. 22324	Ḥujja issued by al-Bāb al-ᶜĀlī.

Royal Library, Copenhagen

MS Cod. Arab. 159	Muṣṭafā ibn Ibrāhīm al-Qinalī, *Kitāb Tārīkh Miṣr.*

Printed primary sources—legal texts and documents

Babinger, Franz (ed.), *Das Archiv des Bosniaken Osman Pascha: nach den Beständen der Badischen Landesbibliothek zu Karlsruhe* (Berlin: Reichsdruckerei, 1931).

Barkan, Ömer Lûtfi, "Mısır Kanunnamesi," in Ömer Lûtfi Barkan (ed.), *XV. ve XVIinci Osmanlı İmparatorluğunda Zirai ve Ekonominin Hukuki ve Mali Esasları* (Istanbul: Bürhaneddin Matbaası, 1943), 355–87.

Düzdağ, M. E. (ed.), *Şeyhulislam Ebussuud Efendi Fetvaları Işığında 16. Asır Türk Hayatı* (Istanbul: Enderun Kitabevi, 1983).

Horster, Paul, *Zur Anwendung des Islamischen Rechts im 16. Jahrhundert: Die „juristischen Darlegungen" (ma*ᶜ*rūżāt) des Schejch ül-Islam Ebū Su*ᶜ*ūd (gest. 1574) herausgegeben, übersetzt und untersucht* (Stuttgart: W. Kohlhammer, 1935).

Ibn ᶜĀbidīn, Muḥammad Amīn (ed.), *al-*ᶜ*Uqūd al-durriyya fī tanqīḥ al-fatāwī *ᵓ*l-Ḥāmidiyya* (Beirut: Dār al-maᶜrifa, 1970).

Ibn Nujaym, Zayn al-Dīn ibn Ibrāhīm, *al-Baḥr al-rā*ᵓ*iq, sharḥ Kanz al-daqā*ᵓ*iq* (Beirut: Dār al-kutub al-ᶜilmiyya, 1997).

Majer, Hans Georg (ed.), *Das osmanische Registerbuch der Beschwerden (Şikayet Defteri) vom Jahre 1675: Österreichische Nationalbibliothek Cod. mixt. 683* (Vienna: Verlag der Österreichischen Akademie der Wissenschaften, 1984).

Al-Ramlī, Khayr al-Dīn, *Kitāb al-Fatāwā ʾl-khayriyya li nafʿ al-bāriyya* (Būlāq: Maṭbaʿat Muḥammad Saʿīd Bāshā, 1273 AH).

Shaykhzāda, ʿAbd al-Raḥmān ibn Muḥammad, *Majmaʿ al-anhur, sharḥ Multaqā ʾl-abḥur* (Beirut: Dār al-kutub al-ʿilmiyya, 1998).

Tyser, C. R., D. G. Demetriades, and Ismail Haqqi Effendi (trans.), *The Mejelle: Being an English Translation of Majallah el-Ahkam-i-Adliya and a Complete Code on Islamic Civil Law* (Kuala Lumpur: The Other Press, 2001).

Ursinus, Michael (ed.), *Grievance Administration (Şikayet) in an Ottoman Province: The Kaymakam of Rumelia's "Record Book of Complaints" of 1781–1783* (London: RoutledgeCurzon, 2005).

Printed primary sources—historical, biographical, and travel literature

Al-Damīrī, Ḥusayn ibn Muḥammad, *Quḍāt Miṣr fī ʾl-qarn al-ʿāshir wa ʾl-rubʿ al-awwal min al-qarn al-ḥādi ʿashar al-hijrī li ʾl-Damīrī*, ed. ʿAbd al-Rāziq ʿAbd al-Rāziq ʿĪsā and Yūsuf Muṣṭafā al-Maḥmūdī (Cairo: al-ʿArabī li ʾl-nashr wa ʾl-tawzīʿ, 2000).

Al-Damurdāshī, Aḥmad, *al-Durra al-muṣāna fī akhbār al-Kināna*, ed. ʿAbd al-Raḥīm ʿAbd al-Raḥmān ʿAbd al-Raḥīm (Cairo: Institut français d'archéologie orientale, 1989).

Al-Damurdāshī, Aḥmad, *Al-Damurdashi's Chronicle of Egypt: al-Durra al-musana fi akhbar al-Kinana*, trans. Daniel Crecelius and ʿAbd al-Wahhab Bakr (Leiden: Brill, 1991).

Evliyā Çelebi, *Evliya Çelebi Seyahatnamesi*, 10. kitap, ed. Seyit Ali Kahraman, Yücel Dağlı, and Robert Dankoff (Istanbul: Yapı Kredi Yayınları, 2007).

Ḥuseyn Efendi, *Ottoman Egypt in the Age of the French Revolution*, ed. and trans. Stanford J. Shaw (Cambridge, MA: Center for Middle Eastern Studies, 1964).

Ibn ʿAbd al-Ghanī, Aḥmad Shalabī, *Awḍaḥ al-ishārāt fī man tawallā Miṣr min al-wuzarāʾ wa ʾl-bāshāt*, ed. ʿAbd al-Raḥīm ʿAbd al-Raḥmān ʿAbd a-Raḥīm (Cairo: Maktabat al-Khānjī, 1978).

Ibn Iyās, Muḥammad ibn Aḥmad, *Badāʾiʿ al-zuhūr wa ʾl-waqāʾiʿ al-duhūr*, ed. Muḥammad Muṣṭafā (Cairo: Maṭbaʿat Dār al-kutub wa ʾl-wathāʾiq al-qawmiyya, 2008).

Ibn Riḍwān, ʿAlī (attrib.), *Zubdat ikhtiṣār tārīkh mulūk Miṣr al-maḥrūsa 922–1113 H / 1516–1701 M*, ed. Bashīr Zayn al-ʿĀbidīn (Cairo: Dār al-faḍīla, 2006).

Al-Jabartī, ʿAbd al-Raḥmān, *al-Tārīkh al-musammā ʿAjāʾib al-āthār fī ʾl-tarājim wa ʾl-akhbār* (Būlāq: n.p., 1297 AH).

Al-Jabartī, ʿAbd al-Raḥmān, *ʿAbd al-Raḥmān al-Jabartī's History of Egypt: ʿAjāʾib al-athār fī ʾl-tarājim wa ʾl-akhbār*, ed. and trans. Thomas Philipp and Moshe Perlmann (Stuttgart: Franz Steiner Verlag, 1994).

Al-Muḥibbī, Muḥammad Amīn, *Khulāṣat al-athar fī aʿyān al-qarn al-ḥādī ʿashar*, ed. Muḥammad Ḥasan Ismāʿīl (Beirut: Dār al-kutub al-ʿilmiyya, 2006).

Al-Murādī, Muḥammad Khalīl, *Silk al-durar fī aʿyān al-qarn al-thānī ʿashar*, ed. Muḥammad ʿAbd al-Qādir Shāhīn (Beirut: Dār al-kutub al-ʿilmiyya, 1997).

Al-Rashīdī, Aḥmad, *Ḥusn al-ṣafā wa ʾl-ibtihāj bi dhikr man waliya imārat al-ḥājj*, ed. Laylā ʿAbd al-Laṭīf Aḥmad (Cairo: Maktabat al-khānjī, 1980).

Al-Shādhilī, ᶜAlī ibn Muḥammad, "Dhikr ma waqaᶜa bayna ᶜaskar al-maḥrūsa al-Qāhira (sana 1123 H = 1711 M)," ed. ᶜAbd al-Qādir Aḥmad Ṭulaymāt, *al-Majalla al-tārīkhiyya al-Miṣriyya* 14 (1968), 321–403.

Secondary works

Abacı, Nurcan, *Bursa Şehri'nde Osmanlı Hukuku'nun Uygulanması, 17. Yüzyıl* (Ankara: T. C. Kültür Bakanlığı, 2001).

ᶜAbd al-Maqṣūd, al-Sayyid Sāmir, *al-Shawām fī Miṣr mundhu ʾl-fatḥ al-ᶜuthmānī ḥattā awāʾil al-qarn al-tāsiᶜ ᶜashar* (Cairo: al-Hayʾa al-Miṣriyya al-ᶜāma li ʾl-kitāb, 2003).

Abu-Lughod, Janet L., *Cairo: 1001 Years of the City Victorious* (Princeton: Princeton University Press, 1971).

ᶜAfīfī, Muḥammad, *al-Awqāf wa ʾl-ḥayā al-iqtiṣādiyya fī Miṣr fī ʾl-ᶜaṣr al-ᶜUthmānī* (Cairo: al-Hayʾa al-Miṣriyya al-ᶜāma li ʾl-kitāb, 1991).

Agmon, Iris, "Women's History and Ottoman Sharīᶜa Court Records: Shifting Perspectives in Social History," *Hawwa* 2 (2004), 172–209.

Agmon, Iris, *Family and Court: Legal Culture and Modernity in Late Ottoman Palestine* (Syracuse, NY: Syracuse University Press, 2006).

Ahmed, Shahab and Nenad Filipovic, "The Sultan's Syllabus: A Curriculum for the Ottoman Imperial Medreses Prescribed in a Fermān of Qānūnī I Süleymān, Dated 973 (1565)," *Studia Islamica* 98–9 (2004), 183–218.

Akarlı, Engin Deniz, "Law in the Marketplace: Istanbul, 1730–1840," in Muhammad Khalid Masud, Rudolph Peters, and David S. Powers (eds), *Dispensing Justice in Islam: Qadis and their Judgments* (Leiden: Brill, 2006), 245–70.

AlSayyad, Nezar, *Cairo: Histories of a City* (Cambridge, MA: Belknap Press, 2011).

ᶜĀmir, Umniyya, "Niẓām al-iltizām: al-Taḥawwul min al-milkiyya al-ḥukūmiyya ilā ʾl-milkiyya al-khāṣṣa," *al-Rūznāma: al-Ḥawliyya al-Miṣriyya li ʾl-wathāʾiq* 1 (2003), 267–85.

Arabi, Oussama, "The Dawning of the Third Millennium on Sharīᶜa: Egypt's Law No. 1 of 2000, or Women May Divorce at Will," *Arab Law Quarterly* 16 (2001), 2–21.

Atcil, Abdurrahman, "The Route to the Top in the Ottoman İlmiye Hierarchy of the Sixteenth Century," *Bulletin of the School of Oriental & African Studies* 72 (2009), 489–512.

Atcil, Abdurrahman, The Formation of the Ottoman Learned Class and Legal Scholarship (1300–1600), PhD dissertation, University of Chicago, 2010.

Ayalon, David, "Studies in al-Jabartī I: Notes on the Transformation of Mamlūk Society in Egypt under the Ottomans," *Journal of the Economic and Social History of the Orient* 3 (1960), 148–74.

Ballanfat, Paul, "Nîyâzî Mısrî: l'Égypte, station mystique pour un soufi turc du XVIIᵉ siècle," in Rachida Chih and Catherine Mayuer-Jaouen, *Le soufisme à l'époque ottomane, XVIᵉ–XVIIIᵉ siècle* (Cairo: Institut français d'archéologie orientale, 2010), 249–73.

Baldwin, James E., "Prostitution, Islamic Law and Ottoman Societies," *Journal of the Economic and Social History of the Orient* 55 (2012), 117–52.

Baldwin, James E., "Petitioning the Sultan in Ottoman Egypt," *Bulletin of the School of Oriental & African Studies* 75 (2012), 499–524.

Baldwin, James E., "The Deposition of Defterdār Aḥmed Pasha and the Rule of Law in Seventeenth-Century Egypt," *Osmanlı Araştırmaları* 46 (2015), 131–61.

Baldwin, James E., "Elite Conflict and the Urban Environment: Eighteenth-Century Cairo," in Nelida Fuccaro (ed.), *Violence and the City in the Modern Middle East* (Stanford: Stanford University Press, 2016), 41–60.

Barakat, Nora, "Regulating Land Rights in Late Nineteenth-Century Salt: The Limits of Legal Pluralism in Ottoman Property Law," *Journal of the Ottoman and Turkish Studies Association* 2 (2015), 101–19.

Barbir, Karl, *Ottoman Rule in Damascus, 1708–1758* (Princeton: Princeton University Press, 1980).

Barkey, Karen, *Bandits and Bureaucrats: The Ottoman Route to State Centralization* (Ithaca, NY: Cornell University Press, 1994).

Barkey, Karen, "Aspects of Legal Pluralism in the Ottoman Empire," in Lauren Benton and Richard J. Ross (eds), *Legal Pluralism and Empires, 1500–1850* (New York: New York University Press, 2013), 83–107.

Barnes, John R., *An Introduction to Religious Foundations in the Ottoman Empire* (Leiden: Brill, 1986).

Behrens-Abouseif, Doris, *Islamic Architecture in Cairo: An Introduction* (Cairo: American University in Cairo Press, 1989).

Behrens-Abouseif, Doris, *Egypt's Adjustment to Ottoman Rule: Institutions, Waqf and Architecture in Cairo, 16th and 17th Centuries* (Leiden: Brill, 1994).

Ben-Bassat, Yuval, *Petitioning the Sultan: Protests and Justice in Late Ottoman Palestine, 1865–1908* (London: I. B. Tauris, 2013).

Benton, Lauren, *Law and Colonial Cultures: Legal Regimes in World History, 1400–1900* (New York: Cambridge University Press, 2002).

Berkey, Jonathan, *The Transmission of Knowledge in Medieval Cairo* (Princeton: Princeton University Press, 1992).

Berman, Paul Schiff, *Global Legal Pluralism: A Jurisprudence of Law beyond Borders* (New York: Cambridge University Press, 2012).

Black-Michaud, Jacob, *Feuding Societies* (Oxford: Basil Blackwell, 1980).

Boogert, van den, Maurits, "Redress for Ottoman Victims of European Privateers: A Case against the Dutch at the Divan-i Hümayun (1708–1715)," *Turcica* 33 (2001), 91–118.

Braude, Benjamin, "Foundation Myths of the Millet System," in Benjamin Braude and Bernard Lewis (eds), *Christians and Jews in the Ottoman Empire: The Functioning of a Plural Society* (New York: Homes and Meier, 1982), I: 69–88.

Brockelmann, Carl, *Geschichte der arabischen Litteratur* (Weimar and Berlin: Felber, 1898–1902).

Brown, Nathan, *The Rule of Law in the Arab World: Courts in Egypt and the Gulf* (Cambridge: Cambridge University Press, 1997).

Burak, Guy, *The Second Formation of Islamic Law: The Ḥanafī School in the Early Modern Ottoman Empire* (New York: Cambridge University Press, 2015).

Burak, Guy, "Between the Kānūn of Qāytbāy and the Ottoman Yasaq: A Note on the Ottomans' Dynastic Law," *Journal of Islamic Studies* 26 (2015), 1–23.

Burak, Guy, and Jonathan Brown, "Justice between Scholars and the State," unpublished paper delivered at the Hagop Kevorkian Center for Near Eastern Studies, New York University, May 2015.

Buzov, Snjezana, The Lawgiver and His Lawmakers: The Role of Legal Discourse in the Change of Ottoman Imperial Culture, PhD dissertation, University of Chicago, 2005.

Canbakal, Hülya, *Society and Politics in an Ottoman Town: ᶜAyntab in the Seventeenth Century* (Leiden: Brill, 2007).

Carroll, Stuart, *Blood and Violence in Early Modern France* (Oxford: Oxford University Press, 2006).

Casale, Giancarlo, "The Ottoman Administration of the Spice Trade in the Sixteenth-Century Red Sea and Persian Gulf," *Journal of the Economic and Social History of the Orient* 49 (2006), 170–98.

Chamberlain, Michael, *Knowledge and Social Practice in Medieval Damascus, 1190–1350* (Cambridge: Cambridge University Press, 1994).

Chaudhry, Ayesha S., *Domestic Violence and the Islamic Tradition* (Oxford: Oxford University Press, 2013).

Cheta, Omar Youssef, Rule of Merchants: The Practice of Commerce and Law in Late Ottoman Egypt, 1841–1876, PhD dissertation, New York University, 2014.

Chih, Rachida and Catherine Mayeur-Jaouen (eds), *Le soufisme à l'époque ottomane, XVIᵉ–XVIIIᵉ siècle* (Cairo: Institut français d'archéologie orientale, 2010).

Clarke, Morgan, "The Judge as Tragic Hero: Judicial Ethics in Lebanon's Sharīᶜa Courts," *American Ethnologist* 39 (2012), 106–21.

Cohen, David, *Law, Violence and Community in Classical Athens* (Cambridge: Cambridge University Press, 1995).

Coşgel, Metin M. and Boğaç A. Ergene, "The Selection Bias in Court Records: Settlement and Trial in Eighteenth-Century Kastamonu," *Economic History Review* 67 (2014), 517–34.

Coşgel, Metin M. and Boğaç Ergene, "Law and Economics Literature and Ottoman Legal Studies," *Islamic Law and Society* 21 (2014), 114–44.

Crecelius, Daniel, *The Roots of Modern Egypt: A Study of the Regimes of ᶜAli Bey al-Kabir and Muḥammad Bey Abu al-Dhahab, 1760–1775* (Minneapolis: Bibliotheca Islamica, 1981).

Crecelius, Daniel (ed.), *Eighteenth-Century Egypt: The Arabic Manuscript Sources* (Claremont, CA: Regina Books, 1990).

Cuno, Kenneth, "The Origins of Private Ownership of Land in Egypt: A Reppraisal," *International Journal of Middle East Studies* 12 (1980), 245–75.

Cuno, Kenneth, *The Pasha's Peasants: Land, Society and Economy in Lower Egypt, 1740–1858* (Cambridge: Cambridge University Press, 1992).

Cuno, Kenneth, *Modernizing Marriage: Family, Ideology and Law in Nineteenth and Early Twentieth-Century Egypt* (Syracuse, NY: Syracuse University Press, 2015).

Daly, M. W. (ed.), *The Cambridge History of Egypt*, vol. 2: *Modern Egypt from 1517 to the End of the Twentieth Century* (Cambridge: Cambridge University Press, 1999).

Darling, Linda, *Revenue-Raising and Legitimacy: Tax Collection and Finance Administration in the Ottoman Empire, 1560–1660* (Leiden: Brill, 1996).

Darling, Linda, *A History of Social Justice and Political Power in the Middle East: The Circle of Justice from Mesopotamia to Globalization* (New York: Routledge, 2012).

Di-Capua, Yoav, *Gatekeepers of the Arab Past: Historians and History Writing in Twentieth-Century Egypt* (Berkeley: University of California Press, 2009).

Doumani, Beshara, *Rediscovering Palestine: Merchants and Peasants in Jabal Nablus, 1700–1900* (Berkeley: University of California Press, 1995).

Dupret, Baudouin, Maurits Berger and Laila al-Zwaini (eds), *Legal Pluralism in the Arab World* (The Hague: Kluwer Law International, 1999).

Eldem, Edhem, *French Trade in Istanbul in the Eighteenth Century* (Leiden: Brill, 1999).

Ergene, Boğaç, *Local Court, Provincial Society and Justice in the Ottoman Empire: Legal Practice and Dispute Resolution in Çankırı and Kastamonu, 1652–1744* (Leiden: Brill, 2003).

Ergene, Boğaç, "Document Use in Ottoman Courts of Law: Observations from the Sicils of Çankırı and Kastamonu," *Turcica* 37 (2005), 83–111.

Ergene, Boğaç, "Social Identity and Patterns of Interaction in the Sharīᶜa Court of Kastamonu (1740–44), *Islamic Law and Society* 15 (2008), 20–54.

Ergene, Boğaç, "Why did Ümmü Gülsüm go to Court? Ottoman Legal Practice between History and Anthropology," *Islamic Law and Society* 17 (2010), 215–44.

Ergene, Boğaç, "Qanun and Sharīᶜa," in Rudolph Peters and Peri Bearman (eds), *The Ashgate Research Companion to Islamic Law* (Farnham: Ashgate, 2014), 109–20.

Fadel, Mohammad, "The Social Logic of Taqlīd and the Rise of the Mukhtaṣar," *Islamic Law and Society* 3 (1996), 193–233.

Fahmy, Khaled, *All the Pasha's Men: Mehmed Ali, His Army and the Making of Modern Egypt* (Cambridge: Cambridge University Press, 1997).

Fahmy, Khaled, "The Anatomy of Justice: Forensic Medicine and Criminal Law in Nineteenth-Century Egypt," *Islamic Law and Society* 6 (1999), 224–71.

Fahmy, Khaled, "The Police and the People in Nineteenth-Century Egypt," *Die Welt des Islams* 39 (1999), 340–77.

Fahmy, Khaled, *Bodies of Law: Science and Religion in Modern Egypt* (Berkeley: University of California Press, forthcoming).

Faraḥāt, Muḥammad Nūr, *al-Qaḍāʾ al-sharᶜī fī ʾl-ᶜaṣr al-ᶜUthmānī* (Cairo: al-Hayʾa al-Miṣriyya al-ᶜāma li ʾl-kitāb, 1988).

Faraḥāt, Muḥammad Nūr, *al-Tārīkh al-ijtimāᶜī li ʾl-qānūn fī Miṣr al-ḥadītha*, 2nd ed. (Kuwait: Dār saᶜād al-ṣabāḥ, 1993).

Faroqhi, Suraiya, "Political Initiatives 'From the Bottom Up' in the Sixteenth- and Seventeenth-Century Ottoman Empire: Some Evidence for their Existence," in Hans Georg Majer (ed.), *Osmanistische Studien zur Wirtschafts- und Sozialgeschichte: In Memoriam Vanco Boskov* (Wiesbaden: O. Harrassowitz, 1986), 24–33.

Faroqhi, Suraiya, "Political Activity among Ottoman Taxpayers and the Problem of Sultanic Legitimation (1570–1650)," *Journal of the Economic and Social History of the Orient* 35 (1992), 1–39.

Faroqhi, Suraiya, *Pilgrims and Sultans: The Hajj under the Ottomans* (London: I. B. Tauris, 2014).

Fay, Mary Ann, "Women and Waqf: Property, Power and the Domain of Gender in Eighteenth-Century Egypt," in Madeline Zilfi (ed.), *Women in the Ottoman Empire: Middle Eastern Women in the Early Modern Era* (Leiden: Brill, 1997), 28–47.

Fay, Mary Ann, "From Concubines to Capitalists: Women, Property and Power in Eighteenth-Century Cairo," *Journal of Women's History* 10 (1998), 118–40.

Fitzgerald, Timothy J., Ottoman Methods of Conquest: Legal Imperialism and the City of Aleppo, 1480–1570, PhD dissertation, Harvard University, 2008.

Fuess, Albrecht, "Ẓulm by Maẓālim? The Political Implications of the Use of the Maẓālim Jurisdiction by the Mamluk Sultans," *Mamluk Studies Review* 13 (2009), 121–47.

Gambetta, Diego, *The Sicilian Mafia: The Business of Private Protection* (Cambridge, MA: Harvard University Press, 1993).

Gelder, van, Geert Jan, "Shihāb al-Dīn al-Khafājī," in Joseph E. Lowry and Devin J. Stewart, *Essays in Arabic Literary Biography: 1350–1850* (Wiesbaden: Harrassowitz, 2009), 251–62.

Gerber, Haim, "Social and Economic Position of Women in an Ottoman City: Bursa, 1600–1700," *International Journal of Middle East Studies* 12 (1980), 231–44.

Gerber, Haim, "The Muslim Law of Partnerships in Ottoman Court Records," *Studia Islamica* 53 (1981), 109–19.

Gerber, Haim, *State, Society and Law in Islam: Ottoman Law in Comparative Perspective* (Albany: State University of New York Press, 1994).

Gerber, Haim, *Islamic Law and Culture, 1600–1840* (Leiden: Brill, 1999).

Gerber, Haim, *Crossing Borders: Jews and Muslims in Ottoman Law, Economy and Society* (Istanbul: Isis Press, 2008).

Gerber, Haim, "The Public Sphere and Civil Society in the Ottoman Empire," in Miriam Hoexter, Shmuel N. Eisenstadt, and Nehemia Levtzion (eds), *The Public Sphere in Muslim Societies* (Albany, NY: State University of New York Press, 2002), 65–82.

Ghazzal, Zouhair, *The Grammars of Adjudication: The Economics of Judicial Decision-Making in fin-de-siècle Ottoman Beirut and Damascus* (Beirut: Institut français du Proche-Orient, 2007).

Al-Ghitani, Gamal, *Zayni Barakat*, trans. Farouk Abdel Wahab (Cairo: American University in Cairo Press, 2006).

Ghobrial, John-Paul A., A Word of Stories: Information in Constantinople and Beyond in the Seventeenth Century, PhD dissertation, Princeton University, 2010.

Gilsenan, Michael, "Law, Arbitrariness and the Power of the Lords of North Lebanon," *History and Anthropology* 1 (1985), 381–98.

Ginio, Eyal, "The Administration of Criminal Justice in Ottoman Selānik (Salonica) during the Eighteenth Century," *Turcica* 30 (1998), 185–209.

Ginio, Eyal, "Living on the Margins of Charity: Coping with Poverty in an Ottoman Provincial City," in Michael Bonner, Mine Ener and Amy Singer (eds), *Poverty and Charity in Middle Eastern Contexts* (Albany, NY: State University of New York Press, 2003), 165–84.

Ginio, Eyal, "Patronage, Intervention and Violence in the Legal Process in Eighteenth-Century Salonica and its Province," in Ron Shaham (ed.), *Law, Custom and Statute in the Muslim World: Studies in Honor of Aharon Layish* (Leiden: Brill, 2007), 111–30.

Girgis, Magdī, *al-Qaḍā᾽ al-Qibṭī fī Miṣr: Dirāsa tārīkhiyya* (Cairo: Mīrīt li ᾽l-nashr wa ᾽l-maᶜlūmāt, 1999).

Goldish, Matt, *Jewish Questions: Responsa on Sephardic Life in the Early Modern Period* (Princeton: Princeton University Press, 2008).

Gradeva, Rossitsa, "Orthodox Christians in the Kadi Courts: the Practice of the Sofia Sheriat Court, Seventeenth Century," *Islamic Law and Society* 4 (1997), 37–69.

Gradeva, Rossitsa, "On Judicial Hierarchy in the Ottoman Empire: The Case of Sofia from the Seventeenth to the Beginning of the Eighteenth Century," in Muhammad Khalid Masud, Rudolph Peters, and David S. Powers (eds), *Dispensing Justice in Islam: Qadis and their Judgments* (Leiden: Brill, 2006), 271–98.

Gradeva, Rossitsa, "A Kadi Court in the Balkans: Sofia in the Seventeenth and Early Eighteenth Centuries," in Christine Woodhead (ed.), *The Ottoman World* (Abingdon: Routledge, 2012), 57–71.

Griffiths, John, "What is Legal Pluralism?" *Journal of Legal Pluralism and Unofficial Law* 24 (1986), 1–55.

Guenther, Alan M., "Hanafi Fiqh in Mughal India: The Fatāwā-i ᶜĀlamgīrī," in Richard M. Eaton (ed.), *India's Islamic Traditions, 711–1750* (New Delhi: Oxford University Press, 2003), 209–30.

Hallaq, Wael B., "Was the Gate of Ijtihād Closed?" *International Journal of Middle East Studies* 16 (1984), 3–41.

Hallaq, Wael B., "The Qāḍī's Dīwān (Sijill) before the Ottomans," *Bulletin of the School of Oriental & African Studies* 61 (1998), 415–36.

Hallaq, Wael B., *Sharīᶜa: Theory, Practice, Transformations* (Cambridge: Cambridge University Press, 2009).

Hallaq, Wael B., *The Impossible State: Islam, Politics, and Modernity's Moral Predicament* (New York: Columbia University Press, 2013).

Hanna, Nelly, *Construction Work in Ottoman Cairo* (Cairo: Institut français d'archéologie orientale, 1984).

Hanna, Nelly, *Habiter au Caire: la maison moyenne et ses habitants aux XVIIe et XVIIIe siècles* (Cairo: Institut français d'archéologie orientale, 1991).

Hanna, Nelly, "The Administration of Courts in Ottoman Cairo," in Nelly Hanna (ed.), *The State and its Servants: Administration in Egypt from Ottoman Times to the Present* (Cairo: American University in Cairo Press, 1995), 44–59.

Hanna, Nelly, *Making Big Money in 1600: The Life and Times of Ismaᶜil Abu Taqiyya, Egyptian Merchant* (Syracuse, NY: Syracuse University Press, 1998).

Hanna, Nelly, "Coffee and Coffee Merchants in Cairo, 1580–1630," in Michel Tuchscherer (ed.), *Le commerce du café avant l'ère des plantations coloniales: espaces, résaux, sociétés, XVe–XIXe siècle* (Cairo: Institut français d'archéologie orientale, 2001), 91–101.

Hanna, Nelly, "The Chronicles of Ottoman Egypt: History or Entertainment?," in Hugh

Kennedy (ed.), *The Historiography of Islamic Egypt, c. 950–1800* (Leiden: Brill, 2001), 237–50.

Hanna, Nelly, *In Praise of Books: A Cultural History of Cairo's Middle Class, Sixteenth to the Eighteenth Century* (Syracuse, NY: Syracuse University Press, 2003).

Hanna, Nelly, *Artisan Entrepreneurs in Cairo and Early Modern Capitalism, 1600–1800* (Syracuse, NY: Syracuse University Press, 2011).

Hashmi, Irfana, Patronage, Legal Practice and Space in al-Azhar, 1500–1650, PhD dissertation, New York University, 2014.

Hathaway, Jane, "Sultans, Pashas, Taqwīms and Mühimmes: A Reconsideration of Chronicle Writing in Eighteenth-Century Ottoman Egypt," in Daniel Crecelius (ed.), *Eighteenth-Century Egypt: The Arabic Manuscript Sources* (Claremont, CA: Regina Books, 1990).

Hathaway, Jane, "The Role of the Kızlar Ağası in 17th–18th Century Ottoman Egypt," *Studia Islamica* 75 (1992), 141–58.

Hathaway, Jane, "The Wealth and Influence of an Exiled Ottoman Eunuch in Egypt: The Waqf Inventory of ᶜAbbas Agha," *Journal of the Economic and Social History of the Orient* 37 (1994), 293–317.

Hathaway, Jane, *The Politics of Households in Ottoman Egypt: The Rise of the Qazdağlıs* (Cambridge: Cambridge University Press, 1997).

Hathaway, Jane, "Exiled Harem Eunuchs as Proponents of the Hanafi Madhhab in Ottoman Cairo," *Annales islamologiques* 37 (2003), 191–9.

Hathaway, Jane, *Beshir Agha: Chief Eunuch of the Ottoman Imperial Harem* (Oxford: Oneworld, 2005).

Heller, Daniella Talmon, "The Shaykh and the Community: Popular Hanbalite Islam in 12th–13th Century Jabal Nablus and Jabal Qasyūn," *Studia Islamica* 79 (1994), 103–20.

Heyd, Uriel, "Some Aspects of the Ottoman Fetvā," *Bulletin of the School of Oriental & African Studies* 32 (1969), 35–56.

Heyd, Uriel, *Studies in Old Ottoman Criminal Law*, ed. V. L. Ménage (Oxford: Clarendon Press, 1973).

Heywood, Colin, "The Red Sea Trade and Ottoman Wakf Support for the Population of Mecca and Medina in the Later Seventeenth Century: Notes on an Unpublished Ottoman Shipping Register," in Abdeljelil Temini (ed.), *La vie sociale dans les provinces arabes à l'époque ottoman* (Zaghouan: Markaz al-dirāsāt wa ᵓl-buḥūth al-ᶜuthmāniyya wa ᵓl-mūrīskiyya wa ᵓl-tawthīq wa ᵓl-maᶜlūmāt, 1988), 165–84.

Heywood, Colin, "The Via Egnatia in the Ottoman Period: The Menzilhanes of the Sol Kol in the Late Seventeenth / Early Eighteenth Century," in Elizabeth Zachariadou (ed.), *The Via Egnatia under Ottoman Rule, 1380–1699* (Rethymnon: Crete University Press, 1996), 129–44.

Hoexter, Miriam, "Qāḍī, Muftī and Ruler: Their Roles in the Development of Islamic Law," in Ron Shaham (ed.), *Law, Custom and Statute in the Muslim World: Studies in Honor of Aharon Layish* (Leiden: Brill, 2006), 67–85.

Holt, P. M., "The Exalted Lineage of Riḍwān Bey: Some Observations on a Seventeenth-Century Mamlūk Genealogy," *Bulletin of the School of Oriental & African Studies* 22 (1959), 221–30.

Holt, P. M., "The Beylicate in Ottoman Egypt during the Seventeenth Century," *Bulletin of the School of Oriental & African Studies* 24 (1961), 214–48.

Holt, P. M., "The Career of Küçük Muḥammad (1676–94)," *Bulletin of the School of Oriental & African Studies* 26 (1963), 269–87.

Holt, P. M., *Egypt and the Fertile Cresecent, 1516–1922* (London: Longmans, 1966).

Ibrahim, Ahmed Fekry, School Boundaries and Social Utility in Islamic Law: The Theory and Practice of Talfīq and Tatabbuᶜ al-Rukhaṣ in Egypt, PhD dissertation, Georgetown University, 2011.

Ibrahim, Ahmed Fekry, "Al-Shaᶜrānī's Response to Legal Purism: A Theory of Legal Pluralism," *Islamic Law and Society* 20 (2013), 110–40.

Ibrahim, Ahmed Fekry, *Pragmatism in Islamic Law: A Social and Intellectual History* (Syracuse, NY: Syracuse University Press, 2015).

Ibrahim, Ahmed Fekry, "The Codification Episteme in Islamic Juristic Discourse between Inertia and Change," *Islamic Law and Society* 22 (2015), 157–220.

Imber, Colin, *The Ottoman Empire, 1300–1650: The Structure of Power*, 2nd ed. (Basingstoke: Palgrave Macmillan, 2009).

Imber, Colin, *Ebuʾs-suᶜud: The Islamic Legal Tradition* (Stanford: Stanford University Press, 2009).

İnalcık, Halil, "Maḥkama / Ottoman Empire / Early Centuries," *Encyclopaedia of Islam*, 2nd ed. (Brill Online).

İnalcık, Halil, "Şikayet Hakkı: Arz-ı Hal ve Arz-ı Mahzarlar," in *Osmanlı'da Devlet, Hukuk, Adalet* (Istanbul: Eren, 2000), 49–71.

Irwin, Robert, "The Privatization of Justice under the Circassian Mamluks," *Mamluk Studies Review* 6 (2002), 63–70.

ᶜĪsā, ᶜAbd al-Rāziq Ibrāhīm, *Tārīkh al-qaḍāʾ fī Miṣr al-ᶜUthmāniyya, 1517–1798* (Cairo: al-Hayʾa al-Miṣriyya al-ᶜāma li ʾl-kitāb, 1998).

İslamoğlu-İnan, Huri, *State and Peasant in the Ottoman Empire: Agrarian Power Relations and Regional Economic Development in Ottoman Anatolia during the Sixteenth Century* (Leiden: Brill, 1994).

Ivanova, Svetlana, "The Divorce between Zubaida Hatun and Esseid Osman Ağa: Women in the Eighteenth-Century Sharīᶜa Court of Rumelia," in Amira El Azhary Sonbol (ed.), *Women, the Family and Divorce Laws in Islamic History* (Syracuse, NY: Syracuse University Press, 1996), 112–25.

Ivanova, Svetlana, "Muslim and Christian Women before the Kadı Court: Marriage Problems," *Oriente Moderno* n.s. 18 (1999), 161–76.

İzgi, Cevat, *Osmanlı Medreselerinde İlim* (Istanbul: İz, 1997).

Jackson, Sherman, "Kramer versus Kramer in a Tenth/Sixteenth-Century Egyptian Court: Post-Formative Jurisprudence between Exigency and Law," *Islamic Law and Society* 8 (2001), 27–51.

Jennings, Ronald, "The Office of Vekil (Wakil) in 17th-Century Ottoman Sharīᶜa Courts," *Studia Islamica* 42 (1975), 147–69.

Jennings, Ronald, "Women in Early 17th-Century Ottoman Judicial Records: The Sharīᶜa Court of Anatolian Kayseri," *Journal of the Economic and Social History of the Orient* 18 (1975), 53–114.

Jennings, Ronald, "Kadi, Court and Legal Procedure in 17th-Century Ottoman Kayseri: The Kadi and the Legal System," *Studia Islamica* 48 (1978), 133–72.

Jennings, Ronald, "Zimmis (Non-Muslims) in Early 17th-Century Ottoman Judicial Records," *Journal of the Economic and Social History of the Orient* 21 (1978), 225–93.

Jennings, Ronald, "Limitations of the Judicial Powers of the Kadi in 17th-Century Ottoman Kayseri," *Studia Islamica* 50 (1979), 151–84.

Jennings, Ronald, *Christians and Muslims in Ottoman Cyprus and the Mediterranean World, 1571–1640* (New York: New York University Press, 1993).

Jennings, Ronald, "Divorce in the Ottoman Sharīᶜa Court of Cyprus, 1580–1640," *Studia Islamica* 78 (1993), 155–67.

Jennings, Ronald, *Studies on Ottoman Social History in the Sixteenth and Seventeenth Centuries: Women, Zimmis and Sharia Courts in Kayseri, Cyprus and Trabzon* (Istanbul: Isis Press, 1999).

Johansen, Baber, *The Islamic Law on Land Tax and Rent: The Peasants' Loss of Property Rights as Interpreted in the Hanafite Legal Literature of the Mamluk and Ottoman Periods* (London: Croom Helm, 1988).

Johansen, Baber, "Verité et torture: Ius commune et droit musulman entre le Xe et le XIIIe siècle," in François Héritier (ed.), *De la violence* (Paris: Odile Jacob, 1996), 123–68.

Johansen, Baber, "Legal Literature and the Problem of Change: The Case of the Land Rent," in Baber Johansen, *Contingency in a Sacred Law: Legal and Ethical Norms in the Muslim Fiqh* (Leiden: Brill, 1999), 446–64.

Johansen, Baber, "Signs as Evidence: The Doctrine of Ibn Taymiyya and Ibn Qayyim al-Jawziyya on Proof," *Islamic Law and Society* 9 (2002), 168–93.

Judd, Stephen C., *Religious Scholars and the Umayyads: Piety-Minded Supporters of the Marwānid Caliphate* (Abingdon: Routledge, 2014).

Kafadar, Cemal, Yeniçeri–Esnaf Relations: Solidarity and Conflict, MA thesis, McGill University, 1981.

Kaminsky, Howard, "The Noble Feud in the Later Middle Ages," *Past and Present* 177 (2002), 55–83.

Kermeli, Eugenia, "Ebūʾs-suᶜūd's Definitions of Church Vaḳfs: Theory and Practice in Ottoman Law," in Robert Gleave and Eugenia Kermeli (eds), *Islamic Law: Theory and Practice* (London: I. B. Tauris, 1997), 141–56.

Kermeli, Eugenia, "The Right to Choice: Ottoman, Ecclesiastical and Communal Justice in Ottoman Greece," in Christine Woodhead (ed.), *The Ottoman World* (Abingdon: Routledge, 2012), 347–61.

Khoury, Dina Rizk, *State and Provincial Society in the Ottoman Empire: Mosul, 1540–1834* (Cambridge: Cambridge University Press, 1997).

Kracke, Edward A., Jr., "Early Visions of Justice for the Humble," *Journal of the American Oriental Society* 96 (1976), 492–8.

Kuran, Timur, *The Long Divergence: How Islamic Law held back the Middle East* (Princeton: Princeton University Press, 2011).

Laiou, Sophia, "Diverging Realities of a Christian Vakıf, Sixteenth to Eighteenth Centuries," *Turkish Historical Review* 3 (2012), 1–18.

Lamdan, Ruth, *A Separate People: Jewish Women in Palestine, Syria and Egypt during the Sixteenth Century* (Leiden: Brill, 2000).

Lange, Christian, "Legal and Cultural Aspects of Ignominious Parading (Tashhīr) in Islam," *Islamic Law and Society* 14 (2007), 81–108.

Lange, Christian, "Changes in the Office of Ḥisba under the Seljuqs," in Christian Lange and Songül Mecit (eds), *The Seljuqs: Politics, Society and Culture* (Edinburgh: Edinburgh University Press, 2011), 157–81.

Leeuwen, van, Richard, *Waqfs and Urban Structures: The Case of Ottoman Damascus* (Leiden: Brill, 1999).

Lellouch, Benjamin, *Les ottomans en Égypte: Historiens et conquérants au XVIe siècle* (Leuven: Peeters, 2006).

Lellouch, Benjamin and Nicolas Michel (eds), *Conquête ottoman de l'Égypte (1517): Arrière-plan, impact, échos* (Leiden: Brill, 2013).

Mandaville, Jon E., "Usurious Piety: The Cash Waqf Controversy in the Ottoman Empire," *International Journal of Middle East Studies* 10 (1979), 289–308.

Marcus, Abraham, "Privacy in Eighteenth-Century Aleppo: The Limits of Cultural Ideals," *International Journal of Middle East Studies* 18 (1986), 165–83.

Marcus, Abraham, *The Middle East on the Eve of Modernity: Aleppo in the Eighteenth Century* (New York: Columbia University Press, 1989).

Margoliouth, G., *Catalogue of the Hebrew and Samaritan Manuscripts in the British Museum* (London: British Museum, 1899–1915).

Marino, Brigitte, "Les correspondances (murāsalāt) adressées par le juge de Damas à ses substituts (1750–1860)," in Brigitte Marino (ed.), *Études sur les villes du Proche-Orient, XVIe–XIXe siècle: hommage à André Raymond* (Damascus: Institut français d'études arabes, 2001), 91–111.

Marsot, Afaf Lutfi al-Sayyid, *Egypt in the Reign of Muhammad Ali* (Cambridge: Cambridge University Press, 1984).

Marsot, Afaf Lutfi al-Sayyid, "Power and Authority in Late Eighteenth-Century Egypt," in Nelly Hanna and Raouf Abbas (eds), *Society and Economy in Egypt and the Eastern Mediterranean, 1600–1900: Essays in Honor of André Raymond* (Cairo: American University in Cairo Press, 2005), 41–9.

Marsot, Afaf Lutfi al-Sayyid, *A History of Egypt from the Arab Conquest to the Present Day*, 2nd ed. (Cambridge: Cambridge University Press, 2009).

Masters, Bruce, *Christians and Jews in the Ottoman Arab World: The Roots of Sectarianism* (Cambridge: Cambridge University Press, 2001).

Masters, Bruce, *The Arabs of the Ottoman Empire, 1516–1918: A Social and Cultural History* (New York: Cambridge University Press, 2013).

Masud, Muhammad Khalid, Rudolph Peters, and David S. Powers (eds), *Dispensing Justice in Islam: Qāḍīs and their Judgments* (Leiden: Brill, 2006).

Merry, Sally Engle, *Getting Justice and Getting Even: Legal Consciousness among Working-Class Americans* (Chicago: University of Chicago Press, 1990).

Meshal, Reem, "Antagonistic Sharīᶜas and the Construction of Orthodoxy in Sixteenth-Century Ottoman Cairo," *Journal of Islamic Studies* 21 (2010), 183–212.

Meshal, Reem, *Sharia and the Making of the Modern Egyptian: Islamic Law and Custom in the Courts of Ottoman Cairo* (Cairo: American University in Cairo Press, 2014).

Messick, Brinkley, *The Calligraphic State: Textual Domination and History in a Muslim Society* (Berkeley: University of California Press, 1993).

Michel, Nicolas, "Les paysans et leur juge dans la campagne d'Esna (Haute-Egypte) au XVIIIe siècle," *Studia Islamica* 90 (2000), 125–51.

Mikhail, Alan, "An Irrigated Empire: The View from Ottoman Fayyum," *International Journal of Middle East Studies* 42 (2010), 569–90.

Mikhail, Alan, *Nature and Empire in Ottoman Egypt: An Environmental History* (New York: Cambridge University Press, 2011).

Mīlād, Salwā ᶜAlī, *al-Wathāʾiq al-ᶜUthmāniyya: Dirāsa arshīfiyya wathāʾiqiyya li sijillāt maḥkamat al-Bāb al-ᶜĀlī* (Alexandria: Dār al-thaqāfa al-ᶜilmiyya, 2001).

Mīlād, Salwā ᶜAlī, *al-Qaḍāʾ wa ʾl-tawthīq fī ʾl-ᶜaṣr al-ᶜUthmānī: Dirāsa wathāʾiqiyya arshīfiyya li sijillāt maḥkamat al-Ṣāliḥiyya al-Najmiyya* (Alexandria: Dār al-thaqāfa al-ᶜilmiyya, 2008).

Miller, William Ian, *Bloodtaking and Peacemaking: Feud, Law and Society in Saga Iceland* (Chicago: University of Chicago Press, 1990).

Minkov, Anton, *Conversion to Islam in the Balkans: Kisve Bahası Petitions and Ottoman Social Life, 1670–1730* (Leiden: Brill, 2004).

Müller, Christian, "Redressing Injustice: Maẓālim Jurisdictions at the Umayyad Court of Cordoba (Eighth–Eleventh Centuries CE)," in Albrecht Fuess and Jan-Peter Hartung, *Court Cultures in the Muslim World: Seventh to Nineteenth Centuries* (Abingdon: Routledge, 2014), 93–104.

Murphy, Jane H., Improving the Mind and Delighting the Spirit: Jabarti and the Sciences in Eighteenth-Century Ottoman Cairo, PhD dissertation, Princeton University, 2006.

Murphy, Jane H., "Aḥmad al-Damanhūrī (1689–1778) and the Utility of Expertise in Early Modern Ottoman Egypt," *Osiris* 25 (2010), 85–103.

El-Nahal, Gamal, *The Judicial Administration of Ottoman Egypt in the Seventeenth Century* (Minneapolis: Bibliotheca Islamica, 1979).

Necipoğlu, Gülrü, *Architecture, Ceremonial and Power: The Topkapı Palace in the Fifteenth and Sixteenth Centuries* (Cambridge, MA: MIT Press, 1991).

Nielsen, Jorgen, *Secular Justice in an Islamic State: Maẓālim under the Baḥrī Mamlūks 662/1264–789/1387* (Leiden: Nederlands Historisch-Archaeologisch Instituut te Istanbul, 1985).

Othman, Aida, And Ṣulḥ is Best: Amicable Settlement and Dispute Resolution in Islamic Law, PhD dissertation, Harvard University, 2005.

Othman, Aida, "And Amicable Settlement is Best: Ṣulḥ and Dispute Resolution in Islamic Law," *Arab Law Quarterly* 21 (2007), 64–90.

Peirce, Leslie, *Morality Tales: Law and Gender in the Ottoman Court of Aintab* (Berkeley: University of California Press, 2003).

Peters, Rudolph, "The Battered Dervishes of Bab Zuwayla: A Religious Riot in 18th-Century Cairo," in Nehemia Levtzion and John Voll (eds), *Eighteenth-Century Renewal and Reform in Islam* (Syracuse, NY: Syracuse University Press, 1987), 93–115.

Peters, Rudolph, "Murder on the Nile: Homicide Trials in 19th-Century Egyptian Sharīᶜa Courts," *Die Welt des Islams* 30 (1990), 95–115.

Peters, Rudolph, "Islamic and Secular Criminal Law in Nineteenth-Century Egypt: The Role and Function of the Qāḍī," *Islamic Law and Society* 4 (1997), 70–90.

Peters, Rudolph, "For His Correction and as a Deterrent Example for Others: Mehmed ᶜAlī's First Criminal Legislation (1829–1830)," *Islamic Law and Society* 6 (1999), 164–92.

Peters, Rudolph, "Administrators and Magistrates: The Development of a Secular Judiciary in Egypt, 1842–1871," *Die Welt des Islams* 39 (1999), 378–97.

Peters, Rudolph, "An Administrator's Nightmare: Feuding Families in Nineteenth-Century Bahariyya Oasis," in Baudouin Dupret, Maurits Berger, and Laila al-Zwaini (eds), *Legal Pluralism in the Arab World* (The Hague: Kluwer Law International, 1999), 135–44.

Peters, Rudolph, "From Jurists' Law to Statute Law or What Happens When the Sharīᶜa is Codified," *Mediterranean Politics* 7/3 (2002), 82–95.

Peters, Rudolph, *Crime and Punishment in Islamic Law: Theory and Practice from the Sixteenth to the Twenty-First Century* (Cambridge: Cambridge University Press, 2005).

Peters, Rudolph, "What Does it Mean to be an Official Madhhab? Hanafism and the Ottoman Empire," in Peri Bearman, Rudolph Peters, and Frank E. Vogel (eds), *The Islamic School of Law: Evolution, Devolution and Progress* (Cambridge, MA: Harvard University Press, 2005), 147–58.

Petry, Carl, "Royal Justice in Mamlūk Cairo: Contrasting Motives of Two Sulṭāns," in *Saber religioso y poder político en el Islam: actas del simposio internacional, Granada, 15–18 octubre 1991* (Madrid: Agencia española de cooperación internacional, 1994), 197–211.

Powers, David S., "On Judicial Review in Islamic Law," *Law & Society Review* 26 (1992), 315–41.

Powers, David S., "Kadijustiz or Qāḍī-Justice? A Paternity Dispute from Fourteenth-Century Morocco," *Islamic Law and Society* 1 (1994), 332–66.

Powers, David S., *Law, Society and Culture in the Maghrib, 1300–1500* (Cambridge: Cambridge University Press, 2002).

Al-Qattan, Najwa, "Dhimmīs in the Muslim Court: Legal Autonomy and Religious Discrimination," *International Journal of Middle East Studies* 31 (1999), 429–44.

Rabbat, Nasser, *The Citadel of Cairo: A New Interpretation of Royal Mamluk Architecture* (Leiden: Brill, 1995).

Rafeq, Abdul-Karim, "City and Countryside in a Traditional Setting: The Case of Damascus in the First Quarter of the Eighteenth Century," in Thomas Philipp (ed.), *The Syrian Land in the 18th and 19th Century: The Common and the Specific in the Historical Experience* (Stuttgart: Franz Steiner Verlag, 1992), 295–332.

Rafeq, Abdul-Karim, "The Syrian ᶜUlamāᵓ, Ottoman Law, and Islamic Sharīᶜa," *Turcica* 26 (1994), 9–32.

Rafeq, Abdul-Karim, "Relations between the Syrian ᶜUlamāᵓ and the Ottoman State in the Eighteenth Century," *Oriente Moderno* n.s. 18 (1999), 67–95.

Rafeq, Abdul-Karim, "The Application of Islamic Law in the Ottoman Courts in Damascus: The Case of the Rental of Waqf Land," in Muḥammad Khalid Masud, Rudolph Peters, and David S. Powers (eds), *Dispensing Justice in Islam: Qāḍīs and their Judgments* (Leiden: Brill, 2006), 411–25.

Rapoport, Yossef, "Legal Diversity in the Age of Taqlīd: The Four Chief Qāḍīs under the Mamluks," *Islamic Law and Society* 10 (2003), 210–28.

Rapoport, Yossef, "Royal Justice and Religious Law: Siyāsah and Sharīᶜah under the Mamluks," *Mamluk Studies Review* 16 (2012), 71–102.

Raymond, André, "Essai de geographie des quartiers de residence aristocratique au Caire au XVIIIᵉ siècle," *Journal of the Economic and Social History of the Orient* 6 (1963), 58–103.

Raymond, André, "Une revolution au Caire sous les mamelouks: la crise de 1123/1711," *Annales islamologiques* 6 (1966), 95–120.

Raymond, André, "The Opuscule of Shaykh ᶜAli al-Shadhili: A Source for the History of the 1711 Crisis in Cairo," in Daniel Crecelius (ed.), *Eighteenth-Century Egypt: The Arabic Manuscript Sources* (Claremont, CA: Regina Books, 1990), 25–38.

Raymond, André, "Soldiers in Trade: The Case of Ottoman Cairo," *British Journal of Middle Eastern Studies* 18 (1991), 16–37.

Raymond, André, *Artisans et commerçants au Caire au XVIIIᵉ siècle* (Cairo: Institut français de l'archéologie orientale, 1999).

Raymond, André, *Cairo*, trans. Willard Wood (Cambridge, MA: Harvard University Press, 2000).

Raymond, André, "Une famille des grands négociants en café au Caire dans la première moitié du XVIIIᵉ siècle: les Sharāybī," in Michel Tuchscherer (ed.), *Le commerce du café avant l'ère des plantations coloniales: espaces, résaux, sociétés, XVᵉ–XIXᵉ siècle* (Cairo: Institut français d'archéologie orientale, 2001), 111–24.

Reichmuth, Stefan, *The World of Murtaḍā al-Zabīdī: Life, Networks and Writings* (Cambridge: Gibb Memorial Trust, 2009).

Reinhart, A. Kevin, "Molla Hüsrev: Ottoman Jurist and Uṣūlī," in Andreas Christmann and Robert Gleave (eds), *Studies in Islamic Law: A Festschrift for Colin Imber* (Oxford: Oxford University Press, 2007), 245–80.

Repp, Richard, *The Müfti of Istanbul: A Study in the Development of the Ottoman Learned Hierarchy* (London: Ithaca Press, 1986).

Repp, Richard, "Qanun and Sharīᶜa in the Ottoman Context," in Aziz al-Azmeh (ed.), *Islamic Law: Social and Historical Contexts* (London: Routledge, 1988), 124–45.

Rosen, Lawrence, *The Anthropology of Justice: Law as Culture in Islamic Society* (Cambridge: Cambridge University Press, 1989).

Rubin, Avi, "Legal Borrowing and its Impact on Ottoman Legal Culture in the Late Nineteenth Century," *Continuity and Change* 22 (2007), 279–303.

Rubin, Avi, *Ottoman Nizamiye Courts: Law and Modernity* (New York: Palgrave Macmillan, 2011).

Salzmann, Ariel, "An Ancien Régime Revisited: Privatization and Political Economy in the Eighteenth-Century Ottoman Empire," *Politics & Society* 21 (1993), 393–423.

Salzmann, Ariel, *Tocqueville in the Ottoman Empire: Rival Paths to the Modern State* (Leiden: Brill, 2004).

Sartori, Paolo and Ido Shahar, "Legal Pluralism in Muslim-Majority Countries: Mapping the Terrain," *Journal of the Economic and Social History of the Orient* 55 (2012), 637–63.

Schacht, Joseph, *An Introduction to Islamic Law* (Oxford: Clarendon Press, 1982).

Shaham, Ron, "Shopping for Legal Forums: Christians and Family Law in Modern Egypt," in Muhammad Khalid Masud, Rudolph Peters and David S. Powers, *Dispensing Justice in Islam: Qāḍīs and their Judgments* (Leiden: Brill, 2006), 451–69.

Shaham, Ron, "Women as Expert Witnesses in Pre-Modern Islamic Courts," in Ron Shaham (ed.), *Law, Custom and Statute in the Muslim World: Essays in Honor of Aharon Layish* (Leiden: Brill, 2007), 41–65.

Shaham, Ron, *The Expert Witness in Islamic Courts: Medicine and Crafts in the Service of Law* (Chicago: University of Chicago Press, 2010).

Shahar, Ido, "Legal Pluralism and the Study of Sharīʿa Courts," *Islamic Law and Society* 15 (2008), 112–41.

Shalakany, Amr, "Islamic Legal Histories," *Berkeley Journal of Middle Eastern & Islamic Law* 1 (2008), 1–82.

Shaw, Stanford J., *The Financial and Administrative Organization and Development of Ottoman Egypt, 1517–1798* (Princeton: Princeton University Press, 1962).

Shūmān, Muḥsin ʿAlī, *al-Yāhūd fī Miṣr al-ʿUthmāniyya ḥattā ʾl-qarn al-tāsiʿ ʿashar* (Cairo: al-Hayʾa al-Miṣriyya al-ʿāma li ʾl-kitāb, 2000).

Singer, Amy, *Palestinian Peasants and Ottoman Officials: Rural Administration around Sixteenth-Century Jerusalem* (Cambridge: Cambridge University Press, 1994).

Sirriyeh, Elizabeth, *Sufi Visionary of Ottoman Damascus: ʿAbd al-Ghanī al-Nābulusī, 1641–1731* (Abingdon: RoutledgeCurzon, 2005).

Smail, Daniel Lord, *The Consumption of Justice: Emotions, Publicity and Legal Culture in Marseille, 1264–1423* (Ithaca, NY: Cornell University Press, 2003).

Sonbol, Amira, "Rape and Law in Ottoman and Modern Egypt," in Madeline C. Zilfi (ed.), *Women in the Ottoman Empire: Middle Eastern Women in the Early Modern Era* (Leiden: Brill, 1997).

Sonbol, Amira, "Women in Shariʿah Courts: A Historical and Methodological Discussion," *Fordham International Law Journal* 27 (2003), 225–53.

Sood, Gagan, "The Informational Fabric of Eighteenth-Century India and the Middle East: Couriers, Intermediaries and Postal Communication," *Modern Asian Studies* 43 (2009), 1085–116.

Staffa, Susan Jane, *Conquest and Fusion: The Social Evolution of Cairo,* A.D. *642–1850* (Leiden: Brill, 1977).

Stilt, Kristen, *Islamic Law in Action: Authority, Discretion and Everyday Experiences in Mamluk Egypt* (Oxford: Oxford University Press, 2011).

Tamdoğan, Işık, "Sulh and the 18th-Century Ottoman Courts of Üsküdar and Adana," *Islamic Law and Society* 15 (2008), 55–83.

Taylor, Scott K., *Honor and Violence in Golden Age Spain* (New Haven: Yale University Press, 2008).

Tezcan, Baki, *The Second Ottoman Empire: Political and Social Transformation in the Early Modern World* (New York: Cambridge University Press, 2010).

Tillier, Mathieu, *Les cadis d'Iraq et l'état Abbasside (132/750–334/945)* (Damascus: Institut français du Proche-Orient, 2009).

Tillier, Mathieu, "Qāḍīs and the Political use of the Maẓālim Jurisdiction under the ᶜAbbāsids," in Christian Lange and Maribel Fierro (eds), *Public Violence in Islamic Societies* (Edinburgh: Edinburgh University Press, 2009), 42–66.

Tillier, Mathieu, "The Qāḍīs of Fusṭāṭ-Miṣr under the Ṭūlūnids and the Ikhshīdids: The Judiciary and Egyptian Autonomy," *Journal of the American Oriental Society* 131 (2011), 207–22.

Tillier, Mathieu, "Judicial Authority and Qāḍīs' Autonomy under the ᶜAbbāsids," *al-Masāq* 26 (2014), 119–31.

Tillier, Mathieu (ed.), *Le pluralisme judiciaire dans l'Islam prémoderne*, special edition of the *Bulletin d'études orientales* 63 (2014).

Tillier, Mathieu, "Le pluralisme judiciaire en Islam, ses dynamiques et ses enjeux," *Bulletin d'études orientales* 63 (2014), 23–40.

Toledano, Ehud, *State and Society in Mid Nineteenth-Century Egypt* (Cambridge: Cambridge University Press, 1990).

Trivellato, Francesca, *The Familiarity of Strangers: The Sephardic Diaspora, Livorno and Cross-Cultural Trade in the Early Modern Period* (New Haven, CT: Yale University Press, 2009).

Tuchscherer, Michel (ed.), *Le commerce du café avant l'ère des plantations coloniales: espaces, résaux, sociétés, XVᵉ–XIXᵉ siècle* (Cairo: Institut français d'archéologie orientale, 2001).

Tucker, Judith, *Women in Nineteenth-Century Egypt* (Cambridge: Cambridge University Press, 1984).

Tucker, Judith, *In the House of the Law: Gender and Islamic Law in Ottoman Syria and Palestine* (Berkeley: University of California Press, 1998).

Tucker, Judith, *Women, Family and Gender in Islamic Law* (Cambridge: Cambridge University Press, 2008).

Tuğ, Başak, Politics of Honor: The Institutional and Social Frontiers of Illicit Sex in Mid-Eighteenth-Century Ottoman Anatolia, PhD dissertation, New York University, 2009.

Tuğ, Başak, "Ottoman Women as Legal and Marital Subjects," in Christine Woodhead (ed.), *The Ottoman World* (Abingdon: Routledge, 2012), 362–77.

Tyan, Emile, *Histoire de l'organisation judiciaire en pays d'Islam* (Leiden: Brill, 1960).

Ursinus, Michael, "Petitions from Orthodox Church Officials to the Imperial Diwan, 1675", *Byzantine and Modern Greek Studies* 18 (1994), 236–47.

Uzunçarşılı, İsmail Hakkı, *Osmanlı Devletinin İlmiye Teşkilatı* (Ankara: Türk Tarih Kurumu Basımevi, 1988).

Varese, Federico, *The Russian Mafia: Private Protection in a New Market Economy* (Oxford: Oxford University Press, 2001).

Voll, John, "Old ᶜUlamāᵓ Families and Ottoman Influence in Eighteenth-Century Damascus," *American Journal of Arabic Studies* 3 (1975), 48–59.

Wakin, Jeanette A., *The Function of Documents in Islamic Law: The Chapters on Sales from*

Ṭaḥāwī's Kitāb al-shurūṭ al-kabīr (Albany, NY: State University of New York Press, 1972).

Wilkins, Charles, *Forging Urban Solidarities: Ottoman Aleppo, 1640–1700* (Leiden: Brill, 2010).

Winter, Michael, *Society and Religion in Early Ottoman Egypt: Studies in the Writings of ᶜAbd al-Wahhāb al-Shaᶜrānī* (New Brunswick, NJ: Transaction Publishers, 1982).

Winter, Michael, *Egyptian Society under Ottoman Rule, 1517–1798* (London: Routledge, 1992).

Wittman, Richard, Before Qadi and Grand Vizier: Intra-Communal Dispute Resolution and Legal Transactions among Christians and Jews in the Plural Society of Seventeenth-Century Istanbul, PhD dissertation, Harvard University, 2008.

Yerasimos, Stephane, *Les voyageurs dans l'empire ottoman, XIVᵉ–XVIᵉ siècles* (Ankara: Imprimerie de la société turque de l'histoire, 1991).

Yılmaz, Gülay, The Economic and Social Roles of Janissaries in a 17th-Century Ottoman City: The Case of Istanbul, PhD dissertation, McGill University, 2011.

Zaman, Muhammad Qasim, *The Ulama in Contemporary Islam: Custodians of Change* (Princeton: Princeton University Press, 2002).

Zarinebaf, Fariba, *Crime and Punishment in Istanbul, 1700–1800* (Berkeley: University of California Press, 2010).

Zarinebaf-Shahr, Fariba, "Women, Law and Imperial Justice in Ottoman Istanbul in the Late Seventeenth Century," in Amira el-Azhary Sonbol (ed.), *Women, the Family and Divorce Laws in Islamic History* (Syracuse, NY: Syracuse University Press, 1996), 81–95.

Zečević, Selma, "Missing Husbands, Waiting Wives, Bosnian Muftis: Fatwa Texts and Interpretation of Gendered Presences and Absences in Late Ottoman Bosnia," in Amila Buturović and İrvin Cemil Schick (eds), *Women in the Ottoman Balkans: Gender, Culture and History* (London: I. B. Tauris, 2007), 335–60.

Ze'evi, Dror, *An Ottoman Century: The District of Jerusalem in the 1600s* (Albany, NY: State University of New York Press, 1996).

Ze'evi, Dror, "The Use of Ottoman Sharīᶜa Court Records as a Source for Middle Eastern Social History: A Reappraisal," *Islamic Law and Society* 5 (1998), 35–56.

Zmora, Hillay, *The Feud in Early Modern Germany* (Cambridge: Cambridge University Press, 2011).

Zubaida, Sami, *Law and Power in the Islamic World* (London: I. B. Tauris, 2005).

INDEX